ANTHONY
WAYNE

Anthony Wayne, by Edward Savage, oil painting executed in 1795, after the general's triumphant return to Philadelphia from his Indian campaign in the Northwest Territory. *The New-York Historical Society, New York City.*

Anthony *Wayne*

SOLDIER OF

THE EARLY REPUBLIC

Paul David Nelson

Indiana University Press

BLOOMINGTON

Library of Congress Cataloging in Publication Data

Nelson, Paul David, 1941 –
    Anthony Wayne, soldier of the early republic.

    Bibliography: p.
    Includes index.
    1. Wayne, Anthony, 1745 – 1796. 2. Generals — United
States — Biography. 3. United States. Army — Biography.
4. United States — History — Revolution, 1775 – 1783 —
Campaigns. 5. Wayne's Campaign, 1794. I. Title.
E207.W35N34 1985   973.3'3'0924 [B]   84-48543
ISBN 0-253-30751-1

1   2   3   4   5   89   88   87   86   85

For my Parents

Contents

ILLUSTRATIONS

MAPS

PREFACE

THE MOST INTERESTING thing about Anthony Wayne's life, I think, is that it presents us with an important case study in the development of a "military mind." To use this phrase, however, is not to accept the way it is sometimes defined today, as embracing militaristic values, pomp, and ceremony and rejecting all things liberal. It is true, of course, that Wayne had a romantic, almost childlike, attachment to the trappings and glory of service as an army officer during the Revolution and later as commander of the United States Legion. It is also true that his views on the role of the military, both as an officer and as a quondam politician, were products of a fundamentally conservative cast of mind. Nevertheless, to describe the "military mind" of Anthony Wayne is to show the complex interplay between a set of conditions—political, social, economic, cultural, ideological—that motivated him to choose a military career as the most eligible way of defending his convictions about what ought to be a man's relationship to government.

In this context, Wayne's service in the military and in the legislative processes of Pennsylvania and the United States government can be seen as attempts to preserve the best of Whig political doctrine, as it had manifested itself in American republicanism during the Colonial era, while at the same time giving outlet to his deep-seated romanticism. What saves his efforts from being merely reactionary or facile is that the Whiggism and republicanism for which he contended were not conservative in the context of eighteenth-century European politics. On the contrary, they were a profoundly new, and essentially untested, assertion—embodied in the American political experiment—that the individual must be guaranteed *by* government his personal and economic liberty *from* government. Proponents of this viewpoint, Wayne included, were radical indeed, and all the soldiers and politicians of the early American republic who accepted this ideology were considerably more complicated than they have often been delineated.

WITHOUT THE ASSISTANCE that I received from many institutions and individuals, this book could not have been written. I am particularly indebted to Berea College for generous financial grants in support of my research and writing. I also owe an incalculable debt of gratitude to the staffs of many libraries and manuscript repositories, including the Historical Society of Pennsylvania, the American Philosophical Society, the New-York Historical Society, the Massachusetts Historical Society, the Margaret I. King Library of the University of Kentucky, the Filson Club, the Detroit Public Library, the Georgia Historical Society, the Library of Congress, the New York Public Library, the Charles Patterson Van Pelt Library of the University of Pennsylvania, the Newberry Library, the Ohio Historical Society, the Greene Library of West Chester State College, the State Historical Society of Wisconsin, the Presbyterian Historical Society, the Alderman Library of the University of Virginia, the Chester County Historical Society, the Chicago Historical Society, the Joseph Regenstein Library of the University of Chicago, the Duke University Medical Center Library, the Henry E. Huntington Library, the Kentucky Historical Society, the New Jersey Historical Society, the University of Georgia Libraries, the Historical Society of the County of Montgomery (Pennsylvania), the American Baptist Historical Society, the Cincinnati Historical Society, the Robert Hutchings Goddard Library of Clark University, the Connecticut State Library, the New Hampshire Historical Society, the North Carolina State Department of Archives and History, and the Morristown National Historical Park. I owe a special word of thanks to Mattie Russell of the Perkins Library, Duke University; Arlene Shy of the William L. Clements Library; Eric Pumroy of the Indiana Historical Society; John F. Reed, King of Prussia, Pennsylvania; and Henry Gershwin Mazlen, Brooklyn, New York.

I must take this opportunity to express my deep gratitude to Orrin June, who at the time I was doing research on Wayne's life resided at Waynesborough (the general's ancestral estate in Paoli, Pennsylvania) and invited me to visit with him. Not only did he and his wife welcome me into their home and give me a special tour, but Mr. June also made available to me original Wayne manuscripts in his possession. These were acts of great generosity.

I am also grateful to the editors of the *Pennsylvania Magazine of History and Biography* and the *Northwest Ohio Quarterly* for permission to draw upon copyrighted materials in their journals. I am much obliged to Michael and Kathleen Burke and their children for hospitality to my family and me while I conducted research in Philadelphia. My largest debt I owe to my wife, Rebecca P. Nelson. Her constant support of my work—and her very practical skills as a typist and editor—are for me an unfailing source of comfort.

Paul David Nelson

ANTHONY
WAYNE

"Fighting was constitutional with him."

Anecdote about Anthony
Wayne during the Revo-
lutionary War.

"General Wayne had a constitutional attachment
to the sword, and this cast of character
had acquired strength from indulgence."

Henry "Light Horse Harry"
Lee, *Memoirs*, 420.

CHAPTER *1*

Genesis of a Soldier
1745–1776

IT WAS Anthony Wayne's good fortune to live in the latter half of the eighteenth century, a time so unsettled by the American Revolution and by wars against the Indians of the Northwest Territory that he could practice the only two professions — army command and politics — for which he possessed any natural ability or temperament. The maelstroms of this period, occurring while Wayne was at the height of his bodily and mental powers, were not for him unhappy disruptions in the normal routine of life, as they were for thousands of other Americans who were caught up reluctantly, but rather an opportunity for him to rise above his humdrum life as a Pennsylvania farmer-businessman and give full rein to the deepest romantic urgings of his restless spirit. Had he lived during many another age of American history, it is possible that he would not have become famous, or experienced personal fulfillment, by acting the swashbuckling military hero and serving as a Pennsylvania politician of some distinction.

Of Wayne's two great gifts, his military leadership is by far the better known, although not well understood. Contrary to common belief, his ability as a soldier rested not upon some wild-eyed enthusiasm but a natural flair for leading troops and a sensible recognition that his success as an army commander hinged upon adherence to military fundamentals such as planning and logistics. It is true, of course, that in 1781, during the Revolutionary War, Wayne acquired among Continental soldiers the nickname "Mad," in the sense of possessing a foolhardiness in battle that went beyond prudence, and the

1

cognomen *seemed* to fit so well that it endured. James McHenry, for instance, in commenting upon Wayne's part in the battle of Green Spring Farm in 1781, wrote Nathanael Greene that Wayne was "impetuous," and Greene replied that the Pennsylvanian certainly had his share of "military ardor, which no doubt is heated by the fire of the Modern Hero." George Washington also thought Wayne a bit rash, once characterizing the man as "more active and enterprising than judicious and cautious," and General Comte de Rochambeau assessed Wayne as being a *"brave homme, mais très ardent."*[1]

Even Wayne himself contributed to his image as a fire-eater by his use of florid, impetuous, language. As an example, he was given to phrases such as "A Bloody track will mark my Setting Sun" should he be killed in battle, and he was a terrible swearer, perhaps the greatest among the general officers. During the Canadian expedition in 1776, one of his outbursts was described by Lieutenant Ebenezer Elmer: "Col. Wayne. . .finding no sentry (as we have not kept one in the day time) he damned all our souls to hell, and immediately ordered two by night and one by day, which I immediately put in execution — but shall not forget his damns, which he is very apt to bestow upon people; but my great consolation is that the power thereof is not in his hands, blessed be God for it."[2]

Despite the assessments of his contemporaries, despite his continuing reputation of "madness," Wayne was nevertheless a prudent and careful officer, whose military record belies the myth. He was a systematic organizer, who paid careful attention to basic military problems such as the supply, training, and comfort of his men in the field. He never undertook an operation, whether it be against Stony Point in 1779 or the Indians of the Northwest Territory in the 1790s without minute attention to all details of the operation. Learning from experience and from the study of military history and science, Wayne made every effort in all his martial activities to avoid the mistakes of generals who preceded him on fields of battle. While it is certainly true that Wayne was first and foremost a dashing military figure, who possessed those subtle qualities of leadership that inspire men on the battlefield and whose first ambition was to be in the thick of the fight where the danger was greatest, nonetheless he was far more than merely a fighting general. As Nathanael Greene noted, Wayne might be given to playing the Modern Hero, but he was also "by the by. . .an excellent officer." The Marquis de Chastellux, who met Wayne at the American army's encampment of the Hudson River in 1780, characterized the Pennsylvanian by the single word "sensible." Washington also appreciated Wayne's abilities, as can be seen in the commander in chief's constant reliance upon Wayne to carry out difficult and important assignments during both the Revolution and the war against the Northwest Indians a decade later. And Alexander Graydon, who observed Wayne at Washington's headquarters in June 1777, noted that the Pennsylvanian was "somewhat addicted to the vaunting style" but "could fight as well as brag."[3]

Temperamentally, as well as by aptitude, Wayne was drawn toward the martial life, for he possessed a streak of romanticism and dash which inclined him to love the pomp and show of the profession of arms. Always proud of his own military appearance, he took great pains to appear in a splendid uniform, neatly turned out in all respects. As Graydon once described his appearance, "General Waynes. . .uniform as colonel of the Fourth Battalion was. . .blue and white, in which he had been accustomed to appear in exemplary neatness." Because of this fastidiousness about his own figure, he became known in some circles as "Dandy Wayne." This same martial appearance he also wanted to effect among the men under his command, and he was constantly trying to get better uniforms for his soldiers or issuing orders to have the troops groom themselves. He especially abhorred long hair as unmilitary, and in general orders of July 7, 1776 (in the midst of hard field service in Canada), he decreed, "A barber for each company is. . .to be nominated, for the purpose of shaving the soldiers and dressing their hair." With considerable vanity, Wayne wrote Washington shortly before the raid on Stony Point, "I must acknowledge that I have an insuperable prejudice in favor of an Elegant uniform & Soldierly appearance, so much so that I would rather risk my life and reputation at the head of the same men in an attack, clothed and appointed as I could wish, merely with bayonets and a single charge of ammunition, than to take them as they appear in common with sixty rounds of cartridges," for good uniforms promoted among the troops a "Laudable pride. . .which in a soldier is a Substitute for almost every other Virtue."[4]

While he emerged as a dynamic military romanticist and a dashing soldier during his lifetime, Anthony Wayne also played another, less known role as a politician in one of the great ages of American politics. He was a shrewd, flamboyant, articulate politician who often showed ability in organizing, leading, and dominating his fellow citizens to achieve what he believed was in their, and his own, best interests.

During his times of army service (and again belying his reputation as a rash, impulsive officer who acted first and thought later), he exercised deeply ingrained habits of care toward civilians in his department and total subordination to civil authority, both national and state.

In all these political activities, Wayne displayed little consistent ideology, except to remain true to republicanism and a conviction that military men should always be subordinate to civilian power. At the commencement of the war, he expressed a sort of Whiggish faith in both governmental and military amateurism, and just as he would organize armies based upon a notion of short-term militia service for all citizens, he also would arrange affairs of state along the same democratic lines. His wartime experiences, however, changed his mind about the desirability of trying to run either army or state in such essentially "radical" or democratic ways (to him the terms were synonymous). For once the revolutionary conflict got under way, by far the greatest amount of his time and correspondence as a soldier was taken up by attempts to persuade officials in Pennsylvania and the Continental Congress to give him necessary supports to keep his battalions in the field. Disgusted when inadequate assistance was forthcoming, he came to believe that the politics of the Revolution had taken too sharp a turn toward a decentralization and radicalism that had created dangerous inefficiencies in governmental affairs.

As time wore on, therefore, General Wayne expressed views that were more and more at variance with his earlier, more democratic positions on how government, society, and the army ought to be organized and who should dominate these institutions. In short, within the framework of his larger republican ideals, he was converted in the 1770s to the political and military stance, which he advocated until the end of his life, that strong central government ought to be instituted by, and maintained in the interests of, the propertied and "aristocratick" elements of the nation. From this same galaxy of perceptions, he concluded that the officer corps of the army ought likewise be recruited from these same elites. Since he was a member of that small social group which in his scheme would run things, and since he might be helped personally by securing a "place" in such a structuring of government, it is not surprising that he became a Federalist in the last years of his life. In the last analysis, then, Wayne was a man with an innate sense of how to conjoin in his political arguments and activities at one and the same time deeply felt principles of government and crass practicality in order to gain office or sway men to his purposes. Thus, he was typical of many other successful American politicians during his lifetime (or any other time).

The same qualities that made Wayne a good soldier and a modestly gifted political figure led him to fail in many other of life's pursuits. As shown by the derangement of his financial affairs in the 1780s, he could make dismal business decisions. His family life was also a muddle, largely because of his own glaring faults as a husband, son, brother, and father. His relationship with his wife, Mary Penrose Wayne, was greatly strained by his romantic attraction to other women, especially Mary Vining, a Delaware belle, and he was estranged from Mary Wayne before her death in 1793.[5] His mother, whom he had neglected and treated meanly in her last years, cut him almost entirely out of her will, and in maturity he also got on poorly with one of his sisters, Hannah. His wife accused him of neglecting his two children, Margaretta and Isaac, and near the end of his life he admitted that he had been remiss in their upbringing.

Anthony Wayne was born on January 1, 1745, at the family estate of Waynesborough in Easttown Township, Chester County, Pennsylvania. He was part of the third generation of Waynes to have their home in Chester County. Anthony Wayne, grandfather of the general, had been the first to settle in the region. The grandfather, born in 1666 in Yorkshire, England, moved early in his life to County Wicklow, Ireland, where he became a settled agriculturalist and executed some civil and military responsibilities for the government. Being a Protestant, he served under William of Orange in 1690 at the Boyne as commander of a squadron of dragoons. While in Ireland, he married Hannah Faulkner, by whom he had nine children. Being a republican in sentiment, he found it increasingly unpleasant to live under monarchical government, and so in 1722 he moved with his family to America. Two years later, he purchased 380 acres at Easttown, in Pennsylvania, and lived there until his death in 1739.[6]

Waynesborough, home of the Wayne family in Chester County, near Paoli, Pennsylvania. It was begun about 1715 by Anthony Wayne, the general's grandfather, and expanded by Isaac Wayne, his father. *Historical Society of Pennsylvania.*

Grandfather Anthony Wayne's sons, Isaac and Francis, whom he had left in Ireland, also migrated to Pennsylvania in 1724 and purchased one hundred acres of land in Easttown. In 1739, Isaac bought out his brother and in the same year inherited his father's estate. Isaac Wayne, the father of the general, was a prominent man in Chester County affairs. He was an active member of St. David's Church, in Radnor Township, and he served from 1757 to 1763 as a member of the Provisional Assembly from Chester County. During the Seven Years' War, he held a militia commission and saw three tours of active duty on the frontiers of the province. He married Elizabeth Iddings, the daughter of Richard and Margaret Iddings of Chester County, and in 1742 finished construction of the first part of the Wayne family's home, which he expanded in 1765 to its full size. The house, constructed of brown stone and pointed with white mortar, had capacious rooms, eleven fireplaces, and broad entranceways. It was built in a beautiful setting and was an imposing seat for Anthony Wayne after he inherited the estate from his father in 1774.[7]

There is little in the records of the Wayne family to indicate that young Anthony Wayne had an eventful or unusual childhood. On the contrary, his life seemed to move along smoothly and conventionally in an orderly family setting. In the Wayne household were two children besides Anthony, an elder sister named Hannah, who later married Captain Samuel Van Leer, and a younger sister, Ann, who would become the wife of William Hayman. While a boy, Wayne clashed from time to time with his father, a man of "strong mind, great industry and enterprise." Isaac Wayne's plan for his son was to bring young Wayne up in his own profession of agriculture, but the father "soon discovered that the labors of the field did illy accord with his son's propensities." It was not clear, to be sure, exactly what the son's propensities were, but since Isaac Wayne's resources gave him "the means of indulging the bent of his son's genius" — once it might be discovered — Anthony Wayne was allowed to study with his uncle, Gabriel Wayne, a schoolmaster who possessed "considerable erudition and mental acquirements."[8]

Although Wayne spent much time with his uncle in pursuit of education, he had made no progress at all. In fact, his presence among the other pupils was distracting them from their studies and bringing chaos to the whole school. Hence, Uncle Gabriel Wayne wrote Anthony's father.

> I really suspect that parental affection blinds you, and that you have mistaken your son's capacity. What he may be best qualified for, I know not—one thing I am certain of, he will never make a scholar, he may perhaps make a soldier, he has already distracted the brains of two-thirds of the boys under my charge, by rehearsals of battles, sieges, &c.—They exhibit more the appearance of Indians and harlequins than students. . . . During noon, in place of the usual games of amusement, he has the boys employed in throwing up redoubts, skirmishing, &c.

Isaac Wayne was vexed by this account of young Wayne's behavior at school and decided to take matters in hand. At the next meeting of father and son, Isaac scolded the youngster, threatening to take him out of school and put him to work at Waynesborough, doing the worst tasks a farm has to offer. Wayne, "knowing the decisive character of his father," now realized that unless he wanted to start shoveling manure he had better delay his military games for a time and labor longer at his studies. Hence, he began to give serious attention to his school work, especially mathematics, and within eighteen months had learned all that his uncle had to teach.[9]

Uncle Gabriel Wayne was so impressed with his nephew's academic progress and potential at this point that he advised his brother to continue the young man's education. Isaac Wayne concurred, and so at the age of sixteen Anthony Wayne was enrolled in the Philadelphia Academy, "for the purpose of acquiring an academical education." For two years he lived and studied in the bustling environment of Philadelphia, a city only twenty miles from his home in Chester County but far removed in terms of its activity and gaiety. Still, his head was not turned from his school work, and he pursued mathematics with considerable zeal. He was less successful in mastering Latin and Greek, for he would not try to grasp these languages even though urged by "the united solicitations of friends and tutors." At the age of eighteen, after experiencing the life of an academician for longer than he had really desired, Wayne returned to Easttown and began a career as a surveyor.[10]

As Anthony Wayne entered adulthood, he was an attractive young man embarked on a useful and necessary career. At about this time, he was described by a contemporary as "above what is commonly termed the 'middle stature,' and well proportioned. — His hair was dark; his forehead was high and handsomely formed; his eyes were dark hazel, intelligent, quick and penetrating; his nose inclined to the aquiline; the remainder of his face was well proportioned, and his whole countenance fine and animated." In his "natural disposition," he "was very amiable," while remaining "ardent and sincere in his attachments." Finally, "his morals were chaste and his manners refined." With these attributes to assist him, Wayne quickly became a popular surveyor. There was much of that work to be done in Chester County, for the region was rapidly increasing in settlement and improvements, and surveyors were needed to run disputed or poorly defined boundaries between properties, to locate public roads, to prepare private sites for houses and barns. Soon Wayne was busy with all the work he could accept. In his leisure time, he pursued the avocations of astronomy and engineering. Quickly making a reputation for competency, thoroughness, and dependability in his line of work, Wayne's circle of acquaintances expanded to include many of the more famous Pennsylvanians of the age.[11]

One such person was Dr. Benjamin Franklin, who among his other numerous and diverse activities speculated in Nova Scotia lands. In 1764, Franklin suggested to Wayne that the latter join in an association being formed among a number of prominent Pennsylvanians for the purpose of purchasing and colonizing lands in Nova Scotia. Wayne agreed to the plan, apparently with the understanding that his part of the financial responsibilities of the scheme would be discharged by his assuming the role of company agent on the scene at Halifax. As agent, his tasks would be to select, survey, and buy the land most eligible to the purposes of the associators and to report to John Hughes, a partner in the venture and a close friend of Dr. Franklin. In possession of a twelve-point list from Hughes of things to look for in the lands to be chosen, Wayne on March 16, 1765, embarked at Philadelphia for Halifax.[12]

After a stormy passage in which Wayne's ship was caught in a three-day tempest off the east end of Long Island, the waterlogged Pennsylvanian arrived at his destination on March 29. Shortly after recovering from his unpleasant voyage, he was received pleasantly by Alexander McNutt, a co-speculator, and introduced to Governor Montague Wilmot and the Council. Two days after that, he dined with the governor and "several other gentlemen of the province" and then, with his "connexions" with the powerful men of the colony made, got down to business. In his first report to Hughes, written on April 10, he noted that he could give no account of the land as yet, except from hearsay, but what he heard was certainly encouraging. Wayne was preparing to send out emissaries, and he was going himself as soon as possible, to check the veracity of these reports.[13]

For the next two months, Wayne assayed the lands available for survey and occupation in Nova Scotia, reporting to Hughes from time to time on what he had found. Hughes was pleased and urged his young partner to continue improving the company's "advantage" with Governor Wilmot, the Council, and other prominent men of the province, who could be instrumental in helping the company secure from the provincial government a favorable charter for the intended "plantation." By July 9, Wayne was reporting that he had reserved five townships and that "16 townships is left to me to choose which can't be attended with any Disadvantage to our Side." A month later, he was angrily noting that the government's terms for granting these lands were unfavorable to the company. While he had urged that the partners be required to settle only one hundred families per 100,000 acres every four years, the Nova Scotians were insisting that twice that number be domiciled. "Mankind," he noted disgustedly, "is hard to Lead," and as to politicians, "I always thought some of them acted in a double Capacity. Experience now Confirms me in that thought."[14]

Subsequent governmental decisions about the grants did nothing to alleviate Wayne's disgust. Although Hughes wrote his young colleague a number of letters insisting that Wayne must secure better terms from the governor and Council, Wayne, despite all his efforts, was not successful. First, he wrote a memorial to the Council, "but they declined it." Then, he sounded out the councilmen one by one on altering the terms, but when they met — despite a majority having said they would "do what they could" — the original governmental plan was declared "reasonable and just." Hence, the final form of the land grants, issued on October 31, 1765, contained not all the terms the associators could wish. All in all, however, they were generous, allotting to Franklin, Wayne, McNutt, and twenty others a grant of 100,000 acres on the St. John's River and another 100,000 acres on the Peticoodiack River. On the same day, Wayne, John Hughes, and Lester Falkner received a separate grant of 1,000 acres each in Annapolis County — a tidy piece of land for the young Pennsylvanian in and of itself. After these settlements were made with the government of Nova Scotia, Wayne returned to Philadelphia for the winter, bearing "a satisfactory report" of all his activities in Canada.[15]

Wayne spent the next five months quietly at his father's fieldstone house in Easttown, in the company of family. On at least one occasion (December 23, 1765) he rode out on a fox hunt with his neighbors, and he was also finding time to court "a young lady of modest demeanor and amiability" named Mary Penrose. Mary, or "Polly," as she was nicknamed by her suitor, was the nineteen-year-old daughter of Bartholomew Penrose, a prominent Philadelphia merchant, and a friend of Wayne's younger sister, Ann. Quickly a deep affection sprang up between Anthony and Polly, and although it was destined to wane in later years, for the first decade it remained strong. On March 25, 1766, after only a very short courtship, Anthony Wayne and Mary Penrose were married in Christ Church, Philadelphia, the Reverend Richard Peters presiding.[16]

Shortly after their nuptials, the Waynes were separated when Anthony returned to Nova Scotia in his capacity as superintendent of the company's lands. He took with him a number of settlers, implements for farming and for house construction, seeds, and other items necessary for completing the task of colonizing the associators' lands. Not much is known of his activities there during the summer, except that he charged some bills, which he did not finally pay until the following year, and that he continued to hold title upon his share of the grant of 3,000 acres made to him and two partners the year before. In late autumn, he returned to Pennsylvania, rejoining his wife and kin, and he never returned to the settlements in Canada, although he did continue to act as superintendent of the land company until its ill-starred colonization venture collapsed in the following year.[17]

The next few years found Wayne living sedately with his wife on the family's Easttown estate, attending to agriculture, developing a tanning business, and continuing to survey for his neighbors. His numerous enterprises established him as a well-to-do farmer and businessman, and his neighbors, who prized such accomplishments, held him in high regard. As his fortune and reputation increased, so also did his family. In 1770, his first child was born, a daughter whom he christened Margaretta and promptly nicknamed "Peggy." Two years later, his second and last child, a son, entered the world and was given the name of Isaac, in honor of Wayne's father and the baby's grandfather. In 1774, Anthony Wayne was propelled into full control of the family's estate of Waynesborough when his aging father consigned it to his only son's care and ownership. The sole caveat in the agreement was that Wayne must pay his mother, Elizabeth Iddings Wayne, £500 plus an annuity of £50 per year until her death. He willingly agreed to this arrangement, although within two years (a year after his father's death) he was neglecting to pay the annuity, and his unhappy mother had moved in with her sister at Newtown.[18]

In the early 1770s, Wayne had much more to occupy his time than business and family matters. Like all English Americans, he must try to make sense of the activities of British ministries that seemed determined to alter long-standing imperial constitutional arrangements to the seeming detriment of American liberties. From the beginning of the colonies' troubles with Britain to the successful completion of the Revolution and the establishment of American independence, Wayne wavered not the slightest in support of republican principles. In the political arrangement of the American colonies by 1774, he perceived a *de facto* if not *de jure* republicanism that had been nurtured in "American liberty" and which "a despotic Parliament" would now attempt to destroy piecemeal. These measures he would oppose "by every moderate, constitutional means within our reach," or if necessary by arms.[19]

Given the romanticism and love of things martial within Wayne's character, it is not surprising that he was not so bothered by the prospect of war as were some of his more cautious brethren. Warfare offered for him an escape from the prosaic existence of rural life. From early childhood, he had imbibed his father's tales of military life and glory during the latter's militia service in the Seven Years' War. Perhaps even more influentially, he had been told the stories of Grandfather Anthony Wayne's service as a cavalryman under William at the Boyne, stories he was already repeating to his own young son. Hence, as early as the first month of 1775, while he and most other colonists pursued redress of their grievances by peaceful protest and petition (all carried on through political processes), Wayne was striving to create what amounted to a revolutionary militia in eastern Pennsylvania. Never was there any doubt that the fiery-eyed, passionate Anthony Wayne would play the role of soldier rather than statesman should the unpleasantness between Britain and America degenerate into warfare.

In 1774, Wayne entered upon the stage of public life from which he did not retire until his death more than two decades later. At that time, Pennsylvanians were organizing protests against Britain's so-called Coercive Acts against Massachusetts, which were designed to punish that colony for the destructive work of a few who had thrown tea into the harbor at Boston the year before. In mid-1774, Pennsylvania's counties elected delegates to attend a Provincial Convention in Philadelphia to discuss ways of protesting Britain's coercion of a sister colony. Wayne, as Easttown's representative, was one of thirteen men sent by the electors of Chester County. When the Convention met, it organized Committees of Correspondence and of Safety and voted trade restrictions against England in response to the alarming state of affairs then existing between England and the colonies. Later, following the lead of the Provincial Convention, Pennsylvania localities, including Chester County, began to condemn the British ministry's activities against Massachusetts. Wayne was in the forefront of such activities in his county. In July 1774, he chaired a county committee, whose task was to draft resolutions repudiating Prime Minister Frederick Lord North's policies, and he had the pleasure of seeing his committee's handiwork adopted by the Chester County voters. It was as chairman of the county's committee of Safety that he began to examine the state of preparedness of the Chester County militia during that active summer. Additionally, in August, he subscribed money for relief of "the Poor of Boston" as a humanitarian — and political — gesture of support for his fellow colonists to the North.[20]

Wayne's outspoken and bold style of public conduct immediately attracted the attention of his Pennsylvania neighbors, as can be seen in the way they responded to his dynamic, magnetic personality in the summer of 1774, and so continued to do for the rest of his life. Although he was only twenty-nine years old when he appeared in the limelight, he was a handsome, virile character, and there was clearly something about him — perhaps the way he carried himself, or the fierceness with which he expressed his well-formed opinions on public issues, or the certainty with which he declared that this or that point was undeniably correct — that drew attention to him and made him a popular figure. His education and knowledge of the world helped also, for in both he was more advanced than most of his fellow citizens. Moreover, it was known to one and all that in personal fortune he had little to gain and much to lose by taking an outspoken stand against the mother country. His willingness to risk both life and estate for the "cause of American Liberty" created for him a great reservoir of good will among his neighbors. He certainly had his glaring faults — among them, vanity, overconfidence, boastfulness, impatience, and impetuosity — but his colleagues, both civilian and military, were willing to overlook these in light of his better points.

Wayne's success at winning support for himself from his fellow citizens in protest politics decided him in August 1774 to stand for election to the Provincial Assembly as a member from Chester County. As a part of his campaign he issued to the freemen of his district an exhortation to attend a preelection meeting in which he would instruct them on the best men for whom to vote, that persons "of first abilities both for learning, prudence and unshaken fortitude" might be chosen, "as the time is drawing to a Crisis" and the next Assembly might be called upon "to withstand and ward off the impending blows big with the fate of British America." Although Wayne had signed his missive merely as "A Freeman of Chester County," his neighbors probably knew who the author was. In any case, when the caucus met, Wayne took the floor and made the first political speech of his career.

He began by apologizing for his relative youthfulness, then launched into a tirade against Britain's intention to tax Americans unconstitutionally and to destroy their ancient charters. The mother country's policy, he said, was plain to see: the undermining of the colonies one at a time, while hoping the others would not rise to assist the one being attacked. " 'Divide and conquer' is the sum of politics," he asserted, and "One of the chief members of the British Senate has said that this was meant to enslave America." Would Pennsylvanians, then, "remain idle and tame spectators whilst a despotic Parliament are making a footstool of a sister colony to mount and trample on the high reared head of American liberty? Forbid it, Virtue, and forbid it, Shame." Instead, "Let us modestly, yet manfully, show our decent protest, and by every moderate, constitutional means within our reach, let us endeavor to obtain our redress and that equitable independency which as part of the British Empire we are indubitably entitled to." On the basis of these sentiments, Wayne won election to the Assembly and took his seat in October 1774.[21]

For the next few months, Wayne played no conspicuous role in the Pennsylvania legislature, only acting with John Dickinson, Thomas Mifflin, Charles Thomson, George Gray, Edward Biddle, and others as they steered a course of support for the First Continental Congress while repressing more conservative measures advocated by Joseph Galloway and the Philadelphia merchants. In January 1775, he attended a second Provincial Convention, which encouraged the Assembly to adopt a measure supporting nonconsumption of British goods. Some members of the Convention, himself included, also urged, without success, that the extralegal body prod the Assembly to form a revolutionary militia, outside the structure of the regular Royal militia system prevailing in the province at the time. When the Assembly received the Convention's proposals, it accepted (over the opposition of Galloway and others) a plan for "Associators" to enforce nonimportation and nonconsumption of British goods as a protest against the Ministry's coercion of Massachusetts.[22]

Meantime, Wayne and other Assemblymen continued to advocate that a province-wide Committee of Safety be organized, empowered to see to the colony's defenses and to enforce a tax on the Associators to pay for supplies, fortifications for Philadelphia, and other warlike paraphernalia. Others resisted this idea, believing (correctly) that a committee appointed to carry out these measures would prove more powerful than the Assembly itself. However, under the impetus of the outbreak of war in Massachusetts, in April 1775, the Assembly finally went along with the proposal, and on June 30, Wayne, Dickinson, Thomson, and twenty-two other representatives were embodied as a Committee of Safety with power to spend £35,000 for essential military supplies, including five thousand muskets and bayonets, and to tax the Associators for the expenses. The zealous young Wayne, and a close friend and ally from Chester County, Benjamin Bartholomew, who had supported the struggle, were exultant at the outcome of the vote.[23]

From that time on in the colonial rebellion against Great Britain, Wayne devoted practically all his time to the military aspects of the struggle. Throughout the summer of 1775, he met regularly with the Committee of Safety, constantly urging that the Assembly provide more money, provisions, and arms for the Associators. On August 19, with Wayne absent, the Committee drew up a set of uniform rules and regulations for the Associators, which were accepted by the Assembly on November 25 in the form of thirty-eight articles. At this point, the militia system of revolutionary Pennsylvania was born. But the Assemblymen were not finished helping the military arm of the colony, for they also voted in the same session £80,000 in additional financial supports for the Associators and expanded the membership of the Committee of Safety to include thirty-two men, headed by Benjamin Franklin.[24]

Meanwhile, Wayne pursued his personal predilection for things military. He devoured every piece of martial literature he could lay his hands on, paying special attention to Marshal Saxe's *Campaigns* and Caesar's *Gallic Wars*. He also began to organize and drill a regiment of volunteers in his spare time, and bemoaned what he saw as weaknesses in the militia law, which left membership a voluntary matter and allowed non-Associators between the ages of sixteen and fifty to escape service by paying an exemption fee of £2 10s. This penalty Wayne felt was far too low. But even worse, he said, men over fifty paid nothing at all, and usually the wealthiest citizens of Pennsylvania fell into that category. At the present moment, however, his appeals fell upon deaf ears.[25]

Although Wayne's attention in the latter half of 1775 was being drawn ever more certainly toward military matters, he nonetheless continued to serve in the Assembly — if for no other reason than that he might retain his position on the Committee of Safety. In late September, as he stood for reelection in his home county of Chester, a small political incident was created by some opponents, seemingly Quakers, who accused him and the other members of the Chester County Committee of Safety of seeking independence from Britain. Wayne vehemently denied such an intention, declaring that the notion "could not originate but among the *worst of men* for the *worst of purposes*." In fact, the whole idea of independence, he asserted, was "pernicious in its nature," and he declaimed that his hearty wish was "for nothing more than a happy and speedy reconciliation, on constitutional principles, with that state from which [we] derive [our] origins." Wayne was reelected, continuing to serve on the Committee of Safety through the rest of the year and into January of 1776.[26]

Wayne's service on the Committee, however, was becoming more erratic, and soon ceased entirely, because his attention was diverted elsewhere. First, he was called home to Easttown in December by news that his father, Isaac, was dead. After spending some time at Waynesborough attending to personal and business matters relating to the old man's death, he returned to the busy scenes of Philadelphia to continue his public career. Second, Wayne was now a full-fledged colonel in the regular Continental Army, having been unanimously recommended for that position by the Pennsylvania Committee of Safety on January 2, 1776, and approved the following day by the Continental Congress. The colonel was given command of the 4th Battalion of the Pennsylvania line, which consisted almost entirely of Associators who volunteered into his regiment in order to serve under his specific charge. At this point, Colonel Wayne resigned all his civilian posts in order to conform to the Whiggish doctrine, which he heartily endorsed, that civil-military affairs be kept distinctly separate in any well-ordered state.[27]

Although Wayne was delighted with his new rank, one aspect of his appointment was aggravating and created subsequent tensions between himself and a fellow Pennsylvanian, Arthur St. Clair. Congress, following a British tradition that first-commissioned officers were senior in the chain of command (even if they held similar rank), appointed St. Clair and John Shee on January 3 to the rank of colonel in battalions that were "older" than Wayne's. Since Congress had previously commissioned Thomas Mifflin, William Thompson, and John Bull as colonels from Pennsylvania, Wayne now found himself sixth in line of seniority among Pennsylvania's Continental officers. Wayne had no quarrel with the status of those men appointed prior to 1776, or with the appointment of Shee, for he recognized them as being deserving of their seniority by virtue of talents and social rank. He objected, however, to St. Clair's higher status and complained bitterly to anyone who would listen that it was unfair. His pleas were to no avail, for it was not by coincidence that Congress and the Pennsylvania Committee of Safety had ranked Wayne below St. Clair; the latter gentleman, as both bodies knew, had served with distinction as an ensign under Sir Jeffery Amherst in the Seven Years' War. Wayne was not placated by this reasoning and in fact continued to berate his fellow colleague throughout the war. Before long, St. Clair, usually a modest and condescending fellow, reciprocated Wayne's ill feeling, and a simmering feud broke out between the two that poisoned their relations into the 1790s. The responsibility for this fruitless, uncomfortable, and slightly ridiculous state of affairs was almost entirely Wayne's.[28]

Throughout the months of January and February 1776, Colonel Wayne was deeply involved in a chore that hundreds of other new officers in America were stuggling with as well, trying to organize a regiment of troops into some semblance of a fighting force. On January 12 he and most of the other Pennsylvania officers sent a "Representation" to Congress complaining about the company organization of their battalions, and he instructed his captains to continue their efforts to recruit the regiment to full strength. In early February, Congress ordered the 4th Battalion "to quarter. . .in or near Chester" and appointed a committee chaired by John Morton to see that Wayne's men were provided for in their new station. On the eighth, Colonel Wayne informed Morton that when his troops arrived in Marcus Hook, where they decided to locate, they found no preparation whatsoever for their coming. Since they had no barracks, they must live in houses, and Wayne hoped that he could find blankets for his men. A few days later, as he informed John Hancock, president of Congress, his troops were still "in want of almost every necessity," and he doubted that Congress was exerting itself to help him alleviate the regiment's suffering. (The colonel was wrong, for the legislators were requesting the Chester County Committee of Safety to assist the 4th Battalion.) Meanwhile, Wayne in general orders encouraged his men to exercise great care not to harm the houses in which they were living.[29]

While his troops at Marcus Hook went through the vicissitudes of training for war, Wayne remained in Philadelphia, leaving to his good friend, Lieutenant Colonel Francis Johnston, the day-to-day administration of the regiment. On February 12, Wayne continued to berate Pennsylvania's militia law, arguing that as the statute was written, "The burthen of the Association falls chiefly on the poor and middling sort of the inhabitants — while the opulent are, for the most part, exempt." Additionally, all militiamen must supply their own gun and equipment, and this was a cost which few could afford. Certainly, with the fine for non-Association being so low, it was cheaper for some men to pay than to serve, and in any case, all those over fifty were exempt. Therefore, said the colonel, as bare minimums "all able-bodied men, from sixteen to sixty, [should be] obliged to associate or pay the fine," and the public should be required to bear the expense of muskets and other military equipment.[30]

Wayne's concern with the militia law went beyond the question of equity, for he was convinced that the statute retarded recruitments and hindered discipline of those men already in the ranks. By February 17, his battalion numbered 462 men, but these were not enough to fill allotments, and the soldiers on hand at Marcus Hook were a rowdy and undisciplined lot. As Lieutenant Colonel Johnston noted to Wayne on February 26, many of the privates, being apprentices released by their masters because of the workings of the militia law, were the most unruly people imaginable. "The puritanical spirit was unknown among us," said Alexander Graydon, a Pennsylvania soldier at Marcus Hook; "capacious demijohns of madeira were constantly set out in the yard where we formed, for our refreshment before marching out to exercise."[31]

Conditions such as these persuaded Wayne early on in his career that his military discipline must be strict in order to redress the intemperance of the only soldiers he could secure under the bad law of his civilian masters. Thus, he began to punish troopers severely for breaches of military regulations under Pennsylvania's Articles of War. Deserters were handled with special severity, and six of them in less than three months received between fifteen and thirty-nine lashes each. Ever afterward in his career, Wayne was widely known as a strict disciplinarian, and some even came to view him as a martinet. Yet, Wayne's discipline did unquestionably instill efficiency and a martial mien in his troops. As the colonel noted in April, after his command had marched to New York City, the 4th Pennsylvanians were held "in high esteem" by his colleagues there, "especially as to appearance and discipline."[32]

This movement of troops had occurred in early April, after the Pennsylvanians were deemed by Congress well enough trained to take the field. In fact, Colonel Wayne's command was a motley crowd of untried, unmilitary rural men and boys, for whom the legislators had trouble finding arms. But Congress was so desperate by early 1776 that it must use whatever soldiers it had available, for the British army under General William Howe at Boston might move to New York momentarily, since New York and the Hudson River Valley were believed to be the strategic center in America at which English forces would lunge. In addition, New York was the staging base that the patriots were using to send supplies and reinforcements to their army in Canada, an army which had invaded the previous winter, besieged Quebec, and now faced imminent peril from British reinforcements arriving in the St. Lawrence River. Although Wayne did not know it, he and his 4th Battalion were destined almost immediately to march into Canada and try to assist Americans there in retaining a toehold on the north bank of the St. Lawrence.[33]

Wayne's soldiers left for New York without him, for he was detained in Philadelphia by both public and private business. He was wheedling the Pennsylvania Committee of Safety to give him more money to outfit his battalion, and on March 16, he received from that body £2,000 in extra financial support. He was also placating his wife, Polly, who was distraught at his absence. She was troubled, she said, "haveing you So far of and So long absent from me and your Little Daughter and Son that So often asks after you. . . . My Dear I am in great hops this will be the last letter i Shall have to rite to you till i have the pleasure of Seing that fase i So long have loocked for. I remayn with the greatest Love yours till Death."[34] This letter from Polly to Wayne is typical in that it shows the depth of feeling the woman had for her husband in the early stages of the war, and that it was rather coldly turned aside by its recipient. Before long, his coldness was reciprocated, and the relationship between Anthony and Mary Penrose Wayne lapsed into a sort of distant and businesslike formality. That Wayne was responsible for this state of affairs cannot be in doubt after an examination of the correspondence between them during their long years of separation.

When Colonel Wayne arrived in New York City in mid-April, he was welcomed by Generals Washington, Nathanael Greene, Lord Stirling, and other Continental officers. He found his battalion encamped on Long Island. The men were still poorly armed and clothed, as he pointed out to Congress on the twenty-sixth, although the legislators four days earlier had voted $1,000 more on supplies for these troops. To his wife, he noted that the Pennsylvanians were now busy working on defensive fortifications around the city. As for himself, he declared immodestly, his "presence here was absolutely necessary as engineers are much wanted." In a letter to his most intimate friend and neighbor, Dr. Sharp Delany, he described his activities since his arrival, especially his participation in a fox hunt with the "Gentlemen of Long Island" and General Greene. Another hunt, he said, was planned for "Sunday next," with General Israel Putnam and Colonel Mifflin to join the gang that he had ridden with before.[35]

But Wayne's fox hunting and other pleasures quickly came to an end, for he was ordered by Washington to prepare his brigade "for immediate embarkation for Canada," along with five other regiments under the command of a New Hampshire man, General John Sullivan. To his wife on the twenty-eighth of April, he wrote melodramatically, "Whatever may be my fate I can answer for this, that my children will never have reason to blush for the conduct of their father. . . . Adieu my Dear Girl. . . ." Poor Polly, however, was dismayed at the prospect of Wayne's marching to Canada. "The very thought of your going to Quebeck has almost Deprived me of what little Currige i had," she wailed, "for I greatly fear your Constitution will not hold out with your Currige."[36]

Although now fully prepared to set out for parts north, Colonel Wayne suddenly found himself forced into a long wait, while the wheels of military organization turned slowly to accommodate Washington's orders. He blustered to Francis Johnston on May 6 that he hoped "in three weeks. . .to date my next in *Quebeck*," but he was merely daydreaming. Shortly thereafter he received a sweet little letter from Sally Robinson, the young sister of his friend, Thomas Robinson, asking that he care for her brother while both officers were in Canada. Sally Robinson was one of a number of young ladies, among whom were Hetty Griffits and Ann Biddle (who later married James Wilkinson), that Wayne had gotten to know earlier in Philadelphia society. Finally, on May 10, he boarded a ship for Albany and scribbled a last hasty note to Polly: "kiss my little Girl and Boy for me—Tell them their dady sent each of them two—farewell once more—God bless and protect you adiew my Dear Polly."[37]

CHAPTER *ii*

Canada and Ticonderoga
1776–1777

DURING THE NEXT three weeks, Wayne and his battalion wended their way toward Canada. On May 13, the colonel entered Albany and was impressed with neither the town nor its inhabitants. The latter, he said, were "Hollanders who could speak no English," a people "shy of strangers, impolite and mulish." Fortunately, he was not obliged to seek quarters there, for General Philip Schuyler met him and invited him to stay at the Schuyler mansion. When he reached Schuyler's home, "The General's daughters" immediately caught his eye, as he noted to Thomas Robinson. They were, he said appraisingly, "Accomplished, fine, sweet girls, and very handsome." Therefore, he was "necessitated to pass four or five evenings out of six (being the time I was in Albany) in their company."[1]

The day after his arrival in Albany, Colonel Wayne set about to put his battalion on a more martial footing. First, he ordered the men "Shaved, washed Powder'd &c," so they would cut a fine figure on parade. Soon he was boasting about the "soldierly appearance" of his Pennsylvanians, they "made a formidable & pleasing appearance to the Whigs—but—to the *tories.* . . ." Their impressiveness was multiplied by the fact that Wayne, pursuant to Washington's orders, had requisitioned from Schuyler arms enough for the remainder of his troops, and the 4th Pennsylvania Battalion was now fully outfitted for war.[2]

A few days later, Colonel Wayne received orders from General Sullivan to push his men northward once again. In late May he arrived at Fort Ticonderoga, on the south end of the lake, there to be greeted by

21

General Benedict Arnold. Tarrying at Ticonderoga only long enough to see John Trumbull prove that a cannon shot could reach the fort from the top of undefended Mount Defiance (a bad omen for the future ability of Americans to hold Ticonderoga against a determined enemy), on May 27 he pressed on with his troops down Lake Champlain. The barges carrying his army, about two hundred in number, were impressive, according to Captain John Lacey, who was serving under Wayne. "The whole," he said, "made a most formidable and beautiful appearance—I presume, something like the Gretian Fleet going to the Seage of Troy." By June 1, the American forces were in St. Johns and two days later had reached Sorel, on the south bank of the St. Lawrence River. At that place they rendezvoused with patriot troops under command of General David Wooster, who were retreating up the St. Lawrence from Quebec, to escape the dual scourges of smallpox and a mortal fear that hordes of British soldiers, recently arrived in the St. Lawrence Valley, were breathing down their necks. For a day or two afterward, Wayne's attention was taken up by an inconsequential tiff with Captain Lacey, who believed the commander had reneged on an earlier promise to allow the captain to command his own company. But after that matter was settled, more or less amicably, Wayne focused his attention on the growing likelihood of an imminent American confrontation with the British forces in Canada.[3]

Meanwhile, General Sullivan was working himself into a state of mild disgust over the retreat of the patriot army from the walls of Quebec. He declared to Congress, "I am Surprized that an Army should Live in Continual fear of & Even retreat before an Enemy which no person among them has Seen." Itching for a fight, as was his equally zealous subordinate Wayne, Sullivan shortly afterward heard with pleasure from General William Thompson that a British force of 800 regulars was at Trois Rivières on the north bank of the St. Lawrence River, about 45 miles away, under command of Colonel Allen Maclean. Here was a number the Americans could deal with, and if a subsequent intelligence report from Thompson on June 6 was true, the actual number of the enemy might be only 300. Therefore, on June 6 Sullivan issued detailed orders to Thompson for a raid in force on Maclean's British troops. It was the opinion of both Sullivan and Wayne that all thought of American retreat from Canada should be suppressed, at least until British might in the province could be tested. Perhaps the enemy would prove no impediment to an American advance toward Quebec.[4]

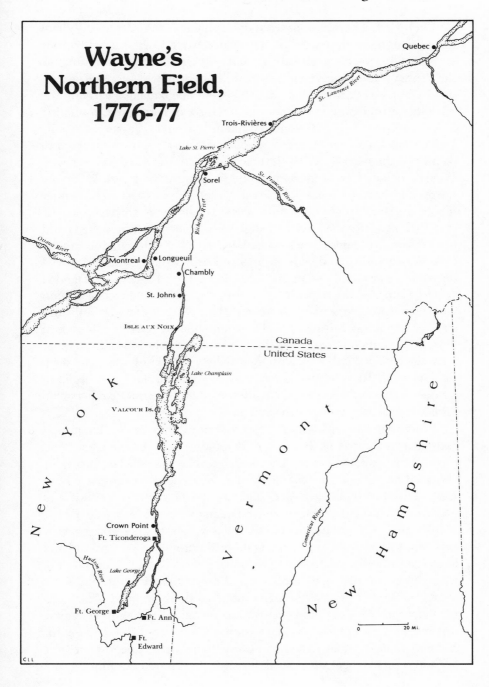

Wayne's Northern Field, 1776-77

Quebec

St. Lawrence River

Trois-Rivières

Lake St. Pierre

St. François River

Sorel

Ottawa River

Richelieu River

Montreal • • Longueuil

• Chambly

St. Johns •

ISLE AUX NOIX

Canada
United States

Lake Champlain

NEW YORK

VALCOUR IS.

Vermont

New Hampshire

Connecticut River

Crown Point •

Ft. Ticonderoga ▪

Hudson River

Lake George

Ft. George ▪

▪ Ft. Ann

▪ Ft. Edward

0   20 Mi.

CLL

On June 7, Thompson ordered the regiments of Wayne and William Irvine to embark down the St. Lawrence River toward a rendezvous with St. Clair's troops, already at Nicolet. Arriving there at midnight, the Pennsylvania officers and General Thompson held a council of war, in which it was decided that an attack would be launched early on the morning of June 9, with the Continental force of 1,450 men, consisting of five divisions led by Colonels William Maxwell, Wayne, St. Clair, Irvine, and Lieutenant Colonel Thomas Hartley, who was ordered to command the reserve. With all their plans laid, the American officers, Wayne included, waited throughout the long day of June 8 for the upcoming clash of arms. For Colonel Wayne this was his first test under fire, and although his personality seemed designed to thrive under the stimulus of warfare, he still had slight misgivings about how he would react to command under such conditions. Finally, night came on and the time for action arrived. The troops reboarded their bateaux, moved downriver to a point about nine miles above Trois Rivières, and landed at two o'clock on the morning of June 9, under the guidance of *habitats* who were hired to lead them toward the town. Following Sullivan's strict admonition to keep open a secure line of retreat, Thompson detached 250 men under Major Joseph Wood to guard the bateaux that were the patriots' only link with their fellows farther up the wide, deep St. Lawrence River. After about an hour's march, daybreak began to lighten the eastern horizon and to illuminate the American soldiers who "proceded swiftly towards the town."[5]

From that moment onward, the American force under Thompson experienced a series of disasters. The guides, said Wayne later, "had mistook the road, the Enemy Discovered and Cannonaded us from their ships." The Americans, still far from Trois Rivières, would have been well advised to withdraw, but, said Colonel Hartley, "no one would propose it." Instead, the army moved inland from the river to avoid the British ships' fire and floundered for the next four hours through waist-deep mud. At last, Wayne's men emerged onto dry, open ground and began to form into a battle line, but they were still under constant fire from cannon on British men-of-war in the river to their right. Suddenly a large body of English "Regulars marched down in good Order Immediately in front of me to prevent our forming," whereupon Wayne ordered his light infantry to skirmish with them until he could get his troops arranged. Finally, he advanced with his battle line, directed the left and right to wheel and flank the enemy, and poured a deadly fire into the redcoats facing him. Under this intense attack, the British attempted to retire with formations intact, "but in a few minutes [they] broke and ran in the utmost Confusion." Wayne had passed his test as a military officer commanding men under enemy fire, for he had directed the hot little fight with coolness and intelligence. According to a description of the colonel at this time, his very person seemed to expand, his high forehead to gleam as he swung his hat, his dark eyes to flash, his voice to ring in bugle tones, and his mind to work like a clock, despite the danger.[6]

Meanwhile, as Wayne later recorded, "the Other Divisions began to emerge from the swamp, except Maxwell who with his was advanced in a thicket a Considerable distance to the left." All the patriot troops now suffered an extremely rude shock, as described by Hartley, for "the great body of the enemy, which we knew nothing of, consisting of two or three thousand men covered with intrenchments and assisted with the cannon of the shipping and several field pieces," under command of British General John Burgoyne, suddenly opened "a furious fire, and continued it upon our troops in the front." Despite these odds, Wayne advanced his regiment against the enemy and was soon joined in battle by the troops of St. Clair, Irvine, and Maxwell. Hartley also entered the affray with his reserves, pushing some of his troops to within eighty yards of the enemy in a position "exposed to the fire of the shipping, as hot as hell." These conditions the Continentals could not tolerate for long, and indeed they soon began to withdraw in reasonably good order until only Wayne's "small Battalion. . .amounting in the whole to about 200 were left exposed to the whole fire of the shipping in the flank and full three thousand men in front with all their Artillery." Then the 4th Battalion retreated as well, "back into the woods which brought us to a Road on the far side of the Swamp"— but not before an enemy ball had given him a "Slight touch in my Right leg."[7]

Although Wayne had managed to extricate himself from the field, his troubles were far from over. The British had detached a force of about 1,500 men to march westward and cut off the Americans' withdrawal, and Wayne, who on his retreat managed to collect together six or seven hundred of the straggling Continentals, ran into part of this enemy force a few miles from the site of the earlier struggle. Since his troops were too fatigued to give the British a fight, the American colonel marched around the redcoats, who "fired their small arms and artillery on our men as loud as thunder." The Continentals returned a retreating fire as they moved near the place where they had left their bateaux early that morning. To their dismay, they learned that Major Wood's guard of 250 men that was supposed to watch over the boats had been forced to retreat with them to Sorel in order to keep them from falling into British hands. Hence, the Americans were compelled to continue their march on land toward Sorel. Thus, said Wayne, on "the third day almost worn out with fatigue, Hunger & Difficulties scarcely to be paralleled," he arrived opposite Sorel with 1100 men and was ferried across the St. Lawrence to relative comfort and safety of the patriot encampment there. Only then did he learn the extent of the American disaster in the battle of Trois Rivières: fifty men killed and two hundred thirty-six prisoners—among them General Thompson and Colonel Irvine—while the British lost only eight dead and nine wounded.[8]

Wayne and his fellow soldiers were fortunate to escape from the dangerous predicament at Trois Rivières. Indeed, had the patriots not been facing an army commanded by a hesitant Guy Carleton rather than his fire-breathing subordinate Burgoyne the outcome might have been different. Wayne, however, was not about to attribute to British lassitude his having pulled the American bacon out of the fire by his orderly retreat. "I believe it will be Universally allowed," he crowed to Dr. Franklin and other Pennsylvanians in a report of the battle on June 13, "that Col Allen [Lieutenant Colonel William Allen of St. Clair's battalion, who had assisted Wayne in the retreat] & myself have saved the Army in Canada." Sullivan also praised "Colo. Waine" for his "great bravery" on the battlefield. Wayne showed himself to be a bit more humble when he gave praise to his troops for "their spirited conduct in bravely attacking and sustaining the fire from both great and small arms of an enemy more than ten times their number." At the same time, however, he could not resist haranguing his men for coming to parade "dirty, with a long beard, or [their] britches knees open."[9]

In his battle reports, the colonel did not exaggerate the danger to Sullivan's Continentals at Sorel, for the British in Canada now outnumbered the Americans by four to one and were preparing to ensnare the entire Patriot army before it could get back to Lake Champlain. On June 8, Carleton ordered three major thrusts toward the Americans, one under General Simon Fraser against Benedict Arnold's garrison at Montreal, a second under Burgoyne against the patriot lines at Sorel. In personal command of a third drive, Carleton sailed with the bulk of his army up the St. Lawrence River toward Longueuil, at which place he intended to disembark and march eastward, behind Sullivan's forces, to St. Johns. He ordered Burgoyne to remain quiescent until Carleton's main army was in place at St. Johns, lest the patriots scamper away from Sorel before the trap was sprung. General Arnold, however, warned by his aide, Captain James Wilkinson, of Fraser's movement toward him, quickly abandoned Montreal, and struck out for St. Johns, while Sullivan on the night of June 13 retreated as rapidly as possible up the Sorel River. Even then, only a five-day hiatus in Carleton's advance, due to a failure of the wind to push the Briton's troop-laden ships to Longueuil and his curious unwillingness to make his redcoats march that extra distance, saved the American army under Sullivan from entrapment.[10]

Wayne and the other Continental officers, however, were not privy to Carleton's problems with troop movement, and to them it seemed that the enemy might overwhelm them momentarily. Arnold especially desired support in his withdrawal from Montreal, and on the night of June 14 sent his aide Wilkinson riding to intercept Sullivan and ask for assistance. At nine o'clock on the evening of the fifteenth, Captain Wilkinson rode into the main American army encampment at Chambly and informed Moses Hazen of the purpose of his odyssey. Since it was determined by then that the American troops at Chambly were too tired to march to Arnold's assistance, and since "the night was profoundly dark," with rain pouring down in "torrents," Wilkinson was instructed to ride toward Sorel, seek General Baron de Woedtke, the commander of the rear guard, and requisition from him five hundred men for his purpose. Finally, at dawn on June 16, Wilkinson reached De Woedtke's headquarters, only to be informed by Lieutenant Colonel Allen that "the beast" was probably drunk somewhere and that in any case the rear guard was worthless because it was "conquered by its fears." Only Colonel Wayne, commanding the troops nearest the enemy to the north, might be able to help, said Allen.[11]

Thus it was that half an hour later, Wayne was hailed by this strange man Wilkinson, who many years later was to gain a reputation as a thoroughly dishonest rascal and who would cause Wayne much grief and anger during his campaign against the Northwest Indians in the 1790s. At this time, however, Wayne, like everyone else who met Wilkinson, took an instant liking to the man. With Wilkinson the feeling was mutual, for the captain described Wayne as a "gallant soldier," who that day was "as much at his ease as if he was marching to a parade of exercise." When informed of Wilkinson's mission, the colonel immediately agreed to ride to Arnold's rescue, and began collecting a force of men by the simple expedient of posting a guard on a bridge over which the troops must pass, "with orders to stop every man without regard to corps, who appeared to be active, alert, and equipped." In such fashion did he soon have his detachment formed, at which time he immediately set out with it in company with Wilkinson for Longueuil.[12]

Before Colonel Wayne had marched his heterogenous force two miles, he met an express from Arnold with news that the latter had made good his escape from Montreal. The purpose of his mission now negated, Wayne wheeled his men about and marched them southward toward Chambly. As he approached the rear of the main encampment, his forces were espied by Sullivan's troopers and taken for the enemy. "Great alarm and confusion ensued," said Wilkinson, "the drums beat to arms, and Gen. Sullivan and his officers were observed making great exertions to prepare for battle." In response, Wayne merely halted his column and with a sardonic smile pulled his spyglass from its case in order better to observe the scurrying about in the patriot camp that his presence had precipitated. Only after Wilkinson reminded Wayne that this full-scale alert might slow the Americans in their retreat did the colonel order Wilkinson to ride forward and "correct the delusion." Then Wayne joined General Sullivan and proceeded with the commander on the evening of the sixteenth to St. Johns.[13]

For the next two days, American troops continued to straggle into this little town. Then, at last, on the afternoon of June 18, with the van of a British column under Burgoyne only two miles away, Sullivan was forced to abandon St. Johns after putting it to the torch. The same afternoon, the commander and his little army of 2,533 men reached Île-aux-Noix in Lake Champlain, where the determined general decided to remain until ordered by Washington or Congress to budge. However, the place was so unhealthy that soldiers began to fall by scores to various scourges, such as "Fluxes, Fevers, Small Pox. . .Lice and Maggots [which crept] in Millions over the Victims," according to John Lacey. Colonel Wayne's regiment alone, said Sullivan, had sixty of 138 men down with some sort of ague. In all this wretchedness, however, the Americans at Île-aux-Noix could take comfort from one thing, that Carleton had halted the British advance at St. Johns and—to the wonderment of his decimated foes—showed not the slightest sign of recommencing the assault any time soon.[14]

While Wayne's men fell sick about him, the colonel had little to keep him busy in the next few weeks. He got involved with a minor Indian raiding party on June 22, and he also received letters from home. One, from his mother, informed him that the family was in good health and chastised him mildly for having written only one letter to her since he left Pennsylvania. Another, from Polly, gave a heartrending account of her having read in the papers about the battle of Trois Rivières before she received his letter of the thirteenth. She had not known for days, she said, whether the man "who is as dear to me as my own life" was alive or dead, and she was overjoyed to receive his note. The farm was in good condition, she reported, and "I have goan on extremely well in farming this far," but still she wished her husband was at home to help her.[15]

Meanwhile, Colonel Wayne and his battalion, along with the rest of Sullivan's small and wretched army, withdrew on July 1 from Île-aux-Noix southward to Crown Point. There, according to John Trumbull, the army's adjutant general, the men were "dispersed, some few in tents, some in sheds, and more under the shelter of miserable brush huts, . . .totally discouraged by the death or sickness of officers." Four days later, Sullivan was relieved of his command and, much to his disgust (which he broadcast far and wide), replaced by General Horatio Gates, whose commission from Congress said he was to command the patriot army "in Canada." Since Gates's troops were now in Schuyler's area of command, the Northern Department, it was not altogether clear what his authority was to be. In fact, the matter was not cleared up completely between the generals until over a year later, when Gates finally superseded Schuyler as commander of the entire department. Meanwhile, many patriot officers in New York took sides in the altercation over command, and many jealousies were aroused, although not enough, fortunately for the American cause, to weaken the war effort. Colonel Wayne, who at the inception of this quarrel respected all three generals, Sullivan, Gates, and Schuyler, about equally well, attempted to remain aloof from the partisan bickering of their supporters.[16]

Immediately upon taking command at Crown Point, General Gates called a council of war, which Wayne attended, to determine where the Americans must make a stand, should Carleton once more put his army in motion southward. It was the council's decision that Crown Point could not be defended and that the army should move to Fort Ticonderoga, a few miles farther up Lake Champlain. Hence, Wayne shortly found himself at the place where he would spend the following winter and which he would come to despise. But conditions in the patriot army were improving rapidly under Gates's command, and the colonel found his spirits reviving rapidly after the horrors of the recent retreat from Canada. Not even the brigading of the army on July 20, in which the four Pennsylvania battalions, Wayne's included, were constituted the 4th Brigade under command of Colonel Arthur St. Clair, dampened his growing enthusiasm. He was especially delighted to receive word that Congress on July 4 had voted independence from Great Britain. By July 20, Wayne was writing to Franklin, Mifflin, and other friends in Pennsylvania that although his soldiers were destitute of nearly every necessity — shoes, stockings, shirts, soap — their morale was high. In any case, they may not have to fight the enemy, for Gates and Arnold were building boats on Lake Champlain and hoped to get a superior fleet on the water before the British, who were busy as beavers building shipping at St. Johns, could advance.[17]

In the next two months, conditions at Ticonderoga continued to get better for Wayne and the American army. Soon the force had increased to 4,000 men, and the breastworks were complete. To Polly, Wayne said, "Our people have Recovered health and Spirits — have now the finest and best Regiment in the Continental Service." He was disconcerted to learn from his brother-in-law, Colonel Joseph Penrose, that the fortunes of American forces under Washington at New York were not as good as they might be, asserting from his distant vantage point that the commander in chief ought to quit Manhattan. Also trying was word from Franklin that Wayne could expect few resources for his troops in the immediate future, for "America is new at supplying armies" and must learn the game.[18]

On October 11, Wayne's full attention was directed to his immediate military command, for by that time General Carleton had decided at last to drive up Lake Champlain toward Ticonderoga. Beginning that day, a seventy-two-hour running battle between Arnold's American flotilla and Carleton's more powerful naval force resulted by the evening of October 13 in an almost complete annihilation of the Continental fleet. The following day, Wayne wrote excitedly to his wife that a remnant of the shattered patriot force had arrived at Ticonderoga and that Carleton must be close behind. Four days later, he was informing Rush that Carleton was still fifteen miles from Ticonderoga but was awaiting only a fair wind to come southward and attack. He was afraid the patriot forces would be compelled in such an event to fight in the open, for the rear of the American defenses had been neglected because of Gates's dependence upon the fleet.[19]

Soon it became clear to Wayne that he was getting excited for nothing, because Carleton had no serious intention to challenge the patriots at Ticonderoga. After sending a few scouting parties down the lake, the British general withdrew his army toward Canada. On November 5, Wayne was melodramatically declaring that "Honor," "Virtue," and "the Sword" required the Americans to prevent Carleton's "Parasites" from escaping American vengeance — but he, like every other Continental officer at Ticonderoga, was enormously relieved to see the British force depart without a contest. As the colonel knew, and as he told Franklin on the fifteenth, had Carleton invested Ticonderoga the patriots would have been compelled to surrender or face utter annihilation. Yet, he could not resist taking one more rhetorical swipe at his enemies, wondering to Rush in a letter on the twenty-fifth, "What Reason can be assigned those blustering sons of War Carton [sic] and Burgoyne, for their shamefully flying before a people whom they affected so much to Despise."[20]

Colonel Wayne now secured his first independent military command, the patriot army at Ticonderoga. On November 18, General Gates departed for the south with eight Continental regiments, destined to assist Washington's much battered army in New Jersey. Both Gates and Schuyler agreed that in Gates's absence Wayne was the man to leave in charge at the south end of Lake Champlain, for they knew the colonel to be an enterprising and trustworthy officer from his activities at Trois Rivières and during the recent retreat. On November 20, Wayne promised Gates to do the best he could, but he had neither time nor materials enough to effect much. With this assessment Colonel Richard Varick, an officer at Ticonderoga and a close confidant of Schuyler, agreed. But, as he noted to his mentor, he also wondered about Wayne's personal competence. "Tho' Col. Wayne be a brave man," said Varick on November 20, "he is not the character suited to carry into execution the many and various kinds of things that are absolutely necessary to be done, he has been more accustomed to good company & leaving others to superintend, than to deliberate & spend his time in the more necessary employment [of superintending] others."[21] Although Varick's assessment of Wayne's military abilities was shrewd, he was nonetheless somewhat biased against Wayne before he wrote this statement, and his personal antagonism may have contributed to the negative judgments about his fellow colonel. Two days before, Varick had been attacked by a Colonel White, who had somehow come into possession of Wayne's sword and pistols for use in the assault. Upon White's promise to leave Varick alone, both Gates and Wayne had agreed to parole the man while he awaited a military hearing, but Varick was suspicious that Wayne — who was a friend of Gates and therefore automatically not to be trusted — might be trying to set up a situation wherein he could be attacked again. Colonel Varick's suspicions of Wayne were nonsensical, but they do point up how difficult it was for officers in the Northern Department during that trying time to remain neutral between Gates and Schuyler.[22]

In fact, Wayne was by this time beginning to tilt in the direction of support for Gates, and perhaps Varick and Schuyler recognized that this was the case. As early as the previous July, Wayne was hinting in a letter to Franklin that Schuyler was keeping news from him by refusing to send on to Ticonderoga any information that arrived in Albany. Then, early in December, the colonel was rankled by what he considered Schuyler's unnecessary meddling with his command. He fumed to Gates that Schuyler had given him the following orders, "Viz: That sentries were necessary in an Army, that cleanliness was conducive to health; that chimneys ought to be swept; to send advice if soap and candles were wanting, & c. Indeed, the chief purport of them were to let me know that I had no power to do any one act, however necessary, without first obtaining permission in writing from Head Quarters in *Saratoga* or *Albany*." The colonel, however, intended "to recollect the heads of such matters as you recommended to me *viva voce*, and to render this place as tenable as possible during the time I remain on the ground." Given this attitude on Wayne's part, his subsequent relations with Schuyler could not be expected to improve very much.[23]

They did not. On December 16, Wayne questioned whether an order by Schuyler concerning recruiting officers should be published in general orders. A few days later he received a sharply worded note from Schuyler suggesting that the colonel keep his ideas to himself and obey orders, and expressing surprise that such a reprimand was necessary. Wayne responded to Schuyler's censure with an apology, explaining that he had thought the general's commands did not dovetail with his own instructions from Congress. The entire matter was a misunderstanding, he said; otherwise he would not have gotten so severe a reprimand "from a general whom I esteem." Schuyler's answer, stiff and formal, was hardly placatory. The issue, he declared, was more than just Wayne's refusal to publish orders, "it was giving an order contradictory to mine." The general had had no choice but to do his duty by responding as he did, or so he said. This exchange did nothing to alter Wayne's growing perception that Schuyler was something of a tyrant and to reinforce his support for General Gates.[24]

As winter closed about Colonel Wayne and his Pennsylvanians at Fort Ticonderoga, the frigid weather brought much suffering for the cold, debilitated, poorly fed troops. Wayne protested to the Pennsylvania Committee of Safety on December 4 that his soldiers had been paid only twice since they left Philadelphia and that they were now in "wretched condition. . .for want of almost every necessary of the convenience of life, except flour and bad beef." In letter after letter, he complained about the horrible conditions in his army's hospital, "or rather house of carnage." The dead and dying, he said, were mixed together indiscriminantly, there were no beds or bedding for the ailing troops, medicine was nonexistent, and the cold penetrated to the patients' very bones. "Death that *Grisly Horrid Monster* — that Caitiff who Distinguishes neither the Gentleman, nor the Soldier, age Sex, or *State*," he wrote Congressman George Clymer on the tenth of December, "is daily making dreadful Havock amongst the Pennsylvanians." Fifty men from his own regiment had already been buried, he said, and he believed only nine hundred of his two thousand original soldiers would return to their native state. Ticonderoga, he asserted, was "the Ancient Golgotha a place of Skulls — they are so plenty here that our people for want of Other Vessels drink out of them." The number of troops under his command from all states had shrunk in December to only 2,451, including the sick, and although Schuyler was promising that New England would send him more soldiers, the prospect of securing a reinforcement any time soon was not encouraging.[25]

Promotions were on Wayne's mind during these early days of his tenure at Ticonderoga, for both his friends and himself. He was encouraging Congress with vigor to give his close comrade Francis Johnston a full colonelcy, and he also wanted to see Thomas Hartley advanced in rank. Therefore, on November 12, he encouraged his friend Richard Peters in Philadelphia to push in Congress for his colleagues' promotions. For himself, he hinted broadly to General Gates on December 1 that he was willing to accept a brigadier generalship. But he was disturbed by rumors that Congress might promote two other Pennsylvania colonels, Robert Magaw and John P. DeHass, both of whom were "younger in rank" than he was, while leaving him frozen in his present station. These men were good officers, admitted Wayne, but if they were jumped over him in the chain of command, "I shall with the utmost composure retire to my Sabine field, where love, where peace, and all that man can wish fondly, wants my return. I never will submit to be commanded by the man whom I commanded yesterday. I may be wrong, but I have Custom and prejudice in my favor, and a pride common to a soldier, that will not be easily eradicated."[26]

Meanwhile, Wayne was being bombarded with news of Washington's movements to the southward. From Benedict Arnold on November 25 he learned that the enemy had captured Fort Washington on Manhattan with 2,000 prisoners and that the Americans had abandoned Fort Lee on the New Jersey side of the Hudson River. Soon other bad news was filtering up from New Jersey, that General Charles Lee had been captured and that Pennsylvania possibly had been invaded. On January 3, 1777, Wayne in some alarm wrote Polly, instructing her to take care of herself and the family and to be sure that she flee Waynesborough to friends in the "back country" should General Howe occupy Chester County. The "British rebels," he assured her, might be successful for a season, but eventually they would be conquered.[27]

That Colonel Wayne was not merely whistling down the wind with these comments was shown in further elucidation of his military thinking in early 1777, written to friends and acquaintances. He declared to James Moore on January 2, "We shall soon learn to meet [the British] in the Open field — let them Conquer our Maritime towns — they can't Subjugate the free Sons of America — who very shortly will produce a Conviction to the World that they deserve to be free." American defeat, shrewdly observed Wayne to another acquaintance on the third, would eventually prove Britain's ruin, for "our country can absorb much & still rise," while the enemy must import at great expense vast armies and mountains of supplies. In the short run, though, American generals must learn tactics, for they were constantly being outflanked — "thus proving Marshal Saxe's comment that only good lines are the natural & best retrenchment." Patriot troops were "so used to *stand behind works*," declared Wayne to Delany, "that they dare not face the foe in the field — That — that is the Rock we have split on. Our time has been Intirely taken up in making lines &c. and no attention paid to Manoeuvering — our Defenses by some fatality have been so planed that . . .the Enemy could get in our Rear."[28]

As the winter in upstate New York deepened, Colonel Wayne came to despise his inhospitable surroundings and wished with great fervor to march south to where the action was. "Ticonderoga," he groused, "Affords few of the Necessaries less of the Conveniences — and none of the *Desirable objects* of life." To escape his miseries, Wayne during the month of January hinted on two occasions to Schuyler that he and the Pennsylvanians could do much more for America by joining Washington's fight against Howe in their home state and in neighboring New Jersey. Schuyler, however, realized that Wayne was needed at Ticonderoga and would not react to his subordinate's suggestions.[29]

General Schuyler was soon to react, however, to another perceived "slight" (his own word) from Colonel Wayne. The colonel, it seems, was in a terrible quandary by late December 1776, about what course of action he should take regarding Pennsylvania troops whose enlistments were up at the end of the year, who were clamoring to go home, but whose services he might need longer. The problem was being resolved, Schuyler informed Wayne on the twenty-ninth, for a regiment of Massachusetts militia was on the way to relieve part of his men and other replacements would soon follow. Hence, the Pennsylvanians could all soon be discharged. Meanwhile, however, Wayne was not to let any of his soldiers depart the camp until they were relieved, "even tho' their times may be out." But Wayne's replacement troops did not arrive and did not arrive, while all the time his men became ever more insistent on going home.[30]

At last, Wayne deputized two junior officers to attend Schuyler's headquarters with verbal warning that the situation at Ticonderoga was reaching an intolerable state. Not only were the numbers of his troops too few, but the ones he had on hand were about to mutiny because they were ill-supplied, their enlistments were up, and they were demanding to be discharged immediately. When Schuyler heard these words from Wayne's emissaries, he was furious with Wayne, both for their implied censure of his abilities as a military administrator and for the "unusual" way in which they were delivered. For his part, Wayne defended his use of officers to deliver messages, especially since he had unsuccessfully informed Schuyler of his problems before. He conceded the general's right "to enjoin me to do my duty where I was deficit," but in this case he was *not* deficit. Since the matter was, at least for him, one of the head and not of the heart, he was willing to forget it. Schuyler, in a placatory mood, assured Wayne that he was fully aware of the colonel's problems and was doing everything in his earthly power to resolve them.[31]

Wayne proved not to be exaggerating about the dangers of mutiny

among his men, for in late January and early February his command was
racked by a series of such discontents. On January 25, two Pennsylvania
regiments had been finally relieved by Massachusetts troops, and with
Wayne's blessing had marched for home. For the troops of the 6th
Regiment, who were not yet allowed to depart for their hearths, this was
more than they could bear. On the same day that their luckier brothers
started southward, they declared that they would do no further duty
and demanded also to be released from the army. In dealing with this
problem, Wayne realized the distasteful truth that, although he did not
like being compelled to use coercion against his fellow Pennsylvanians,
he might be forced to. Therefore, he immediately proceeded to Mount
Independence and put another regiment on full military alert, in case
they were needed. He then met with the mutineers, harangued them
about their responsibilities, and appealed to their patriotism. When
these rhetorical flourishes did not work he finally had to promise the
regiment that it could go home after two more weeks of service, whereupon the men instantly returned to their duty. Then on February 11, a
second mutiny flared up, this time in a company of riflemen. When
Wayne asked these men what their problem was, he was told in a
"Tumultuous manner" that their terms of service had been up for more
than a month. He then asked the leader of the company to step out and
speak for the others, and when the man advanced, Wayne drew a pistol
and put it to the poor fellow's breast. Falling to his knees, the unfortunate begged for his life, while Wayne ordered the other mutineers
to ground arms, which they immediately did. Wayne then told them
that if they would remain in the army until the twentieth they could
leave peacefully, an arrangement to which they readily assented.[32]

The rifle company had hardly returned to its duty before Colonel
Wayne was confronted by yet another incident. "A certain Josiah
Holida [Holliday]," he wrote Schuyler, was inciting another company,
this time in Colonel Thomas Robinson's regiment, to refuse to work.
Wayne, in confronting Holliday, lost his temper, struck him a blow,
and ordered him to the guardhouse, whereupon Captain Aaron Coe of
the same regiment protested to the colonel in writing that his actions
were unjust, "that every soldier had a right to deliver his sentiments on
every occasion without being punished." For his pains, Coe was also
arrested, and the colonel threatened to pack both of them off to Albany
on the charge of abetting mutiny. Schuyler, however, informed Wayne
that these men ought to be tried at Wayne's own post, by militia officers,

for they were militiamen and the state's articles of war stipulated such a procedure. In the time it took Wayne to receive these instructions, his temper had cooled and he had "released Coe & his Coadjutor Holida." Both, he noted to the general, had "come to their senses." Although the colonel did not say so, perhaps he had as well, for mutinous behavior among his troops was on the decline by then and he felt it was better to let things calm down at Ticonderoga. Nonetheless, he was pretty disgusted with militiamen by this time. "I have been necessitated," he declared shortly afterward, "to put some of the officers in irons, Kick and pull the noses of others, by which means I have brought them to a sense of their duty. To say anything severe to them has just as much effect as if you were to cut up a Butcher's Choping block with a razor. By G-d, they feel nothing but the down Right blows which, with the dread of being whipt thro' the Small Guts keeps them in some awe."[33]

Problems such as Wayne was having with the troops at Ticonderoga in the winter months of 1776–1777 were swiftly altering his views on what form America's revolutionary armies should take. Earlier in the war with Britain, he had expressed "radical" Whiggish views on military and political matters, freely asserting his willingness to fight for "the rights of man" and to preserve "liberty." The army that American Whigs would use to effect these great ends, he felt, must reflect the free society of the United States, which was at once the source and purpose of the revolution. Therefore, the major motive of the soldiers should be a freely chosen willingness to serve, and patriot armies must be ordered and run by officers who understood this point. American soldiers, being free citizens who associated under their commanders for the common purpose of preserving American liberties, must not be strictured by notions of discipline and regularity that would be more appropriate for European peasant armies. A too-severe discipline, in fact, by creating a more traditional, regular army in America — and, more dangerously (as far as the radical Whigs were concerned), a *regular army mentality* — might bring about a paradoxical result: A United States that was independent of Britain but which had lost the very liberties for which it had originally rebelled.

Thus Wayne, while he had found fault in early 1776 with some parts of Pennsylvania's Association, had nonetheless approved of the *principle* of loosely formed citizen armies, membership in which would be voluntary and short term. Even after the Continental Army was organized by Congress, he did not disapprove of having its soldiers serve only until the end of 1776. After all, military service was a privilege which many citizens should have, and when the term of service was up for some, others could come forward to fill the ranks. Discipline in such a force would be no problem, he thought (and on this point he agreed with General Charles Lee), for the troops could learn a few simple military exercises and their ardor for the cause could overcome any "minor" difficulties they may encounter in battle, in camp routine, or on the march.[34]

At Ticonderoga, Colonel Wayne changed his position, maintaining for the rest of his life a new set of notions on the philosophy of warfare. To his friend Sharp Delany, he wrote on December 15, 1776, "in regard to discipline [for our armies as they were being formed in 1775] we understood by this only to put a necessary constraint on the principle of freedom to prevent it growing into licentiousness which it inevitably would if not Curbed in an army." Now, however, he was convinced that liberty for soldiers in an army must be much more severely restricted, for only by limiting individual soldiers' freedoms could the army itself function for its intended purpose. "Here I must once more call in the aid of Marshal Saxe," said Wayne. "He says — *and he says well* — 'that it is a false notion, that subordination, and a passive Obedience to Superiors [debases a man's impulse to liberty or courage] — *so far from it*, that it is a General remark — that those Armies that have been subject to the Severest Discipline *have always* performed the greatest things.' " Declared Wayne, "I shall for my own part Endeavour to put [Saxe's idea] into practice. . .as I am well Convinced that we shall never Establish our Liberties until we learn to beat the *English Rebels* in the field." American armies at present, he noted a few days later, were "no better than so many *Contemptable heaps of Rabble*," but that situation he hoped would change very shortly. Until then, he was "not as yet for putting the fate of America on the Issue of Battle."[35]

Wayne's optimism that the discipline and regularity of his army would soon improve was based upon more than his own irrespressibly ebullient character, for he had now learned that Congress had strengthened his hand as a disciplinarian and military officer. On September 16, even the sternest Whigs in that body had been forced to recognize that America's military forces must be reorganized and enlarged, with the men enrolled "to serve during the present war. . .unless sooner discharged by Congress." These changes, Wayne believed, would eliminate the problems that resulted from short-term enlistments. Moreover, Congress now directed individual states to supply arms and other military necessities to their troops — thus assuring (Wayne was confident) that rich and generous Pennsylvania would furnish its martial sons with every warlike necessity in the future. Finally, on September 20, the legislators had adopted new and stricter articles of war, in order to guarantee that officers' problems with regularity, such as Wayne had encountered at Ticonderoga, could be better dealt with. So Wayne, following up on his notions about improving discipline, wrote a long letter to all his captains, encouraging them to use "Necessary severity" with their troops and render themselves "at once beloved and feared." Consult "military Authors," he lectured, "and be particularly Attentive to the manoeuvering of the men." For his own part, he concluded, "I would much rather lead Gentlemen to their duty by a silken thread than be necessitated to make use of coercive rules."[36]

From the appearance of his command at Ticonderoga in early 1777 the colonel would have a long time to wait, not only for a trained army but for an army to train. He had kept in steady communication with Congress since becoming commandant of the fort, and on February 2 he notified the legislators that conditions were deteriorating there as the winter progressed. The same news he sent to Gates and Schuyler two days later, noting that the fort's defenses must be improved if the rebels intended to hold Ticonderoga in the coming summer. Wayne had done all he could "to render the post tenable," building blockhouses and an abattis, but with only 1,200 troops on hand, little work could be accomplished. With the Pennsylvanians departing as their times expired, the number of soldiers under his command by February 8 was even lower. The colonel was disgusted with this entire arrangement and wanted to be relieved, for his health was being impaired by having to act as quartermaster, commissary, and commander all at once. The only reason why the enemy force in Canada had not already attacked him, he declared to Gates, was because part of Lake Champlain had thawed since December, and the British could not use sleighs they had collected for the purpose. Were the redcoats to come, he certainly could not fight them, since his garrison was "easy prey to the Enemy for want of proper Supplies to maintain an Army. . .owing to a Supineness somewhere."[37]

By March, Wayne still had not received the much promised Massachusetts militia, although he had finally resolved in February to go over Schuyler's head and write Governor James Bowdoin to plead assistance. The governor, like General Schuyler, promised immediate replacements, but a month later no Bay State men had arrived at Ticonderoga. On March 2, Wayne had only 150 Continental regulars in his entire command, and only 850 militia. A week later, his total numbers had not changed, but the number of Continentals had risen to 400. Of his militiamen, he noted with bemusement, many were children twelve to fifteen years old, and fully one-third were "Albany Dutchmen," who could not speak a word of English. It was both hilarious and pitiful, he said, to watch these latter troops drill, for when they were ordered to be quiet they "Gobble dutch," when ordered to rest arms they threw their pieces in the dust with butts and muzzles intermixed, when ordered to march, they made a dash for their huts. But they were good for one thing, standing watch, because since only they knew the passwords, no stragglers entered or left the camp. "Thus go we on," he said with resignation; "Tis said that there is some Consolation in Hell itself."[38]

Throughout most of his tenure at Fort Ticonderoga, Colonel Wayne heard little news from Pennsylvania and received no letters from either family or friends. Since learning of Washington's victories at Trenton and Princeton, he took comfort from the fact that his relations were safe from enemy harm, but he knew little else about their doings. By February he was chastising them all for not writing and threatening — mostly in jest — to quit writing himself. However, he kept up a light-hearted correspondence with Sally Robinson Peters and Hetty Griffits, and he remained in touch with Delany. He also finally got around to writing a short note to his mother, in which he expressed regret that he could not march to her defense when Howe threatened Pennsylvania. He did believe, in any case, that he would shortly be relieved by a general officer at Ticonderoga and ordered to join Washington's army. He sent to Polly another of his impersonal notes, informing her about military affairs in his department and entreating her to see to their children's education. "My son," he said, "must be made the first of scholars."[39]

By mid-March, it was clear that Wayne would soon be allowed to depart despised Ticonderoga. For one thing, Congress on February 21 had finally promoted him (and nine other men) to the rank of brigadier general, and he learned that he was probably to command a brigade of Pennsylvania troops in Washington's main army. For another, General Gates informed him on March 13 that Congress had resolved to send a major general to Albany and two brigadiers to Ticonderoga. When the latter officers arrived, Wayne was to "set out Immediately for Philadelphia." On April 12, he finally received a letter from Washington himself, ordering him to take charge of a Pennsylvania brigade at Morristown as soon as he was relieved of his duty at Ticonderoga. "Your presence here," said Washington, "will be materially wanted, and I persuade myself you will lose no time in complying with my requisition."[40] Indeed, General Wayne was only too happy to leave Fort Ticonderoga — his "Golgotha" — and he set out in mid-May for his new field of adventure to the southward.

···
CHAPTER *iii*
―――――

Trials in Pennsylvania
1777

WHEN GENERAL WAYNE reached Morristown on May 20, 1777, he discovered that his standing in the Continental Army and with Washington was high. His bravery under fire, his skill at leading troops in battle, and his abilities as an army administrator had all been tested in Canada and at Ticonderoga. Therefore, he was respected by military men and was even having his opinions on some matters quoted by the commander in chief himself. In April, Washington had written General Heath, lamenting about field officers not leading their regiments into battle and calling this "a scandalous practice" which "General Wayne complains of. . .with great justice."[1]

While Wayne's training in his previous year of service had prepared him for most of the problems in his new command, his difficulties were magnified by the number of troops he was to lead. For despite the fact that Washington had told him that he was to command a brigade, he would very shortly find himself in charge of a much larger contingent of troops. Not long after Wayne reached Morristown, the commander in chief arranged his army in five divisions, led respectively by Nathanael Greene, Adam Stephen, John Sullivan, Benjamin Lincoln, and Lord Stirling. Under Lincoln, Washington placed two Pennsylvania brigades of four regiments each, one commanded by Wayne, the other by John P. DeHaas, a brigadier general appointed on the same day as Wayne but given lower seniority. Hardly had this arrangement been completed than Washington sent Lincoln to upstate New York to help counter the British threat in that region and gave Wayne command of the entire

42

division of two brigades, numbering in all about 1,700 troops. These Pennsylvanians were enlisted under the law which Congress had enacted the previous September, calling for national troops "to serve during the present war." Thus, Wayne felt assured that he would receive considerably greater personal satisfaction from commanding his "new-modeled" division that he had in serving at Ticonderoga.[2]

As Wayne reflected on his new position in the Continental Army, it became apparent to him that he had taken on the responsibility and work of a major general, without assuming a major general's rank, pay, and privileges. And, in fact, he would not achieve this rank until October, 1783, after the war had come to an end. Why this curious situation prevailed was because there were only two major generals in the Pennsylvania line — Thomas Mifflin and Arthur St. Clair — who might have been eligible for this post, and they were being employed respectively as quartermaster general and commander of Ticonderoga, where apparently they were considered indispensable. Since Wayne could not get Congress to consider promoting him to major general at this time — because he had only four months ago achieved his present rank — there was nothing for him to do but acquiesce in the situation or resign. He chose the former course for two reasons. First, he felt loyalty to the cause of American independence and wanted to do his part for that cause by remaining in the service. Second, he was thrilled to be given such an important and responsible military command, even if he did not enjoy the rank that was supposed to go with it, for he now had a field of action large enough to give full play to his egotistical military romanticism.

His thirst for military glory and his exercise of its more glaring pomposities as a commander, however, did not decrease Wayne's subordination to Washington or weaken his value to the commander in chief. Quickly he fell into the rhythm of camp life and began, as he noted to Polly, "to do the duty of three general officers."[3] The biggest problem facing the American officers was what General Howe intended to do in the upcoming campaign. The previous winter, after the battles of Trenton and Princeton, the British general had withdrawn his army to New Brunswick and the Raritan River line in New Jersey, and there he yet remained. Would he drive forward from there toward Philadelphia by land, or would he push his troops up the Hudson River to meet a British army moving out of Canada, now under command of John Burgoyne? These, to be sure, seemed the most eligible possibilities from which Howe might choose for the campaign of 1777, but Wayne, like all the Continental officers, could only speculate and wait to see what the British commander's strategic decision would be.

Meanwhile, Wayne was preparing his command for the upcoming contest with Howe's redcoated and German minions. Following Washington's orders, he started getting his officers and men to their respective corps, recruiting his brigades up to strength, halting desertions, seeing to the men's arms, drilling his soldiers in battlefield maneuvers, and soliciting from the Board of War arms and clothing for some of his troops who were deficient in both. He wrote to his friend Richard Peters, "I would rather risk my life, my reputation and the fate of America on 5000 men neatly uniformed than on a third more, equally armed and disciplined, covered with raggs and Crawling with Verman." On May 25, in his first brush with the enemy since he had assumed his new post, five hundred of his troopers got in a fire fight with an enemy force of seven hundred from British General James Grant's division and drove it off. This skirmish, he noted proudly, had gained him Washington's "Esteem and Confidence," while dirtying Grant's coat and blowing off his horse's head. On May 31, with the rest of the American army, Wayne's soldiers decamped from Morristown and marched to a new positon at Bound Brook. There, Wayne proudly wrote Delany on the seventh of June, Washington stationed him and his Pennsylvanians "in front" of the camp at Mount Prospect, on the most important pass leading from the British to the American posts. "I can't be spared from camp," he boasted to Polly; "I have the Confidence of the General and the Hearts of the Soldiers who will Support me on the day of Action."[4]

That "day of action" was at hand, for on the fourteenth, General Howe began a long anticipated movement against Washington's army by thrusting a heavy column from New Brunswick toward Somerset Court House, about nine miles away. Along with other Continental officers, Wayne was alerted by the commander in chief to strike camp and be ready to march at a moment's notice, for this might prove to be a major action by the British army. On the twenty-second, Washington had a use for Wayne's troops. By that day, Howe had withdrawn his soldiers from Somerset Court House and was abandoning New Brunswick itself. Suddenly it was clear to the commander in chief that Howe's purpose in his advance all along had been to confuse the Americans and mask a British withdrawal toward New York City. Immediately, the

American commander ordered General Greene to take charge of Wayne's Pennsylvanians and Daniel Morgan's Rifle Corps and assault Howe's rear guard at New Brunswick. Greene moved swiftly to the attack, and although he was outnumbered by the enemy, he allowed Wayne and Morgan to harass the redcoats "from redoubt to redoubt" all the way to Perth Amboy. That night, Washington wrote Congress, describing these activities and praising the "Conduct and bravery of Genl. Wayne and Colo. Morgan and of their Officers and Men. . .as they constantly advanced upon an Enemy far superior to them in numbers." Howe, after a hot skirmish on the twenty-sixth with Lord Stirling's division at Metuchen Meeting House, had quitted New Jersey and withdrawn to New York City.[5]

Given a short hiatus in military duties by Howe's removal from the American front, Wayne used his time to reflect on the political situation in Pennsylvania. Ever since the previous summer, when a convention had been called in Philadelphia to devise a new state constitution, Wayne had received letters from numerous friends and acquaintances disparaging the document as being too democratic. In August 1776, John Morton wrote Wayne that the convention was doing "some things which people did not Expect," such as usurping powers of government and taking authority out of the hands of the old Assembly. A month later, Dr. Benjamin Rush sent Wayne a copy of the constitution, and the general learned that it called for a one-house legislature, a weak executive with no veto power, and frequent elections. The document, a product of the most radical elements of Pennsylvania society, led by men like George Bryan, Timothy Matlack, and James Cannon, was deemed by Rush "to be rather too much upon the democratical order, for liberty is apt to degenerate into luxuriousness, as power is to become arbitrary. . . . But we hope the Council of Censors [a body called for in the new document to suggest amendments to the basic law after seven years] will remedy this defect."[6]

Despite Rush's criticisms of the new constitution, Wayne remained noncommittal about it for some months. In October, he had written his friend Benjamin Franklin, "I observe we have an extraordinary House or Convention in Pennsylvania. . .but the old Adage holds — that a Desperate Disorder — requires a Desperate cure — Our Constitution was Convulsed — these may be the most proper state Physicians to restore it to its native vigor." At his distance from Philadelphia, said Wayne, he could not but be "totally unacquainted with your Politicks I

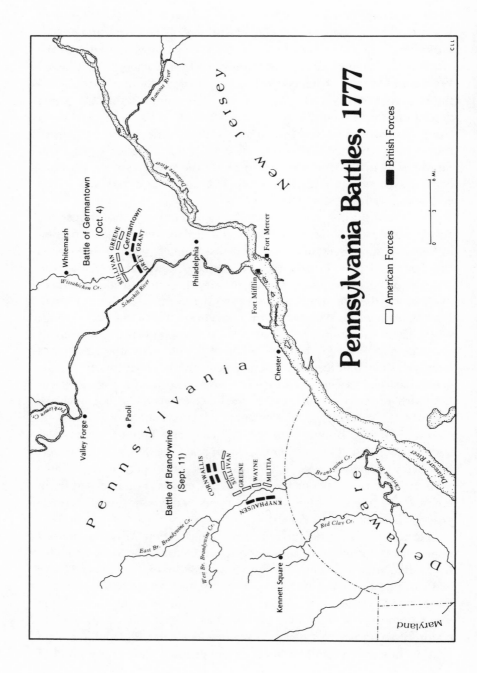

Pennsylvania Battles, 1777

□ American Forces ■ British Forces

0   3   6 M.

shall therefore waive the subject — and like uncle Toby ride my own hobby." But during the winter, the general at his headquarters continued to receive criticisms of the Constitution of 1776, from Richard Peters, James Moore, and of course Rush. By April 1777, these gentlemen had launched a concerted effort to entice Wayne into political opposition to the new basic law. Pennsylvanians, declared Rush to the general, were "intoxicated" with liberty and had produced an "absurd" government; however, support for the constitution was highly organized by its proponents and was widespread, especially among Presbyterians. Would Wayne join his fellow generals, St. Clair and Thompson, in opposing the document, especially in Chester County? "The most respectable Whig characters in the State are with us," the doctor told Wayne; "I need not point out to *you* the danger and folly of the Constitution. It has substituted a Mob Government for one of the happiest governments in the world. . . . A *single legislature* is big with tyranny. . . . Absolute authority should belong only to God. . . . Come, my dear Sir and let us weep together over the dear nurse of our childhood — the protectress of our youth, and the generous rewarder of our riper years." Added Peters to this dolorous chorus, "Our *fallen* Pennsylvania wants you. . . . Some change must be made, or the Power of this important State will never be exerted, for the Salvation of American Liberty."[7]

This barrage of letters to Wayne from the "old Whigs" of Pennsylvania (as Rush called the opponents of the constitution) finally had their intended effect upon the general. The "Melancholy and I fear too just a picture of the Distraction of State," he told Rush on June 2, 1777, "and the folly Obstinacy & Incapacity of those who Influence her Councils," were all matters that a true conservative patriot like himself could not ignore. "Gen'l St. Clair & many Other Gentlemen of the Army can witness for me that at the first view of your Sickly Constitution — I pronounced it not worth Defending." Thus the general took a position on civil politics that was far more conservative than the one he had supported at the beginning of the Revolution, with his new political views dovetailing into his already formed ideas on the need for a regularized military establishment in America and showing an almost total abandonment of his earlier radical Whiggism. A republican Wayne would continue to be, but a republican in the mold of the ancient Roman senator, whose stern sense of obligation to the virtues did not call for allowing much democracy in government. A chosen few of the propertied and "respectable" people, in his view, must keep control of politics, society, and the military establishment, lest all lapse into "anarchy" and "mob rule." It was not the general's intention to lead radical, rabble armies of poorly disciplined citizens in a revolutionary struggle against monarchical tyranny merely to see mob tyranny put in its place. On this point, he agreed with his friend Rush's comment, "I had rather live under the government of one man than of 72."[8]

Turning his attention back to military matters during the first two weeks of July, Wayne found his division, like the rest of Washington's army, engaged in fruitless maneuvering against the enemy, primarily because no one among the patriots could figure out Howe's intentions. Shortly after the British army retreated from New Jersey, the American commander in chief moved his own troops back to Morristown, whence they had started some weeks before. Then, working under the reasonable assumption that Howe would drive up the Hudson River to meet Burgoyne's army coming south from Canada, Washington marched his own divisions, Wayne's included, to the vicinity of Ramapough, where they could interpose upon Howe's line of march should the British general start northward. But by the twenty-fourth, it seemed clear that Howe was embarking his army for a push by sea against Philadelphia, and Washington began shifting his army back toward the Delaware River. He now gave orders to General Wayne "to proceed to Chester County, in Pennsylvania, where your presence will be necessary to arrange the militia who are to rendezvous there," and he gave Lincoln's division into the temporary command of General Horatio Gates. Wayne immediately rode to Philadelphia, where he began to carry out the commander in chief's instructions.[9]

Before long, Wayne's duties took him on to Chester County and, of course, Waynesborough, where he saw Polly, the children, and his mother for the first time in a year and a half. Interspersed with his business of collecting militiamen for duty with the American army, he ruminated to his wife upon the reasons why he must remain in the military service, despite the problems Polly confronted in running the farm alone, and with his mother he lamely explained why he had not paid her any of the debt he owed her for Waynesborough or the annuity to which she was entitled. Neither of these confrontations was pleasant, so it was with renewed enthusiasm that he sought out the more convivial company of younger women like Hannah Griffits. Brigadier General Anthony Wayne simply had never grown up emotionally, and as a result he behaved badly toward those in his life — especially the womenfolk — who were closest to him.[10]

Wayne was not long detained with his duties in Chester County and Philadelphia. As soon as the Pennsylvania militia was embodied, he gave the citizen soldiers a bit of perfunctory training, put them under command of General John Armstrong, and turned his attention to advising the state's officials on a plan for the defense of Philadelphia against attack from the Delaware River. On August 11 he rejoined General Washington's army, which was now encamped in Bucks County on the Neshaminy River, about twenty miles north of Philadelphia, and reassumed command of Lincoln's division because Gates had gone north to replace Schuyler (for a second time) as commander of the Northern Department. Wayne enjoyed this life, for his division had been posted near Gwynedd, on the estate of Elizabeth Graeme Fergusson, and it was in her home that he made his headquarters.[11]

On August 21, Wayne and other general officers in council of war advised Washington immediately to march toward West Point on the Hudson River, and the army broke camp. Washington and his officers were acting upon knowledge that John Burgoyne by that date was threatening to seize Albany, while Howe's army, which until then had been their biggest concern, was now somewhere at sea and presumed to be making for Charleston. Since Washington's men could not possibly reach South Carolina in time to do anything against Howe, should he land there, it seemed sensible to the council of officers to move against an attainable objective. But no sooner had the decision been made than a courier dashed into camp with news that Howe's fleet was sailing into Chesapeake Bay. Hence, Washington rescinded his previous commands and ordered the army southward toward Wilmington, Delaware, directing its line of march through the streets of Philadelphia in order to overawe loyalists and impress waverers in the cause. On Sunday morning, August 24, with drummers and fifers playing "a tune for a quick step," the army marched twelve abreast down Front Street and up Chestnut, with Wayne commanding Lincoln's division in the course of the march. Noted Alexander Graydon of the show, the soldiers, "though indifferently dressed, held well burnished arms, and carried them like soldiers."[12]

That night, the Continental Army went into camp near Chester, practically on the doorstep of Wayne's home at Easttown. Lodging in the Blue Bell Tavern, to the west of Fort Mifflin on the evening of the 26th, he sent Polly a hasty note informing her that he was nearby but unable, because of his military duties, to visit his family. "I must, therefore, in the most pressing Manner," he said, "Request you to meet me tomorrow evening at Naamen's Creek" with "my Little Son & Daughter along." However, when he arrived at Naaman's Creek the following day, he found that Polly had not come; so he scribbled her another note, informing her that Howe's army had landed at Head of Elk, Maryland, and that he was pushing his division on toward Wilmington with the rest of the American army. Within two days, he expected "we shall try the Mettle of the British Troops," for they seemed "Determined to push for Phila." In closing his note to Polly, he asked her to kiss his children for him.[13]

Upon reaching Wilmington, Wayne and the other Continentals began a two-week period of waiting, while General Howe arranged his army of 16,000 for a drive on Philadelphia. Meantime, Wayne began formulating a scheme which he believed would halt the British dead in their tracks. To Washington he proposed to create an elite corp of "2500 or 3000 of our best Armed and most Disciplined Troops (exclusive of the Reserves), who should hold themselves in Readiness on the Approach of the Enemy to make a Regular and Vigorous Assault on their Right and Left flank — or such part of their Army as should then be thought most expedient — and not wait the Attack from them." This maneuver, he was convinced, would so shock the British — who expected the Americans to carry out their usual tactic of fighting from behind well-prepared fortifications and breastworks — that they must retreat. The idea, he admitted modestly, was not his. It had been employed successfully "by *Caesar at Amiens* [and] at *Alesia*," where the Gauls were struck with terror, "which Marshal Saxe *Justly Observes* 'proceeds from the Consternation which is the Unavoidable effect of Sudden and unexpected Events.' " Said Wayne, should these ideas conform to Washington's, "I wish to be of the number Assigned for the business."[14]

The commander in chief gave no serious consideration to Wayne's proposals, for he continued to keep distance between his army and Howe's and waited for the British to initiate action. On September 8, Howe finally began his push by marching toward Christiana, and the following day Washington moved his forces to the east bank of Brandywine Creek, posting them at Chadd's Ford in defensive array. On the left of his line he placed Wayne's division and Colonel Thomas Proctor's Pennsylvania artillery to guard Chadd's Ford from high and defensible ground. In the center stood Greene's corps, and on the American right were stationed Sullivan's veterans. The reserve, consisting of Adam

Stephen's and Lord Stirling's divisions, were posted behind Greene's sector of the line, and across the creek to the west, William Maxwell's light troops were in skirmish formation, awaiting the advance of the enemy. In all, General Washington commanded 11,000 troops, 8,000 of whom were regulars, and Wayne was confident that the patriot force was sufficient to halt Howe's Anglo-German "rebels."[15]

On the foggy morning of September 11, General Howe marched his army forward from Kennett Square to meet the Americans and engaged Maxwell's troops at about 8 o'clock on the west side of Brandywine Creek. Two hours later, when Maxwell was forced to withdraw into the main American line, Wayne and his men got into the battle by engaging the enemy in an artillery duel across the creek. As this cannonade continued for about an hour, without the enemy making any attempt to storm patriot positions on the stream's east bank, Wayne and the other American officers began to suspect that Howe was "amusing" them while preparing to cross the Brandywine elsewhere. Sure enough, at about 11 o'clock Washington began receiving reports that Howe had sent 5,000 men under Lord Cornwallis northward in an attempt to flank Sullivan's corps on the patriot right. The immediate thought of the American officers was that Wayne and Greene might now be facing an inferior force, under General Baron Wilhelm von Knyphausen, which they could assault and drive from the field. Consequently, Washington, ordered these two men, plus Sullivan, immediately to attack across the Brandywine, while Stirling and Stephen took their troops up to Birmingham Meeting House to counter the threat from Howe.[16]

Here at last, believed Wayne, was the opportunity he had dreamed of for months, to lead a head-on assault against redcoats and Hessians in open battle. As noon came on, he excitedly wheeled his men into battle formations and, ignoring the continuing British cannonade, marched the Pennsylvanians out of their earthworks and onto the flats leading toward Chadd's Ford. But Washington had now become convinced that the entire British army was still just across the Brandywine and called off the attack. Unhappily, Wayne obeyed his orders to draw the Pennsylvanians back to their defensive works, and he watched with envy as Maxwell's men pushed forward to skirmish again with the British on the other side of the creek. Thus the battle continued on Wayne's front for the next four hours, while Washington pondered his opponent's intentions and finally deduced that Cornwallis was in fact carrying out a full-scale flanking maneuver on the American right. Since the commander in chief had already ordered Sullivan, Stirling, and Stephen up to Birmingham Meeting House in response to Cornwallis's maneuver, he could only listen anxiously with Wayne and Greene as the crescendo of cannon, musket, and rifle fire mounted in that direction. Not the least of the worries for American officers at Chadd's Ford was the possibility that Cornwallis might force the collapse of the American right wing, trap them between two British forces, and compel them to witness the disintegration or surrender of the Continental Army. When Washington could no longer bear this killing suspense, he set out with Greene's division to support Sullivan and the other generals to the north, leaving Wayne and Maxwell to fend for themselves at Chadd's Ford.[17]

The main weight of battle now had shifted away from Wayne's position, but he and the Pennsylvanians nonetheless were to come in for their share of fighting. As evening came on, General Knyphausen crossed the Brandywine and poured heavy fire into Wayne's position, while the American general returned the musketry with all his might. For about three hours, this engagement continued, as General Wayne fought a holding action to make sure that his German opponent did not break through and get behind the American army's right flank. Then, as daylight began to fade, he learned from the commander in chief that the Continentals at Birmingham Meeting House had broken off battle and were retreating in good order. Wayne, instructed to do likewise, immediately began to disengage his troops and withdraw toward Chester. But all did not go well, for Pennsylvania Colonel William Chambers's artillerymen abandoned many of their pieces in the retreat, and about eleven cannon fell into the hands of the enemy. Still, the general was proud of his division's performance during the battle of the Brandywine, and he boasted of its prowess to Thomas Mifflin in a letter of the fifteenth. Wayne's own reputation as a fighting general was also enhanced by his activities on the eleventh of September, for as John Sullivan noted, "Wain behaved Exceedingly Brave" at Chadd's Ford.[18]

As the American troops withdrew before the victorious British, to Chester, then across the Schuylkill River to Germantown, Wayne and his officer colleagues assessed the damage that the Brandywine battle had done them. Surprisingly enough, they discovered that the Continentals were in good condition, despite total battle casualties of about 1,100 men. As Washington noted, his army seemed to consider "the recent affair. . .as a check rather than as a defeat." Wayne certainly did, and he applauded the commander in chief's decision on September 16 to offer battle to Howe once more at Warren Tavern, about twenty miles west of Philadelphia. This affair came to nothing, however, when a two-day rainstorm wetted everyone's gunpowder and finally forced Washington to withdraw to Reading Furnace. While the American commander was trending northwestward in his movements toward the Schuylkill (in order to protect American military supplies at Reading Furnace), Howe marched from Warren Tavern toward a Schuylkill crossing called Swede's Ford, which was between Washington's army and Philadelphia. Although the British army now posed a severe threat to that city, all the commander in chief could do in response was detach Wayne, Maxwell, and Brigadier General William Smallwood from his army in separate units to act independently against Howe's rear and right as the British army moved northward. Perhaps, he said, these three officers could slow the enemy's advance long enough for the main army to rest and once more challenge Howe's drive on Philadelphia.[19]

Wayne was delighted with this assignment. With haste and stealth, on the evening of the eighteenth he moved his division of 1,500 men south and east around the British rear, taking post between two old familiar haunts, Paoli and White Horse Taverns, just off the Lancaster Road and only about two miles from Waynesborough. In this encampment, Wayne had positioned his detachment only four miles from the right flank of the entire British army, a force that outnumbered his by ten to one, and he was in a situation that might have unnerved a general less confident than himself. Wayne, however, was not the least bit disconcerted by his exposed position, for he believed that his presence was unknown to the enemy. His first idea was that he might combine his force with Maxwell's and conduct a joint operation against Howe, but when that general, despite Wayne's request to him, had not appeared at Wayne's encampment by reveille on the morning of the nineteenth, Wayne decided to march his own division to within half a mile of the British cantoment in order to carry out a surprise raid on the rear of what he hoped would be a decamping enemy.

The American general learned upon reconnaissance, however, that the British were remaining at their post and were "too compact to attack with prudence." Therefore, Wayne, after drawing his men off to his own encampment, wrote Washington in mid-morning a letter encouraging him to take advantage of Howe's "supineness" by rushing the main army forward for a general assault. "For God's sake," he exclaimed to the commander in chief, "Push on as fast as possible." Three hours later, he was repeating to Washington that Howe's troops, engaged in the prosaic chores of laundering clothes and cooking, were open to attack. With General Maxwell expected soon to arrive on their left flank, he said, with himself on their right, and with the commander in chief in their rear, the Americans could "complete Mr. Howe's business." Washington's army did not arrive however, during that day or the next, and by evening of the twentieth, Wayne was preparing his division for the night by posting a routine number of pickets and mounted patrols about his camp. On the morrow, support or no from either Washington or Maxwell, General Wayne intended to assail the British rear guard as his orders called for him to do so. His hopes for success were bolstered by one piece of news, that General Smallwood was marching toward his camp and would join him momentarily.[20]

An uneasy quiet settled over Wayne's camp on the night of September 20–21, for officers and privates on the eve of conflict are always wakeful and restless. But tonight there was an unusual tenseness, brought on by the men's knowledge of their proximity to the enemy's army. To be sure, Wayne believed that his presence was unknown to Howe, but all the same one could never be absolutely certain about these things. Hence, with a special alertness he received in his quarters at about eight or nine o'clock that evening a neighbor of his, Mr. Morgan Jones, father of his chaplain, David Jones, who told him that the British were apprised of his presence and intended to attack him that night. Immediately, Wayne responded to his old friend's warning by "Ordering out a number of Videttes [horse guards] in Addition to those already fixed with Orders to patrol all the Roads leading to the Enemy." Additionally, he "planted two new pickets," to join the four that were already doing guard duty, and he sent out a special "horse Picket. . .well advanced on the Swedesford Road — and on the Very Road the Enemy Advanced." It was extremely fortunate for Wayne and his soldiers that Mr. Jones alerted his camp, for in fact General Howe had instructed Major General Sir Charles Grey, commanding three regiments, to carry out a surprise assault against the Americans. To assure the stealth of his enterprise, Grey ordered his men to attack with bayonets only, and he required some of his men to remove their musket flints — thus acquiring the nickname "No Flint" Grey. As Grey's men marched westward out of their camp that night at about nine or ten o'clock by Swede's Ford Road, Lieutenant Colonel Thomas Musgrave, upon Howe's command, proceeded southeast with the 40th Regiment to Lancaster Road, and posted his men to block Wayne's path, should the American commander attempt by that route to escape Grey's cold steel.[21]

At about 11 o'clock that night, Wayne heard firing from one of his "Out guards" on Swede's Ford Road — the signal that the enemy had been sighted — and he now knew for certain that the British intended to attack him. Immediately he ordered his men under arms, and within ten minutes he heard firing on his right flank, "where our Artillery was planted." Not aware of the size of the British force that attacked him, Wayne now decided that his most prudent course of action was withdrawal. (Why he had not reached the same decision two hours earlier some critics found hard to fathom.) Consequently, he ordered the division to file off westward along White Horse Road, and he instructed Colonel Richard Humpton, his artillery officer, to remove the American cannon by the same route. In the meantime, the general had taken personal command of the Light Infantry, the 1st Regiment and the cavalry, all of which formed into line to oppose Grey's redcoats while the rest of his men made good their retreat. "These troops," he declared, "met and Rec'd the Enemy with a Spirit becoming free Americans," fighting at times "not more than ten Yards distant — a well directed fire *mutually* took place, followed by a change of Bayonet — numbers fell on each side." At last Wayne's men were compelled to give way to the weight of the British attack, and the American general commenced withdrawing his shielding force from the field. However, his maneuver was cut short when he discovered that Humpton, either through "neglect or misapprehension," had not gotten the artillery clear, and so Wayne was "Necessitated to form the fourth Reg't to Receive the Enemy and favour the Retreat of the Others." These troops, though, General Grey chose not to assault, and before many minutes had elapsed Humpton finally had his cannon on the road to White Horse Tavern behind the protective shield of the 4th Regiment's battle deployment.[22]

With the rest of his division finally clear of the battlefield and in full retreat, Wayne, still in personal command of the now-disorganized 4th Regiment, began his own withdrawal. When he was about a thousand yards up White Horse Road, he attempted to rally this unit, as well as other members of his command, and impose some semblance of order upon the milling chaos about him. To his dismay, however, he discovered that many of his soldiers had taken "a Contrary way" from the place of attack, due in large part, he believed, to Humpton's incompetence in

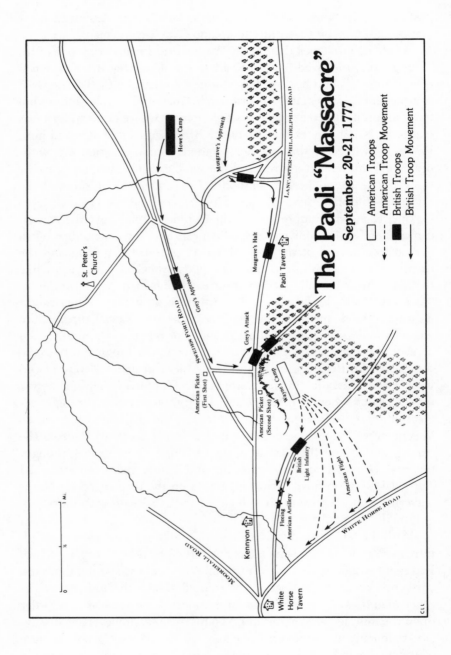

The Paoli "Massacre"
September 20-21, 1777

☐ American Troops

---→ American Troop Movement

■ British Troops

⟶ British Troop Movement

Howe's Camp

Musgrave's Approach

LANCASTER-PHILADELPHIA ROAD

St. Peter's Church

Grey's Approach

SWEDES FORD ROAD

Musgrave's Halt

Paoli Tavern

Grey's Attack

American Picket (First Shot)

American Picket (Second Shot)

Wayne's Camp

British Light Infantry

American Flight

Kennyon

Fleeing American Artillery

WHITE HORSE ROAD

MOOREHALL ROAD

White Horse Tavern

1 Mi.

forming the men to protect his cannon. In any case, he continued to move westward through the darkness until at last he reached Red Lion Tavern. There, he was greeted by General Smallwood, who had been only a mile from Paoli at the time of Grey's attack but who had "Order'd his people to file off toward this place" when he realized that his raw, untrained troops could be of no assistance to Wayne in fending off British regulars in a night assault. At his new post, Wayne reported the battle to Washington, noting that he still was not sure how many casualties his division had suffered but that he had saved all his artillery and baggage, "except one or two waggons belonging to the Commissary's Department." Also, he said, most of his division had now straggled in, and his present plan was to rest his troops for a few hours, then "follow the Enemy who I this moment learn. . .are marching for the Schuylkil."[23]

Wayne never got to chase General Howe, for his command, he learned on the twenty-first, was more battered than he had believed. Nearly two hundred of his troops had been bayoneted to death by Grey's soldiers, and about one hundred were wounded (the redcoats had suffered only a dozen casualties); these dead and maimed he must give first attention. Thus he lingered another day at the Red Lion, taking the occasion to write Polly. "The Enemy made a hard push to camp on the night before last," he said, "some loss and thought prudent to halt." The same day, Abner Robinson, a neighbor at Easttown, informed him that the British had visited Waynesborough, surrounding his house and searching for him. But except for their having absconded with a couple of servants, one of them Wayne's overseer, nothing was disturbed, and the British had "behaved with the utmost politeness to the Women." Finally on September 23, Wayne received orders from Washington, who was near Potts Grove, to march his own and Smallwood's commands immediately to the main army. Consequently, Generals Wayne and Smallwood directed their troops northward, rejoining Washington's command just as General Howe rode with his conquering army into Philadelphia.[24]

No sooner had Wayne reached Washington's camp on the twenty-sixth than he realized that the Paoli affair was to have serious repercussions for his and Grey's reputations. Quickly he was made aware that what he was calling the *battle* of Paoli other patriots, perhaps for purposes of anti-British propaganda, were referring to as the Paoli *massacre*. With considerable exaggeration, some Americans were lambasting "No

Flint" Grey as a bloodthirsty murderer, who had allowed his men during the night of September 20–21 indiscriminately to bayonet poor Continental soldiers who were trying to surrender. So fixed became this notion, in fact, that within days after the battle most patriots accepted it as the gospel truth, and in the future another generation of Pennsylvanians would erect a monument at Paoli in memory of the poor "victims of coldblooded cruelty," who had died there as a result of "British barbarity." To be sure, Wayne did not worry overmuch about the reputation of Grey, and had this matter been one of mere justice for an enemy general, he would not have been too concerned about it. The problem for him was that the same Americans who berated Grey's "barbarity" also condemned Wayne for his having "allowed" the enemy to perpetrate such a disgraceful "atrocity" upon American soldiers. Such gossip was everywhere. Congressman John Adams, riding westward toward York on the twenty-fifth with other legislators who had decamped Philadelphia just before Howe's occupation of the town, heard it from Colonel Thomas Hartley in a German tavern at Reading Furnace. "Hartley thinks," said Adams, "that the Place was improper for Battle, and that there ought to have been a Retreat." Similar comments, Wayne learned, were being bruited about casually by many people who had no notion (in his view) of what had really happened at Paoli. Therefore, on September 27, he demanded that the commander in chief order a formal inquiry into his conduct at Paoli, and Washington promised him that one would be held as soon as military affairs would allow.[25]

Meantime, the war continued. In early October, the commander in chief received intelligence that some of Howe's army was at Germantown, where it might be struck by the Americans with telling effect. So, he declared that the time had come to give the enemy battle. While preparations for this conflict were being made in camp at Skippack Creek, about fifteen miles from Germantown, Wayne took time out to write Polly a belated letter of encouragement about the American situation, for although Mrs. Wayne was turning out to be an excellent farm manager (doing a better job, in fact, than Wayne ever had), she had sunk into despondency since the battle of Paoli. That the enemy possessed Philadelphia, noted Wayne, "is of no more Consequence than their being in possession of the City of New York or Boston — they may hold it for a time — but must leave it with Circumstances of shame and Disgrace before the Close of the Winter." From the northward, he said, came word that "Gen'l Gates is Victorious — matters looked much more Gloomy in that Quarter four weeks ago — than they do at this time here — it is our turn next — and altho' appearances are a little Gloomy at present — yet they will be soon Dissipated and a more pleasing prospect take place."[26]

By October 3, Washington's plans for his attack on the British at Germantown were laid. On the American right, Sullivan was to push down the main road from Chestnut Hill to Germantown with his and Wayne's divisions. Farther to the right and nearest the Schuylkill River, Pennsylvania militia under General Armstrong was supposed to move forward and give support to the regulars under Sullivan's command. The patriot left, under Nathanael Greene, was to consist of Wayne's division and that of Adam Stephen, both of which would move directly down Skippack Road. Even farther to the left, militiamen under Smallwood and David Forman were to push forward. Lord Stirling was to command the reserve, composed of the brigades of Maxwell and Abner Nash, and was to follow Greene's men down Skippack Road. With his division ready to march by late afternoon on the third, Wayne sat down to compose one of his florid prebattle letters to Polly. "I have often wrote to you on the eve of some unexpected and uncertain event," he said, "but never on any equal to the present — before this reaches you, the Heads of many Worthy fellows will be laid low — dawn is big with the fate of thousands." However, "My Heart sets lightly in the mansion — every Artery beats in unison and I feel unusual Ardour." His letter finished, Wayne at seven o'clock joined Washington and Sullivan at the head of their divisions and along with the rest of the American army commenced his march toward Germantown.[27]

That Wayne's mental state before and during the battle of Germantown was conditioned by his desire to avenge the defeat at Paoli cannot be doubted. As the general rode throughout the night of October 3–4, ever closer to the British lines which he would assault on the morrow, he savored the retribution he would visit upon his enemies. Thus he was not discouraged when his troops encountered thick fog just before dawn, a murky white blanket that obscured all objects beyond a distance of three hundred feet. As he neared the British pickets at about six o'clock, he was delighted when firing on Sullivan's front signaled that the column in which he rode would be the first to engage the enemy. Soon General Thomas Conway's men were exchanging hot fire with the British Light Infantry, which had reinforced the enemy's lines at the first sign of trouble from the Americans, and Sullivan was ordering Wayne into the affray, instructing him to form a battle line on the left of Sullivan's own men, who were supporting Conway's brigade. Sullivan was compelled to make this maneuver because Greene's column, which was supposed to occupy that position, was still four miles to the rear and thus incapable of giving the New Hampshire general any assistance. After disposing Colonel Stephen Moylan's light horse on Wayne's left, Sullivan ordered a general advance of his entire division, and the Continentals drove forward against the British Light Infantry with Wayne's men screaming, "Have at the bloodhounds, revenge Wayne's affair." Soon the enemy troopers gave way under this assault and began to withdraw, maintaining as they did a steady, harassing fire against Wayne's and Sullivan's men from behind every fence, tree, or ditch that offered them cover. The Americans, who groped forward in the fog while under the galling fusillade, discovered that they must remove fences and climb over obstructions, and it was indeed lucky for them that obscuring mist lay so heavily over the landscape. Declared Wayne, the fog "together with the smoke Occasioned by our Cannon, and Musketry — made it almost as dark as night."[28]

As Wayne's men drove ahead through these confusing conditions, the British army prepared behind the protective screen of the skirmishing light infantry to receive the Pennsylvanian's charge. Said an officer of the 40th Regiment, all these men were perfectly aware that they faced a rebel horde bent on revenge for "the surprise we had given them" at Paoli and were therefore doubly alert. When Wayne's soldiers broke from the fog and smashed against this powerful British force, according to the American general's own account, a series of charges and countercharges took place before "the Unparalelled bravery" of the Continentals "surmounted every difficulty, and the enemy retreated in the utmost Confusion — Our People. . .pushed on with their Bayonets — and took Ample Vengeance" for the Paoli defeat. Although American officers "Exerted themselves to save many of the poor wretches who were Crying for Mercy," it was to little purpose, for "the Rage and fury of the Soldiers were not to be Restrained for some time — at least not until great numbers of the Enemy fell by our Bayonets." By that time, Wayne's advance, which Sullivan said was conducted "with great Bravery & Rapidity," had brought the Pennsylvanians abreast of Sullivan's right wing, which had surged ahead of the Americans to the left. The division had now moved forward one and a half miles under almost constant enemy fire, and still it showed no signs of slowing down. In fact, Wayne and Sullivan learned at this point that General Greene's column was finally approaching on Wayne's left, and the two generals were encouraged to believe that the fresh troops of Greene and Stephen would give new impetus to their own singular drive.

At this point, however, things began to go badly wrong for Wayne and his colleagues on the field at Germantown. General Maxwell, whom Washington ordered to bring up reserves to support Wayne's and Sullivan's rapid advance, instead got held up by enemy fire from a large stone house named Cliveden, owned by Benjamin Chew. Although this edifice had been easily bypassed by Sullivan's men in their drive forward, its reduction now became the object of a half hour debate between Washington, Henry Knox, Timothy Pickering, and other patriot officers before a decision was finally made that it would be left alone. Meanwhile, Wayne, who had continued his advance until he was three miles from his starting place and was "in possession of [the enemy's] whole Encampment," suddenly descried "a large body of troops. . . Advancing on our left flank." Already, he and his men were skittish, because in the fog and smoke Americans frequently had mistaken each other for the enemy and "Exchanged several shots before they discovered the Error." Additionally, he and they had listened with considerable unease to the staccato of musketry and cannon fire directed against Chew House to their rear, not knowing whether the shooting was from friend or foe. Consequently, the unexpected appearance of unidentified soldiers in the murk and gloom on the Pennsylvanians' left caused Wayne's men to conclude that they were the enemy. Suddenly, despite anything Wayne could do to stop them, his men began a panic-stricken retreat. "The fog and this mistake," said Wayne disgustedly, "prevented us from following a victory that in all Human probability would have put an end to the American War."

After a headlong withdrawal of about two miles, Wayne finally brought his men under control by convincing them that "it was our own people" they had been running from. But his retrograde motion had totally uncovered Sullivan's left flank, and that general's own men also became unnerved and fell back. Unknown either to Sullivan or Wayne at this point, the Americans were now facing General Howe himself. The British commander in chief, who had rushed from Philadelphia to Germantown with reinforcements while the battle was going on, arrived on the scene at about noon, and began berating his regulars for retreating before "a scouting party." Howe soon had formed four regiments and a brigade to counterattack the exhausted patriots (who had been fighting now for more than three hours) and began to push the rebels back vigorously.[29]

With great disappointment, Wayne now faced the fact that the American army was once more defeated and must not hazard its existence by lingering near the British forces. As the Continentals drew off, he was ordered to cover the withdrawal, which he did for a while with ease, since the British "for a long time could not persuade [themselves] that we had run from Victory." However, the fog cleared, the redcoats advanced, and Wayne gave them "a few Cannon shot with some Musketry — which caused [them] to break and Run with the utmost Confusion — this ended the Action for that day." Then, Wayne followed the American army to Pawling's Mill, twenty miles north of Germantown, where Washington set his men down to rest from their arduous labors of the past two days and to count his losses, which came to about 1,100 men as over against half that number for the British. From there, on October 6, Wayne wrote Polly an extensive account of the battle, with studied casualness near the end of this letter mentioning "that my Roan Horse was killed under me within a few yards of the Enemy's front — and my left foot a little bruised by one of their Cannon shot — but not so much as to prevent me from walking — my poor horse Received one Musket Ball in the breast — and one in the flank at the same Instant that I had a slight touch on my left hand — which is scarcely worth mentioning." Upon the whole, he said, "it was a Glorious day — Our men are in the highest Spirits — and I am Confident we shall give them a total Defeat the next Action; which is at no great Distance."[30]

With a few days' quietude in view for the American army after the battle of Germantown, Wayne reminded General Washington that he had been promised a hearing on the Paoli incident. The general was now more insistent about such an inquiry than he had been a few days before, for rumors continued to circulate that he had been negligent in his duties on the evening of September 20. Moreover, Colonel Humpton had filed formal charges against Wayne, "Viz: 'that he had timely notice of the enemy's intention to attack the troops under his command. . .and notwithstanding the intelligence, he neglected making a disposition until it was too late either to annoy the enemy, or make a retreat without the utmost danger and confusion.' " Therefore, Washington in general orders on October 11, appointed a formal court of inquiry, with Lord Stirling as chairman, to hear the charges and determine their validity. For three days, from October 13 to 15, Stirling and his fellow board members Alexander McDougall, Henry Knox, and two colonels sat, then concluded that Wayne had been guilty of no misconduct. At the same time, however, the court *was* disturbed that the general had camped so near the enemy, and its report implied that while Wayne had succeeded in getting off his cannon he had done so only in the nick of time, after being remiss in not ordering the artillery to safety earlier.[31]

When Wayne learned of the court's conclusions, he was baffled, for instead of that body clearing him of suspicion it had raised new issues. Indignantly, he wrote Washington on the twenty-second, demanding a full court martial and explaining the things that had bothered Stirling and his colleagues. There were two good reasons, declared Wayne, why his army had encamped so near the enemy at Paoli and kept that post. First, "The Distance between the nearest part of the Enemy's camp and where I lay — was near four miles which was greater than from their Camp to the Fatland ford, and Richardson ford on the Schuylkill. . . . Consequently had I been farther Distant it would have put it out of my power to Comply with your Excellency's Orders — i.e. to harass their Rear," which Wayne had fully intended to do at dawn on the twenty-first of September, for he "had Information that the Enemy would march for Schuylkill the next Morning." Second, he had expected Smallwood to arrive at any time "from two OClock in the Afternoon until we were Attacked" and had sent out guides to conduct him to *that specific* camp. As for the charges about the cannon, said Wayne, that he personally had managed "to Rally a Body of troops" on the ground and cover the retreat of both artillery *and* the division was proof in itself that the guns had never been in such danger as the court seemed to think.[32]

The reasonableness of Wayne's concern for his military reputation persuaded Washington that the Pennsylvanian deserved a general court-martial in order thoroughly to air his side of the incident. Therefore, on October 24, the commander in chief appointed a panel of thirteen field-grade officers, with Sullivan as chairman, to hear the case. Over the next week, the court heard evidence from a dozen Pennsylvania officers that Wayne might have done more between ten and eleven o'clock on the evening of September 20 to prepare for an enemy assault. Others, however, especially Thomas Hartley and Michael Ryan, declared that Wayne had not been remiss. In his own defense, Wayne read a long document, outlining the ways in which he had responded to Mr. Jones's intelligence, pointing out how Colonel Humpton's own bungling had lengthened the American stay on the field. To close his defense, he said, "Let me put a Question — Suppose after. . .repeated orders from [Washington to attack Howe's rear], I had Retreated, before I knew whether the Enemy Intended to Attack me or not, . . . would not [the] very Gentlemen [who now condemn me for staying put] have been the first to default me — would not His Excellency with the Greatest Justice have Ordered me in Arrest for Cowardice and Disobedience of his Repeated peremptory and pointed Orders — would I not have stood Culpable in the eyes of the World — would I not Justly merit either Immediate Death or Cashiering? I certainly would." The court, on November 1, unanimously concluded that General Wayne was "not guilty of the charge exhibited against him," that he had in fact done at Paoli "everything that could be expected from an active, brave and vigilant officer," that he was acquitted "with the highest honor." Immediately, General Washington approved the sentence, and the matter was officially at an end.[33]

CHAPTER *iv*

Valley Forge and Monmouth
1777–1779

WHILE WAYNE'S TRIAL proceeded, he and other American generals turned their attention to maintaining patriot posts on the Delaware River below Philadelphia, for although the city had fallen to Howe, the British commander had trouble furnishing his army with supplies as long as the American forts Mercer and Mifflin, on either side of the river, prevented the British from severing a heavy iron chain across the shipping channel that closed the Delaware to enemy commerce. General Howe had constructed batteries on Providence Island, on the Delaware's west side, that threatened Fort Mifflin, and these the rebels must eliminate if they were to keep control of the river. Therefore, Wayne petitioned General Washington for permission to assault Howe's positions on Providence Island, spike the enemy's guns, and destroy his works. The commander in chief, however, felt that he had not the necessary forces to carry out this operation, and he decided to wait until expected reinforcements arrived from Gates's army in upstate New York before attempting to relieve Fort Mercer. While he waited, that bastion fell, and the Delaware was opened to the British navy.[1]

Wayne was furious at this turn of affairs. His own hot-blooded approach to warfare had no room for the kind of calculation that Washington must always exercise, and he never made any attempt to understand that his commander in chief, with responsibility for the success of the Revolution riding upon his every decision, must act with caution. Therefore, he lambasted Washington furiously in a letter to Richard Peters on the eighteenth of November. "Six weeks Investiture and no

Attempt to raise the seige," he fumed, "will scarcely be Credited at an Other day." The reason for this "Supineness? " Why "an over stretched caution, which is oftentimes attended with as fatal Consequences, as too much rashness, the *present*, as well as some *past* events, fully evinces the truth of this position." And although "his Excellency [finally] had Determined to act the General," by ordering Wayne to the assault, the fort had had to be evacuated the day before the attack was to proceed. "It was a saying of one of the first of Generals," declared Wayne, that calling a council of war "was the surest way to do nothing," and nothing the American army had so far mostly done. Soon "Our poor naked soldiers" must be driven from the field by cold, and only "the doubtful state we are in" kept Wayne himself "a Single Moment in the Service that has become almost Intolerable."[2]

That General Wayne's confidence in his commander in chief had been eroded during the campaign of 1777 was clearer in other letters than the one to Peters that he was writing by the end of the year. On October 18 to his wife Polly he praised the success of General Gates against Burgoyne at Saratoga and wished that he could give Howe a dose of the same medicine. Even before he had written his angry letter to Peters, Wayne declared to his Pennsylvania colleague, Thomas Mifflin, on the tenth of November, "There are certain Generals, as Lee, Gates, Mifflin, who will point out by their conduct the line which I shall follow next campaign." Two weeks later, he was writing General Gates, criticizing Washington's handling of the troops at Germantown and reiterating his disgust at the outcome of the Fort Mifflin affair. However, in this last note he moderated his criticism of the commander in chief somewhat by declaring that all would yet be well "if our worthy General will but follow his own good judgment without listening too much to some counsel." These few documents constitute the sum total of Wayne's censorious remarks about Washington, and they hardly support assertions by some Americans that the Pennsylvanian was involved in the so-called "Conway Cabal" during the winter of 1777–78 against Washington's leadership. In fact, it is extremely unlikely that any highly organized attempt to remove Washington as commander in chief during this time ever involved *anyone*.[3] However, that General Wayne was momentarily indignant at the course of events since the fall of Philadelphia to Howe was not to be doubted.

Wayne's attention in October and November of 1777 was not entirely directed toward the Delaware forts and Washington's caution in their defense. Like the rest of the American officers in the main army, he was concerned with trying to dislodge Howe from Philadelphia. Unlike some of them, he was willing to fight for the objective, and whenever asked by the commander in chief for his opinion, always opted for action. Bold self-confidence, he felt sure, was an officer's duty and would ever justify itself in victory. Timidity could only have the opposite result. Hence, he was willing to take calculated risks in operations that depended "not on the numbers, but the vigor of the men engaged." In all he did as a commander, from emphasizing military demeanor to praising his men, he attempted to infuse in his soldiers this winning attitude. Nothing disgusted him more than to hear his own colleagues denigrate Continental troops, for when they did, he declared, they sounded like the arrogant officers of the British army. Give the Continentals real soldiers' work, he argued, and they would act like real soldiers. Hence, in three long letters, on October 27, November 25, and December 4, Wayne urged, pleaded, and cajoled Washington in one manner or another (with accompanying detailed plans) to "[give] the enemy Battle," "Attack," carry out a modest winter campaign. "It is not in our power to Command Success," he said, "but it is in our power to produce a Conviction to the World that we deserve it."[4]

In the end, however, Wayne was compelled to allow his martial blood, like the temperatures in eastern Pennsylvania, to cool with the coming of winter. Both General Washington and a vast majority of American officers were persuaded that the Continental Army, rather than attacking Howe, must go into winter quarters, and it only remained to decide where. In a council of war on November 30, Wayne joined with Greene, the Marquis de Lafayette, Smallwood, and others in recommending a site near Wilmington. When Washington made his decision, however, he opted for an easily defended site called Valley Forge, on the south side of the Schuylkill River, about eighteen miles from Philadelphia. Wayne reconnoitered this position and found adequate, and early on the morning of December 11 he began marching his division from Whitemarsh toward the new position. During that day, after he had crossed to the south side of the Schuylkill on a bridge, some of his men espied a body of the enemy observing the American march from a height on the north side of the stream. Two days later, the British force removed to Philadelphia, and Wayne's men proceeded on uneventfully to Valley Forge. At the end of December, as he told his friend Richard Peters, he was busy helping to form "a new city at this place," and he noted that his Pennsylvanians would soon be ensconced in huts for the winter. His outdoor activities, however, had given him a deep cold that settled in his throat and lungs. As he told Peters, he now had been on duty constantly for twenty-three months without leave, and he was desperately tired. Could Peters lay his case before Congress and get him a five- or six-week furlough?[5]

As it turned out, Wayne did not need to leave the army in order to find rest, for the quietude of winter now closed over him and the American forces at Valley Forge, and he found much leisure there. Still, while action against the enemy was for the next few months minimal, Wayne found much to occupy himself. With his sister, Ann Wayne Hayman, Richard and Sally Peters, and other friends and acquaintances he kept up a steady correspondence. To his delight, Richard Peters informed him that Sally had had a baby boy, thus making him a *"grandfather,"* and his sister congratulated him on his success at "Jarmentown Battle and Likewise Burgirns Capitulation." Wayne also sent a few letters to Polly, and in fact, he even got around to asking her to join him at Valley Forge, but she pleaded sickness and would not budge from Waynesborough. Wayne's mother, on the other hand, was desirous of seeing him and even made a trip to his headquarters on one occasion during the winter. It seems that Elizabeth Wayne and her son had a pleasant visit, but apparently this outcome was despite, not because of, his attending to their earlier financial agreements.[6]

As he kept up with his private affairs, Wayne paid attention to military business as well. A particularly irksome problem for him was the criticism he continued to receive from junior officers about the Paoli incident. Two of his colleagues, Sullivan and Maxwell, commiserated with Wayne on this point, for they too had been tried by courts-martial and acquitted, only to continue receiving censure from inferiors who they believed wanted "to clear the Stage for their own advancement." At last the three officers conjointly inscribed a letter to Washington, complaining that junior officers continued "to Arraign the Conduct of their Superiors" without knowing what they were talking about. The generals hoped that the commander in chief would put a stop to this carping, lest they all be forced to resign in order to seek redress. Passing on to other matters, Wayne informed Washington on December 26 that many civilians near Valley Forge were complaining that the deputy quartermaster general was stealing their grain, fodder, and hay. It was particularly sad, he noted, that families of citizen soldiers were "stripped" while their menfolk were in military service. Washington, in reply, noted that his staff officers denied the truth of Wayne's intelligence, and he asserted that standing orders were in place to head off such practices.[7]

While Wayne served at Valley Forge, he inevitably was drawn back into the roiling politics of his home state of Pennsylvania. A very important aspect of his duty as a general was to recruit his regiments to their allotted strength by replacing deserters, sick, and wounded, to keep his men supplied with clothing, and to see to the discipline and moral well-being of his soldiers. Since Congress had voted the previous year that states were to provide their own men with certain kinds of supplies, such as clothing, Wayne must deal with the civilian government of Pennsylvania for that business. He must also try to convince these same men that certain militia laws were hurting his recruiting of Continental regulars. As the months passed and none of General Wayne's concerns for his men were adequately addressed by the state's politicians, he became more and more convinced that the fault lay with the radical, democratic nature of the government itself and the people who controlled it. Already he despised the Pennsylvania government on philosophical and ideological grounds, but now he came to dislike it even more for its niggardliness toward Pennsylvania's poor, suffering soldiery. Before long, he came to believe that he and the politicians were caught up in an enormous paradox, in which he was refused the very supports necessary to defend the government by politicians who seemed to fear militarism among their own people more than they did the English army. That he was probably wrong in his assessment and that Pennsylvania was more forthcoming in assistance for its troops than most states was of small comfort to him, and he complained bitterly to Pennsylvania politicians in letter after letter during the winter of 1777–78.[8]

Recruiting problems were uppermost in Wayne's mind during most of his stay at Valley Forge. Earlier, the general had blasted Pennsylvania's militia law for its inequities against "the poor and middling sort of the inhabitants." Now, however, his concern lay not in the realm of citizens' justice but in getting his battalions populated with able bodied, acquiescent, disciplined soldiers. The problem was one of inducing Pennsylvanians to enlist in the regular Continental Army rather than in the state militia. Under the law a man could get a bounty of $100 for serving for two months in the militia but only $20 and a $45-per-month salary for enlisting as a regular for the duration of the war. Thus, the tendency was for the worst ne'er-do-wells of society to join the Continentals, and few even of these. He growled to Thomas Wharton, president of the Pennsylvania Assembly, in November, 1777, "Next Campaign, we will take the Field with not one-fifth of Our Quota of Troops," while other states will fill theirs. Pennsylvania soldiers were second to none in the field, he said, and this situation could continue to be the case, but only if the Assembly would give them proper support to bolster "the sinking Credit of this State." Otherwise, the Commonwealth soon would be the laughing stock of the union.[9]

President Wharton was aware of General Wayne's recruiting problems and promised that the Assembly would revise the law to eliminate its more glaring deficiencies. The legislators, however, liked the statute, precisely because it favored recruitment of citizens into short-term militia forces rather than long-term regular battalions, and they proceeded only at a carefully measured pace to examine the militia law in light of Wayne's complaints. Thus, Wayne in May 1778 lashed out in his most venomous attack thus far. His two brigades, he declared to John Bayard, speaker of the Assembly and a political ally, were deficient by 1,763 men, a paucity which he attributed almost entirely to bounties that militiamen still received by avoiding the Continental service. Pennsylvania's division, said Wayne with mortification, was being called by other generals "a Dead Weight on their hands," and these officers sometimes used "other Language not quite so Respectful" when discussing Pennsylvania's troops. "For God sake," he thundered, "by some means Complete your Regiments," even if the only recourse was to a draft. Meantime, all Wayne could do was carry on his own recruiting service, by instructing his recruiters to enroll practically any man who was strong enough to walk and carry a weapon. The Assembly's response finally was to appoint a committee to study the problem and to have Wharton write him letters expressing skepticism that the general's burdens were as weighty as he proclaimed. Beyond that, for the moment, the government of Pennsylvania was not willing to budge.[10]

If recruiting was Wayne's biggest problem while at Valley Forge, difficulties in the procurement of clothing certainly ran a close second. By the beginning of the new year, however, Wayne's clothing problem was not cosmetic but a fundamental deficiency in coats, breeches, shoes, stockings, blankets, shirts — everything his men must have to keep warm in the freezing January temperatures at Valley Forge. That the entire army suffered the same glaring needs did not reduce Wayne's boiling anger at the Pennsylvania Assembly for his own troops' wants, and his letters to the legislators practically seethed with fury over the situation. At last, Wayne decided that he simply could not wait for the Assembly to act in this matter, for his men were suffering from nakedness, so in January he received permission from Washington to visit Lancaster and York in a search for clothing for his soldiers. He had some success in finding some bolts of cloth, which he intended to take back to camp and have his men tailor into some semblance of uniforms, but the cloth was held by the state clothier general, James Meese, who refused to issue it to Wayne on the pretext that the general had no authorization from the Assembly to draw these goods. Hence, a distressed General Wayne returned to Valley Forge without "an Iota of Clothing," as he told Lord Stirling in February. Over the next few months, the situation worsened, and by May 13, he was entreating his friend Richard Peters of the Board of War, "For God sake give us — if you can't give us anything else — give us linnen," so that he might protect his "Worthy fellows from vermin which are now Devouring them." By that time, Wayne had finally secured enough coats, breeches, hats, stockings, and shoes to clothe about a fourth of his men, but as these figures indicate, he still suffered glaring deficiencies in uniforms for his troops. He was far indeed from fulfilling his desire to lead a division of men bedecked with an "Eligent Uniform" and presenting the clean, neat, short-haired well-groomed appearance that he thought fulfilled the soldierly ideal.[11]

Surprisingly enough, considering the catalog of horrors that Wayne must contend with in the dark days of early 1778, the general's own spirit and morale remained high. He continued to breathe fire against the British, hoping that the enemy would not give up the fight "untill we have an opportunity to Burgoyne him." And he also found time to reflect on the deeper philosophical motivations of the patriots in their time of trial. The New Englanders, he disgustedly noted to Wharton in April, were falling "into a torpid supineness" toward the cause, so absorbed in getting and spending that they had become insensitive to patriotism. The army of General Washington, however, was becoming an example for civilians to emulate on the points of morality and patriotism — which for Wayne went hand in hand. The Continental Army, he told Gouverneur Morris, was the most moral military force that had ever existed on earth, and it remained embodied "only because we love our Country and Freedom." Therefore, while the radical Whig politicians on the national or state level might worry that the military life encouraged authoritarian values and an attitude that was antithetical to liberty, it was the army as an institution that most *preserved* the very values for which the Revolution was being waged.[12]

Given this view, Wayne rejected an argument made by Morris (one widely held by civilians at this stage of the Revolution) that the army remained true to the cause, and did not get lax in its morals, because politicians saw to it that the soldiers did not receive any unnecessary "luxuries" while in camp. Anyone familiar with the true condition of the army, declared Wayne, would know that the soldiers were genuinely deprived, and if they remained at their posts it was for reasons that transcended material values. That these views on the motivation of the soldiery seemed to contradict Wayne's earlier insistence that only discipline would keep troops in the field for the duration did not seem to occur to him. Perhaps it was clear to Wayne by now that the soldiers' motivation for staying the course was a mixture of things — patriotism, pride, stubbornness, hatred of the enemy, group loyalty, and (like Wayne himself) love of the pomp and horror of war itself. Given Wayne's patriotic feelings during early 1778, and knowing that he always accepted the Whig notion of military acquiescence to civilian authority, it seems unlikely that he made the comment in June that Howe's military secretary, Ambrose Serle, attributed to him — "that He & his Corps wd. turn [out the Pennsylvania government] or 'cut the Throats of the Rascals, he did not care wch.' " Shabbily treated by both national and state politicians Wayne certainly felt the Pennsylvania battalions to be, but that he felt a military *coup d'etat* was a solution to the army's problems is arrant nonsense. Thus, it was with an easy conscience and great willingness that Wayne, in early 1778, swore an oath of allegiance to the United States, as prescribed by a recently enacted law of Congress.[13]

As Wayne dealt with the many problems of recruiting, clothing, and troop morale at Valley Forge, he kept an attentive eye on military operations and the arming of his soldiers. Shortly after his return to camp in February from his clothing expedition to Lancaster and York, he wrote his friend Peters, asking the Board of War to exchange all the rifles in his division for muskets. "I don't like Rifles," he declared. "I would almost as soon face an Enemy with a good Musket and Bayonet without Ammunition — as with Ammunition without a bayonet." He conceded that there were not many cases in battle where bayonets got bloodied, but that was because both sides were armed with them and they mutually checked each other. Riflemen, however, having no bayonets, often fled in panic when they were assaulted by soldiers armed with this weapon. Replying, Peters noted that the Board of War did not disagree with Wayne's reasoning, but it could not fulfill his request because there were not enough muskets in American armories to cover the swap. Hence, some of Wayne's soldiers remained embodied as riflemen, but as late as May 1778 the general still was attempting to lay his hands on muskets, both to arm newly arriving recruits and to replace as many rifles as he could.[14]

In early February, General Wayne was ordered by Washington to lead 500 Pennsylvanians on an extended foraging expedition into southern New Jersey. It was Wayne's prosaic but nonetheless important assignment from the commander in chief to round up cattle to help feed the hungry army at Valley Forge. Hence, Wayne said good-bye to a brace of new lady friends, Priscilla Stephens and Priscilla Walker, that he had become acquainted with in his residence at Valley Forge, and rode away from camp on a horse that Polly recently had sent him to replace a mare that had been stolen. Trending southeastward toward Wilmington, he rode with his troops near Waynesborough but did not stop, and after making sure the Delaware River was clear of enemy shipping, crossed that stream to the Jersey shore on the nineteenth. For the next few days, Wayne and his troops combed the region between Bordentown and Salem for cattle and horses. This was not easy work, for the citizens of the area had learned from hard experience that if they intended to keep their animals they must secrete them in the forests, far from the prying eye of either redcoat or patriot. After considerable riding, Wayne and his men finally rounded up 150 cows, plus 30 fine horses, and started them northward by quiet country roads, far to the east of Philadelphia and (hopefully) British patrols, toward Coryell's Ferry, where he intended to cross the Delaware and then push westward to Valley Forge with his herd.[15]

Unknown to Wayne, however, an enemy spy had informed the British of his presence, and Howe had ordered a detachment of about 4,000 men across the Delaware into New Jersey to apprehend the rebels. When Wayne and his troops reached Haddonfield with their livestock, they were warned by a New Jersey militiaman that they were in danger of being entrapped by this vastly superior force of British soldiers, which was commanded by Lieutenant Colonel Thomas Stirling. Consequently, Wayne hastily marched his men northward to Mount Holly, which he reached on February 26, wrote Washington a report of his situation, and sent an order to Count Casimir Pulaski, a Polish officer in command of a tiny body of dragoons at Trenton, to come to his assistance. Immediately, Pulaski set out with fifty horsemen, and upon reaching Burlington on the twenty-eighth attacked an enemy outpost without much result — except, as Wayne noted, to convince Stirling that the rebel force arrayed against him numbered in the thousands. Now "the *North Briton* thought it prudent to Retreat under Cover of the Shipping" on the Delaware "and Arrived at Cooper ferry before day" on the twenty-ninth.[16]

That same morning found General Wayne and Count Pulaski pushing their now-combined force toward the British camp at Cooper Ferry. Approaching their objective, the officers rode forward to reconnoiter, hoping to find most of the British soldiers withdrawn and only a small rearguard to attack. Although the enemy commander certainly had every intention of departing the shores of New Jersey, he had been held up in getting across the Delaware River by high winds. Thus, his entire detachment remained on the ground, "covered and flanked by their shipping." Nevertheless, Wayne and Pulaski attacked Stirling's position with such vigor that the badly shaken British commander "took the Horrors" and that night withdrew to Philadelphia, convinced, said Wayne, that he had been assaulted by a vastly superior American army. The American commander praised Pulaski, who "behaved with his usual bravery," and the infantry, he declared, had acted "with a Degree of bravery that would have done Honor to the Oldest Veterans."[17]

After this small battle with the British in New Jersey, "Drover" Wayne (as he now was being referred to by his redcoated enemies) collected his cattle and horses and continued a leisurely march northward. Soon he sent off most of the livestock toward Valley Forge, but he lingered on the east side of the Delaware River for another week or two, seeking shoes to replace those worn out by his men. In mid-March he returned to Pennsylvania by fording the Delaware far above Philadelphia. For a time he foraged in Bucks County, but while there he received orders from Washington to return to the main camp. Consequently, he proceeded westward to Valley Forge, thus finally completing a month-long march that had encircled the British-occupied city of Pennsylvania. Wayne now learned with pleasure that the horses that he had sent on were put to good use by his young friend Henry Lee to mount some of his dragoons. In return for the horses, Lee presented Wayne with a barrel of malt liquor, which the cavalryman had stolen while foraging in Maryland. The general considered it a fair swap.[18]

The reason why Washington had summoned Wayne back to headquarters so suddenly was because certain gentlemen in Congress wished to consult the Pennsylvanian, even though he was a mere brigadier general, about rearranging his state's line. This curious situation had come about because Wayne was now the senior officer of his state still on active duty (Thomas Mifflin, the quartermaster general, had resigned, and Arthur St. Clair had been suspended while awaiting a court-martial for his surrender of Fort Ticonderoga to John Burgoyne during the previous campaign). Being the center of attention appealed to Wayne, and it was with considerable conceit that he presented his well-groomed person at York in late March to give the legislators his advice. The outcome of the deliberations there were about what Wayne recommended, that the Pennsylvania troops be embodied in one division of ten regiments, due to the fact that the state would provide no larger number of troops. Writing to President Wharton to announce this decision, Wayne noted that he was not particularly proud of Pennsylvania's performance in enrolling Continental regiments and that the new arrangement was the best he could propose under the circumstances. From Wharton and the legislators of his home state, Wayne received only an icy silence for his accurately stated rebuke of them.[19]

As spring arrived at Valley Forge, General Wayne and his military colleagues began to give thought to operations for the coming campaign. To their amazement, the Continental Army after its hard winter was vigorous, numerically almost equal to the enemy force in Philadelphia, and well trained — thanks to the ministrations of a Prussian drillmaster with a fake title, Friedrich Wilhelm, "Baron" von Steuben. On April 20, Washington sent a query to all his general officers, asking their advice on three possible courses of action for the American army: to attack Philadelphia, to attack New York, or to remain in camp while training and recruiting for a later test with the enemy. The generals were greatly divided in their counsel on these matters, but Wayne was sure in his own mind and the following day wrote the commander in chief that any attack, against any objective — Philadelphia, New York, or enemy-held fortifications in the Hudson Highlands — was better than keeping on the defensive and allowing the enemy to follow a well-ordered plan, "(perhaps) already formed in England [to] harass us at pleasure." But by

April 23, he had become convinced, and so informed the commander in chief, that the objective of the Continental forces ought definitely to be "Philadelphia and Howe's Army." Washington, despite Wayne's fire-breathing advice, decided for the moment to stay put at Valley Forge and await events, allowing the army in the meantime on the sixth of May a grand celebration in honor of the Franco-American treaties of recognition and alliance. General Wayne found this party delightful and some recompense for having to remain idle in camp — especially Washington's serving him and his fellow generals a "cold collation" of "fat meat, strong wine and other liquors" under a bower erected for the occasion. [20]

For the rest of May and on into early June, Wayne fussed and fumed at Valley Forge while he awaited some motion from the British army (now commanded by Sir Henry Clinton) that would set the Continentals into action. Meantime, he meditated upon England's attempts to negotiate with Americans on the subject of rejoining the empire. Commissioners, he had heard, were in Philadelphia for the purpose, and if it were true that the ministry had sent over "Lord Amherst, Admiral Kepple and Gen. Murray," as rumor had it, why, they sounded to him more like *Heralds of War* — than *Ambassadors of Peace*! " Then, on May 21, he wrote his friend Delany that the British were about to evacuate Philadelphia and that he expected a battle soon, since Clinton would not retire without a fight. Was it true, he asked, that some "Caitiffs" in Philadelphia still slandered him about his conduct at Paoli? If so, he was almost disgusted enough with this continuing carping to throw up his commission, like some other officers, and "Retire to my *Sabine* field." [21]

Of course, Wayne was about to do no such thing, and why should he? Waynesborough was thriving under the careful attention of Polly, and the general had no abiding desire to be with his family. General Washington and the Pennsylvania troops needed his gifts as a military commander. His remaining in the army was the most sensible thing he could do, for by June 17 it was clear to the Americans that Clinton intended to withdraw from Philadelphia toward New York by land, and the only question for the patriots was what course of action they could pursue to the benefit of their cause and harm to the enemy. In a council of war on that date, Washington polled his officers on whether to attack Clinton immediately, and most agreed with the commander in chief that the Continental Army should await more definite news of enemy intentions. Wayne, however, favored an immediate assault. [22]

One day after the council was held, news arrived at Valley Forge that Clinton was on the march. Although the enemy's route through New Jersey was not clear, Wayne and General Charles Lee, who had recently been released from British captivity, were ordered by Washington to cross the Delaware at Coryell's Ferry with their divisions, determine Clinton's line of march, and interpose themselves between the enemy and the Highlands in order to block any attempted movement in that direction. Since it was soon apparent that the Royal army was directing its march toward South Amboy and New York City, Wayne and Lee bided their time until the twenty-third, while the entire Continental force crossed the Delaware and Washington moved his headquarters to Hopewell, about twelve miles northwest of Princeton. The following day, the commander in chief called a council of war and as usual found his generals in divers frames of mind about how to use the army. General Lee believed that the British ought to be allowed to retreat unmolested, for nothing could better favor America's strategic position than to allow Clinton to lock himself up in New York City. Lord Stirling and Knox agreed with this view. But Wayne, Greene, Von Steuben, and Colonel Louis Duportail favored assaulting the enemy while he was in motion, and Lafayette vehemently argued in favor of an attack by a strong American force on some part of the British column. Finally, Washington decided to send 1,500 men to attack "the enemy's flank and rear" while the main army remained nearby in case an occasion for its use arose. This "solution" Wayne found so disgusting that he refused to sign the document, although his colleagues did, and on the twenty-fifth, along with Greene and Lafayette, he begged the commander in chief to reconsider his plans.[23]

By June 25, it was manifest to Washington that Wayne and the dissenters were correct in advocating stronger actions against the British if the Americans intended truly to annoy Clinton. Small parties of militia, and Colonel Daniel Morgan's riflemen, were giving the redcoats some trouble, but not enough to suit the commander in chief or his more fiery generals. Hence, he advanced his army to Kingston and decided to reinforce the 1,500 men he had detached the day before under Charles Scott with Anthony Wayne's division of 1,000 Continentals. He also decided that this powerful force should be commanded by a senior officer, and he chose Lafayette for the task. Charles Lee, however, interposed a claim to lead these troops, and Washington had to cobble up a curious arrangement in which Lafayette would relinquish command of the force to Lee once contact with the British was made. Working under this awkward scheme, Wayne on the twenty-sixth joined Lafayette's command, which was posted near Allentown, about twelve miles closer to the enemy than was the main army's camp. The general's division upon arrival rested and ate, while Wayne, Alexander Hamilton, and some other American officers set off to reconnoiter Clinton's camp, which was about seven or eight miles away. That evening they returned to Lafayette's headquarters just in time to begin executing Washington's order of the same day to join Charles Lee and some other patriot troops on the following morning at Englishtown. Thus, on June 27, Wayne went under the command of Lee, who now headed a force of 4,200 Continentals and who was under orders from Washington to attack the enemy's rear guard on the twenty-eighth as it marched clear of a village named Monmouth Court House.[24]

On the evening of June 27, Wayne met with Generals Lee, Lafayette, and Maxwell at Lee's headquarters to formulate "a plan of attack on the enemy" for the following day. This meeting took place upon Washington's order, because the commander in chief had given Lee no specific instructions on how to proceed with the assault. Since none of the officers present knew the size or disposition of the British army, it was decided that a plan would have to be put together on the morrow. None ever was, however, unfortunately for the Americans, because there was a misunderstanding between Wayne and Lee as to the tenor of Washington's orders to strike Clinton's army. "I understood," said Wayne later, "that we were to attack the enemy on their march at all events," even if it brought on a general engagement, while Lee felt he had leeway to decide on the scene whether conditions were such as to allow or preclude an assault. In any case, at about eight o'clock on the morning of the twenty-eighth, Lee's "flying army," after a three-hour march, came in view of the enemy at a distance of about one-half mile from Monmouth Court House, and the commander ordered Wayne to push ahead against the unprepared and confused British forces. Meanwhile, he directed Maxwell's men to take post on Wayne's left and went himself with a detachment of Scott's troops even farther left along the developing front. As Wayne thrust his men forward, however, the enemy, commanded by Lord Cornwallis, quickly formed into line of battle and themselves advanced. Hence, Wayne ordered his men to receive this charge and dispatched an officer with a request to Lee for reinforcements and a suggestion that Lee's whole force might be formed

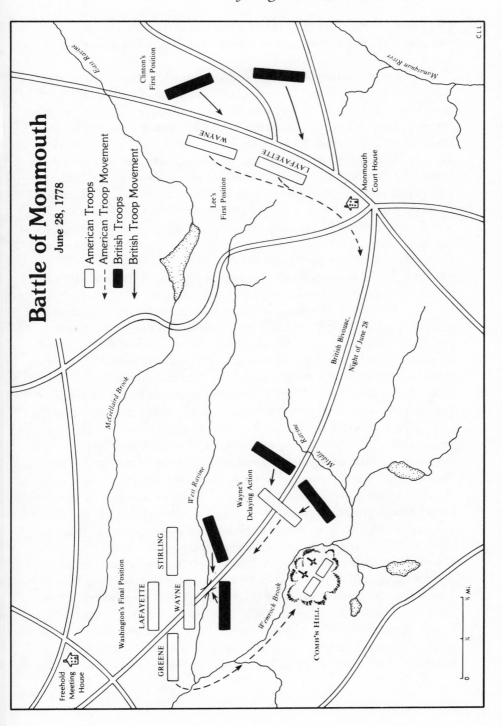

Battle of Monmouth
June 28, 1778

American Troops
American Troop Movement
British Troops
British Troop Movement

Clinton's First Position

East Ravine

Manasquan River

WAYNE

LAFAYETTE

Monmouth Court House

Lee's First Position

British Bivouac, Night of June 28

McGellaird Brook

Middle Ravine

West Ravine

Wayne's Delaying Action

STIRLING

Washington's Final Position

LAFAYETTE

WAYNE

GREENE

Wemrock Brook

COMB'S HILL

Freehold Meeting House

¼ Mi.

½

¼

0

to good advantage "on the edge of a deep morass, which extends from the east of the Court-house on the right a very considerable distance to the left."[25]

The ground he now occupied, said Wayne, was "the best formed by nature for defense of any, perhaps, in this country," and for about an hour after he had sent his request and hint to Lee, he kept the British forces in his front at bay. Then American reinforcements arrived, and these Wayne disposed to his right along the morass. Additionally, General Scott's men, who had fallen back once, came forward again and raised the number of Continentals under fire to about 2,500. Since at this point in the battle the enemy had only 2,000 troops engaged, Wayne, ever the optimist, believed that the battle was going well for the Americans. Suddenly, however, the soldiers to Wayne's right began to fall back, and Wayne sent Major Benjamin Fishbourn, an aide, seeking General Lee with a request that Lee order those men to stand fast. While awaiting Lee's assistance, Wayne ordered Colonel Richard Butler's regiment to hold the line on his right.

Soon Fishbourn returned, with no answer from Lee "than that he would see Gen. Wayne himself " — which he never did. The troops on the right, meantime, continued to withdraw, despite Butler's best efforts, while the rapidly reinforcing enemy pushed forward not only there but also through "an opening on the right of General Scott." Now desperate for assistance, Wayne and Scott both sent to Lee "to request him at least to form, to favor General Scott's retreat." But this requisition "met with the same fate as the last." Finally, Scott was forced to order a general withdrawal, and Wayne, totally unsupported, also pulled back, finally rejoining the main body of the "flying army" after "being often hard pushed and frequently surrounded." Thus, said Wayne, "were these several select detachments unaccountably drawn off without being suffered to come to action, although we had the most pleasing prospect, from our numbers and position, of obtaining the most glorious and decisive victory." Wayne conveniently failed to mention that the enemy force he and the other battle-thirsty generals felt so certain they could trounce had vastly increased in numbers and was, as Lee noted, "the whole flowr of the British Army, Grenadiers, Light Infantry, Cavalry & Artillery amounting in all to 7,000 men."[26]

At that point in the battle, Lee had made the correct decision in withdrawing before such a patently superior enemy force, and it was nonsensical of Wayne to insist after the battle that his retrograde movement from Monmouth Court House "was not occasioned by want of numbers, position, or wishes of both officers and men to maintain the post." But it was just as incorrect on Lee's part to insist that Wayne, by "temerity & folly and contempt of orders," had engaged an enemy force much vaster than his own (it was not at first) while separated by eight miles from the main American army, and that Lee, by his own "presence of mind and courage," had extricated the patriots by a *"masterly manoeuvre."* For both Wayne *and* Lee had received orders from Washington to engage the rear guard of the withdrawing British army. In any case, it was General Lee's misfortune that Washington arrived on the field with the rest of the Continental Army before Lee had had an opportunity to re-form his struggling command, which had fallen back about a mile from its original positions. "His Excellency," said Wayne, ". . .was surprised at our Retreat, knowing that Officers as well as men were in high Spirits and wished for Nothing more than to be faced about and meet the British fire." It was true that Washington jumped to the conclusion that Lee had withdrawn his troops from battle for no reason at all, although Lee justifiably insisted that he had freedom within his instructions to react to conditions which the commander in chief could not possibly know anything about. Unmollified by Lee's explanation, Washington was livid with rage that his subordinate had "disobeyed" orders, and the two men exchanged hot words. Immediately afterward, the commander in chief wheeled his horse and rode quickly away to rally the retreating American soldiers.[27]

To this point in the battle of Monmouth Court House, General Wayne had not particularly distinguished himself as a tactician, even if he had shown his usual courage and *élan* under fire. However, under Washington's immediate command, he now began to perform better. By order of that general, Wayne organized a line of battle about two miles west of his morning post, using three regiments and two pieces of artillery. With these forces, he was admonished to hold the enemy in the broiling heat until Washington could re-form the remainder of the army and restore order on another line about a thousand yards behind Wayne's position. "We had but just taken post," said Wayne, "when the Enemy began their attack with Horse & foot & Artillery." These enemy troops, Clinton's elite light infantry and grenadiers, supported by two regular regiments and the Hessian grenadiers, were simply too much for Wayne's hodgepodge defense line. "The fire of their whole united force," he said, "soon Obliged us after a Severe Conflict to give way." By then, Washington had managed to form his last line of the day, posting Lord Stirling on the left, Lafayette in the center, and Greene on the right, and these officers were making "every possible Exertion. . .to Spirit up the Troops and to prepare them for an other Tryal." American artillerists, who had gotten a few pieces in place and who cannonaded advancing British forces for about four hours, gave them enough time to accomplish this task. During this bombardment, Wayne got his men back to the center of Washington's well-formed line, in advance of Lafayette's position, and was ready when "the Enemy began to Advance again in a heavy Column." Stirling's men on the left received a powerful attack, as did Greene's on the right, but both positions held. Then the fire of enemy infantry began to abate, and Wayne decided to test the redcoats in his front by ordering his Pennsylvanians to advance. The ensuing action "was Exceedingly warm and well Maintained on each side for a Considerable time," but finally Wayne — and Washington — had the extreme gratification of seeing England's finest troops fall back before Wayne's veterans and at last disengage from the fight.[28]

Wayne's success in pushing back the enemy encouraged Washington to order his entire line to move forward against the now-retreating British soldiery. Although the American troops tried to respond to their commander's injunction, they were, as one officer noted, too "beat out with heat and fatigue." Therefore, they paused on the steaming-hot field, staring across a ravine at the enemy force until darkness ended this recreation. Next morning, they discovered that Clinton had withdrawn his troops and was continuing on his march toward New York City. Although Wayne wanted to pursue the British army, Washington correctly deduced that his men were too worn down by heat and fatigue to do any more damage to the enemy. So the troops stayed put. It only remained for the Americans to count their losses (about 325 casualties, as over against 385 for the British) and to ruminate upon their performance during the previous day's fighting. Assessments of Wayne's conduct — except for the one written by General Lee — were uniformly favorable. John Laurens specifically noted the Pennsylvanian's bravery, as did Alexander Hamilton, who commented that the general "was always foremost in danger." Washington, in a letter to Congress, expressed a general obligation to all his officers for their support on the battlefield but added, "I cannot. . .forbear mentioning Brigr Gen Wayne, whose good conduct and bravery thro' the whole action deserves particular commendations."[29]

To a degree, both the favorable comments, and Lee's unfavorable one, about Wayne's behavior at Monmouth Court House were warranted — even after discounting the growing partisanship of the assessors — for the statements were actually directed toward two different battles. Lee was not wrong in charging Wayne with being impetuous, even to foolhardiness, in trying to fight an elite British corps that was ultimately reinforced to twice the size of his own in the opening phase of the conflict (even if Lee was incorrect in accusing the Pennsylvanian of disobeying orders). But Washington, Hamilton, and Laurens were also not wrong to praise Wayne's performance in the latter stages of the battle. That General Wayne combined a dashing bravery with tactical intelligence in handling his forces under Washington's direct orders is clear. In fact, it is arguable that his holding action, which gave the commander in chief desperately needed time to re-form the shaken Continental forces, saved the American army from being routed on the twenty-eighth of June 1778.

If Wayne's battlefield performance was being discussed and analyzed, even more so was General Lee's. Hardly had the smoke of musket and cannon cleared from the battle than Lee was complaining to Washington about the latter's treatment of him. If the commander had charges of disobedience, misconduct, or cowardice to lodge against him, said Lee on June 30, he wished to see the complaints in writing, "that I may prepare for my justification." But in fact, he said, neither Washington nor anyone else who was not at the scene of action during the early hours of the twenty-eighth had warrant to "judge of the merits or demerits" of his behavior. When the commander in chief received this letter, he instantly called upon Generals Wayne and Scott to inform him of what had "really" occurred near the court house, whereupon both men assured Washington that they had faced a numerically inferior and disorganized enemy, taken a post suited for defense, twice petitioned Lee fruitlessly for reinforcements when their line started crumbling, and been forced to withdraw when left unsupported. These facts, asserted Wayne and Scott, should "convince the world" that their retreat was occasioned by no other reason than Lee's unexplained refusal to supply them with assistance at a critical time. "We also beg leave to mention," concluded the two generals, "that no plan of attack was ever communicated to us, or notice of a retreat, until it had taken place in our rear, as we supposed by General Lee's order." Satisfied that this letter confirmed the correctness of his battlefield behavior toward

Lee, Washington now wrote his subordinate that he might have his hearing, "as soon as circumstances will permit." To this note, Lee replied that he must have a court martial instead, and the commander in chief thereupon placed him under arrest, on charges that he had disobeyed orders, conducted "an unnecessary, disorderly and shameful retreat," and shown "disrespect to the Commander in Chief."[30]

From July 4 to August 12, Lord Stirling, as president of Lee's court martial, held session after session of the trial, while the American army moved from New Brunswick to Paramus, then to Haverstraw, and finally to White Plains. These proceedings took up a great deal of Wayne's time, for not only was he a principal witness in the trial but also — like everyone else in the army — curious about what would be the ultimate fate of the unique Charles Lee. Early in the inquiry, Wayne was called by Lee, who acted as his own defense lawyer, to give testimony. With careful questions, Lee attempted to maneuver Wayne into admitting that he (Lee) had acted under no ironclad orders from Washington to attack the enemy on the twenty-eighth of June, but the Pennsylvanian insisted that these *were* his *precise* orders. It may be true, as has been charged, that Wayne gave this testimony about his orders to "avert criticism" from his own conduct upon the battlefield. But a more likely explanation is that Wayne — whether correct or not in his interpretation — truly *believed* that these were his and Lee's orders, and that he (Wayne) was carrying them out by vigorously engaging the enemy, come what may. After Wayne had completed his participation in the trial itself, he continued to watch with fascination as the flamboyant Lee went on with his defense. "A note of his [about Wayne] to the printer of the Burlington papers," mused Wayne to Greene on July 14, "savors of Insanity — or flows from *a worse cause*."[31]

Finally, however, Wayne's diversion with the eccentric goings on of his colleague came to an end, for on August 9, Lee summed up his defense. In a lengthy, handwritten document he touched on many matters, but he gave pointed attention to refuting Wayne's damaging testimony by asserting that the Pennsylvanian on June 28 had himself been overconfident, that his call for reinforcements — if he had made one (Lee could not recollect having received this request) — was unnecessary, that he mistook a British feint for a retreat, that his lack of concern about the danger of enemy cavalry was wrong, and that in general he had behaved as though *he*, and not Lee, were the overall commander of the advanced corps. Despite these facts, conceded Lee, his purpose in limning them was not to deprecate Wayne's courage or his sincerity but merely to note that the general's testimony was muddled. Three days later, the court, ignoring Lee's comments about Wayne, found him guilty of all the counts against him and suspended him from command for a period of twelve months.[32]

As General Lee's exciting trial had proceeded through the summer of 1778, Wayne and the Continental Army remained peacefully in "a strong camp" at White Plains. General Clinton's British minions kept quiet within their lines around the city of New York, and not much immediate concern with the enemy disturbed Wayne's repose. The British, noted Wayne, were "too strong to touch" and they themselves would only venture forth from their entrenchments to forage for supplies. Hence, there was a stalemate between Washington's and Clinton's armies. To the eastward, however, General Sullivan conducted operations against a British base in Rhode Island, and Wayne was pleased that a French fleet and army, first fruits of the Franco-American alliance (which Wayne had declared would assure the "Establishment of the Declaration of Independence"), operated there in cooperation with Sullivan. His ony disappointment in this arrangement was that Washington and the Comte d'Estaing, commander of the French fleet, had concluded that a combined operation against New York would not be feasible. He and his colleagues did become concerned in August that Clinton might try to relieve Rhode Island, for Wayne, as he told his wife, devoutly wished that Sullivan might destroy the British forces there before they could receive assistance, then join Washington's army at New York to crush that post as well. In a council of war on September 1, Washington asked his generals whether the army at White Plains ought to assist Sullivan by marching east itself, or perhaps attacking New York City. The vast majority of the generals desired no action at all, with only Wayne advocating an assault on New York as a diversion. Washington did not heed Wayne's advice, even though Clinton had weakened the British position in the city by sending reinforcements to Rhode Island. In any case, by that time Sullivan had been compelled to lift the siege, the French fleet having withdrawn its support of his operations.[33]

Although Wayne was left in peace and quiet by the British at White Plains in 1778, he had many things of a military and personal nature to occupy his time. He sat on two courts-martial, one in August for his Pennsylvania colleague, Arthur St. Clair, who was charged with negligence in ordering the evacuation of Fort Ticonderoga in July 1777, and the other for Schuyler, who was accused of dereliction of duty in being absent from Ticonderoga in the weeks prior to that fortress's fall to Burgoyne. In both these trials, Wayne was sympathetic to the problems that the defendants had faced in their commands and voted with the majority to exonerate the generals of all charges. From Polly and Elizabeth Wayne came a number of letters, expressing concern for his welfare and worrying about his complaints that he was not receiving their letters, which they assured him they wrote often. Polly also noted that their son, Isaac, had been missing some school because his teacher was ill, a comment which (inevitably) brought from Wayne in his next letter to her a lecture about making sure the children got an education and not "indulging" them.[34]

During the fall of 1778, Wayne began once more to have problems with the government of Pennsylvania on the issue of support for the state's troops. In October, Wayne wrote Robert Morris pleading for the Assembly to provide uniforms for "our poor Worthy fellows. . . — their distresses are great." He sent the same heartrending appeal to Peters, noting that not only soldiers but officers as well were being "beggared." Many of the latter were threatening to quit the service, and Wayne himself declared, "I wish from my very Soul that affairs may be in such train as to permit me to Retire to my *Sabine fields* at the end of this campaign without the Imputation of *fear* or want of Patriotism." That the Pennsylvania regiments were undermanned the general proved to the Assembly on the twenty-sixth of October by sending a return showing a total deficit of 1,767 men and expressing a certainty that since other states were recruiting their troops up to strength Pennsylvania would want to do so as well. Through November and December 1778 and January 1779, Wayne pleaded over and over again for blankets, shoes, shirts — all the items of clothing and bedding that might give a bare modicum of comfort to his men in their rude-hutted encampment, which now had been located at Middlebrook, New Jersey. Little or no assistance was forthcoming from the Assembly, for the state's treasury, noted President Joseph Reed to Wayne on January 14, was bare; a petition to Congress, he hoped, would bring Pennsylvania some much-needed cash; meantime, Wayne and his soldiers were to do the best they could.[35]

When Wayne warned the Pennsylvania Assembly about the officers of his state quitting the service, he was not exaggerating in order to scare the legislators into compliance with his demands, for many colonels and majors did resign. Wayne himself had his own special reason for seriously threatening resignation in mid-October, and although he had made insincere threats about leaving the service in the past, this time he was seriously contemplating defecting. The catalyst for this thinking was his loss of command of the Pennsylvania line to St. Clair, who, after being cleared by the very court-martial upon which he had sat, assumed overall command of the Pennsylvania troops and relegated Wayne to control of a battalion. St. Clair was an officer whom Wayne had come to dislike more and more as the Revolutionary War progressed, for not only did the man continue to speak disparagingly of Wayne's conduct at Paoli, fumed the brigadier, but he also had refused to send troops to Wayne's assistance when he requested them at Monmouth. "Add to this," commented Wayne, that Colonel Irvine must be deprived of his brigade command if he (Wayne) were demoted, and the situation was hardly bearable. This criticism of St. Clair, insisted Wayne, was not to be construed as a demand for his own promotion, for he would willingly remain a brigadier general — but only if he were not "superseded at this late hour" in command of the division "by a man in whose conduct and candor I can have no confidence." To St. Clair's leadership, he said, "I can never submit. . .I have therefore determined to return to domestic life, & leave the blustering field of Mars to the possession of gentlemen of more worth."[36]

It can hardly be doubted that General Wayne heartily felt all the things he had said about his new commander, but they did not lead to his resignation. The comments were contained in a draft of a letter that Wayne seems to have composed for Congress, and had the letter been sent to the legislature his resignation must have followed. But apparently, Wayne's romantic attachment to the military service overrode his immediate scruples about accepting orders from St. Clair, and he chose to hold his peace for the moment, while trying to work out an arrangement to secure an independent command. Meantime, he swallowed his pride and took over Irvine's brigade. While he was preparing to take a long-delayed furlough in Philadelphia, a statement from Charles Lee in the local papers caught his eye. In the article, Lee made comments about Wayne which the Pennsylvanian decided were aspersions upon "the Military Character of a Gentleman," and on January 7, 1779, he wrote Lee, demanding an accounting. In a conciliatory letter of response, Lee informed Wayne that he always spoke highly of the latter's character and bravery, and while the two men had honest differences of opinion about Monmouth Court House, they certainly did not involve the honor of either one. Wayne retorted to these comments that he still felt wounded in his character, and he wanted to meet Lee for a duel whenever it was convenient for that officer. However, both men now allowed the issue to lapse into silence and never brought it up again.[37]

In early February 1779, General Wayne at last began a leave in Pennsylvania's capital, far from the oppressive strictures of St. Clair's command or other military aggravations. The city to which he returned after months of absence was one transformed by the corrupting influence of British money and manners. Before Wayne's arrival, Colonel Walter Stewart had written him that in "dress, manners, & customs of the town's people, great alterations have taken place since I was here. It is all gaiety, and. . .every lady and gentleman endeavours to outdo the other in splendor & show. The manners of the ladies are likewise much changed. They have. . .lost that native innocence which was their former characteristic & supplied in its place. . .an Easy behavour. . .The manner of entertaining in this place has likewise undergone a change. . . You will hardly dine at a table but they present you with three courses & Each of them in the most elegant manner. 'Tis really flattering to the officers of the Army, the attention paid them by the people. . .God knows we deserve it. Much have we suffered while these people were enjoying all the luxury and ease of life." Wayne gave hearty assent to this last sentiment, and he accepted the lionization of society as a military hero whose hard-won reputation in many battles made him a favorite of hostesses.[38]

Public business, however, was General Wayne's predominant concern in Philadelphia — specifically, seeking assistance from the state Assembly for the Pennsylvania line and its officers. The condition of the colonels, majors, and captains especially grieved Wayne. Two months earlier, he had declared that their "distressed situation beggars all Description," and he laid the cause of their difficulties at the door of an Assembly elected under a bad constitution. "Lenient government," he insisted, was not congruent with martial necessity, for how could armies be maintained by a state that was afraid to tax its people because its legislators faced annual elections? Wayne, in any case, felt he must do something to improve conditions in the Pennsylvania line, and in the fall of 1778 he and his colleagues had organized into a committee to seek better pay, supplies, and pensions from the Assembly. Even before that time, in the previous May, he and other Continental officers had already won from Congress enactment of legislation providing seven years' half pay (with the reimbursement never to exceed that of a colonel's rank) at the end of the war. But, as Wayne had noted then, "I am sorry to say that it falls far short of giving satisfaction. . . . For my own part I have a Competency and neither look nor wish for an Gratuity, other than Liberty and Honor — but the Discontented say that 7 years half pay would not make up for the Depreciation of the Money & the high price of every Article for this last year being on the Average at least five to one — which would Require three years half pay to do even justice to them for the Deficiency of the Last — How just this mode of Reasoning may be I shall not Attempt to say nor do I mean to Advocate their cause — if they want more I doubt not but Congress will make the proper provision — if not they will be Justifiable in adhering to what they have Done."[39]

Six months after writing these words, Wayne clearly had changed his mind and was advocating the dissident army officers' cause in the Pennsylvania Assembly. Looking toward a legislative battle, Wayne in October 1778 had begun to take great interest in the annual Assembly elections, writing friend Peters to send him news of the election results. What he learned after the returns came in could hardly be comforting to him, for the proconstitution people, whom Wayne and his officer friends called the "Yellow Whigs," headed by George Bryan, won a handy majority. Of the fifty-nine members elected, only nineteen, led by Robert Morris, refused to swear an oath of allegiance to the present constitution. In November, however, twenty-three anticonstitution members were active in the legislature, and one, James Wilson, wrote Wayne seeking the general's support in overthrowing the present system by campaigning against it in state politics.[40]

The general certainly was receptive to Wilson's entreaties, for he still despised the Constitution of 1776, calling it in November "that usurpation & tyranny (sometimes called a Government)" which "Oppressed" poor Pennsylvania. But he could hardly take an active part in trying to destroy the very government to which he and his officer colleagues were appealing for military assistance. Therefore, he reluctantly declined Wilson's offer and worked instead as a lobbyist for his proposals, which in November 1778 he had his "agent," William Irvine, introduce to the Assembly (since he was still with the Continental Army in New Jersey). These proposals, later embodied in a bill for consideration by the Pennsylvania Assembly, were that (1) Pennsylvania's army officers would receive half pay from the state for life when the war was terminated; (2) foodstuffs for the officers would be distributed at a set price, regardless of inflation; (3) each officer in the line would receive a full uniform ("set of Regimentals") each year at the rate of 1776; (4) all state land grants to officers, in lieu or excess of salary, would be free of taxes as long as the property remained in the soldier's family; and (5) all widows of army officers would receive their husband's half pay, whether their spouse died in the service or later.[41]

When Wayne arrived on the scene in Philadelphia, the Assembly — despite General Thomas Mifflin's earlier view that "Affairs now wear a very pleasing aspect in Penn'a" because "A majority of the members elected to the Assembly are sincerely & warmly disposed" toward the patriotic army officers' grievances — was making no progress on the military bill. Therefore, Wayne went before the assemblymen in person on the tenth of March 1779, and made a pathetic speech, appealing for their support of and sympathy toward his claims. Probably his address had little effect in swaying the Assembly, since it was already moving rapidly toward accepting the army's arguments. In any case, the bill shortly thereafter became law, and a delighted Wayne on the fourteenth wrote a letter to the field officers of the Pennsylvania line, announcing that the officers' reforms had been ratified by the Assembly "with a great majority." The Pennsylvania establishment, he boasted, was now superior to any in the continent and equal to Britain's, and there may be more legislative delights still in store for the military. The Assembly, he said, was still working on proposals from him and other officers regarding improvements in the services of supply and in recruiting. No longer need Wayne or any of his fellow Pennsylvania officers consider returning to their "Sabine fields" because of civilian neglect.[42]

As events were to prove, Wayne was overly optimistic about the future of civil-military relations among Pennsylvanians in the Revolutionary period, but for the present his republican faith in civilian control of the army was restored. Even in the darkest hours of legislative neglect during the previous two years, Wayne had insisted on a strict compliance by his soldiers with civilian law. On one occasion he had confined some soldiers to their tents because they had ignored "the superior power of the *Civil Law* over the military" and had exercised "*Military Law* over the peacable & Unarmed Inhabitants of this State [New York]." The governor, he said, "who is the Guardian of the Civil

Liberties of the People over which he presides, has Demanded you to be given up to the Civil Power," and Wayne intended to comply. But the general insisted on adhering to the letter of the law in these matters, for on another occasion in January 1779, at Middlebrook, he was not so polite to the civil authority. In that case, a fellow calling himself a magistrate burst into Wayne's headquarters and demanded the arrest of a Pennsylvania officer for a supposed breach of New Jersey law.[43]

The "dirty looking" character, who had roused the grumpy Wayne from his bed, was rude and had no warrant, so Wayne ordered him to depart from camp. When he refused to leave, the general unceremoniously had him arrested "until he produced his authority (I had had a case a day or 2 before of a spy in the middle of camp)." The character was not released until a fellow citizen came the following day with an acceptable arrest warrant. When Governor William Livingston of New Jersey was apprised of Wayne's actions, he protested to Washington that they were "a breach of *decorum*, — and *Indignity* to the Civil Authority — . . .a *violation* of the articles of war." They were none of these, insisted Wayne to the commander in chief, who asked his subordinate to give his side of the story, for the scruffy arrogant character whom Wayne had arrested possessed no civil warrant to support his claims. "I have as high an Idea of Civil Liberty as Gov. Livingston or any other Gentleman," declared Wayne, and his sacrifices for the principle, he said, proved the assertion. However, he had not given up his own right of citizenship by becoming a soldier. At that point, both Washington and Livingston let the matter drop quietly into limbo.[44]

With the season for military campaigning drawing near in the spring of 1779, General Wayne put aside civil politics and became more active in the military variety. Not wishing ever again to be under the command of General St. Clair, Wayne began casting about for employment in the army outside the Pennsylvania line. In early 1779, it was being bruited about among American officers that Washington planned to organize an elite light infantry corps for special temporary service during the following year, and Wayne immediately queried the commander in chief about whether he might have charge of this special unit. Although he "sincerely esteemed" St. Clair, said Wayne disingenuously in his application, he did not wish to interfere with the positions of colonels who now commanded Pennsylvania's brigades. Immediately, Washington agreed to appoint Wayne to the new position — a telling indication of the respect with which he viewed the military abilities of the Pennsylvanian — "as soon as the arrangements of the army. . .permit the formation of that corps." Consequently, Wayne, after receiving a heart-warming letter of appreciation from a number of the officers of the Pennsylvania line, said good-bye to his old command. Wayne's new light infantry corps, which was to be composed of 2,000 veterans from the finest companies of each regiment in Washington's army, was a choice position, much desired by many officers. Among those who thirsted for the new position was Daniel Morgan of Virginia, and when the new corps was not given into his charge he resigned from the army in protest. Jealousies such as these caused Wayne on May 18 to write Washington, "I had better be absent [from camp] (while the corps is being organized)," lest officers find cause to criticize him for influencing the commander's choice of companies and officers to make up the new corps.[45]

Besides politicking to secure an independent command in the army, Wayne was also attempting to gain promotion to the rank of major general. In early October 1778, Wayne had thrown out to Assembly-man Robert Morris of Pennsylvania a broad hint that he and other Pennsylvania officers were being held back in rank more than other states' officers. The Pennsylvania line, he noted pointedly, had "but one Brig'r General for the three Brigades," and throughout the winter of 1778–79, he suggested to other men on other occasions that he ought to be promoted. When nothing came of his efforts, finally in March 1779, he made a point-blank requisition to Washington that he be advanced in his rank, but the commander in chief refused to violate his long-standing rule not to recommend officers for promotion — although he did note that in this case he wished he could. Returning to his petition of civilians, Wayne in April assured some friends in Congress that while his "only ambition was to have continued a Brigadier Commanding the Penn'a line," that recourse was no longer available to him, and should the legislators choose to promote him he would "be glad to accept." A month later, a congressional committee made a specific proposal that Wayne be given the rank of major general — but there the issue died, for the legislators feared that such action would invite too many state jealousies.[46]

Nevertheless, the general enjoyed himself mightily in his continuing visit to Pennsylvania. But the adulation of a fawning public having finally palled upon him after many weeks of parties, suppers, and other social amusements in Philadelphia, Wayne in May at last betook himself to Waynesborough, where he seemed for a time to revel in the pleasures of family life and rural leisure. He wrote to his friend Richard Butler on June 7, "I must try to get away from this place — the Luxurancy of the soil — the Domestick Rewards & other Pleasures & amusements, which hourly present themselves, have almost debouched me from the field." Despite his protestations about enjoying rural Chester County's springtime delights, Wayne was soon chafing to get back to the army and take over his new light infantry corps. "I don't know what to do till I hear from [Washington]," he told Henry Archer, and to Butler and Walter Stewart he expressed "impatience" to return to "the field of Mars."[47]

CHAPTER *V*

Stony Point and Stormy Politics
1779–1780

BELIEVING THAT "sanguine God is rather thirsty for Human Gore," Wayne in mid-June departed from home and friends to rejoin the army. Wayne's catalyst to action was a letter from Washington, calling him at last to take command of the light infantry at West Point. For a while, he lingered in Philadelphia, saying good-bye to acquaintances there, but then, scrawling a final hasty note to Polly, he rode north to the Hudson River and assumed his new post. The light corps, composed of Pennsylvania, Connecticut, and Virginia troops chosen by Washington because of their quality and length of service, was organized into two brigades, one under General Irvine, the other under Colonel Francis Johnston. By the time General Wayne reached his new post, Washington had drafted a more specific set of orders for the employment of his subordinate and the light corps: "to make some attempt" upon the enemy posts on Verplanck's Point and Stony Point. These positions, rocky promontories jutting into the Hudson River respectively from the stream's east and west banks across from each other just below Peekskill, had been seized by the enemy on June 1 to protect King's Ferry, a major line of communication between New England and the middle colonies. But the points also were important because they were potential hazards to the rebel-held Highlands, and all things considered they would certainly be worth American trouble to eliminate. In response to his orders, Wayne's first duty was to find out whether it would be possible to use the light corps against one or both of these positions before their fortifications became too heavy for the Continentals to assail.[1]

94

General Wayne thus was thrown without ceremony into the very thick of military planning and preparations only days after leaving quiet, peaceful Waynesborough. The American situation was that the main army was scattered in a broad arc from the bank of the Hudson below West Point to Smith's Clove, about ten miles to the west of the river. Washington's headquarters were at New Windsor. Although only one half of Wayne's projected corps of eight battalions had been embodied when he took command, these troops, about 1,300 in all, were considered adequate for their purpose. Wayne immediately began to reconnoiter the enemy's positions, and on July 3 he reported to the commander in chief that it would be impossible to *storm* the defenses of either point. Not to be thwarted from some form of assault, however, Wayne defiantly declared that a *surprise* might work at Stony Point, and he invited his superior to come take a look for himself. General Washington availed himself of that opportunity on the sixth — after which he immediately agreed with Wayne that the commander in chief's staff should proceed with planning for a surprise assault upon Stony Point.[2]

While Washington's headquarters, with Wayne's constant oversight, carefully prepared for this operation, the Pennsylvanian turned his attention to the immediate problem of getting his corps better organized, working from his headquarters, five miles below West Point on the Hudson River, at Sandy Beach. He complained that his corps was deficient in provisions — especially rum — and he asked the commander in chief that his men be issued new uniforms. Washington denied the latter appeal on the reasonable ground that since the light corps was only temporarily embodied it would be impossible to match the many different states' colors in new uniforms. Each man, however, could have a hat or cap, a blanket, two shirts, a pair of overalls, and one pair of shoes. Wayne particularly enjoyed announcing to the soldiers that Congress (upon Washington's request) had just voted each Continental regular a gratuity of $1000.[3]

By the fifteenth of July, Wayne and the commander in chief had completed their plans for a surprise assault upon Stony Point. This sentinel of the Highlands rose one hundred and fifty feet from the water and projected half a mile into the stream, with three sides surrounded by water and the fourth by a swampy morass, bridged by a causeway to the mainland and impassable at high tide. The British fortifications on this point were formidable, consisting of two abatises (matted and sharpened tree branches pointing toward an attacker's force) and three redoubts. These latter held cannon that were so emplaced as to guard all approaches, and the whole was guarded by five hundred soldiers under Lieutenant Colonel Henry Johnson, a capable and brave officer. Washington, as he told Wayne on the tenth, confirmed that the attack should be made in stealth (as Wayne had suggested earlier) by no more than two hundred well-chosen men and officers and that it should take place at midnight. The approach to the post would be made from the south under cover of darkness along the water's edge, "crossing the beach and entering the abattis," to be preceded "by a vanguard of prudent and determined men well commanded, who are to remove obstructions, secure the sentries, and drive in the guard."[4]

All the men, continued Washington, were to advance with fixed bayonets and unloaded muskets toward precisely determined objectives upon their particular path, while other smaller parties would divert enemy attention from the main assault by advancing "to the work by the way of the causeway & the River on the north if practicable." Once the point had been secured, Wayne was to see that no British soldiers escaped by water, or if they did "to annoy them as much as possible." Captured enemy cannon were to be immediately turned on enemy shipping in the river and also Verplanck's Point on the east side of the Hudson opposite, while the same guns were to be shielded if possible from answering British fire. Concluding, the commander in chief told Wayne that these plans could be altered if the Pennsylvanian thought necessary, for Washington reposed full confidence in his subordinate. Wayne, therefore, after a thorough reconnoiter of Stony Point on July 11 proposed to revise the original plan to include two genuine attacks and a feint — one bayonet assault by the south beach, as originally proposed, and another by the north, with a diversion taking place on the causeway in the form of a rapidly firing and noisy party to draw the defenders' attention.[5]

On the morning of July 14, Wayne made a final reconnoiter of enemy positions on Stony Point and informed Washington that he intended to carry out his operation, as amended, on the following day. The commander in chief approved, and so Wayne immediately began to compose battle orders for his subordinate officers. By the time he had gone over all the details that he and Washington had hammered out, these orders ran to six lengthy, handwritten pages. Then, on the morning of the fifteenth, he directed his light corps to be drawn up in camp at Sandy Beach for their first inspection as a completed unit. According to general orders, all the men appeared "fresh shaved and well powdered," with complete equipment and full rations, ready to go into motion. At noon, the inspection completed, Wayne wheeled the corps into column of march on the road southward toward Stony Point, fourteen miles distant, passing Fort Montgomery and turning westward for a few miles away from the river, in order to screen his men from observation from the river and to make sure they did not guess their destination. Then, at Clement's, after a rest, the column turned south once more, finally approaching Springsteel's, less than two miles from Stony Point, where it halted again. The men, admonished to strict silence and to remain in ranks unless accompanied by an officer, now probably guessed their objective. So far all was well, and Wayne's approach had gone undetected, for the evening before he had sent out a number of small parties to patrol and to seize all male inhabitants on the line of march, lest someone see the corps in motion and forewarn the enemy. The general now rode forward to take a last look at the Point's features, just as the evening light began to fail, then returned to his men full of certainty that his bold enterprise would succeed.[6]

With all preparations made, Wayne sat down at eleven o'clock in the evening of July 15 to compose what he believed might be his last letter. Characteristically, it was written not to his wife or mother or sisters but to his friend Delany, to be sent only in case of his death, and it was designed to be a will, an apology for his attitude toward St. Clair, and a final, bitter condemnation of politicians who did not support the military establishment. "This will not meet your eye," he told Delany dramatically "until the writer is no more." Then he referred to certain papers he was enclosing to give Delany ammunition "to defend the Character & support the honor of the man who loved him" against St. Clair and that general's "lackeys." Launching into a critique of the "Supineness & unworthy torpidity" of Congress, he growled about "the choice of difficulties" that Washington was thrown into by legislative pennypinching and noted that the present shoestring operation was a case in point. Even the commander in chief himself might "fall Sacrifice to the folly & parsimony of our WORTHY RULERS." In closing, Wayne asked Delany to see to the education of his children, for he feared "that their mother will not survive this Stroke. Do go to her & tell her her Children claim her kindest offices & protection." With a rhetorical flourish rare even for General Wayne, he concluded, "I am called to Sup, but where to breakfast, either within the enemy's lines in triumph or in the other World! Then farewell my best and dearest friend and believe me to the last moment Yours most Sincerely, Anth'y Wayne." Half an hour later, he gave the order for his corps to advance, and the assault upon Stony Point was at last under way.[7]

In two columns, Wayne's men moved out with pieces of white paper attached to their hats to identify themselves in the heat of battle. No American's gun was loaded, with the exception of those in the party that were to "amuse" the enemy on the causeway. All other men had been told that if they fired a musket they would be instantly put to death by an officer near them. Wayne, accompanying the column on the right (commanded by Lieutenant Colonel François Fleury), moved southward to cross the beach near the river and come upon Stony Point from that direction, while Colonel Richard Butler directed the left column toward the north flank of the post. Meantime, the small party that was to set up a harassing fire at the causeway stealthily moved into place under command of Major Hardy Murfree. With some difficulty, Wayne and his men approached the abatises through water that was two feet deep, but as they neared their objective, Murfree's men began at midnight, precisely as scheduled, to fire tremendous volleys of musketry at the enemy, which tore the heart of silence from the black night and aroused the enemy garrison to station.[8]

As British soldiers answered the Americans' fire, advance parties of men — appropriately called "the forlorn hope" — pushed forward from both Wayne's and Butler's columns to clear out the abatis and other obstructions, that the rest of the patriot soldiers might come on. Although seventeen out of twenty American troopers in one of these "forlorn hopes" were wounded or killed, these brave men made it possible for their comrades to push into the main works. General Wayne himself was in the forefront of the southern column, charging with espontoon in hand up the rocky slopes of the Point — when suddenly he went down with a musketball wound in the head. Fortunately for him, the damage from the shot proved to be relatively minor, so that after he had shaken off his daze he could push forward once again. It was only a short time later that Lieutenant Colonel Fleury seized the British flag that flew over the fort and hauled it down, while Butler's men almost instantaneously met Fleury's troops on the same ground. In all this fighting, not a man of either column had fired a single shot, so great was the discipline that drillmasters such as Von Steuben had instilled in them the previous winter. Shortly after the American columns met,

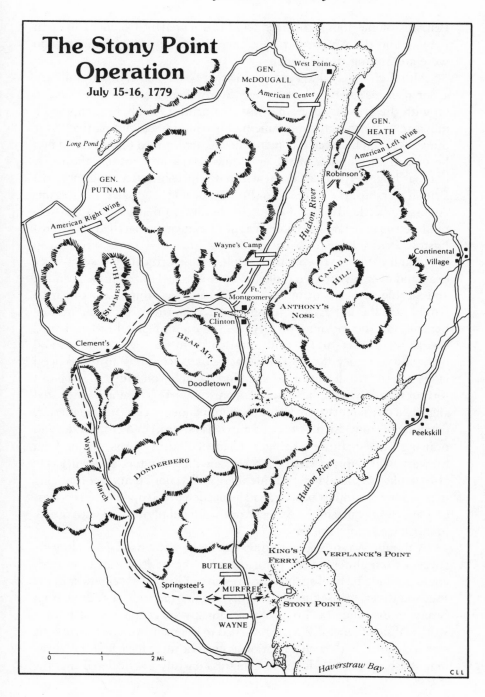

The Stony Point Operation
July 15-16, 1779

GEN. McDOUGALL

West Point

American Center

GEN. HEATH

American Left Wing

Robinson's

Long Pond

GEN. PUTNAM

Hudson River

American Right Wing

Wayne's Camp

CANADA HILL

Continental Village

SUMMER HILL

Ft. Montgomery

ANTHONY'S NOSE

Clement's

Ft. Clinton

BEAR MT.

Doodletown

Peekskill

Wayne's March

DONDERBERG

Hudson River

KING'S FERRY

VERPLANCK'S POINT

BUTLER

Springsteel's

MURFREE

STONY POINT

WAYNE

0   1   2 Mi.

Haverstraw Bay

CLL

British Colonel Johnson surrendered to Lieutenant Colonel Christian Febiger and the American troops gave quarter to Crown soldiers who were attempting to surrender.[9]

Although General Wayne was almost beside himself with military ardor after his splendid victory over Stony Point's garrison, he must go on with the prosaic duties of army command. Quickly he composed a message to Washington announcing his triumph and noting that "Our officers & men behaved like men who are determined to be free." Then he turned the cannon of the erstwhile British fort toward the river, bombarding Verplanck's Point without noticeable effect and forcing a British warship, the *Vulture*, to slip its moorings and sail downstream. Assessing battle losses and gains, he discovered that Johnson had surrendered 442 men, all of whom Wayne immediately marched off toward Easton, Pennsylvania. Casualties among American troops were fifteen killed and eighty-five wounded, while the British suffered sixty-three dead and over seventy wounded. Wayne also had seized fifteen cannon and sizable amounts of military stores, and he promised his men he would sell the latter, with congressional approval, for their mutual benefit. On the morning of July 16, Wayne in general orders issued thanks to his men and warmly praised them for their "coolness and intrepidity" under fire. All these activities, according to the general later, he effected despite a "loss of blood which Continued to Issue in a torrent from my wound," and it was only when this hemorrhage abated slightly a day later that he wrote the commander in chief a longer letter, detailing his movements of the past two days, describing the battle, and praising Fleury, Butler, Febiger, Colonel Return Meigs, Major John Stewart, and Captain Henry Archer, for their conduct under fire. He also thanked General Peter Muhlenberg and Major Henry Lee for being in positions of support nearby, had he needed to call upon their services, and to Lee's cavalry he gave special praise for supplying him with timely intelligence before the battle.[10]

Although Wayne's operation against Stony Point had been a fantastic success from almost every point of view, the position, once secured, could not long be held against the pressure of British navel power in the Hudson River. Consequently, on July 19 the Americans withdrew from Stony Point, and the Royal Army quickly reoccupied its defensive works. When General Wayne returned to the main American army, he was welcomed with such adulation as even he must have found surprising. Washington, in a letter to Congress on July 21, declared that the general's conduct "merits the warmest approbation. . . . He *improved* upon the plan recommended by me, and executed it in a manner that does signal honour to his judgment and his bravery." Congress responded handsomely to this letter on the twenty-sixth by resolving unanimously its commendation of Wayne and his corps for their assault, voting that a gold medal be struck for Wayne and silver ones for Fleury and Stewart, and approving of Wayne's promise of a reward to the troops. John Jay, president of Congress, notified Wayne of these resolves, adding his own congratulations, and Washington on August 15 directed Wayne to distribute to the corps, "according to pay scales," more than $158,000. Other letters also poured in to Wayne from St. Clair, Lafayette, John Armstrong, Sharp Delany, Adam Stephen, Philip Schuyler, Joseph Reed and the Pennsylvania Assembly, Benjamin Rush, and Charles Lee. Responding to the last message, Wayne declared (forgetting his censure of Lee after Monmouth) that Lee's words especially pleased him, coming as they did from a gentleman "whose Military abilities stand high in this age of the World." A final word of praise came from a source that Wayne never knew about, Sir Henry Clinton, who noted in his memoirs that the "bold and well-combined attempt" on Stony Point "procured very deservedly no small share of reputation and applause to the spirited officer (General Wayne) who conducted it."[11]

Not all of Wayne's mail concerning Stony Point was laudatory. The general, in praising some officers in his letters to Washington, had failed to mention others, who now wrote to remind him of his dereliction. One, Major Thomas Posey, declared that although he had led his battalion in the charge, this great contribution to victory had not been mentioned by the commander. Angrily, Wayne reminded Posey that the latter had been behind Fleury and surrounded by superior officers, but if the major was questioning his judgment he would be glad to give him satisfaction in a duel. Posey, taken aback by this reaction on Wayne's part, only insisted that he sought justice not a quarrel. Lieutenant Colonel Isaac Sherman and Major William Hull also complained, noting that some men in the corps were accusing the general of partiality to Pennsylvania officers (which was true and showed). Again, the general reacted harshly, but not so vigorously as against a similar protest by Colonel Meigs. This man, who had been mentioned by Wayne to Washington but also felt slighted, was, he said, writing not only for himself but for other officers who felt the same way. Wayne conceded that Meigs, Sherman, and Hull may be acting from pure motives, but he declared that he knew his own, and the officers were wrong to accuse him of "local prejudice." "I don't wish to Incur any Gentleman's displeasure," he fumed, *"Yet I put up with no mean Insults."* Despite his blustering, however, Wayne did relent toward the soldiers he had not yet officially complimented, and in a letter to Congress thanking that body for its resolutions on Stony Point he included favorable mention of Sherman, Hull, Posey, and, additionally, Major Hardy Murfree.[12]

As the furor over Stony Point died down in the summer of 1779, General Wayne found himself in a military backwater on the Hudson River above New York, for very little of importance occurred there during the remainder of the year. For a time, from his headquarters at the light corps' encampment at Fort Montgomery, Wayne tried to interest Washington in another assault on Stony Point, but the commander in chief showed little interest. It was just as well, for in late October 1779 the enemy withdrew from both Stony Point and Verplanck's Point without the rebels having to fire a shot. Meantime, Wayne continued to move his light corps farther southward, first to Haverstraw, then to Paramus Church, Aquackanock, and finally to Second River in New Jersey. His directives from Washington throughout all these maneuvers were to use his corps, now numbering 523 men, to cover the country against enemy raids or forages and to observe British activities in New York City. Late in the year he was reporting that the British were embarking soldiers in the city, perhaps the entire army, for a movement to Georgia; but on December 18, he warned Washington that Clinton's maneuver might be a ruse to wear down American resistance before launching a winter campaign. Hence, he watched with caution as about 130 transports sailed away from Manhattan with 5,000 British troops on board.[13]

Upon the departure of these enemy soldiers, Washington became convinced that Clinton's campaign was finished for 1779, and near the end of December he ordered General Wayne to disband the light infantry corps. It was an order that came just in time, for Wayne himself knew that the light infantrymen were in terrible straits for supplies. In fact, according to his correspondence in November and December, they were devoid of clothing, blankets, food, forage, rum, arms, and ammunition. As he sarcastically observed to Colonel Irvine apropos Congress's refusal to supply his men with hats, "They mean to leave us uniformly bare headed — as well as bare footed — & if they find that we can *bare* it tolerably well in the two extremes — perhaps they may try it in the *Center*."[14]

It was with considerable sadness that Wayne and Washington observed the end of their special light infantry corps, for it had been successful beyond the hopes of either man. It was understood all along, however, that the unit was temporarily embodied, and by the end of December it had outlived its usefulness. In sending the men back to their own units, Washington asked Wayne to offer them his heartfelt thanks for their gallantry, and to the corps commander himself Washington declared, "Your own conduct on every occasion has justified the confidence which induced me to appoint you to the command." From the officers of the corps also came thanks to Wayne for the way he had comported himself as their leader — to which the Pennsylvanian responded by declaring that their mutual cooperation, though from different states, proved that the British could never divide the people of the United States of America. Replying to Washington's letter of commendation, Wayne noted that the commander in chief 's approbation of his conduct was "very pleasing to an officer whose only merit, is that of having used his best Endeavors to do his duty." With that, he asked for and received leave from the army until the campaign of 1780 opened in the following spring.[15]

In January 1780, on his way home to Pennsylvania, Wayne rode by Washington's headquarters at Morristown, where the American army was encamped for the winter. Fortunately for him he did not long remain with the commander in chief, whose troops suffered horrid deprivations for lack of supplies and from the terrible winter weather. Instead he lived in Philadelphia, where he basked in the attention of the ladies of the city and rested from time to time at his fireside at Waynesborough, enjoying equally well the adulation of his children. Also, he was delighted on January 21 to be chosen by the leading intellectual lights of the city, along with Washington, Henry Laurens, John Adams, Thomas Jefferson, Alexander Hamilton, John Jay, and others, to become a member of the American Philosophical Society.[16] However, his relations with Polly, who had hardly written him at all in the previous year, remained strained. And some of his friends in Easttown, such as Abraham Robinson, were also angry because of his lack of correspondence with them during his recent absence from home.

Polly Wayne, however, had new reasons to censure her errant husband — these having to do with the man's growing enthrallment with a social butterfly in Wilmington named Mary Vining. Poor Polly was already only too familiar with Wayne's "fondness for ladies' society," as he himself put it on one occasion. Yet, she had been persuaded that he would never carry a relationship beyond flirtatiousness. By this time, though, she may not have been so sure, for rumors began to reach her at Easttown that Wayne was dallying with Miss Vining for afternoon teas, visiting her on the sly in Wilmington when he supposedly was out on military business, writing fond letters to her when the two were apart, and exchanging with her handsome, expensive gifts. The rumors remained only rumors, and Polly had little knowledge of the intimacy with which Wayne and Mary Vining had come to know each other at this time. Wayne's first mention of her was in a letter to Colonel Robert Magaw on the twelfth of March 1780, in which the general asked Magaw, a prisoner of war on Long Island, to purchase some fine English cloth in New York and have it made up into clothes for "the very amiable — but too *fascinating* Miss V——g."[17] Aside from the fact that this procedure by Wayne showed questionable fidelity to his wife, the general also knew perfectly well that it was a violation of civil and military laws banning intercourse between patriots and the enemy. Who was the woman that could lead a man as patriotic as Wayne to break a law which he would damn anyone else for defying?

Mary Vining was born in 1756, the daughter of Judge Vining, and grew up a beautiful, rich, socially prominent lady, admired by all. In Wilmington, she lived in Caesar Rodney's house and acted as his hostess, where she welcomed many prominent people to parties, dinners, and other social occasions. To some of these functions after 1776 came Anthony Wayne, Lafayette and other officers, many of whom fell in love with the coquette but all of whom she supposedly rejected — until 1794, when she may have become engaged to Wayne, who had recently become a widower. She was described in 1783 by the Venezuelan patriot, Francisco de Miranda, as a woman whose conversation "is sought after by strangers and men of good taste. . . . A mixture of bizareness and capriciousness in her conduct produce often an almost incomprehensible contrast with her singular knowledge and good ideas."[18] Whatever there was about the woman, it is not to be doubted that General Wayne, for his part at least, was enamored of her by the spring of 1780 (if not before) and that thenceforward he had strong feelings for Mary Vining. It is also highly likely that Polly Wayne knew of his fascination for the other woman and resented it for the rest of her life.

Politics also engaged the attention of Anthony Wayne in the early months of 1780, with about the same intensity that they had a year earlier. In March, he asserted to Francis Johnston, "I have been so much Distracted that I am almost totally Ignorant of the Current politicks in the *Magnum Concilium* of States." But from what he could hear, it was just as well, for political behavior continued to "flow from Interested Motives fabricated by little minds, on the tottering basis of momintary Popularity." Actually Wayne was dissimulating considerably in these comments, for in fact he was deeply involved in the political affairs of Pennsylvania and although he was grateful to President Joseph Reed for the latter's kind words at this time, commending him for keeping the state's soldiers subordinate to civilian authority, he was himself expressing both privately and publicly his resentment toward the Assembly (which he still considered too radical) for its outspoken opposition to "military interference" in legislative affairs — that is, the officers' perpetual lobbying in Philadelphia and their constant carping that they were the only "true patriots." Wayne, and his fellow Pennsylvania officers, were furious at this "ingratitude" by radical, antimilitaristic politicians in the legislature (the "Yellow Whigs") toward their poor, long-suffering military servants, and they began to strike back. "A most wretched & unworthy *torpidity* pervades every publick body," fumed Wayne to Irvine on March 10, and a few days later he warned Johnston, "be assured my dear friend," no matter what the Yellow Whigs may say, "that nothing but the Interposition of providence — the Wisdom, Virtue & fortitude of our great & Good General & army can rescue *America* & themselves from Impending ruin."[19]

General Wayne now believed even more strongly than he had in 1777 that the Assembly's too-tender sensibility for personal liberty was contributing to the demise of revolutionary virtue among the mass of citizens. Of all the agencies of revolution, only the army could still boast of being the repository of correct behavior. Therefore, Wayne declared, soldiers *must* proclaim these points publicly, otherwise the Yellow Whigs would dominate public opinion and continue to foster nonsensical notions among the people that military institutions and values, rather than being the font of all that was good and virtuous in the rebellion against Britain, were a danger to the very freedoms for which the soldiers so righteously fought. With burning indignation in his breast, Wayne on April 6 got together with Walter Stewart, John Stewart, and Henry Lee in Philadelphia's New Tavern to draft a public manifesto on this subject, which appeared two days later in the *Pennsylvania Packet*. "Anxious to give energy so far as our consequence may have force to the future operations of Government," declared the officers, the soldiery believed it was past time in Pennsylvania "to curb the spirit of insolence and audacity manifested by the deluded and disaffected." This problem, they noted, sprang not only from loyalists, but also "a spirit of resistance, which we cannot but apprehend receives encouragement from the lenity of Governments, founded on principles of universal liberty and benevolence." To curb this sullen resistance, they refused to "associate or hold communication with any person or persons, who have exhibited by their conduct an enemical dispositon or even luke warmness, to the independence of America." And should any man attempt to thwart the purpose of this declaration, fumed the officers, he would be held an object of contempt, to be publicly chastised at every opportunity for showing "conduct so *derogatory* to the *dignity* of the Army."[20]

The problems that Wayne faced in 1780 as an army officer in the Pennsylvania line were, to be sure, real enough. But in comparison with how some other military men and their corps were treated by their state legislatures, Wayne and his fellow Pennsylvanians were much better provided for. The Pennsylvanians, while not always kept perfectly clothed or fed, were in so much better condition than their fellows on some occasions that it became a source of worry for Washington, who feared that this situation would create jealousies among troops from other states. As for the way officers were treated, they had by 1780 secured, as Wayne himself admitted, a better pension and provision system than that provided by either the national government or any other state to its officers. What, then, was bothering Wayne and his fellow officers? Likely the answer is to be found in their vague feeling that, despite the material supports that they received from the Assembly, they still did not have the respect or gratitude of its members — especially the Yellow Whigs — for their sacrifices. All they ever heard from these people were complaints about arrogant officers who did not seem to accept their place of subordination to civil authority in a republican system of government and who openly declared fears that regular military forces ("standing armies") might at any time subvert constitutional liberty by martial coercion. President Joseph Reed attempted to explain to Wayne the feeling of some civilians toward the army by noting, "a popular Government must in the nature of things be most generally agreeable to the People of this State," because "property is too casually distributed. . . .ever to permit the Aristocratick influence which some wish and which I admit to be the most natural to the Sentiments of Gentlemen used to the discipline and subordination of an army." Reed's words, however, did not make Wayne feel any better toward Pennsylvania's radically controlled government under the Constitution of 1776, for as far as he was concerned, they gave no explanation of the problem, only a restatement of it.[21]

News from the active theaters of war and elsewhere in the early months of 1780 did little to elevate Wayne's spirits, which were so depressed by the psychic gloom brought on by the perceived ingratitude of rascally politicians and a thoughtless people in his home state. When in May word arrived at Waynesborough that Benjamin Lincoln in South Carolina was on the verge of surrendering Charleston and his army to the enemy, Wayne immediately wrote Washington to urge an attack upon New York City as a relief measure for Lincoln. Certainly, he noted, the politicians in Philadelphia were doing nothing at all about the situation. In reply, Washington noted that his financial condition precluded helping Lincoln or doing "a Thousand things which are now utterly impracticable." On May 18, Wayne heard that a French fleet might relieve Charleston, but not long afterward he finally got the bad news that the city had fallen on the twelfth. He hoped that new attempts by Congress to shore up the nation's tottering finances might now give Washington's army backing enough in the coming campaign to recoup some of America's losses, but he was not optimistic, for while it might be the duty of every citizen "to give [the new economic plan] all the weight in their power," he did not believe some of the "Coffee house politicians" would follow the maxim that "Private will must give way to Public good."[22]

Wayne was more than willing to do his part for the cause by rejoining Washington's army, "either as a volunteer" or in any other capacity in which the commander in chief might find him useful. But the desire of Wayne's life was to be put at the head of a reembodied light infantry corps, and he broadly hinted to Washington in one or two letters that he thought his service in such a unit might be highly useful to the army. However, the commander in chief believed otherwise, for on May 18 he wrote Wayne, asking him to appear in camp at his own convenience to "resume your command in the Pennsylvania line. I know," Washington wrote delicately, "on a former occasion you had some difficulties on this head, but when you consider the point you will see the propriety of the measure." Apparently Wayne did, no matter how much he despised the thought of having to take orders from Arthur St. Clair, for on June 1 he accepted Washington's offer to head a brigade of the Pennsylvania line for the ensuing campaign. Immediately, he rode to Springfield, New Jersey, where he assumed command of the 1st Pennsylvania Brigade, alongside his friend, William Irvine, who commanded the 2nd Brigade, under orders of his nemesis, Major General St. Clair.[23]

General Wayne had rejoined the American army as it loitered in the Short Hills of New Jersey, shadowing an enemy force under Pruissian General Wilhelm von Knyphausen, which was located at DeHart's Point near Elizabethtown. Knyphausen had pushed forward from this position on the seventh of June and assaulted an American troop contingent at Connecticut Farms, only to retreat the following day back to his enclave. On the twenty-third, as Wayne's battalion covered a bridge across the Passaic River at Chatham, the enemy detachment advanced once more toward Springfield, fought a hot skirmish with Greene's forces at that place, then withdrew completely from New Jersey soil, back to Staten Island. Washington, now believing that Clinton intended a stroke against West Point, marched his army (Wayne's battalion included) northward by Pequannock and Ramapo to Preakness, which place they reached by the end of June. Along the route of march, Wayne wrote his daughter, Margaretta (whom he called his "little rustic"), "I steal a moment whilst the troops are getting in motion to ask if you Improve your acquaintance with the young misses."[24]

When in a council of war on July 6 Washington asked his officers for advice on American army operations for the summer of 1780, Wayne in a fifteen-page letter four days later gave his usual response: Attack that "most capital object," New York City. Since the American forces, as Wayne well knew, were not strong enough to carry out operations against Clinton's main army on Manhattan, the Pennsylvanian began hatching another plan. Why not, he proposed to Washington on July 19 from his encampment at Totowa, New Jersey, have Wayne lead a sweep in force into the English Neighborhood, an area between the Hackensack and Hudson rivers south of the ruins of old Fort Lee? This raid, said Wayne to his commander, would have many good purposes, the major ones being to collect cattle and horses for the Continental Army, to destroy a blockhouse at Bull's Ferry, and to lure some of Clinton's soldiers into an ambush near Fort Lee when the enemy commander sent a relieving force over from Manhattan to do battle with Wayne's detachment. (A purpose that Wayne neglected to mention to Washington, but which the commander in chief knew in any case, was that the attack would give the Pennsylvanian something to do militarily and relieve him of the tedium of day-to-day army administration.)[25]

Wayne's plan sounded to Washington reasonably worth the risk, so on the twentieth he told the Pennsylvanian to proceed with the operation, using the 1st and 2nd Pennsylvania Brigades, plus Colonel Stephen Moylan's regiment of dragoons. That afternoon at three o'clock, General Wayne put in motion his force of about 2,000 men, arriving at New Bridge on the Hackensack River at nine, and after a fitful night's rest pushing his men the following day on to the vicinity of Fort Lee. There, he disposed the 6th and 7th Regiments of Irvine's brigade in concealed positions to cover narrow passes that Clinton's men must use to move inland, should the British decide to land at that place. It was Wayne's hope that they would, since the rest of his troops would be operating farther to the south and would appear vulnerable to being cut off by the British if they did bring ashore a party at Fort Lee. Wayne gave orders to the men of these two regiments to hold the redcoats, should they appear, "at every expense of blood" until General Wayne could bring up the remainder of his force in support.[26]

With his ambush laid, Wayne now proceeded southward with the remainder of his troops toward the blockhouse at Bull's Ferry, detaching General Irvine's remaining regiments about halfway between Fort Lee and Bull's Ferry so that they could "move to any point where the enemy should attempt to land, either in vicinity of this post, or Fort Lee." He also left a covering force of Moylan's dragoons and a regiment of infantry to guard a strategic crossroads against possible British attack from the direction of Bergen and Paulus Hook. Then, with most of the 1st Pennsylvania Battalion still under his immediate command, he approached Bull's Ferry blockhouse, which he discovered to be a strong post surrounded by an abatis, stockade, and natural, perpendicular rocks next to the Hudson River. The place was made even more odious to him because it was manned by loyalists — "Refugees & a wretched banditti of Robbers horse thieves & c," as he called them (a "gallant band" who "defended themselves with avidity and spirit," according to Sir Henry Clinton).[27]

Posting two regiments to keep up a constant fire on the blockhouse, Wayne used the cover of their musketry to advance his artillery to within sixty yards of the place, and he commenced a furious bombardment that lasted from eleven o'clock until noon. Although during this hour the general's cannon threw fifty balls into the walls of the blockhouse, the projectiles were not heavy enough to destroy the logs from which the strongpoint had been constructed. Hence, to his intense disappointment, Wayne was compelled by midday to recognize that he was not going to be able to carry the place by storm as he had hoped. Moreover, he was now informed by one of his observation parties, led by Zebulon Pike, that the enemy was embarking 3,000 troops on Manhattan to throw against him somewhere to the north of his present position. Thus it was necessary, said Wayne later, in defense of his action at this time, "to relinquish a lesser for a much greater object; that is, drawing the enemy over towards the [ambush at Fort Lee] and deciding the fortune of the day in the defiles, through which they must pass before they could gain possession of the strong grounds." These ideas in mind, Wayne ordered his Pennsylvanians to disengage from action with the defiant garrison of the blockhouse and retreat. But to his surprise both regiments in action continued to fight and were withdrawn only with the greatest difficulty on the part of their officers and only after three men were killed crossing the abatis. As his men finally drew off, Moylan's dragoons hurried northward toward Liberty Pole with a large drove of cattle that they had been collecting, while some infantrymen destroyed a few sloops and boats which were docked nearby on the Hudson River.[28]

Still hopeful that he might manage a splendid stroke against Clinton's reinforcements at Fort Lee, Wayne now rushed his regiments and artillery northward to catch the enemy landing party "between. . .such fires as no human fortitude could withstand." As he moved his men toward Fort Lee, however, the British officers detected his ruse and refused to land "on the hostile Jersey Shore." It now behooved Wayne to withdraw his own troops lest he tarry too long east of the Hackensack bridges and find himself facing a much superior enemy force barring his route of escape. Hence, he rapidly withdrew his men across New Bridge, continued on to Totowa, and immediately upon reaching that place sat down to write General Washington a report of his foray. After describing his activities in detail, he noted that sixty-four of his men had been killed or wounded and that all of the soldiers had performed bravely under fire. He was only sorry, he declared, that the operation had not achieved as much as he and Washington had hoped. Four days later, Wayne also wrote Joseph Reed, explaining the purposes of the raid and adding to the list that he had probably thwarted Clinton's plans to attack the French in Rhode Island, for his spoiling raid had delayed the enemy's sailing with 6,000 men toward that place and given the French so much time to prepare for a British assault that now it very likely would not take place. The general's purpose in writing this last letter, as he told Reed, was to put the quietus on rumors by his detractors that he had rushed headlong into a useless, wasteful skirmish merely to embellish his own military reputation and that the assault really was worthless from start to finish. Reed thanked him for the explanation and assured him that it cleared up all questions of possible impropriety in reasonable minds. "There is Virtue & Discernment in the World," declared Reed, "sufficient to support a Man in doing his duty," and Wayne could rest assured that he remained in high esteem with the government of Pennsylvania.[29]

There was, alas, no "virtue or discernment" amongst Wayne's British foes regarding his conduct of the Bull's Ferry raid, for they only made merciless fun of the man's efforts. Major John André, aide-de-camp to Sir Henry Clinton, was especially derisive of Wayne in a song called "Cow Chase," which he composed as a parody of the famous fifteenth-century ballad, "Chevy Chace." André's poem, published in three installments in Rivington's *Royal Gazette*, rather leadenly satirized Wayne, Henry Lee, and Lord Stirling as cowboys, drunkards, and cowards, with the worst gibes directed toward the Pennsylvanian. In one stanza, Wayne, like Mark Antony, was lured from duty by a woman, a "lovely hamadryad," who accosts him in a tavern called Three Pigeons:

> So Roman Anthony, they say,
> Disgrac'd th' imperial banner,
> And for a gypsy lost a day
> Like Anthony the Tanner.

Although few of André's lines could be considered epic satire, they were widely read by both British and Americans, and General Wayne suffered not a few pangs of indignity from the poem. It is, however, poignant and ironical that the last of André's verses were published on the day that he was captured as a spy and clapped into an American jail.[30]

During the months following Wayne's foraging expedition into the

English Neighborhood, he lived through one of the most vexing periods of his entire military career. It was a time of bureaucratic paper shuffling, political intrigue with the Pennsylvania Assembly, internecine quarrels between officers of the Pennsylvania line, treason by a colleague, and an apparent weakening of the revolutionary cause in everyone except Wayne himself and a handful of his patriotic army officer friends. His difficulties began when William McPherson, who had already given Wayne problems earlier by being promoted major by brevet at St. Clair's insistence, was now appointed with support from the same officer to command of a light infantry corps to be embodied entirely from the Pennsylvania regiments. When the other majors in Wayne's and Irvine's brigades heard about McPherson's potential new command, they instantly declared that they would resign to a man rather than suffer the humiliation of being overreached in the army by an "interloper." The two generals thereupon outlined the problem to Washington, who insisted that the McPherson appointment was valid but that the gentleman might be prevailed upon to resign the command, since it was creating such a furor. But when Wayne and Irvine petitioned the major to follow the commander in chief 's suggestion, they were told that McPherson would comply only if St. Clair also supported the plan.[31]

Apparently, St. Clair would not go along with this scheme, however, for McPherson retained his position, and Wayne and Irvine were compelled to plead with the other majors to remain in the service despite the perceived slight. "For God's sake, be yourselves," they begged, "and as a band of Brothers — rise superior to every Injury — whether real or Imaginary — at least for this Campaign." With that, the majors relented in their determination to resign, but Wayne emerged from the incident with more rage against St. Clair. That man, he declared to both Washington and President Reed (without, however, mentioning his name), was a venomous snake who attempted to poison relations between him (Wayne) and the commander in chief, and could he but get hard evidence to support his allegations against "the Caitiff, this world would want space to hold us both." Replied Washington, Wayne still held his fullest confidence, and if the man to whom his subordinate alluded was who he thought — Washington knew full well to whom Wayne referred — then the general in question had never said an unkind or derogatory word against him.[32]

While the McPherson incident played itself out to a sordid and inconclusive finish, Wayne once more had come into command of the Pennsylvania division. On September 4, St. Clair was ordered by Washington to assume control of the Continental Army's entire right wing, and as a consequence Wayne, the senior brigadier general of the Pennsylvania line, took charge of the division, which was then encamped at Tappan, New York. Responsibility without rank and pay seemed always to be General Wayne's lot, for although he was again given a major general's command, there was not a hint from either Washington or Congress that he would *ever* be promoted to that rank. He had on his own, however, already tried in August to do something about the erosion of his brigadier's pay, by signing with Greene, Stirling, Steuben, Knox, Alexander McDougall, Irvine, Lafayette, and other officers a memorial to Congress, pleading with the legislators to adjust their salaries in light of the blistering inflation of Continental currency. Money problems aside, as a divisional commander, Wayne's first thoughts were on offensive action against the enemy, and on September 13, he proposed to Washington that he be allowed to lead 1,600 of his men in an attack on Staten Island, thus drawing Clinton's attention toward him and giving the commander in chief a chance to assault the enemy elsewhere. Washington did not accept this proposal, and Wayne was left at leisure for a while.[33]

It was just as well for Wayne that he had managed a short rest, for in late September he was handed all the action he could want. His colleague, Major General Benedict Arnold, as commander of West Point, almost turned that post over to Sir Henry Clinton after months of negotiations with the enemy commander over money and other details of the sellout. The scheme was foiled only when Major John André, who was acting as Clinton's emissary to Arnold, was captured by American irregulars with incriminating documents upon his person. Arnold then fled his post and went over to the British, only hours before an unsuspecting Washington reached the fort after a journey from Hartford, where he had gone to confer with his French allies. The commander in chief quickly became aware of Arnold's perfidy, and after a quick inspection of West Point was appalled at the defenseless state into which Arnold had allowed the place to deteriorate. Fearing an imminent British assault, he ordered Wayne's division, which was then encamped near Haverstraw, to march to West Point's assistance. "At a moments warning," said Wayne later, "leaving our tents standing, Guards & Detachments out," the 1st and 2nd Pennsylvania Brigades set out at eight o'clock in the evening on their march, arriving at Smith's White House during the night. At that place, which afforded protection to West Point from the land side and "with no prospect of any more of the enemy [coming] up the river," Wayne rested his exhausted troops, but on the twenty-seventh he pushed his men on to Washington's exposed post. "When our approach was announced to the General he thought it fabulous," said Wayne proudly, "but when convinced of the reality — he received us like a God — & returning to take a short repose — exclaimed — 'All is safe, & I again am happy.' " Added Wayne, "may he long — very long continue so."[34]

For the next few days, Wayne berated Arnold in every way that he could think of and breathed fire against any enemy that might try an attack on West Point. Long before this incident, declared Wayne, "he had produced a conviction on me. . .that honor & true Virtue were Strangers to his Soul." He was "naturally a Coward, and never went in the way of Danger but when Stimulated by Liquor even to Intoxication." His "dirty — dirty acts which he has been capable of committing," declared Wayne, ". . .are of such a Nature as would cause the *Infernals to blush* — were they accused with the Invention, or execution of them." As for West Point, he would "dispute the Approaches" to that place "*inch* by *inch* and at the point of the bayonet. . .in the Gorge of the Defiles — at every expense of blood, until death or Victory cries — '*bold*' — '*bold*.'" Fortunately, Wayne was not required to defend his post. All his detached service at West Point did was keep him from having to serve with a board of fourteen general officers, assigned by Washington on September 28, to examine evidence against André. Had he been a member of the board, there is little question but that he would have agreed with its recommendation to the commander in chief that the young man be hanged a spy. Although Wayne held no personal grudge against André for the latter's spoofing of him in "Cow Chase," nonetheless the evidence against André for his undercover work against the United States was overwhelming. On the second of October, the amiable gentleman went to the scaffold, while in New York the "caitiff" Arnold already enjoyed the sweet fruits of his bald-faced treason.[35]

CHAPTER *VI*

Mutiny
1780–1781

As the excitement of the Arnold-André affair abated in late 1780, Wayne began to deal with difficulties associated with congressional plans to rearrange his divisions by reducing the number of regiments. This reordering, said the legislators, was necessary because the Pennsylvania line had shrunk to a mere 2,473 troops, and it was manifest that the service was top-heavy with officers. Wayne, however, saw the problem in an entirely different light. "It's a D——d affair," he fumed to Irvine, that some good officers were to be "left without any Command — I am afraid that [they] will *play the* Devil with somebody." To the Board of War on October 13 he raised another objection to shrinking Pennsylvania's line. Remember, he declared, that Georgia and South Carolina remained conquered, that all the states below the Mason-Dixon line *collectively* could raise only 4,000 men. Surely, the Continental Army should depend upon Pennsylvania for *more*, not fewer, troops, and the thrust of Congress should be toward recruiting the existing Pennsylvania regiments to strength — *not* eliminating some of them. After all, the legislators did not wish to make "the freedom of America" dependent upon "the tottering basis of an *ally* [France]," when that freedom ought to be "supported on the firm Ground of our own Virtue and Prowess."[1]

Apparently they did, for Congress now voted to reorganize the army, reducing Pennsylvania's line to six regiments, and, as Wayne noted, giving some officers a chance to retire to private life with a "genteel annuity for life & an exemption from petty offices & Military duty." Still, Wayne was convinced that the reduction in Pennsylvania's strength was wrongheaded, and he urged Irvine in Philadelphia to lobby for at least a seventh regiment. But by December, as a number of Wayne's friends noted to him in letters from Philadelphia, all the decisions had been made, and the Pennsylvania line still was set at six regiments. It only remained, therefore, for the general to carry out the wishes of his civilian masters (bad though he believed they were), decommission many unhappy officers and send them back to their civilian pursuits.[2]

As difficult as were Wayne's problems with army reorganization, they faded into insignificance in comparison with the perennial one of the Pennsylvania Assembly's inability to supply its soldiers in the field. On September 17, Wayne wrote President Reed, "At the commencement of this campaign we had the most flattering expectations from the promised succors of his most Christian Majesty as well as from the exertions of these States," but they had been thwarted by reality. Instead, his "badly paid and worse fed" soldiers, whose enlistments would be up in December, opposed "a well-appointed, puissant and desolating Army" of redcoats, and his only hope was to receive some hard cash to entice his men to reenlist. By the end of the year, his soldiers had been sixty days without rum (except a half-gill per man allowance on one single occasion), his army was almost naked from lack of uniforms, and the politicians were offering him nothing but promises. Truly, he declared to Joseph Reed, the Revolution itself seemed in peril, for it appeared that the French might soon offer peace to Britain on the basis of allowing only those American states in actual exercise of independence to be free, while Britain retained the rest. If that happened, America *must* fight for herself, and only legislative bodies like the Pennsylvania Assembly could supply the needed armies. Therefore, the Pennsylvanians must stop all party bickering — especially about the state's constitution — until the struggle against Britain was successfully terminated. If they did not, there might simply be no state left at the end of the war to which to give a constitution.[3]

Despite Wayne's admonition, he and his officer colleagues were themselves playing the lobbying game with more fervor than before. The issue on this occasion was an adjustment and settlement of the soldiers' pay for the previous three years on the basis of hard currency. That passage of such a law would be much in the officers' favor was obvious, for under the provisions of the new measure they would receive their pay in money valued at preinflationary levels. Also plain, at least to the Yellow Whigs, was that this measure would be vastly expensive, necessitating new taxes upon their antitaxation constituents, and that it seemed to contribute even more to what they viewed as the army's already too-powerful influence upon the civil government. Therefore, while soldiers like Francis Johnston and Josiah Harmar in October and November made the army's case before the Assembly, the radicals attempted countermeasures to thwart the military men, even going so far as to try on one occasion to reduce the army's clothing allowance by £50,000. Such procedures infuriated the officers all the more against radicals who were so lost to shame as not only to support the Constitution of 1776 but also to take the shirts right off the backs of long-suffering soldiers on the front line of the fight for liberty.[4]

In early December, Wayne and his officer friends were worried that this "specie bill" would fail to pass the Assembly. To Irvine, Wayne wrote, "I fear a paper war will (if it has not already) commence between our *Agents* and men in power. . . . I am sorry for it, as in its consequences it may create a Coolness & Jealousy very prejudicial to the General Cause." Over the next few days, as opposition seemed to grow against the bill, Johnston and Major Evan Edwards wrote Wayne despairing letters about how "virulent" members of the Assembly were accusing the army of "wanting to be sole proprietor of the state." Wayne encouraged his friends to keep up their exertions, and on the sixteenth, he wrote President Reed a long letter to explain the officers' attitudes. The men, he declared, "are not devoid of reasoning faculties, nor Callous to the first feelings of Nature. They have now served their Country for nearly five years with fidelity, poorly clothed, badly fed, & worse paid." They had not even seen a paper dollar for more than twelve months, said Wayne, and the enemy was trying to rouse their indignation by circulating appeals for them to desert. But all these problems could be overcome by sending clothing and food to the army and by passing the specie bill, to give the soldiery "a landed property & make their interest the interest of America." Should these measures not be taken, concluded Wayne to Reed, then he shuddered at the consequences and could not answer for the army's behavior. As it turned out, Wayne need not have worried overmuch about the Assembly's opposition to his bill, for on December 16 the legislators passed it with a large majority, and all the soldiers could look forward to receiving their pay for the past three years in specie.[5]

Good news from Philadelphia, however, did not override Wayne's immediate concerns for his army in the field, for although the Pennsylvania Assembly had provided relief for the soldiers in terms of their pay, the measure would take months to implement, and his problems required instantaneous remedy. As the gloomy months of autumn ground slowly onward, Wayne's mood continued to worsen in a macabre lockstep with the deepening crisis of morale among his Pennsylvania veterans. In late November, he marched his restive soldiers from New York to their old winter cantonment at Morristown, and they began to rebuild their huts, in preparation for the coming season of icy weather. Standing "for hours among the poor naked Fellows" as they performed these tasks, Wayne and his brother officers tried by example to show that they suffered the same fate as the wretched troopers. But gestures, no matter how well intended at this late date, were not adequate to rectify the wretchedness of the Pennsylvania soldiers, devoid as they were of anything like a sufficiency of clothing, shoes, blankets, rum, shelter, or pay for their months of service. Not even a number of visits to Wayne by the personable French Major General the Marquis de Chastellux improved the Pennsylvanian's spirits (nor would he have been put in a better frame of mind had he known that Chastellux was criticizing Philadelphia women for using too much rouge, and pointing out that "a certain Miss Vining" was a particularly obnoxious offender).[6]

As the end of the year 1780 approached, General Wayne became more and more uneasy about the growing sullenness of his Pennsylvania veterans. "I sincerely wish," he declared to Colonel Johnston in mid-December, "the Ides of Jany was come & past — I am not superstitious, but can't help cherishing disagreeable Ideas about that period." It was because of this uneasiness on Wayne's part that he intended to remain with the army during the winter, rather than follow his recent practice of furloughing in Philadelphia and (occasionally) Waynesborough. "I know," he said, "that I have the hearts of the soldiers & that my presence is absolutely necessary in camp." But, warned Wayne, he could not alleviate the soldiers' disgust at their predicament, which now was even worse than before, for many of the troopers, who had thought their three-year enlistment was finished on December 31, were being told that they had actually signed on "for the duration of the war." "You may believe me my D'r Sir," said Wayne to Johnston, "that the exertions of the House were never more necessary than at this Crisis to adopt some effectual mode & Immediate plan to Alleviate the distress of the Troops

& to conciliate their minds & sweeten their tempers which are much soured by neglect." These warnings, transmitted by Johnston to the citizenry in Philadelphia, finally had the effect of mobilizing them to charter a private bank to raise money for the soldiers' support, and two women, Esther Reed and Sarah Bache, organized a clothing drive to collect quantities of wearing apparel for the troops.[7]

These gestures of support for the Pennsylvania line by the people of Philadelphia, who took it upon themselves simply to bypass the Assembly entirely, were too little and too late. In fact, Wayne believed that the problems facing not only Pennsylvania's soldiers and civilians but also American revolutionaries in general by December 1780 were not of a nature to be alleviated by any amount of money or goods. For despite the belated benevolence of a few well-intentioned Pennsylvania citizens toward their army, the rebels' crisis had been brought on by a deep spiritual decay, only one of the manifestations being the civilians' disgraceful neglect of the soldiery. The old revolutionary republican virtues of 1776, which American patriots had so abundantly possessed at that time and which had given meaning to the cause of rebellion against Britain, were now sadly eroded. These values, Wayne believed, *must* be restored, and quickly, if (as the general's friend Delany wrote Wayne on December 21) the United States was to survive its present crisis. The republicans of America, both in and out of the army, must learn to cooperate with each other in common cause against the mutual enemy, Britain, and personality conflicts and political enthusiasms must not intrude themselves upon this large and noble undertaking.[8]

While Wayne meditated upon these sentiments in his headquarters at Mount Kemble, near Morristown, his Pennsylvanians on January 1, 1781, rebelled against his authority. "It is with pain," he wrote to General Washington, whose headquarters were at New Windsor, "I now inform your Excellency of the general mutiny and defection which suddenly took place in the Penn'a line between 9 and 10 o'clock last evening." Although all the officers had made "Every possible exertion. . . to suppress it in its rise, . . . the torrent was too Potent to be stemmed." One officer, Captain Adam Bettin, had been killed by the mutineers, and two others, Captain Samuel Tolbert and Lieutenant Nicholas White, were seriously wounded. Many other officers had received less severe hurts from bayonets, stones, and clubbed muskets. The soldiers, too, had suffered deaths and wounds, according to Wayne. "Many of their bodies lay under our horses' feet," he said, "and others will retain with existence the traces of our swords and espontoons." In this melee, the mutineers had seized all four of Wayne's cannon, and after "scouring the grand parade with round & grape shot" had marched from their camp "in solid column with fixed bayonets, producing a diffusive fire of musketry in front, flank & rear."

Swept by this tide of moving, uncontrollable humanity, Wayne, Stewart, and Colonel Richard Butler were carried forward, keeping ever between the soldiers and the roads leading to British positions, until it was clear they were making for Princeton. Thereupon, Wayne and his colonels returned to Mount Kemble, whence at 4:30 on the afternoon of the second the general notified Washington of the uprising and declared his intention of riding immediately with Stewart and Butler to rejoin the mutineers. Then, to the Pennsylvania soldiers, Wayne scrawled a letter requesting that they "Appoint one man from each Reg't to represent their Grievances to the Gen'l who upon the Sacred Honor of a Gentleman & a *Soldier* does hereby solemnly promise to exert every power to Obtain an Immediate redress of their Grievances & he further plights that *Honor* that no man shall receive the least Injury on account of the part he may have taken upon this Occasion, & that the persons of those who may be Appointed to settle this affair, shall be held sacred & Inviolate."[9]

After rejoining the mutinying army and while waiting for the leaders of the uprising to respond to his request for a parley, Wayne marched with the soldiers to Princeton, which he and the troops reached on the fourth. Meantime, Wayne had alerted Congress and the Pennsylvania Assembly to be prepared to depart Philadelphia, for he was told by the mutineers that it was their fixed intention to march on that city. From Washington now came a letter commending Wayne and his officers for their conduct so far. Despite his burning desire to come immediately to New Jersey and take personal charge of the crisis, the commander in chief had decided that he would remain at New Windsor and keep close watch on the troops under his own command. Wayne confirmed the correctness of Washington's decision on the fourth, noting that he was going to encourage President Reed to send a committee of legislators from the Assembly to negotiate with the mutineers, and if the matter could be handled by civilians, "your presence & Influence would be useful where you are."[10]

Working under this plan, Wayne now met with a committee of sergeants who were appointed by the army to represent its interests to the general. From the spokesman of the committee, William Bawser (later described by President Reed as "a very poor creature, and very fond of liquor"), Wayne received a list of the army's requisitions — most of which he recognized as being eminently reasonable, even if he disliked the mutineers who supported them. The list contained three major demands: (1) that all the men enlisted for three years and whose times were up be discharged, (2) that all soldiers receive their pay, which in most cases was over a year in arrears, immediately and in specie as the recently enacted law required, and (3) that the troops be decently clothed and provisioned. All these conditions, Wayne informed the committee, were beyond his power to fulfill, but if the members desired he would send them on to Reed, as he had told Washington he would, with a request that representatives of the Executive Council come to Princeton for negotiations with the mutineers. The sergeants agreed to this procedure, as did Reed, who in fact decided himself to head the civil delegation, and he informed Wayne that he would set out for Princeton as soon as he could. The mutineers promised Wayne that while they awaited the arrival of the civil committee, they would remain quietly encamped near Princeton and make no effort to overawe civilian governments in Philadelphia by marching upon that city.[11]

Wayne was not so sure, however, of the mutineers' intentions about deserting to the enemy, for although spokesman Bawser heartily disavowed any desire on the part of his colleagues to "becom[e] *Arnolds*," the British were holding out enticing blandishments that Wayne feared might get the Pennsylvanians to go over to the other side. Two spies from Clinton had already entered the camp of the mutineers with letters addressed "To the person appointed by the Pennsylvania troops to lead them in their present Struggle for their Liberties & Rights," containing offers to the Pennsylvanians of full payment of their overdue wages and exemption from further military service if they would but desert the rebel cause. Nevertheless, in an action which Washington later called "extraordinary," the mutineers spurned Clinton's generous proposals and clapped the two British emissaries in irons. When Wayne learned of the spies' arrest, he offered to pay a reward of 50 guineas each to the two sergeants responsible for the deed — only to have the money refused on the grounds that the soldiers had done no more than their duty as loyal patriots. At the same time, however, they refused to hand over the captives to the Continental authorities until their demands had been met. Sir Henry Clinton later declared that he had not really expected his appeals to woo the Pennsylvanians over to the British but had thought it his duty nonetheless at least to make the attempt.[12]

On January 7, General Wayne received a letter from President Reed, requesting that the general encourage the Pennsylvania line and its representatives to meet him in Trenton rather than Princeton. Reed adduced a number of reasons for this proposal, but the two most important ones were that the army could be better supplied there with the materials it demanded and that at least a shred of dignity might be salvaged for civil authority if he could "compel" the troops to come to him rather than his going to them. Wayne agreed to this suggestion, prevailing upon the sergeants to go along, and so on the ninth of January the mutineers marched to Trenton, where negotiations immediately commenced between Reed's committee and the spokesmen of the Pennsylvania line. Wayne, meantime, was becoming increasingly more disgusted and less sympathetic with the mutineers, whom he considered to be an altogether insubordinate and sullen lot. While he was bound by his oath not to molest them, as he told Washington and Congress, nonetheless he now felt their demands were so "unreasonable" that they should be instantly dismissed from the service and not a single one of their requisitions met. Washington, however, was expressing to Wayne at the same time an insistence upon keeping the Pennsylvania regiments embodied because of their being needed when the present difficulties were overcome. And while Washington was much afraid that Reed and his committee might be too lenient with the mutineers and set a bad example for the future, he saw no solution to the present dilemma but to allow events already set in motion to play themselves out and to hope for the best.[13]

Finally, on January 9, the issue was settled. That day, after an extensive exchange of proposals and counter-proposals, President Reed and the committee of sergeants agreed to a covenant allowing any Pennsylvania soldier a hearing before a committee of three men, appointed by Reed and the Pennsylvania Executive Council, to determine who should be discharged. Only "three years or the duration" enlistees were eligible for this hearing, but any trooper within that category who presented written proof — or a personal oath — that he was justified in his appeal must be immediately let go. Additionally, *all* Pennsylvania troops were to be issued pay warrants, which the state was legally and honor-bound to redeem as soon as it could get money for that purpose. And, last, all soldiers were guaranteed a shirt, overalls, and shoes as soon as these items, already collected in Philadelphia (by the ladies Reed and Bache), were shipped up the Delaware River to Trenton. No sooner had this deal been struck than the mutineers turned over to Wayne the two British agents who had attempted to subvert the army. These unfortunates on the eleventh were put on trial before a court-martial consisting of Wayne, Irvine, Butler, Stewart, and Fishbourn. Inevitably, they were condemned to death, and before evening on the same day, they were executed by a firing squad. Next day, Wayne wrote Washington to inform him of all these proceedings and to congratulate him on the American officers' good fortune that mutiny had not spread to other troops. The Pennsylvania sergeants, he fumed, had not yet given up command of his brigades, but he before long hoped to regain control of them — "in appearance at least."[14]

For the next few days, Wayne's predominant preoccupation was to watch his beloved battalions shrink in numbers as the soldiers mustered out of the ranks. He agreed with Washington's sentiment of January 20 that Reed's settlement would "not only subvert the Penn'a line but have a very pernicious influence upon the whole army." But he must have been bemused by another assertion of the commander in chief on the same day, that the civil commissioners of Pennsylvania had made an accommodation with the soldiers before he (Washington) could "prosecute such measures with the Pennsylvanians as the case demanded," that is, marching loyal troops against them.[15] The commander in chief's statement seemed curious on two counts, first, because up to that time Washington had approved every measure that Wayne and Reed had taken to negotiate a settlement with the mutineers, and second, because Washington had never so much as hinted to the Pennsylvanians that he could, or intended to, use force to quell the mutiny. That the agreement was lopsided in favor of the mutineers, thought Wayne, should certainly surprise no one, considering his and the civil authorities' helplessness in face of the obvious might of the mutinying army. Given his belligerent attitude toward the soldiers by the eighth, it seems more than likely that he would have applauded a proposal by Washington to put down the mutineers with force — had such a proposal ever been tendered.

In any event, it did no good for Wayne or Washington to dwell upon might-have-beens, nor did Wayne concern himself overmuch with worries about the immediate past. Soon his natural optimism began to assert itself, and he spent his hours cajoling recently discharged Pennsylvania veterans to reenlist. He appealed to the government of Pennsylvania for bonus money in order to take advantage of what he called "the reenlistment Spirit" that now pervaded the troops, at the same time warning his civilian masters that New Jersey recruiters might gain the upper hand in enrolling these soldiers unless he were given authority to act quickly. He also encouraged the Pennsylvania Executive Council to prevail upon the merchants of Philadelphia not to hire any recently discharged soldiers, lest the poor wretches become successes at civilian life and not be compelled to rejoin the army in order to have employment. On January 21, Wayne informed Washington that affairs were now looking better with his command than for some weeks past and that he was expecting soon to have "a *reclaimed* & formidable Line." However, his own figure on the number of Pennsylvanians by then dismissed belied his optimism, for practically all his artillerists had gone home, as had one-third of his infantrymen. Wayne noted facetiously to the commander in chief, in commenting upon his recent difficulties, "I shall only mention that we have not rolled in Luxury, or slept on beds of down."[16]

The next few days saw the final settlements of the Pennsylvania soldiers' grievances. On January 24, Congress approved Wayne's offer of a general amnesty to the mutineers — since it had no other alternative — and the Pennsylvania commander gave a sigh of relief that the settlement would continue. A few days thereafter, he received a letter from Washington containing news of a recently quelled revolt in the New Jersey line and once again had reason to be thankful that affairs were going as well as they were. Then on the twenty-ninth, Wayne wrote the commander in chief a report on the final conclusion of the mutiny, noting that 1,317 privates and artillerists had been discharged, thus leaving him with 1,150 men, including furloughed sergeants "& music." In reply, Washington praised and commiserated with General Wayne, saying "I am satisfied, that every thing was done on your part to produce the least possible evil from that unfortunate disturbance in your line, and that your influence has had a great share in preventing worse extremities — I felt for your situation — Your anxieties & fatigues of mind amidst such a scene, I can easily conceive — I thank you sincerely for your exertions." As for Wayne's present orders, since he was not now needed "in the field," he could simply hold himself ready for future service when the requirement arose.[17]

For the first time in a number of years, Wayne's winter repose in early 1781 was not shattered by bruising political battles with the radicals of the Pennsylvania Assembly. Instead, he spent quiet weeks visiting friends in Philadelphia (including Mary Vining and his daughter, Margaretta, who was enrolled in school there) and from time to time paying perfunctory calls upon Polly at Waynesborough. One incident occurred at about this time which seemed trivial but which had long-lasting consequences for Wayne's reputation. It seems that he had an eccentric private in his army called "Commodore" or "Jimmy the Drover," who was arrested by the civil authorities and who demanded that Wayne intervene in his behalf. When told that the general refused to do so, or had threatened to sentence him to the lash should he be derelict in the future, Jimmy exclaimed, "Anthony is *mad*! Farewell to you; clear the coast for the Commodore, 'Mad Anthony's' friend." This story, like so many anecdotes about men in high places during the Revolutionary War, spread like wildfire through the ranks of America's armies, and thereafter for the troops General Wayne was "Mad Anthony." They, however, unlike later writers such as Washington Irving, meant by the term that the general was impetuous in battle, not insane.[18]

With time on his hands, Wayne reopened his long-simmering feud with Arthur St. Clair, accusing his fellow Pennsylvanian of spreading rumors that Wayne was trying to displace his superior officer. This incident began when St. Clair's aide-de-camp, Major Isaac B. Dunn, told Wayne's friend Fishbourn that Wayne was disloyal to St. Clair. Fishbourn then immediately prattled this gossip to Wayne, who jumped to the conclusion that these slanders must have originated with St. Clair. Thereupon, he wrote his colleague a sharp note, querying him as to whether this suspicion had any basis in fact. In a dignified and somewhat embarrassed reply, St. Clair asserted, "You cannot suppose that I could entertain any Fears of being supplanted in the Command of the Pennsylvania Line, nor is it fair to imagine that if Major Dunn suspected you of intriguing for that Purpose, the sentiment is mine. You must be sensible that there was a Coldness for some time between you and me. . .I may have mentioned. . .to Major Dunn. . .that I thought your Behavior not so candid as I could have wished." Yet, these were not issues that should disturb "Harmony amongst Officers, especially those of high Rank." Wayne, a bit ashamed and entirely mollified, declared in reply, "the Suspicions you harbored were as injurious to me as they were groundless; therefore, we have each been in error." With that, the issue was closed, but for Dunn's issuing Wayne a challenge to a duel after being spoken to rudely by the general or so he said, in "a sacred place." This summons Wayne pointedly ignored.[19]

By early spring of 1781, Wayne's days were taken up more and more with military duties, for he now had his assignment from Washington and Congress for the coming campaign, to join Lafayette's army in Virginia at the head of the troops of the Pennsylvania line (while St. Clair remained in Philadelphia) and once the Old Dominion had been cleared of the enemy, to proceed farther southward and assist General Nathanael Greene against the British there as well. Lafayette had been ordered to Virginia by Washington in February with 1,200 soldiers and instructions to counter a Royal army of 1,600 men, commanded by Benedict Arnold, which had landed at Jamestown on New Year's Day. Arnold's purpose was to create a diversion for Lord Cornwallis, whose army was then wintering at Winnsboro, South Carolina, so that in the coming weeks the earl might overrun North Carolina and add that state to the ones he and Clinton had "conquered" the year before. There was need for Wayne to exercise haste in getting troops into Virginia, for Greene, who faced Cornwallis in the South, needed assurance that Arnold's forces could be neutralized and present no threat to his sources of supply or potential lines of retreat — in the unhappy event that a retrograde maneuver became desirable. Consequently, Lafayette wrote Wayne a number of letters after his own little force reached Virginia in April, encouraging Wayne to do all within his power to prepare the Pennsylvania line for campaigning and bring it forward, "if you lead any detachment whatever." From Washington came a similar exhortation to Wayne to get his men embodied and on the way southward as soon as was humanly possible.[20]

Cajole as they might, Lafayette and Washington could not get Wayne to budge until his battalions were recruited to strength and he was provided adequate supplies for a march. So he told Lafayette on March 7 and three days later he made the same point to Irvine, noting, "I go to join the Marquis in Virginia but don't choose to proceed without a few troops," those armed and clothed. Nor was the Frenchman surprised by Wayne's delay, for as he told the commander in chief in early March, "When I left Philadelphia General Waine was not far from hoping he could soon collect a thousand men but I am not so sanquine in my expectations." Lafayette's was the more realistic assessment. "I experience much anxiety," Wayne told the legislators, to be on his way southward, "as I have the strongest ground" to believe that Washington intended "I should be present in case of an Operation" in Virginia and that at least part of the Pennsylvania troops should by now have joined the Marquis' forces. But he could not move, because his state would not pay off its soldiers, as it had promised in January. "I feel my situation delicate," he said, "duty & Inclination, places me at the point of operations — adverse and intervening circumstances have kept me at a distance." Responding to Wayne's plea, Congress on the same day "recommended" to Reed and his civilian colleagues that they "forward the march of their line in detachments with all possible speed" to join Lafayette. And Washington, on April 8, expressed his "anxiety" that Wayne's soldiers were not yet upon the march.[21]

Despite the prodding of Congress and Washington, Pennsylvania's Assembly moved at a snail's pace to repair the problems of which Wayne reminded them. Through the month of March, and much of April, the general continued to chide Reed for the "unworthy supineness & torpidity which pervades all our civil Councils and prevents the execution of any spirited Operation." As he told Irvine, "I have been knocking at every door from the Assembly up to Congress, to furnish a little money" to pay and clothe the troops, but "they all present me that *Gorgon head* an exhausted treasury." Soon, however, he had gotten full uniforms and shoes for 1,000 men. Moreover, the Pennsylvania legislature had finally gotten the soldiers paid off — with certificates which would draw interest until a later redemption date — after Wayne had shamed Reed by quoting to him Washington's letters declaring that the Pennsylvania troops ought to be mobilized immediately for crucial service in Virginia.[22]

Finally, Wayne's army, 1,000 strong, did in fact march out of its winter camp, but instead of heading in the direction of the Old Dominion it moved westward toward York, searching or better supplies of food and forage. Upon reahcing that town, it lapsed into immobility for the next few weeks, "ruining" for lack of duty, as Colonel Butler told his commander, who remained in Philadelphia. "There is nothing that will rouse [the men] but British Guns and Drums or Jack Hatchway's pipe," declared Butler, "and, Indeed, I wish he'd blow soon, or else their very souls will be petrified so that the Devil himself can't wake them." Wayne, meantime, continued to receive final orders and instructions from St. Clair, Reed, and Washington on how to conduct himself in his southern campaign, not finally setting out to join his command until the eleventh of May, after receiving from the Assembly the good wishes "that you may have Health & long Life to enjoy them."[23]

When he arrived in York two days later, Wayne discovered that it was still impossible for him to march southward, for his men had run out of food, and he had no money — except inflated Continental dollars, which no one would accept as payment — to buy any. In addition, Colonel Moylan's dragoons were bereft of "fittings." He laid these problems before Reed on May 16, begging the Assembly for redress, and shortly thereafter he was informed that the state government would support his new expenses. Even better news arrived from the Board of War, which if belated was nonetheless heartening, for Wayne now learned that on May 18 Congress had empowered him to impress supplies if he could not purchase them with America's almost worthless currency. Wayne had needed this authorization all along, considering the wretched state of Continental money, but he must be polite to his civilian masters, so he thanked the Board of War without adding any gratuitous comments, only noting that the news from Congress came just in time, since "no Article whatever either in the Quarter Master or Comissary Departments (except flour) can be had for Paper Money."[24]

Although the way now seemed clear at last for Wayne to set his "Little well appointed Army" in motion toward Lafayette's corps in Virginia, another delay arose on May 20 in the guise of that continuing anathema, mutinous behavior among the Pennsylvania troops. Trouble had begun when Wayne, forewarned by Butler that his soldiers were become slack in discipline, arrived in camp determined to find examples and put things aright. The soldiers, on the other hand, "influenced by the prior mutiny," as Wayne noted later, were just as determined to yield none of their hard-won personal dignity and freedom to their officers. Soon Wayne was arresting men right and left for petty offenses and imposing harsh sentences upon them. Thus it was that when John Fortescue of the artillery was tried on the twentieth for "mutinous actions" and sentenced to death, the soldiers considered the punishment so monstrous that they began to murmur against their officers. These rumblings of discontent only made Wayne the more determined to bring his army to a just sense of subordination and duty — as he saw it. So within two days more, he had had five other men arrested, tried by a court martial, and sentenced to die with Fortescue for "exciting mutiny," for "mutinous expressions," for saying "God damn the officers, thehbuggers," and for refusing to go peacefully to the guardhouse when put under arrest. Although Wayne relented in his anger towards two of the convicted soldiers at the last moment and pardoned them, the other four he sent to the firing squad. As he told Polly Wayne and his friend Delany, he had been compelled to use harsh punishments to restore a well-disciplined line, and he was now persuaded that the troops had been brought to heel by his stern application of military justice.[25]

Thus, General Wayne prepared on the morning of May 25 to put his army in motion toward the South. "The troops are ready to take their line of march," he wrote Fishbourn happily, "every Impediment to a move is now done away! . . .tell Miss V.——— she will ever live in my fond memory — but mark — the ear piercing fife — the Spirit stirring Drum, & all the humble & Glorious Circumstances of War, summons me to haste." Then to Polly, he composed a more prosaic letter, offering best wishes to "my dear old mother & friends — take care of our Little People — Adieu, believe me yours most Affectionately." Finally, having completed his correspondence, he mounted his horse and rode out to take his place at the head of what he thought were chastened soldiers, who were waiting quietly on parade until he gave the order for them to move out on their march.[26]

But were they? Suddenly a few troopers "on the right of each regiment," as Wayne later described the incident, "called out to pay them in real, not Ideal, Money." No more, they swore, were the Pennsylvania Continentals "to be trifled with," and as another eyewitness, Lieutenant Colonel William Smith Livingston, noted in writing of the incident three days later, "Twelve of the Fellows stepd out and perswaded the Line to refuse to March in Consequence of the Promises being made to them not being complied with." Wayne, furious at this turn of events, reminded all the troops of "the Disgrace they brought on the American Army while in Jersey. . .That the feelings of the Officers on that Occasion were so wounded that they had determined never to experience the like and that he beg'd they would now fire either on him and them or on those Villains in front."[27]

At this point in their recollections of the mutiny, Wayne and Livingston diverge remarkably. Said Livingston, Wayne now ordered a platoon of infantrymen to present arms and fire at the mutineers, which it did, killing six of the "Villains" and wounding another one. This man Wayne "ordered to by Bayonetted," but "The Soldier on whom he caled to do it, recovered his Piece, and said he could not for he was his Comrade. Wayne then drew his Pistol and told him he would kill him. The fellow then advanced and bayonetted him. Wayne then marched the Line by Divisions round the Dead and the rest of the fellows are ordered to be hang'd. The Line marched the next Day Southward, Mute as Fish." As Wayne told it, however, he merely ordered the twelve men "to their tents which being peremptorily refused, the principals were Immediately either knocked down or Confined by the Officers who were previously prepared for this event. A Court Martial was ordered on the spot, the Comission of the Crime, trial and execution were all concluded in the Course of a few hours, in front of the Line paraded under Arms. . . . Whether by design or accident the particular friends and messmates of the Culprits were their executioners and while the tears rolled down their Cheeks in showers, they silently and faithfully obeyed their Orders without a moment's hesitation."[28]

These remarkable stories contradict each other on several important points. While it was unlikely that General Wayne would ignore the Articles of War (which called for any military man inciting mutiny or sedition to "suffer such Punishment as by a general Court-Martial shall be ordered") and command men to be shot without trial, it also seems odd that he would order the mutineers "to their tents" when the army was on full parade, with its tents presumably loaded upon wagons. Perhaps Wayne was only using this term figuratively to mean that the rebels must submit to his orders, for in the final analysis it must be concluded that his seems to be the more accurate account. Given his previous punctilio upon matters legal, both within and without the military establishment, it is odd, to say the least, that he suddenly would override all his previous scruples and command some of his troops to commit what amounted to murder. That he *might* have, however, given the strained circumstances in which he found himself, cannot be entirely dismissed as a possibility.[29]

In any case, Wayne's movement southward was now delayed by one more day, for by the time the "hideous monster" of mutiny had been "crushed in its birth" on May 25 it was too late for his battalions to set out on the march. But the following morning early, Wayne lost no time in rousing his soldiers to the parade and putting them in motion while he sat down to draft letters to various officials. "I steal a moment," he wrote Reed, "whilst the troops are marching thro' the Town," to inform the Pennsylvania government of the previous day's events and to declare that "harmony & discipline" once again reigned supreme, "to which a prompt and exemplary punishment was a powerful, though the necessary prelude." "A liberal dose of niter," he told Washington callously, had worked wonders to purge the "distemper" of rebellion from his troops' systems. He also wrote St. Clair and the Board of War, as a necessary courtesy, to inform them that his army was at last on the march. These duties done, he swung into the saddle and galloped with his aides to the head of a column of soldiers, who marched to new adventures in a part of the world that most (including Wayne himself) had never laid eyes on.[30]

CHAPTER *VII*

The Virginia Adventure
1781

THAT WAYNE'S Pennsylvanians finally were coming to Lafayette's assistance was an enormous relief for the Frenchman, because he was struggling against seemingly insuperable odds in Virginia. As the Marquis was informing Wayne in letter after letter throughout the month of May, the British were building up powerful forces in the Old Dominion, and his tiny army, which now consisted of a mere 900 Continentals, was posted helplessly at Richmond. In early May, Sir Henry Clinton had dispatched Major General William Phillips into Virginia at the head of reinforcements to supersede Arnold in command. Phillips's army, which now numbered 2,300 men, soon took control of the lower James River and on May 20 effected at Petersburg a union with the army of Lord Cornwallis, that had marched into Virginia from Wilmington, North Carolina. By this maneuver, the earl, who had left an army of about 8,000 men under Lord Rawdon in North and South Carolina, had given Nathanael Greene and a small Continental Army there a fighting chance to drive their enemies into Charleston and Savannah. Greene immediately set out to accomplish this result, much to the chagrin of Georgia's royal governor, Sir James Wright, whose province Cornwallis had "left in a defenseless State."[1]

Meanwhile, Cornwallis's already powerful forces in Virginia were reinforced at Petersburg on the twenty-third with three more regiments from New York, and the British general now had under his command more than 7,000 soldiers. With this army, the earl on the twenty-seventh set about driving back Lafayette's puny detachment, which

132

could do no more than skirmish with enemy contingents under John Graves Simcoe and Banastre Tarleton while retreating and awaiting the arrival of Wayne and his Pennsylvanians. Curiously, although Cornwallis knew that Wayne had not yet come to the Marquis's assistance, he for some reason made no real attempt to crush Lafayette's army before Wayne arrived. While he seized Fredericksburg on May 29, he allowed Lafayette to escape unmolested to the north side of Pamunkey River, west of the British positions. In early June, while the Marquis was resting his little army at Culpeper, Cornwallis suddenly thrust a cavalry corps under Tarleton's bold leadership toward Charlottesville and Monticello that came within a hair's breadth of capturing Governor Jefferson and the state legislature. Another force he sent under Simcoe to Point of Fork, west of Richmond, successfully to harass Baron von Steuben, whose troops were guarding vital military stores there. Lafayette responded to these raids by moving his men to Raccoon Ford on the Rapidan River, but because of the weakness of his corps, he remained there while waiting to conjoin his force with Wayne's slow-moving Pennsylvania Continentals from the north.[2]

The Pennsylvania troops came forward but reluctantly, for they were angry with Wayne over his harsh repression of the mutiny at York and were in no mood for a rapid march. Although the general was chagrined that his veterans dragged their feet, he did not dare press them to move faster. Already he rode at the head of troopers who were not even trusted to carry ball, powder, and bayonets, these items (to the delight of Cornwallis and Clinton, who had heard of the recent mutiny) of necessity being kept under constant guard lest the soldiery have at their own officers. But the army was also hindered by constant rains, which turned the roads into quagmires and made the crossing of every swollen stream an adventure. Hence, the Pennsylvania line managed to average only eight or nine miles per day in its march toward Lafayette's army.[3]

One problem that Wayne wrestled with as his troops slogged toward the Potomac River was where he ought to cross that stream. His original intention had been to march by way of Alexandria, where he already had Continental commissaries gathering supplies for his men and horses. But letters from Lafayette, written on the twenty-seventh and twenty-eighth, which reached him at Frederick, Maryland, on May 31, persuaded him that Cornwallis's drive was directed toward Alexandria, and he consequently decided to cross the Potomac at Nowlan's Ferry, which was only seven miles south of the camp he then occupied. It was thus on the first day of June that Wayne entered Virginia and marched, as rapidly as his men would consent to move, to Goose Creek, below Leesburg. Five days after that, in a blinding rainstorm, his drenched army reached the flooded Rappahannock River, where it was forced by the swollen stream to pause while Wayne sent scouts into the country-side to impress flour and cattle. By the time the soldiers had been fed, the river had dropped enough to be crossed without hazard upon a rude raft that local militiamen had constructed for the purpose. Thus, Wayne's soldiers reached the south side of the Rappahannock dry-shod, and after only two more days arrived at Raccoon Ford, where they joined forces with the delighted Lafayette.[4]

The enemies that Wayne faced in Virginia seemed powerful enough to carry all before them, and this was a disturbing enough prospect for the future. But in addition, Wayne must get used to serving under a new commanding officer, Lafayette. Fortunately, he and the Marquis were old friends, and frictions were kept to a minimum, but nevertheless, false rumors soon flew that Wayne disliked Lafayette, and Richard Henry Lee became so alarmed by the reports that he wrote Washington and the Virginia delegates in Congress to report them. As for the Pennsylvania troops, they found Virginia shabby and unkempt, and one veteran reported in disgust that he had seen only one decent house since he entered the state. "Canady is a paradise to this," he snorted; "so much for the grate Dominion."[5]

Wayne was gratified to learn, shortly after his arrival at Lafayette's camp, that Cornwallis was withdrawing his soldiers eastward toward Williamsburg. This maneuver made little sense to Wayne, for he thought the earl should compel the Americans immediately to relinquish possession of re-collected American military stores at Point of Fork, after which Cornwallis could eliminate Greene's army in South Carolina by sheer attrition. But now that Cornwallis was retreating southeastward, Wayne's Pennsylvania troops, ordered by Lafayette to act as the American army's vanguard, were in hot pursuit. On June 22, Wayne and the Marquis attempted to organize an attack on Cornwallis's rear, but they were stymied in this plan when the British marched away from their camp at Bird Ordinary before the assault could be made. Four days later, Wayne, at New Kent Court House, tried to get into position to surprise Simcoe's corps and relieve the cavalry of its stores, but he was thwarted in a skirmish at Hot Water Plantation by his inferior numbers and by the strength of the enemy's positions. By early July, General Wayne was reconnoitering possible campsites for Lafayette's army at Bird Ordinary, sixteen miles from Williamsburg, and reporting to his commander that Cornwallis had taken post on the main road leading from Burnt Ordinary to the former Virginia capital. At that time, Wayne was encamped about five or six miles west of Bird Ordinary, at Hickory Neck, awaiting the arrival of Lafayette's corps at his headquarters before attempting anything else against his redcoated foes.[6]

By July 5, it seemed to Wayne and Lafayette that unless they acted fast they might not have a chance to strike Cornwallis on the north side of the James River. The earl showed every intention to ferry his army southward across that stream, and if such were his purpose then the American commanders were presented with an excellent opportunity for attacking the isolated British rear guard, while the rest of the Royal army was incapable of offering support. Wishing for corroboration of their hopes, Wayne and the Marquis on the sixth received reports from British "deserters" that the chance to strike really existed, and Lafayette ordered Wayne's advance guard of about 500 men to move forward and endeavor to close with the enemy. As Wayne approached Green Spring Farm, he reconnoitered to the southward and discovered that the enemy had posted a large body of cavalry about half a mile to his front and right and had fanned out a line of pickets across his center and left. He also found that the ground favored his foes, for the British flanks were covered on the left by a large morass, reaching the James River, and on the right by a large number of impassable ponds. Between Wayne's position at Green Spring Farm and the British lines was a single narrow causeway, bordered on either side by muddy bogs which, though passable on foot, must certainly hinder the advance of infantry. While Wayne viewed this ground, Lafayette arrived at the farm, and together the two generals agreed that their numbers were more than adequate to deal with the British rear guard that they descried across the swamps. Consequently, they ordered the entire force of Pennsylvanians to wade forward and drive their foes.[7]

Soon a hot fire fight was taking place between Wayne's Continentals and the British troops before them, and all seemed to be going well for the American commander's little army. But after about a two-hour skirmish with the British pickets, Wayne and the Marquis received a very rude jolt, for they discovered that behind the visible enemy line and the small body of cavalry was posted a considerable part of Corn-wallis's army, "ready formed for action, in front of their encampment," as Wayne described the situation later. It was now clear that Lord Cornwallis had laid a neat trap for the Continental vanguard and that the American commanders had fallen into it completely. Neither Wayne nor Lafayette, however, lost their presence of mind, for immediately the Marquis ordered up the remainder of his army, which was en-camped about five miles away, and Wayne directed his riflemen to lay down a galling fire upon the enemy lines. For a time, Cornwallis was content to allow this fight to proceed, but he finally ordered a barrage of grape and canister shot from his cannon and sent out Hessians, light infantry, and Guards regiments to charge Wayne's tiny force. Very soon, the Royal infantry was threatening to turn the American left and get between the small body of Continentals and their line of retreat. Surprised by the intensity of this assault, Wayne was momentarily thrown off balance, but having secured a few reinforcements at last, he decided "among a choice of difficulties" to attempt a subterfuge of his own, by deceiving the British as to his real strength. Therefore, although outnumbered five to one, he ordered three cannon to begin firing, disposed his meager numbers in line of battle, and charged the enemy with fixed bayonets.

As Wayne drove his men forward in this desperate maneuver, Lafayette, observing the advance with utter horror, was convinced that his subordinate was bereft of his wits and ordered him instantly to retire. But, as Wayne noted later, the charge "was done with such vivacity as to produce the desired effect," that is, checking the British in their advance and diverting them from turning his left flank, before he received the Marquis's directive to withdraw. The enemy's forward motion, however, could not be stopped entirely in any case, and Wayne, overwhelmed by numbers, was pushed back with his men to Green Spring Farm. The triumphant redcoats pursued the Americans so closely that at times they were firing at individual targets from a distance of only fifty yards, and in this melee they captured two Ameri-can cannon that had to be abandoned by the Continentals because all the artillery horses had been killed. Fortunately for the rebel troopers, they were not harassed by the British cavalry, because the ground was too swampy to support horsemen, and they were shortly given a reprieve from being chased by the enemy when darkness made it impossible for the British army to advance further in pursuit of the tattered Continentals. Declared Wayne of his major contribution to the battle — his charge into the teeth of the enemy's strength — it was "one of those prudent, tho' daring manoeuvers which seldom fail of producing the desired effect; the result in this Instance fully Justified it."

The battle of Green Spring Farm had a number of important consequences for the Continentals in Virginia, none of them particularly pleasant. In the first place, the American army under Lafayette, which was already puny, had suffered at least ten percent casualties in the fight, while the British had lost only seventy-five officers and men. Therefore, the Continental force was weakened even more in its unequal struggle against its foes. In the second place, Wayne's reputation came under scrutiny once more because of his conduct of the battle, some people lauding, others questioning, his military abilities. Publicly, Lafayette had nothing but praise for his subordinate, both in official letters to Washington and Congress and in general orders after the battle. The commander in chief was also complimentary, noting that perhaps the Pennsylvanian's activities in Virginia would soon free the state of the invader, that he might then march southward and assist Greene in Carolina and Georgia. Privately, the Marquis was declaring that Wayne had made serious blunders in the battle and that accounts of the fight only sounded good "in a gazette" because the enemy quit the ground. General Peter Muhlenberg, who was with Lafayette's army during the battle, was also critical, writing to George Weedon that the American reverse was due to "the impetuosity of our brother Brigadier." Ebenezer Wild, upon hearing of the battle, exclaimed in amazement, "General Wayne, being anxious to perform wonders! attacked the whole British Army with about 1,000 men," and a writer in the *New Jersey Gazette* declared, "Madness — Mad Anthony, by God, I never knew such a piece of work heard of — about eight hundred troops opposed to five or six thousand veterans upon their own ground." Echoing these sentiments, it appeared that Americans, whether soldier or citizen, could hardly decide after the battle whether to admire Wayne for his brave and impetuous character or to condemn him as a foolhardy adventurer.[8]

A period of relative quiet now enveloped General Wayne, as he rested his tatterdemalion troops and attempted to penetrate the intentions of Lord Cornwallis. The earl completed his crossing of the James on July 6–7, marched his men to Portsmouth, and began fortifying that seaport town. Lafayette, noting that this maneuver placed

Cornwallis in position to send raiding parties westward toward the vital American stores at Point of Fork, ordered Wayne to leave his encampment at Holt's Forge on the Chickahominy River, ferry his men across the James River at Westover, and take post near Amelia Court House in such a way as to counter any British attacks in that direction. By mid-July, Wayne's forces were encamped at Goode's Bridge, on the Appomattox River, in readiness to respond to whatever the British army on the Chesapeake might attempt. As he carried out these marches, he corresponded with friends and politicians in Pennsylvania about the battle of Green Spring Farm, boasting to Polly, Richard Peters, Robert Morris, William Irvine, and Joseph Reed about the prowess of the Pennsylvania troops. Wayne also heaped praise upon his soldiers in personal addresses to them in camp. Noted one private, "Our general gave us great applause for our fortitude and good conduct [in] attacking the whole British army with Spirit." In this way, the commander restored with his Pennsylvania soldiers the prestige and rapport that he had badly damaged during his harsh repression of the mutiny at York.[9]

For a short time in mid-July it appeared to Wayne that his peaceful repose on the quiet banks of the Appomattox might be shattered. From Lafayette at Richmond came word to him that Cornwallis was detaching Simcoe and 900 men for some mischief or other, probably either a raid on the stores at Point of Fork or a march to reinforce Lord Rawdon in South Carolina. Whatever Simcoe's mission, Wayne was immediately to join Greene — a heartening prospect for the action-loving Pennsylvanian, but also frightening in view of his army's generally poor condition. He dispatched letters on the sixteenth to Washington, Reed, Irvine, and St. Clair, bemoaning his need for reinforcements, shoes, needles, and thread and noting that he was reducing his battalions to two, thus releasing some officers for recruiting service. Before he could carry out his orders, however, news arrived that apparently the entire British army was embarking at Portsmouth, and he was left in a quandary as to what he should do next. As he told Virginia's newly elected governor, Thomas Nelson, on the twenty-second, if Cornwallis intended to depart the state he might still leave behind Tarleton's cavalry to operate between the Potomac and Rappahannock rivers, in which case Wayne ought not to join Greene in South Carolina. Consequently, he asked Lafayette for freedom to remain in Virginia if British cavalry forces did, or to follow them southward should their intention be to move in that direction.[10]

Over the next few days, Wayne received only contradictory orders from the Marquis. First, the Frenchman wished him to stay put as long as Cornwallis's destination remained obscure, then he wanted him to march on to join Greene as originally ordered. At last, on July 31, Lafayette notified Wayne that the earl's army was sailing up Chesapeake Bay, believed to be headed for Fredericksburg. Thus, it behooved American forces to march immediately in that direction, and while the Marquis hurried north with his troops Wayne was also to set out in the same direction, effecting a junction with the main Continental army somewhere between Richmond and Fredericksburg. Although both Wayne and Lafayette suspected that Cornwallis might be feinting, that his real destination was either New York or Charleston, still they felt American military stores at Fredericksburg were too valuable to be left uncovered. Hardly had the patriot corps gotten in motion than Lafayette learned on August 4 that the British, instead of doing anything they had been expected to do, were landing at Yorktown. Bemused by this operation and still suspicious that Cornwallis was trying to trick him, the Marquis ordered Wayne to halt his march at Bottom's Bridge, about twenty miles west of his own position at New Castle, and await further orders. By August 6, the Marquis at last became convinced that Cornwallis was making Yorktown his main post and ordered Wayne to join him at his new headquarters. Wayne offered to comply with Lafayette's instructions but noted that his present encampment offered more food and forage for his army, whereupon the Marquis allowed him for the moment to remain where he was.[11]

During this brief respite, General Wayne turned his attention to a number of matters that demanded, or drew, his interest. For one thing, he still had received no assistance from the civil officers of Virginia or Pennsylvania in supplying his troops, and as he told Irvine on July 29, he was tired of seeing his men barefoot in "*the Antient Dominion.*" A day later he declared angrily to Daniel Morgan that his troops' health was being ruined because of their nakedness to the elements. Taking matters into his own hands, on the sixth of August he rode to Richmond and began impressing clothing from Virginia commissary William Davies, who vigorously protested that only the governor had the authority to make such distributions. Since Nelson was out of town until the following day, said Davies, Wayne ought to have patience enough at least to await the governor's return. Wayne scornfully retorted to this advice, "it may be well to advise Lord Cornwallis to have *patience* 'until the Governor arrives,' " and he continued to seize stores. When Nelson heard of Wayne's activities, he angrily protested to Lafayette that they were an infringement on civil authority and that other members of the Pennsylvania line were following the lead of their commander and "comitting excesses on private property." Lafayette, upon receiving this sharply worded note from the governor, forwarded it to Wayne under cover of a noncommittal note from himself.[12]

Replying to the Marquis's letter and Governor Nelson's reprimands, Wayne angrily described to Lafayette the plight of his wretched Pennsylvanians for want of clothing, and while he agreed to return to Virginia's commissary officers the garments he had purloined, he also promised to withdraw the Pennsylvania troops from active service until they should be supplied from their own state's stores. The governor's insinuations, he barked, were insulting, especially since Pennsylvanians had come southward to assist Virginia in repelling an invader and since the stores certainly would have been destroyed had he not made a forced march to save them from the enemy. After venting his anger to Lafayette, however, Wayne did not carry out his threat to disengage his troops from service. Instead, he wrote Governor Nelson two rigidly polite letters, one asking him to send an emissary to take charge of the clothing, the other explaining that his men were bereft of food because the state commissary general was not providing any. In the course of the past two weeks, he noted, the Pennsylvania line had lived on Indian corn and water, without any salt, spirits, bacon, or flour to improve their lot. He sent the same tale of uninterrupted woe to Irvine and President Reed in Pennsylvania, only to receive from the latter fair words (and little more) that his home state would soon be forthcoming with mounds of supplies and at least 1,000 more Continental recruits.[13]

The optimism of Reed regarding future successes in enlisting Pennsylvanians into the army was based (as Wayne now knew) upon recent changes in the state's militia law. This statute General Wayne had attempted for years to get the Assembly to change, so that Continental service would be at least as attractive as militia duty. Finally, as William Irvine wrote the general in July, the radicals in the Assembly had swallowed their fear of standing armies long enough at least to modify the law and allow certain classes of citizens to be exempt from militia duty if they would furnish recruits for the Continental line. While this was hardly a ringing endorsement by the radicals of the officers' point of view on the necessity of encouraging long-term military enlistments, nevertheless it was, as Wayne and Irvine recognized, at least a step in their direction. But even this small concession, noted Irvine with disgust, "goes down hard with *people* who are fond of *Militia*." Thus, it was as clear to Wayne in 1781, as it had been in 1777, that his natal state still groaned under a government that would never accept his conservative views on how politics, society, and the army ought to operate. And although the Assembly made even more changes in the law during September, he still looked forward to the time when he might do his part to excise the radicals from government by eliminating their major bulwark, the Constitution of 1776.[14]

Turning his mind from Pennsylvania politics to considerations of grand strategy, Wayne reflected in July and August upon some of the implications of military activity in the American South. He mused to Washington and Morgan on July 27 about Lord George Germain's announcement to the governments of Europe that Virginia had been restored to "peace & good order," thus setting the stage to claim the province for Britain should peace talks occur. "It is therefore the business of America," he said, "to dispossess them of every post they hold in the United States, at every expense of blood & treasure," lest they make similar ridiculous claims to other states' territory in a general peace conference. He noted to William Irvine on the fourteenth that the Continentals had finally had the last laugh over Cornwallis, for he, after moving "some hundreds of miles by Land & sometimes by water" since July 6, had "returned to the spot he left about six weeks since." And what were his future plans? Well, since "the affair at James Town," he had shown no desire to fight, nor was it at all clear where he intended to go next, but Wayne believed he would be reinforced by "*John Murray* (alias) Earl Dunmore" and then attempt something or other.[15]

Although General Wayne was not aware of the fact, events in places far removed from his quiet encampment were fast sealing Cornwallis's fate. As Lafayette informed Wayne in two letters, on August 22 and 25, George Washington and General Comte de Rochambeau were coming from New York to Virginia with 5,000 Continental and French regulars to entrap Cornwallis at Yorktown. This maneuver, Lafayette told Wayne in strictest confidence, was made possible because a French fleet under Admiral de Grasse, bearing 3,000 soldiers was to sail from the West Indies to the Chesapeake in mid-August and preclude any chance that Cornwallis's army might escape by sea or be relieved by Sir Henry Clinton's forces in New York City. At all costs, the Marquis anxiously informed Wayne, it was General Washington's strict admonition that

Continental forces already in Virginia prevent Cornwallis from escaping by land into North Carolina while the trap was being laid. Wayne's task, then, was to ferry his army to the south side of the James River at Westover, "take an healthy position" on the other bank, and thwart the British earl should he try to move southward. By August 31, Wayne had fulfilled these orders, and from Prince George County he wrote Lafayette that he was in a position to "dissuade" Cornwallis from trying to escape in his direction. The Marquis, much relieved that his subordinate had successfully executed this seemingly vital operation, sent Wayne a reinforcement of forty dragoons, 300 riflemen, and a similar number of militia to assist him in his duty.[16]

Wayne's presence upon the south side of the James was not consequential, however, for upon the arrival of de Grasse's fleet in the Chesapeake Bay on August 30, the admiral (at Lafayette's suggestion) anchored frigates in the James River to guard all fords that Cornwallis might use to flee his growing entrapment. Wayne's station now being redundant, he was ordered by the Marquis on September 1 to recross the river at Jamestown and meet with him near Williamsburg to coordinate the junction of their two armies. The following day, having effected the ferrying operation, Wayne at eight o'clock in the evening set out with his aides for a rendezvous with Lafayette at the main American camp about ten miles away. Two hours later, as he was approaching Lafayette's pickets, he was challenged (as he told Polly later) by a sentry, and although he "made the usual answer" he was mistaken by the "poor fellow" for an enemy and shot in the middle thigh (of which leg he did not say). Fortunately for him, the ball only grazed the bone before finally lodging in the leg, but he was almost riddled by a volley from the "whole advanced guard" before he could rally from his daze and convince the terrified soldiers that he was an American. Finally, he was carried into Lafayette's thoroughly aroused camp, given first aid, and under these less than fortuitous circumstances reunited with the commander whom he now referred to as "one of the best Officers and first of men."[17]

During the next few weeks, Wayne was for the most part a mere spectator to events, directing his energies to convalescing and throwing off the effects of illnesses triggered by his wound. On September 12 he wrote Polly that a "very extraordinary" consequence of being shot was "that although I never had a symptom of gout before," his being injured had "brought it upon me, as quick as electricity, so much so that I thought I was wounded in the foot, which continued more Painful than my Thigh." Although the "complaint" had left him, he still felt sore and could only get about in a carriage. Wayne bantered on the same day to his friend Peters, "Your D——d Commissary of Military *plays false*. He has put too little powder in the musket Cartridges." A consequence, said Wayne to Lafayette, was that the ball was still in his leg, causing a lingering "Caitiff fever" through his entire body. It was only slowly that he recovered his strength, and in the meantime he missed ceremonies celebrating the arrival of the French fleet in the Chesapeake. However, on the fourteenth of September he was well enough to dine with General Washington, who had that day reached Williamsburg, and to listen to the Marquis de Saint-Simon's military band play Grétry's opera, "Lucille." He also took time to write a touching little note to his daughter, Margaretta, telling her about his infirmities and urging her to excel in her study of dancing, drawing, and music, that she might become a lady and hold up her head in society.[18]

On September 28, Wayne watched as General Washington marched his Franco-American army to Yorktown and began formal siege operations against the British forces there. Two days later, to Wayne's delight, Cornwallis fell back to his inner defense works and the allies seized the old British lines. But Wayne was not sanguine that subsequent operations would go smoothly, for as he told President Reed on October 3, the earl's "political and military character are now at stake," since he had "deceived" the British ministry with talk about subjugating the Carolinas, "and his manoeuvre into Virginia was child of his own creation, which he will attempt to nourish at every risk and consequence." Despite the Pennsylvanian's worries that Cornwallis would put up a good fight before capitulating, the earl remained supine within his works, and matters proceeded smoothly for American and French troops before Yorktown. On October 6, the allies began approaches to the enemy's lines, with General Wayne doing a small share of commanding the covering troops. By the ninth, Washington had implanted siege guns and was bombarding British positions.[19]

General Wayne was minimally involved in the dénouement at Yorktown, only occasionally commanding his Pennsylvanians as they dug a second and final parallel trench. During this operation, according to an anecdote that later became popular among American soldiers, Wayne and Von Steuben accompanied the troops in their work on the night of the eleventh and were silhouetted on a rampart when an enemy shell suddenly screamed through the air nearby. Both generals, it was said, immediately tumbled into the partially dug trench, with Wayne falling upon the Baron in the process. "Ah ha, Wayne," the German was supposed to have said, "You cover your general's retreat! " Three days later, the second parallel was finished, two British redoubts triumphantly stormed, and Cornwallis had attempted unsuccessfully to withdraw his army across the York River to Gloucester. That failing, he had no choice but to surrender, and on October 19, with General Wayne, his fellow officers, and the Franco-American army looking on, 8,000 British soldiers marched into captivity, while their "musick" played "The World Turned Upside Down." Fortunately for Wayne, he had recovered from his wound well enough to sit astride a horse during these ceremonies; but as he had told Governor Thomas Burke of North Carolina shortly after being injured, he would participate in "the glory of *Burgoyning* Lord Cornwallis" on this "*grand festive day*" even if he had to be "borne on the shoulders of my trusty Veterans."[20]

Although the Pennsylvanian was delighted with this event and relished letters of congratulations which began to pour in from friends like Benjamin Rush, he hastened to write Robert Morris that the Pennsylvania government must not let down its guard because of the victory. "If we suffer that unworthy torpor & supineness to seize us, which but too much pervaded the Councils of America after the Surrender of Gen'l Burgoyne," he warned, "we may yet experience great Difficulties." America must not depend upon France for its salvation, insisted Wayne, but must harness its own great resources in order to "produce a Conviction in the World that we deserve to be free." As for his own part, "I am such an Enthusiast for Independence, that I would hesitate to enter heaven thro' the means of a secondary cause unless I had made the utmost exertions to merit it."[21]

Despite Wayne's warnings to civilians that the war must continue after Yorktown, his worst fears were realized in Philadelphia on the issue of support for the military. Colonel Walter Stewart wrote in December, "As you dreaded our chimney corner soldiers in this place immediately on the capture of Cornwallis took up the opinion that the war was at an end." Similar grim messages about politics in Pennsylvania came from David Jones, Wayne's chaplain, who was on leave at home. "Nothing," he said, "is done by our civil officers that answer any good purpose for the Army — Our taxes are insupportable, and all seems likely to be consumed in support of civil government. The old adage is true, 'Out of sight out of mind.'" While civilian officers continued to receive their pay, "no period is fixed to pay the Army. . .I have no pleasure in Penn'a at present. In the Army there is some Virtue still."[22]

Civilian support or no, Wayne in November 1781 was under orders to march his Pennsylvania line south and join General Greene in ridding Wilmington, Charleston, and Savannah of British occupation. He had received a letter from Greene in late September urging him to come on quickly, once the "modern Hannibal" capitulated at Yorktown, and Governor Burke had offered him all the support that North Carolina could muster to assist the Pennsylvania troops in freeing Wilmington of enemy control. Also, Dr. Benjamin Rush gave his friend medicinal advice on how to survive a southern campaign, noting that "death from a fever or a flux may be natural to a citizen, but a soldier can only die naturally and professionally of a ball or a bayonet." If disease did not get him, however, declared Rush, Wayne would surely be triumphant in his service with Greene. After all, had this same warrior not "forced laurels out of the rocks of Stony Point?" The general's native state, declared the doctor, "watches you with an affectionate eye. She has services and honors in store for you when you have sheathed your sword."[23]

Although it was clear to Wayne in late 1781 that many of his fellow Americans expected him instantly to grasp (as he always had before) any chance for active military service, he was for once in his life surfeited with the military life. His old nemesis, Arthur St. Clair, had arrived in the South, interposed his claim to command the Pennsylvania line, and once again relegated Wayne to leadership of only a part of his former division. Although St. Clair had already marched with the Pennsylvania line toward Greene's headquarters at Round O, South Carolina, Wayne had declined to accompany his fellow Pennsylvanian.[24]

Instead, on November 4, General Wayne petitioned Washington either for winter leave or permission "to advance by slow degrees" to join Greene, citing as necessity for either one of these concessions his wounded leg and the fact that the present campaign was at an end. The commander in chief conceded that it was up to Wayne to determine his own duty for the winter, but the latter request was "more consonant with military propriety." At that, Wayne bristled slightly, declaring to Washington that his adduced reasons for wanting to leave were offered as a "*friend*," but since the commander in chief had "put it on a ground that keeps me from accepting," and "as a *soldier* I obey orders," Wayne was setting out immediately by "slow stages" in the wake of the Pennsylvania line toward Greene's headquarters. Washington accepted this arrangement in a friendly reply to his subordinate's slightly frosty note, but the commander in chief retreated not an inch from his previously stated reasons for wanting Wayne to go south, and he made no apology for holding firmly to his position.[25] After finishing his business dealings and having one final pleasant meal with Washington and the Frenchmen Rochambeau and Chastellux, Wayne on November 8, in company with his aides, departed the now-famous village of Yorktown and set his face toward further military adventures in the South.

Anthony Wayne, attributed to John Trumbull, engraving from the original. It shows Wayne as a young brigadier general, around 1776 or 1777. *State Historical Society of Wisconsin.*

Sharp Delany, by an unknown artist. Delany, a Philadelphia doctor and apothecary, was Wayne's closest and dearest friend, and looked after the general's affairs when he was away from home. *Historical Society of Pennsylvania.*

George Washington, by James Peale. Both as commander in chief of the Continental Army and as president of the United States, Washington was instrumental in advancing Wayne's career. *Independence National Historical Park Collection.*

Arthur St. Clair, by Charles Willson Peale. St. Clair was Wayne's superior officer in the Pennsylvania line during the Revolutionary War and governor of the Northwest Territory while Wayne was commander of the Legion Army. *Independence National Historical Park Collection.*

William Irvine, etching by H.B. Hall from the original portrait by James R. Lambdin. Irvine was a brigadier general of the Pennsylvania line with Wayne during the Revolutionary War and a conservative colleague in postwar Pennsylvania politics. *Historical Society of Pennsylvania.*

Nathanael Greene, by Charles Willson Peale. Greene was commander of the Southern Department when Wayne served there from 1781 to 1783; he was one of Wayne's closest friends and strongest supporters. *Independence National Historical Park Collection.*

Anthony Wayne, engraving of original painting by Alonzo Chappel of the brigadier general in the Continental Army. *Indiana Historical Society Library*.

John Trumbull's "Surrender of Lord Cornwallis," oil on canvas, 1787–1794. Identifying individuals important in Wayne's life: General Lincoln (center) accepts the surrender while Washington looks on; Wayne is sixth from the right among the mounted American officers; third to his left is Henry Knox, fifth is Timothy Pickering; fifth to his right is Baron von Steuben, sixth is Lafayette; among the standing American officers, second from the right is Walter Stewart and fourth from the right is Alexander Hamilton. *Yale University Art Gallery.*

James Jackson, a Georgian, served with Wayne in the Revolutionary War, contested (successfully) Wayne's election to Congress from Georgia in 1790, and later became governor of his native state. *Georgia Historical Society.*

Anthony Wayne, painting by James Sharples, probably from the period after the general was appointed commander of the Legion Army in 1792. *Independence National Historical Park Collection.*

Pittsburgh, 1790, engraving of a drawing by Seth Eastman. General Wayne arrived at the settlement two years later to command the Legion Army. *Carnegie Library of Pittsburgh.*

Cincinnati, 1802. Fort Washington (14) is located in the right rear. The town changed little in the ten years since General Wayne had arrived there with his army. *Indiana Historical Society Library.*

James Wilkinson, engraving from a painting by Charles Willson Peale. Wilkinson, a friend of Wayne during the American Revolution, later became a bitter opponent and a schemer for Wayne's position as commander of the Legion Army. *State Historical Society of Wisconsin.*

Fort Washington, near Cincinnati, Ohio, headquarters of the Legion Army in 1792. *Indiana Historical Society Library.*

John Graves Simcoe was commander of the Queen's Rangers during the American Revolution; he fought against Wayne in Virginia in 1781. He was governor of Upper Canada, including Detroit and Niagara, while Wayne was commander of the Legion Army in the Northwest Territory. *State Historical Society of Wisconsin.*

Fort Greeneville was built by General Wayne in 1793. It was the site of treaty negotiations with the Northwest Indians in 1795. *State Historical Society of Wisconsin.*

Battle of Fallen Timbers, August 20, 1795. In this early illustration General Wayne is brandishing his sword as he leads his troops into action. *Indiana Historical Society Library.*

Battle of Fallen Timbers. A fanciful, nineteenth-century view of Legion Dragoons bearing down on the Indians. *Indiana Historical Society Library*.

Fort Wayne was founded by General Wayne in 1795. An unknown artist made this drawing that same year. *Indiana Historical Society Library*.

"The Treaty of Greeneville, 1795," oil painting by an unknown artist who is thought to have been a member of General Wayne's staff. The general is surrounded by aides and an interpreter. The Indian chief is Little Turtle. *Chicago Historical Society, Negative No. 1914.1.*

Detroit, 1794, watercolor by an unknown artist. General Wayne took possession of the settlement a year later and made it his headquarters. *Burton Historical Collection, Detroit Public Library.*

Mary Vining, from a miniature portrait. Vining was a society belle of Philadelphia and Wilmington, who apparently formed a liaison with General Wayne in 1793 and became engaged to him in 1796, a few months before his demise. *Historical Society of Delaware.*

Anthony Wayne, probably by Henri Elouis, painted in oil in 1796 when Wayne was courting Mary Vining. *Historical Society of Pennsylvania.*

CHAPTER *viii*

Southern Triumph
1781–1783

FOLLOWING THE Pennsylvania line's route of march toward Petersburg, Wayne reflected to General Greene some days later that this agreeable course of travel through populated country, rich with stores, had been made possible by the enemy. For had the British not evacuated Wilmington shortly after the surrender of Cornwallis's army on October 19, the Pennsylvania line — and Wayne who followed after — must have moved directly southward from the Chesapeake toward that city through "exhausted country" — a most unhappy prospect. As it was, the general could make leisurely, restful stops, along the way to Petersburg, at Galt's Ordinary and Blandford, home of Congressman Theodorick Bland, and when he reached Petersburg itself he could take plenty of time to write Margaretta another of his admonitory notes (now becoming somewhat tiresome) about studying and becoming a fine lady.[1]

Continuing to ride on at a sedate pace, Wayne in early December crossed the line between Virginia and North Carolina and picked his way southward over roads worn rough by the army that preceded him. At Guilford Court House, he surveyed the scene of Greene's battle with Cornwallis nine months before, and then pushed on to Salisbury and Harrisburg. At the former town, on December 14, he wrote a self-pitying letter to an old soldier friend, Captain Henry W. Archer, bemoaning his fate at "having to ride the ball out [of his wound] in a barren wilderness," when he might have spent the winter by a roaring fire in Philadelphia. But willingly or not, he soon was pushing on toward Greene's camp, and six days later, at the Waxhaws in South Carolina, he overtook and passed General St. Clair's slow-moving soldiery. After spending Christmas at Camden, eating dinner with rich planters of the neighborhood and looking over battlefields near the place, he rode on toward his destination. At last, on January 4, 1782, he crossed the Edisto River, the final barrier between himself and General Greene's camp, and joined the Rhode Islander's headquarters at the tiny town of Round O. A day later, St. Clair arrived at the same place with the Pennsylvania troops, and Greene gave a lavish dinner in honor of his colleagues' safe arrival. At the same time, Greene was also celebrating his own brightening prospects for eliminating the enemy from South Carolina and Georgia before premature peace terms ended the war unfavorably for the revolutionaries in those states.[2]

After only a short rest from his two-month-long ride across three states, General Wayne — much to his delight, for he dreaded having to serve under St. Clair — was ordered by Greene on January 9, 1782, to assume an independent command in the state of Georgia for the next few months. Upon assuming this new duty, Wayne was instructed to lead about a hundred of Colonel Moylan's dragoons, a small detachment of artillery, 300 mounted men from General Sumter's brigade under command of Colonel Richard Humpton, and about 170 Georgia volunteers across the Savannah River with the purpose of covering the country and ending the "malignant warfare" between Whigs and Tories within that unhappy state. Empowering Wayne to correspond with newly elected Governor John Martin in order to assure civilian cooperation in this venture, Greene also authorized Wayne to take command of whatever militiamen the government of Georgia could embody for his use. Greene carefully informed Governor Martin about his arrangement, to avoid any misunderstanding about the authority his subordinate was to wield in Georgia. General Wayne, although bothered by the paucity of troops under his command as he set out on his newest adventure, nevertheless looked forward to securing more soldiers for his army once he entered the sovereign state of Georgia, and so he immediately rode out of Greene's camp at the head of his tiny army.[3]

Upon reaching the Savannah River, Wayne went into temporary residence on the South Carolina side while corresponding with Georgians about his upcoming campaign. He introduced himself to Governor Martin on January 14 and outlined ways in which the state of Georgia could assist him in carrying out his orders. Militarily, he requested that the governor enlist militia for two months' service and organize a system of supply for his troops. Politically, he suggested that the state government open wide the door of pardon to citizens who might have been compelled against their will to swear allegiance to the British Crown. By the seventeenth, Wayne was informing Greene and Henry Lee that enemy numbers in Georgia were much larger than the Continental commanders had believed, and that there were at least 900 men (there were, in fact, 1,000) under arms for Britain. Yet, Wayne was undaunted, and he continued with plans to ferry his corps across the Savannah as soon as possible. Meantime, many prominent Georgians, civilian and military, sent him letters welcoming him to their state. Also from Governor Martin came a message promising Wayne that he and the Georgia Legislature would do all within their power to help the general "reinstate, as far as may be possible, the authority of the Union, within the limits of Georgia."[4]

On January 19, General Wayne entered Georgia at Ebenezer, about fourteen miles upstream from the city of Savannah, Britain's major military post in the province. Although he now learned from Governor Martin that neither men nor supplies would be forthcoming any time soon from exhausted Georgia, he vigorously set about to improve the position of the revolutionaries in that distressed state. Quickly, he made arrangements to draw supplies for his few troops from South Carolina commissaries, then marched forward to challenge the mettle of his enemy counterpart, Brigadier General Sir Alured Clarke. While a nervous General Greene warned his hotblooded subordinate to use caution and avoid "a misfortune" ("Brilliant actions may fade, but a prudent conduct never can"), Wayne on the twenty-fourth of January successfully drove enemy forces from Mulberry Grove, Gibbons, and Ogechee. That he could not prevent the enemy from burning stores of rice before they retreated, he told Greene disgustedly two days later, was owing entirely to his having no foot soldiers, and he begged his commander (without success) for a reinforcement of *"natural Infantry."* On the twenty-eighth, Wayne directed Colonel William McCoy and his South Carolina Dragoons to ambush an Indian pack train, which they did, and he ordered out Major Joseph Habersham for like duty, but with a lack of success. Meanwhile, his troop strength had fallen even lower, because the Carolina Dragoons had gone home, and he pleaded with Greene on February 6, "For Gods sake reinforce us the moment possible."[5]

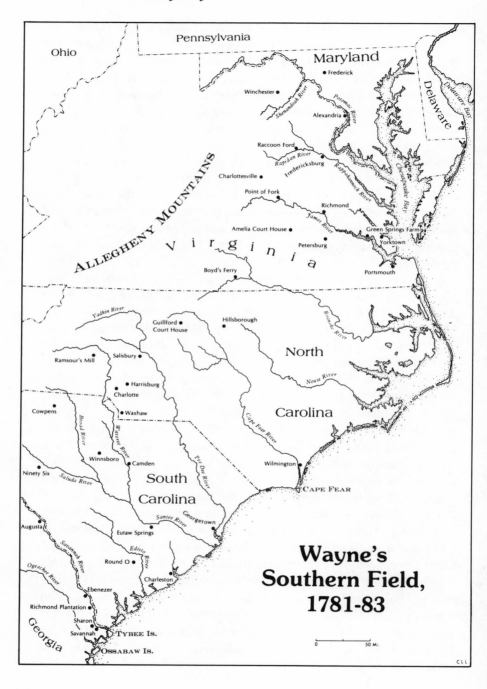

Ohio

Pennsylvania

Maryland
• Frederick

Winchester •
Alexandria •

Shenandoah River
Potomac River

Delaware

Chesapeake Bay

Delaware Bay

Raccoon Ford •
Rapidan River
Fredericksburg •
Charlottesville •
Rappahannock River

Point of Fork •
Richmond •
James River

ALLEGHENY MOUNTAINS

V i r g i n i a

Amelia Court House •
Green Springs Farm •
Petersburg •
Yorktown

Boyd's Ferry •
Portsmouth •

Roanoke River

Yadkin River
Guillford •
Court House
Hillsborough •

North

Ramsour's Mill •
Salisbury •

• Harrisburg
• Charlotte

Neuse River

Cowpens •
• Waxhaw

Carolina

Broad River
Wateree River

Cape Fear River

Ninety Six •
Winnsboro •
• Camden

Wilmington •

Saluda River
Pee Dee River

South
Carolina

CAPE FEAR

Georgetown •

Augusta •
Santee River
Eutaw Springs •

Savannah River
Edisto River
Round O •

**Wayne's
Southern Field,
1781-83**

Ogeechee River
Charleston •

Ebenezer •

Richmond Plantation •
Sharon •
Savannah •
TYBEE IS.

Georgia

OSSABAW IS.

0   50 Mi.

CLL

As Wayne attempted to cope with Clarke's soldiers and Indian allies, he also dealt with civil matters. On February 13, he repeated his suggestion to Governor Martin and the legislature that the state offer lenient pardons to the loyalists in order to effect a reduction in political strife in the state. Six days later, he sent Governor Martin drafts of statements he believed the General Assembly of Georgia should adopt, one calling for pardons for everyone (except those on a proscribed list) who would join Wayne's army by March 15, another offering land to Hessians who would desert the Royal army in Savannah. The legislature approved these proclamations on February 20, and their effect was gratifying to all supporters of the Revolution. Within less than a month, large numbers of loyalist militia deserted the enemy, as did a group of 38 irregular cavalrymen and their leader, Sir Patrick Houstoun. Noted Wayne to Polly in a letter of March 2, he was delighted to be the agent of peace and happiness without being compelled to shed blood, "So that you find my Dear Girl, that Sterne's observation 'that a soldier is of a profession that tends to make bad men worse' is ill natured and unjust; on the Contrary, I am satiate of this horrid trade of blood; & would much rather shame one poor *Savage* than destroy twenty."[6]

Although General Wayne conceded that proclamations of pardon had their place in warfare, nonetheless as a military man he felt that they did not take the place of a well-ordered body of soldiers for forcing one's will upon an enemy. Hence, he continued to berate Governor Martin and General Greene for their part in perpetuating his weaknesses in supplies and in numbers of infantry and horsemen. On February 11, while pleading with Greene for reinforcements, he reported that the state of Georgia had at last furnished him with some soldiers — but only one hundred — and by the twenty-eighth he was grumbling, "The duty we have done in Georgia was more difficult than that imposed upon the children of Israel. They had only to make bricks without straw, but we have had provision, forage, and almost every other apparatus of war to procure without money: boats, bridges, & c. to build without materials except those taken from the stump: and, what was more difficult than all, to make *Whigs* out of *Tories*." He made similar comments to his friends Irvine and Stewart, and to the latter he also exclaimed, "Would to God you were with us at the head of one thousand stout fellows as used to parade with Infantry Caps decorated with flowing red hair near the falls of Passaick."[7]

Instead of these well-dressed soldiers, Wayne could muster at the close of February only about 300 ill-clad, stinking men who had not even attempted to undress (so he told Greene) since they had arrived in Georgia. With these poor few soldiers he must cow not only General Clarke's regulars but also the *"copper coloured Gentry,"* the Creeks and Choctaws. However many entreaties Wayne made for reinforcements, he could not get Greene to relent, for Greene correctly noted on March 6 that should Wayne be compelled to retreat, he could do so with no injury to the American position in the South, whereas if the same happened to Greene at Charleston, great mischief might ensue. "Duty falls a little hard upon you," commiserated Greene, "but you don't risque capitally by that. . . To detach two hundred men to you would be madness."[8]

Although Greene had insisted that Wayne did not need reinforcements as badly as he needed to keep his men in South Carolina, nevertheless he finally relented to his subordinate's insistence that troops were a necessity in Georgia. On March 12, Greene promised Wayne that he would send to Ebenezer a force of Virginians that was embodied under Colonel Thomas Posey and expected to arrive shortly. Although Wayne declared that he would "be content with a Battalion of Pennsylvanians," he was glad to hear this news, for since Governor Martin could furnish him with no militia, his military activities against Clarke had ground to a halt. While awaiting Posey's arrival, he idled away the month of March at Ebenezer, writing his wife Polly a short letter with its usual lecture about seeing to the children's education and one to Richard Peters commenting upon the birth of the Peters's second child, a daughter, whom he hoped had inherited her mother's features since they were "rather more pleasing to the eye, & better suited to a female than that *Phiz* of Yours."[9]

Meanwhile, Wayne continued to augment his army and prepare for offensive actions against General Clarke at Savannah. On March 29, his force consisted of 523 men, infantry and cavalry combined, and a few days later he was petitioning the Georgia legislature for the acquisition of 200 riflemen, which that body resolved to raise and which Governor Martin immediately set out to recruit for two months' service (even though the governor, as he noted to Wayne shortly thereafter, had exceeded his authority under a state constitution that gave the executive no emergency powers). Then on April 4, Posey's long-awaited Virginians arrived, and although their uniforms were in rags, the Continental commander in Georgia quickly set in motion a plan to march from

Ebenezer nearer to the enemy's lines and put pressure on the British soldiers holding Savannah. Greene expressed some concern about Wayne's moving too near the British with inferior forces, and Wayne on April 28 laid to rest any fear that his superior might have about his taking too great risks. "I have always adopted the opinion of those Military writers," he said, "who lay it down as a maxim; that an officer never ought to hazzard a Battle where a defeat would render his situation much worse, than a retreat without it." Therefore, for the present he would remain where he was and await more promising circumstances for an advance — a good decision, as it turned out, for a day later Greene reduced Wayne's army by ordering some cavalry back to South Carolina. Meanwhile, Wayne sadly noted in numerous letters the death of his friend, Major Francis Moore, who had been killed in a skirmish with British forces, after Moore had himself killed two of the enemy. To die in action as Moore had, believed Wayne, was the most noble of all deaths for a soldier and one that he could wish for himself.[10]

Although his corps was sadly decimated by Greene's call for a return of cavalry to his own command ("Do you know my Dear Sir how much you have weakened us," complained Wayne plaintively to his commander on May 7), the Pennsylvanian made the best of his continuing enforced quietude on the Savannah's peaceful banks by writing more friends in Pennsylvania. To Thomas Moore, he laughingly described his army as a "heterogeneous" mixture of "British, Hessians, new levies, out layers, Tories, Crackers, Ethiopians & Indian *allies* to the number of thirteen tribes." With these latter folk, he said, he had become so friendly that "was I so Inclined might form an Alliance with the *Charming* Princess of the lower Creek Nation, which honor I shall decline, having business of a Very Sanguinary nature to settle in a few days." Wayne also wrote his old friend Rush, addressing the letter dramatically from "the dreary desarts between Georgia & Florida." The general thanked Rush for his kind sentiments about the gratitude of Pennsylvania for his services and for the free medical advice. The latter, however, Wayne declared he could not follow, for his diet consisted of "cold beef & rice," washed down with "*Alegator* water," and he had no "covering to screen me from the burning ray's of the meridian sun, the rude thunder storms, & baneful evening air." His only shelters were "the concave heavens, & a horse mens cloak; which probably will be the case for the chief part of the campaign." And if these did not kill him he still might fall prey to "the British bullet & bayonet, the tommyhock, or scalping knife of less *Savage* allies, the Chickasaws, Choctaws, Tapoock-aws, Tuknebatches, Nutahoorits, Makatasas, Apalaches, Sakuspagas, Timmokahs, Okmulghes, *Cherakees* & Owaguaphenogas." With all these things against him, concluded Wayne in feigned distress, he had "no flattering prospect of seeing Pennsa. in *health* & safety."[11]

Other reasons also seemed likely by mid-1782 to keep Wayne from returning to his native state. For one thing, he learned from Governor Martin and Samuel Dalton, speaker of the Georgia General Assembly, that the legislature on May 1 had "Resolved that a high Sense of the great merits and Services rendered by the Hon'ble Brigadier General Anthony Wayne is entertained by this House" and that the sum of 4,000 guineas be granted to three commissioners for the purpose of purchasing an estate for Wayne "in any part of the state he may appoint." At the same time, the General Assembly also granted General Greene 5,000 guineas for a similar purpose. Wayne gratefully responded to the legislature and to Martin on May 14, noting that he was "highly flattered" that Georgians wished him to remain within their midst, and to Greene he gleefully noted that perhaps they could be neighbors once the war was ended. Possibility became reality when on July 31 the General Assembly informed Wayne it was giving him a rice plantation of 847 acres, named Richmond, which the state had confiscated from a loyalist, Alexander Wright, son of Royal governor Sir James Wright. To this piece of land, with its fine old house and numerous outbuildings, located about twelve miles upriver from Savannah, was later added another estate named Kew. General Greene was given the splendid nearby plantation of Mulberry Grove, worth £7,000, within easy visiting distance of Wayne's own rich acres. Both Wayne and Greene had become committed (although they did not know it at the time) to living after the war as rice farmers and incurring debts that would disturb their peace long after the Revolutionary War was at an end.[12]

On May 21, a military opportunity arose for Wayne when he learned that General Clarke had sent out two days before a detachment of 350 infantrymen and a squadron of cavalry under Lieutenant Colonel Thomas Browne to escort a party of Indians into Savannah. By the time Wayne received this news, Browne's party had already advanced to the Ogechee River, and there finding that the expected Indians had not arrived, had collected a few cattle and begun its return march to Clarke's main lines around the city. Immediately, Wayne began preparations to intercept this party, for here was just the opportunity he had been awaiting: to attack an enemy force roughly equal in size to his own small corps. With his entire force of about 500 men, he marched from Ebenezer on the evening of the twenty-first, hastening ahead with Captain Alexander Parker and a vanguard consisting of sixty infantry and a squad of forty dragoons to seize a four-mile-long causeway over which Browne must pass on his way to Savannah. Meanwhile, Colonel James Jackson, a semi-independent cavalry officer, was reporting to Wayne at about six o'clock that the enemy was "in force" on the Ogechee Road at Harris's Bridge, about seven miles from Savannah, and that a small advance party was guarding Ogechee Ferry, which he intended to attack.[13]

As Wayne rode with the vanguard of his small army toward the causeway on the evening of May 21, he reflected on the "*delicacy*" of his situation, moving a force the size of his corps on a night march through swamps, into a position between Clarke's main army at Savannah and Browne's detachment to the southwest. Compounding his problem, he had with him only Captain Parker's small guard and could expect no support from his main body for some time should he engage with the enemy on the causeway. With these matters weighing on his mind, Wayne at about midnight reached the Ogechee Road with his van at a place about four miles southwest of Savannah, and waited anxiously to see which force, Browne's or the rest of his own, would arrive first upon the scene. Before long, Wayne and his tiny corps with sinking heart espied Browne's men coming forward "in close & good order," and the general might at that point have been forgiven had he decided a hasty withdrawal was in order, for his entire military future "depended upon the moment." But instead of retreating he ordered his forty dragoons to charge the front of the closely filed British, whose march was led by a troop of cavalrymen, while his sixty infantrymen laid down a fire upon their flanks. This attack, as Wayne noted proudly, coming as it did unexpectedly upon the British and conducted with "vivacity," caused Browne's cavalry and a large part of his infantry to disperse into the surrounding swamps, so that no other American forces even managed to get into the skirmish with the utterly demoralized redcoats and Hessians.

Pursuit of the enemy being impossible at night in the morasses to which they had fled, Wayne now called off his triumphant dragoons and infantrymen, rounded up about eighteen enemy troopers and thirty horses, collected his own five dead cavalrymen,[14] and turned the march of his now-reunited total force of 500 men toward Savannah. Although he allowed his men to rest overnight at Gibbon's Plantation, Wayne in the early morning of the twenty-third of May advanced his corps in line of battle within view of General Clarke's entrenchments, sent skirmishers forward to draw his foes from their works, and taunted Clarke to come out and fight. The British general, however, would not take the bait, for by then he had been constrained by act of Parliament from initiating any "offensive actions" against the rebels. Moreover, as he was aware, his new commander in chief, Sir Guy Carleton, who had supplanted Clinton on May 5 at New York City, was under orders from the Rockingham ministry to evacuate all military posts in America, including Savannah, and more bloodshed in defense of the place at this late date seemed pointless. So his only response to Wayne's provocation was to send out a few "Indians & negroes to the skirt of a swamp from which they commenced an ineffectual fire" upon their enemies. The American general, seeing that Clarke would not rise to the challenge, turned his back upon the lines at Savannah and returned his corps to Gibbon's Plantation, where he spent the night before moving the following day by an easy march back to Ebenezer.

Although Wayne's army continued to be too weak to assault Clarke in Savannah, the American general, given the right circumstances, nevertheless was willing to bluff at it. "Desertions," he told Greene "prevails from *Savannah*," and he mused that it would be wonderful to receive assistance from "the [Spanish] Dons" (who had reconquered West Florida) to assault Britain's ever-weakening forces in Georgia. "Do let us dig the Caitiffs out," he pleaded to Greene on May 27, "it will give an eclat to our arms to effect a business in which the armament of our great & good ally failed." But Greene would have none of this hyperbole, reminding Wayne over and over again that he did not have the strength to force the enemy from Savannah and noting that, from all appearances, the British would soon be evacuating the city in any case.[15] For Greene, as for General Clarke in Georgia, military operations seemed more and more beside the point. Of all the commanders in the South by 1782, therefore, only Anthony Wayne, despite his assertion to Polly that he was "satiate of this horrid trade of blood," lusted for more military service. His was a personality that flourished on those very things of war — glory, splendor, pomp, excitement, blood hatreds, destruction, and danger — repellent to other men, even soldiers, after they had become surfeited by conflict.

On May 29, Wayne received from Brigadier General Clarke and Sir James Wright, royal governor of Georgia, news that peace negotiations were going on in Europe and that both officials wanted a cessation of hostilities around Savannah in order to avoid unnecessary effusion of blood. Wayne declared to these men that approval for such a plan must come from higher authority but that he was notifying Greene (who had received a similar request from General Alexander Leslie in Charleston eight days before) and Governor Martin that he had gotten the proposal. Greene, on June 5, replied to Wayne that this was a matter that fell under the civil authority of Congress and that he was sending all the relevant papers on to Philadelphia. Wayne so informed Wright and Clarke, and there the matter rested until a month later, when it became moot because of British withdrawal from the state. While he dickered with the Britons about terms of a cease fire, Wayne also conducted a vigorous campaign to lure enemy soldiers in Savannah to desert, by offering them 200 acres of land and citizenship in the state of Georgia, as Governor Martin had promised in February, if they would come over to his army. He needed these men desperately, for a number of his Georgia cavalrymen were mustering out on June 7 with no replacements coming to fill the gap and, as he told his friend Peters on the 8th, he expected the enemy at any time to give him another battle to redress their losses from the *recontre* of May 21.[16]

While he negotiated with British leaders in Savannah, Wayne also became involved with his comrade Greene in a tiff over army stores. It seems that in April Greene had sent congressional inspectors to Wayne's camp to take account of whether clothing, accouterments, forage, and food were being husbanded with the rigor that "the Financier," Robert Morris, would wish. When the report on Wayne's operations was completed in early June, it showed him to be fiscally responsible in all matters except subsistence, and on the sixth, Greene warned him that his army's consumption of ratios was too high. When Wayne received this reprimand, he was furious that anyone could suggest that his poor, strapped soldiers were wastrels, and in a seven-page letter to Greene on June 13, he carefully explained that he had always followed strict military procedure in apportioning foodstuffs. Then, he launched into a three-page recapitulation of his entire service record in Georgia to show his superior that the state had always gotten more from his men and himself than it ever gave in return. "I am warranted," he declared, "in asserting that no army was ever supported for less expense, or more service rendered in proportion to numbers, than on the present occasion." General Greene responded to this sulfurous blast with placating words, declaring that it was never his intention to chastise his friend, only to caution him to exercise future economies, and if Wayne could but see the letters Greene was receiving from Morris he would understand why Greene harped on economy. "I think you have conducted your command with great prudence," declared Greene, "and with astonishing perseverence, and in so doing you have fully answered the high expectations I ever entertained of your Military ability from our earlier acquaintance." These soothing words balmed the tender spirit of General Wayne, and he said no more about this incident.[17]

That Greene did not exaggerate Wayne's success in Georgia since January was not to be disputed (although one may argue with another assessor of his campaign of 1782, who declared that "his achievements made him worthy to rank as a strategist with Turrenne or the Duke of Marlborough"). His military operations, conducted under the most trying circumstances, had forced General Clarke to withdraw his forces into Savannah and had made his cooperation with Britain's up-country Indian allies extremely difficult. The fact was, however, that much of Wayne's success was due to Clarke's own self-imposed restraint, because of the British general's knowledge that the war was drawing to a close and because he did not wish to shed any unnecessary blood. Also, the American commander had been for a time on the receiving end of fortune's whimsical favor — much longer, in fact, than perhaps was healthy for a man of his self-conception. As Henry Lee observed in his *Memoirs*, such good luck as Wayne's "encourages the ardent soldier to put himself upon his fortune and his courage — overlooking those numerous sure, and effectual aids to be drawn from accurate intelligence and due circumspection." Destiny, said Lee, eventually forsakes such a soldier, and after that "no prop remains to support him but courage, and he falls victim to his own presumption."[18]

Such, noted the able cavalryman Lee, was soon to be the fate of Anthony Wayne, for either from ignorance or apathy Wayne had not made himself aware of the reason why General Clarke in mid-May had sent out Browne's detachment. Therefore, Wayne with a confidence born of self-imposed blindness marched his army in early June out of its secure encampment at Ebenezer and took post at Sharon, only five miles from Savannah, on the road from that place to the Ogechee River. In this new camp, he placed himself directly in the vicinity of a band of

Creek warriors and their proud leader Guristersigo, who were to have formed a junction with the British earlier but who had arrived on the Ogechee a day after Browne turned back. No sooner did Guristersigo learn that his American foes were at Sharon than he decided to carry out a surprise raid upon the American pickets in the early morning hours of June 24. As fate would have it, Wayne on the evening of the twenty-third, following a custom he had instituted after Paoli, switched his picket camp with his main bivouac and marched the body of his corps to the place recently vacated by the pickets. This diversion, designed to reduce his chances of being attacked in his camp, would under normal circumstances work to the Americans' advantage, for a surreptitious enemy assault would be directed straight into the midst of alert guards instead of sleeping soldiers, and the attackers would themselves receive a rude surprise. But in this case, Guristersigo intended to attack Wayne's pickets first, and the general, as a consequence of switching his camps around, laid himself open for another surprise night attack against totally unprepared men.[19]

Early in the morning hours of June 24, a surprise attack is exactly what General Wayne and his corps got. Out of the surrounding swamps the Indians formed themselves into a war party upon the road to the west of the American position. In utter silence, they approached the unguarded rear of Wayne's sleeping men and quietly dispatched the lone sentinel guarding that entire side of the Continental camp. Seconds later, Guristersigo, with a whoop, rose to his feet and led his yelling warriors into the midst of the sleep-dazed Americans. As quickly as he could under these circumstances, a surprised Wayne leaped upon his horse, and believing that the garrison of Savannah had surrounded his corps, ordered his men to fix bayonets and die with him, weapons in hand. At that point his horse was killed beneath him, but he continued to rally his men on foot. Finally, the camp fully alerted, Wayne, who had remounted, led the infantry and cavalry in charges against the Indians, scattering them into the surrounding bogs and killing eighteen, including Guristersigo.[20]

After the battle, Colonel Posey chased the Indians through the surrounding countryside, finally capturing twelve of their chiefs, whom he brought next morning under guard into the American camp. "The general," said Posey, "appeared in a good humor until he discovered the Indian prisoners, his countenance then changed, and he asked [me] in a very peremptory manner, how [I] could think of taking those savages prisoner. . .; he said they should not live, and they were accordingly put to death." The general then buried five of his own dead soldiers, bound up the wounds of eight more, "and finding," said Lee, "that he had an enemy in the rear as well as in front, he became more circumspect in his future arrangements." If Wayne was chastened by his recent experience, however, he gave no sign of it in his report to Greene on the same day as the battle. "Our trophies," he boasted, "are an elegant standard, 107 horses with a number of packs, arms, & c. . . . Such was the determined bravery with which the Indians fought that after I had cut down one of their chiefs, with his last breath he drew his trigger and shot my noble horse dead under me."[21]

A calm now fell upon Wayne's army at Sharon, while signs of an imminent British evacuation of Savannah continued to mount. Already Greene and Governor Martin on at least one occasion had been misinformed that Wright and Clarke had withdrawn, and Greene issued orders for Wayne to join him near Charleston immediately after the actual event had taken place. In response to this requisition, Wayne informed his superior that he would come on as quickly as possible but that he must first rest his exhausted cavalry horses, "cover the naked country" against a threatened Indian carnage, "& arrange matters." Angry that Clarke supposedly was threatening both to "unleash" his Indian allies against the rebels and "put to the sword any American officer that might be captured," Wayne on June 27 wrote his British counterpart in Savannah, warning that these things had better not happen. With indignation, General Clarke replied that it was dastardly of the American general to countenance such mad rumors, but Wayne was not appeased and quickly ordered militia officers to be wary of native Americans seeking the blood of "Innocent & defenseless Women & Children." Although Wayne notified Greene of all these proceedings and used them as excuse for keeping a Continental force in Georgia after the British had departed, Greene would not be dissuaded from having his subordinate return to South Carolina, and so he informed both Wayne and Governor Martin on the fourteenth of July.[22]

Finally, Wayne had the pleasure on July 11 of seeing the last British forces in Savannah retire to Tybee Island, where they would remain for a few days before finally quitting the state of Georgia entirely. At twelve o'clock noon, he ordered Colonel James Jackson's "Partisan Legion" of Georgia cavalrymen to lead his army, under strict admonition not to loot the inhabitants, into the city. To Wayne's delight, the British themselves had carried out no destruction, either of military works or of civilian real estate, and he quickly notified Governor Martin and the legislature, at Ebenezer, to move in and assume control of the populace. Meantime, the general put into operation a plan that he had devised some weeks before with the merchants of Savannah to protect their property while the changeover was taking place. Under this arrangement, agreed to by Martin and the legislature, all merchants who chose to remain in the city after the Whigs regained control would have their goods "resigned inviolate into the Hands of the Civil Authority of this State which must ultimately decide" the fate of each trader's property. Additionally, all loyalists, except murderers, who had helped the British but who now wanted to remain as citizens could repair their past conduct by enlisting in the Georgia Continental battalion for a term of two years or the duration of the war.[23]

Most of Wayne's proclamations on matters concerning the future relations of Georgia's citizens to their government were confirmed by the state's legislature when it reached Savannah. The civilian leaders quickly announced that all American merchants who had cooperated with the British were forgiven, contingent upon their willingness to supply the American army with all necessities that might be requisitioned, with just compensation, by the state. Also, British businessmen were to be given six months, as Wayne had promised, to wrap up their affairs and move their stocks of goods elsewhere (no mention was made of whether they would be allowed to continue in active trade during this period). But on the question of the general's blanket pardon of all loyalists save those who had committed murder (if they would but enlist in the Georgia Continentals) the legislature reneged upon its prior acceptance of Wayne's proclamation. After some reflection, the General Assembly decided on July 26 that the general's pronouncement would "class good and wretched together indiscriminantly and subvert justice"; therefore, the patriots of Georgia must approach this matter with considerable caution. They were not, in a word, about to let bygones be bygones, as Wayne wished. The passions unleashed in Georgia by the past few years of civil war were too great to be downed by one interloping soldier's easy proclamation.[24]

Even though Wayne was under strict and pointed orders from Greene to march toward South Carolina after Savannah had been secured, he continued for almost a month to loiter in and about the pleasant riverport town. As he told Greene on the seventeenth of July, since the enemy was still at Tybee Island, the Georgia government must not be left unprotected, and in any case these troops had not yet joined Leslie in Charleston, so Greene had nothing to fear from superior enemy numbers for some time to come. While Wayne remained in Georgia, he improved the American military position by issuing threatening speeches to Britain's Indian allies and proclamations to the English inhabitants of East Florida, both designed to coax these people into surrendering to him at Savannah. He also worked with the town's merchants to stabilize his and their relationship on the question of supplies for the American army, and he tried to force the British on Tybee to return some slaves they had "stolen" from Savannah merchants. When Greene received copies of Wayne's Indian speeches and proclamations, he wrote his subordinate with amusement that such statements ought always to be "within supporting distance of facts. However, I hope you are in little danger of meeting with Burgoyne's fall."[25]

At last, on July 26, Wayne was ready to march northward to join Greene — when suddenly he received intelligence that once again delayed his departure from Georgia. On that day he learned that "a motley crew" of 500 loyalists under Colonel Thomas Browne, which supposedly had gone overland from Savannah to St. Augustine after the British evacuated Savannah, were "Skulking" only nine miles from the city. Therefore, on the twenty-sixth he must turn his line of march with his light infantry and dragoons southward, rather than the opposite direction toward Charleston, in order to drive Browne away. Three days later he had succeeded in this task, scaring the loyalists into retreating to Ossabaw Island, twenty miles below Savannah, and he reported to Greene that Brown's force now posed little threat to the city. But the Georgia General Assembly had become so thoroughly skittish, because of the organized loyalist presence in the state, that on July 31 it petitioned Greene to allow Wayne and his army to remain for a time in Savannah and protect the government. Greene reluctantly agreed to this requisition on August 2, but he grumbled to Wayne that the Americans in the South risked defeat by detachment. Frederick II was correct, he declared, in noting that an army that tries too much generally loses all, and if he suffered a defeat in South Carolina the Georgians would feel the loss a great deal more than most other Americans.[26]

In early August, Wayne had become persuaded to Greene's point of view, and so he informed the Georgia General Assembly on the third.

Browne's men, he iterated to the legislators, were only a slight offensive threat, and any danger they might pose could easily be handled by Jackson's legion and a newly embodying battalion of Continentals under Major John Habersham. Therefore, he was ordering his men to march for South Carolina and would himself soon join them on their march. The legislature reluctantly acceded to this news, and on August 4 the assemblymen honored departing General Wayne by expressing "the high Sense this House entertain of his important services already rendered the State" as well as its continued support of his future exertions. Five days later, Wayne carried out his last official function in the state by issuing a proclamation — which proved to be controversial — expanding his original agreement with Savannah merchants who were British subjects to allow them to carry on active business without being molested by the patriots until their six months' time to move their property was exhausted. Angry Georgia Whigs, who only days before had heaped praise upon Wayne, were so disgruntled with this measure that they insisted it could only become operational if Congress approved it. And there the matter rested, as the general on the evening of August 9 departed Savannah.[27]

If General Wayne was angry or upset at the furor he had created in Georgia, he showed no sign of it as he enjoyed a pleasant, leisurely journey of six days northward toward Greene's encampment near Charleston. His only thought as he happily rejoined his friend on August 15 at Ashley Hill was to secure some sort of detached service, away from St. Clair's domination, preferably at the head of Greene's light infantry corps, then commanded by General Mordecai Gist. While Greene expressed strong faith in Wayne's abilities as a general ("I think no man can execute a command better than yourself"), he would not give "personal affront" to Gist by removing that gentleman in favor of the Pennsylvanian. So Wayne tried another tack, proposing that Greene give into his charge a detachment of troops that he could march into the area of the Combahee River, south of Charleston, to prevent enemy foraging there. But Greene informed him that the troops Wayne proposed for this duty were already scheduled for other service. Wayne next proposed, on August 29, that Greene let him use a detachment of Georgians for patrolling between the Ashley and Cooper rivers, northwest of General Leslie's defensive positions at Charleston. The American commander also reluctantly refused this request, noting that the value of such an operation would not be worth its expense and that all military undertakings should be for the good of the public which was paying the army's upkeep. Finally, on August 31, Wayne simply announced to Greene, without asking the commander's approval, that he intended to use his own Georgia troops, plus a small number of "reclaimed citizens" from General Francis Marion's irregular corps, to create a "flying or reconnoitering party" to harass the enemy between the Ashley and Cooper rivers.[28]

Whether General Greene would have allowed Wayne to get away with this cheeky assumption of authority is not known. For on September 2, General Wayne was stricken by an illness that interrupted his immediate military plans, seemed for a time about to kill him, and from which he never fully recovered. Considering the malignancy of such diseases among unacclimated persons living on the low-lying coasts of the American southland at that time, it was a miracle that Wayne had not already contracted some form of fever. Although he had taken the advice of his friend, Benjamin Rush, and dosed himself liberally with "Peruvian bark" (from the South American chinchona tree), in this case the specific had failed. As he sat, on the 2nd of September, writing Robert Morris a letter, he had completed a paragraph about "Our little Army mouldering away to a handful by the baneful effects of short Inlistments & the fatal fevers natural to this inhospitable climate," when suddenly the letter stopped. Twenty-seven days later, it recommenced, with Wayne declaring, "My pen was wrested from me by a Caitiff & Dangerous fever before I could finish." During that entire time, he had done nothing whatsoever but battle "that disorder which I really dread much more than I do the D——l, a musket and cannon ball." A local doctor, he told Benjamin Rush in December, "after trying the powers of almost his whole Materia Medica without effect," had instituted a regimen of "moderate exercise," which finally began to have some effect.[29]

But even at the time he was writing Rush, almost four months after he had been first stricken, General Wayne still suffered chest congestion, "like *consumption*," and a low-grade fever. Although he did not believe his constitution had been permanently impaired (on this point he was wrong), nonetheless he was "broken down & exhausted." As he declared to Richard Butler during the same month, December, his health was so low that "was the wealth of India to be the reward I would not walk a mile in one hour to obtain it." He told another friend, Major James Moore, on January 1, 1783, "I am a *cripple* call & see me." By late

September of the year before, Wayne had recovered at least a part of his strength, and he mustered the will to compose letters to Polly, from whom he had heard nothing for months, and to Governor Martin of Georgia, explaining to them both the reason for his total lack of communication during September.[30]

The military reality to which General Wayne returned in October was almost as bad as the feverish nightmares that he had suffered the month before, for a host of vexations and disappointments weighed down his spirit over the next few weeks. For a start, he received from his commander, Greene, on October 5 a terse reprimand for trying to draw forage for too many horses on his personal account. Then, at about the same time, Wayne received from the Whigs of Georgia a battery of complaints about his proclamation of August 9, and he angrily declared to them that if they must question his judgment — as they seemed determined to do — then he would accede to their request that Congress decide the validity of his manifesto. Hence, he had General Greene forward all the relevant papers toward Philadelphia. Finally to dampen his weakened vitality even further, on November 2 he was chastised again by Greene, this time because he was accused by Colonel Thaddeus Kosciuszko, commander of an American checkpoint on the Ashley River, of not exercising care in granting permits for the state's inhabitants to pass into Charleston for purposes of trade, thus allowing some persons to smuggle army supplies to the enemy.[31]

Wayne, indignantly jumping to the conclusion that Greene was accusing him of cooperating with criminals, furiously lashed out to his superior that such a charge was a vicious lie and a wanton slander against his reputation. The only passes he had issued, he swore, were for "sundry inhabitants" who wanted to take a few necessary articles to sick family members in the city. In any case, who in the American army would be swinish enough to send supplies to the enemy, starved as all patriot soldiers were for even the barest necessities of life? While it may be true that Wayne had issued passes — without malicious intent — to a few persons who abused their privilege and that he had himself received a few of the "common comforts and necessities of life," such as wine, port, and medicine from Charleston for his "family" and himself, these facts did not warrant Greene's conclusion that Wayne was a common outlaw, trafficking in stolen public American stores with the enemy. Of course, Greene had concluded no such thing, and his response to his subordinate's almost hysterical diatribe against him only gently noted that his friend's letter had given him pain and that the Pennsylvanian was overreacting. Soon the two men got together and ironed out their differences, with Greene taking by far the more conciliatory role in the proceedings, and after that Wayne was mollified.[32]

Throughout November, Wayne's long period of gloom and short temper, which was probably due in part to his illness, showed signs of ending as his physical health and the Whig military posture around Charleston improved. Soon, therefore, he had resumed his normal military duties. Growing signs that the British intended to evacuate Charleston, including the arrival of forty-five naval transports in the harbor on October 21, compelled the general to believe that soon the enemy would be out of South Carolina. But, as he told Robert Morris, the British Ministry could always change its plans, and the Americans ought to be prepared for the worst. In this frame of mind, he lectured politicians Richard Hawley in Philadelphia and John Martin in Georgia to get their respective state legislatures out of their "supineness & torpidity" and support the army. The poor Pennsylvania line was especially prostrate, he told Butler, having suffered the death of one in eight of its numbers because of fevers since marching south. To his dismay, however, the people's representatives, rather than trying to improve America's military posture, were weakening it, and on November 7 he was appointed by Greene to the sad duty of reducing the lines of Pennsylvania, Maryland, and North Carolina to one regiment each.[33]

As the cool weather of late autumn in 1782 spread like a balm over the plains and morasses of coastal South Carolina, General Wayne began to look forward to surcease from his military labors and a return to the pleasures of life at Waynesborough. He predicted to Polly in late September that he would be leaving the South by New Year's Day, 1783, unless ordered by Greene to lead an expedition against Florida. Homesick for his friends in Philadelphia, he groused to Peters in November that none of "your great men" were writing him. Nonetheless, he was delighted a few days later to receive from Rush a letter congratulating him on the American occupation of Savannah and pleading with him not to let even a princely rice plantation in Georgia "tempt you to abandon" Pennsylvania. His native state loved him, declared Rush; "You are one of her legitimate children." Come home, and assist the lovers of good government in getting rid of those "Vagabonds" who had usurped power in the state's Assembly. Wayne, replying to his friend's solicitations, assured Rush that he had a "fixed determination to revisit my Sabine field" when the war was over, not because of any honors or offices that might await him — "they have lost the power to please" — but because he hoped to pass many happy hours on his estate "with a few choice friends, unfettered by public employ."[34]

Dream as he might of Pennsylvania fields and the hearty, loving companionship of friends and family, Wayne must focus his attention on the military object of seeing the British out of Charleston. On November 26, Greene gave him command of the light infantry at last (but only because General Gist was ill) and a legionary corps formerly commanded by Wayne's old friend Henry Lee, with orders to occupy the South Carolina capital upon the retirement of the British. Although Wayne over the next two weeks lusted for one last chance to draw English blood in the present war, Greene refused to free him for such worthless histrionics, and finally, on December 13, the conflict ceased in South Carolina. That day, Wayne, with Greene's approval, accepted a plan sent him by General Leslie that was designed to let the British depart in peace from Charleston the following morning, in return for which the city would be left unharmed. Therefore, at nine o'clock, on December 14, 1782, the last of the British troops left their entrenchments and marched to the Royal Navy's transports, to be followed into the city two hours later by General Wayne's motley vanguard. That evening, as the redcoats on board their ships dropped down the harbor toward the Atlantic Ocean, a proud General Wayne bragged to his friends about his role in Britain's final withdrawal from United States territory south of New York City. But his happiness was quickly dampened by illness, which forced him to bed while other of his compatriots, soldier and civilian alike, fell to celebrating the occasion with gala revels.[35]

With Wayne now convinced that America's war with Britain was drawing to a successful close, the general in 1783, although he continued for some months to serve in the Continental Army, began more and more to turn his thoughts to civil affairs. In January, he wrote both Washington and Rush that his health was shattered and that it was Greene's opinion he ought to return to Pennsylvania as soon as possible. Looking toward that happy event, in February he tried to get the Georgia General Assembly to give him a clear deed to Richmond, his rice plantation, before he departed, but he was not to be successful in that venture for three more years. In the same month, he learned from friends in Philadelphia that Congress the previous December had taken up the matter of his proclamation to Savannah merchants of August 9, 1782, and while the legislators had reluctantly accepted his action as an irreversible fait accompli, many of them looked upon it as being open to "infinite abuses" and a dangerously militaristic transgression of civil authority. As though this were not enough for Wayne to have to swallow, the general also became aware that a large number of Georgia's Whigs thought that he had been altogether too lenient toward Tories and that if he ever attempted in the future to become active in the state's politics, they intended to use his politically ill-conceived proclamations against him.[36]

Angry civilians, however, were the least of Wayne's worries in February 1783, for the Continental Army under Greene at Charleston was on the verge of starvation and was about to mutiny. Under the plans of Robert Morris, America's Superintendent of Finance, South Carolina was supposed to support all Continental soldiers within the confines of that state, but the treasury of the state was empty, and no food or forage could be purchased. Finally, Morris proposed to Greene that he contract with Carolina merchants to supply the troops, and as a consequence the general advertised for bids. To his surprise, only one person, a John Banks of Virginia, came forward with a bid to supply the army, and Greene was forced to accept his terms, although they were expensive. Moreover, Greene was required to become Banks's security for certain purchases of supplies in Savannah, and soon the merchant was using the general's name rather haphazardly for all sorts of questionable personal deals. Furiously, Greene ordered the "infamous scoundrel" to cease this business and forced him to swear before a notary, with Wayne and Colonel Edward Carrington as witnesses, that Greene was not involved in the shady transactions. These matters would later come back to haunt Greene and his widow, Catherine Greene, but at the time Wayne was sure that "a calamity [was] avoided that appeared to us dreadful, and order, discipline and control restored" among American soldiers, who were again being fed.[37]

Not only near-mutiny in the army but a last-minute military assignment from General Greene delayed Wayne's plans for a quick departure from the South in early 1783. Since by April he had recovered his health to the point of being able to lead an army in the field, Greene prevailed upon him to march south into Georgia with a small cavalry force and Major Joseph Habersham's infantry to protect that state from threatened enemy incursions from Florida. When he arrived, it became clear to him immediately that no such incursions were forthcoming, and so to improve his time he proceeded on to Augusta, where he intended "to meet the Creeks, Cherokees, and other Indians in treaty. . .with Commissioners from Georgia, North and South Carolina," in hopes of ending the vicious border warfare that had been conducted by the tribes for the last few years and which showed no sign of abating, despite the fact that the Indians' erstwhile ally, Britain, was on the verge of making peace with America. When the Indians refused to join Wayne's pow-wow, he could only return empty-handed to Savannah, with nothing to show for his foray into diplomacy.[38]

Through June and July of 1783, General Wayne concluded the last of his military and civil duties in the South and made ready to return home. Regarding army matters, it now only remained for him to write Governor Lyman Hall of Georgia a final, formal note that his duty in that state was at an end; to return to Charleston and assist Greene in demobilizing the Continental Army as Congress had directed; and to see his own veteran Pennsylvanians on board transports that he had arranged previously with Governor John Dickinson of Pennsylvania to provide for their return to the North. Turning to his personal affairs, he paid a last visit to his rice plantation, Richmond, and spent some time putting the estate into operation by attempting to purchase slaves to work the place. Because he did not have clear title to the land as yet, he had to finance his plans by drawing upon his capital in Pennsylvania and by borrowing money from people in that state. To Jonathan Penrose, a relative of Polly's, and to John Nesbit, a Philadelphia merchant, he had earlier made application for loans, using as collateral his future army pay and money owed him by the state of Georgia. For some reason, these loans did not go through and he was consequently unable to "procure Negroes to work Richmond." Hence, as the time drew near for him to depart Georgia, he made plans to leave his estate under the watchful care of a friend, William Gibbons, who had volunteered for this service. With all his business conducted, Anthony Wayne returned once more to Charleston and on July 27, 1783, took passage on a transport from that city, bound for the Delaware River.[39]

CHAPTER *ix*

Politics and Debt
1783–1786

GENERAL WAYNE'S welcome home confirmed for him Robert Morris's earlier assurance that "The Laurels you have gathered in the Southern Swamps will bear our Frosts,"[1] for he was lionized by everyone in Philadelphia and the surrounding counties of eastern Pennsylvania. Besides Morris, Richard and Sally Robinson Peters, Stewart, Irvine, Rush, Hartley, Johnston, Governor Dickinson, Delany, and even St. Clair tried to outdo each other in the joyousness of their greetings. Wayne also was delighted to get reacquainted with his thirteen-year-old daughter, Margaretta, and his young son, Isaac, and he was happy to embrace his wife Polly and his aging mother in gladness at returning home safely. While the record is silent on this matter, in all likelihood he also made haste as soon as decently possible to visit his most ardent love interest, Mary Vining, who still held social court in Wilmington and Philadelphia.

Given the weakened state of Wayne's constitution by late 1783, it was not surprising that all the excitements of the past few months — his demobilization of the army in the South, his sea voyage home, his roisterous welcome by friends and loved ones — led to another gravely serious bout with his now-chronic malady. Shortly after he arrived in Philadelphia, as he told Joseph Habersham in a letter of October 1, he was forced to bed with agues and "bilious Vomiting" which "nearly made my Quietus," and to James Jackson on the same day he wrote with black humor, "A very troublesome fellow — commonly known by the name of Death took the liberty to call frequently at my Quarters to know

186

if I was ready for *payment*, my friends were of Opinion that the *bond* would not be due until some 33 or 40 years hence, notwithstanding their opinion the fellow continued an Importunate din until a Certain Doct. Jones Issued a Nolle Proseque & I have just obtained a Habeas Corpus for my Liberation from my Chamber, to which I have been confined for Seven Weeks i.e. Forty two days or 1008 Hours." From the ravages of this "D——d fever" he recovered, but slowly, over the next several weeks.[2]

But not even life-threatening disease could deter Wayne in 1783 from yielding to a growing lust for easy fortune as a Georgia rice planter. Despite his decision in July to depart the banks of the Savannah, half his heart and most of his head were still there with his beloved Richmond. He now promised Habersham that Georgia would be his home for the next winter, "if the *Curly heads* can be procured at any reasonable rate," and he asked a number of his friends in the state to buy slaves for him if they could be found in a market that was suffering inflation in prices because of a scarcity of slaves for purchase. Finally, in the fall of 1783, he received a letter form one of his agents, James Penman, telling him that even "common field Negroes" were fetching £50–£70 if bought with cash, even more if acquired on credit. These astronomical prices, confirmed in a note from Habersham, were simply beyond Wayne's ability to pay, and he decided that without laborers to work his land it was useless to return to Georgia any time soon. Therefore, despite his continuing efforts throughout the winter of 1783–84 not only to buy slaves from James Budden in Barbados but also to secure a government job as Commissioner of Indians in Georgia — that he might be financed by the taxpayers when he moved there — Wayne finally was compelled in May 1784 to write Gibbons, instructing him to rent the estate "for a year or two."[3]

Meanwhile, Wayne continued to serve as a general in the fast-disappearing Continental Army, doing the few martial tasks that still remained to him before his retirement from the service. In October, when it finally no longer mattered, he was promoted major general by Congress, an increase in rank that rankled as much as it pleased, coming as it did so many years after he had assumed the duties and responsibilities of that office. With Leonard Cecil, a Savannah merchant, he settled a debt accumulated by his Pennsylvania officers during the war by paying it out of his own pocket and billing it to Congress — although he did not expect to be reimbursed unless "the Public shows more gratitude than at present" toward its military (an indication that he did not believe the army was being treated fairly as it was demobilized). In early December, while he lay sick at Waynesborough with a new ailment, gout, he learned from Delany that General Washington was in Philadelphia for a visit, as the commander in chief wended his way home to Mount Vernon at the war's end. Wayne wrote to Washington on the fourteenth, "Long want of health occasioned by the extreme of fatigue and loss of blood in assisting to vindicate the rights and Liberties of America from her Coldest to her hottest Sun deprives me of the honor and pleasure of attending your Excellency." In reply, Washington expressed regret at not seeing his old comrade, whom he had come to appreciate as an officer only slightly inferior in ability to Greene, Knox, and Lafayette, and invited him to visit Mount Vernon.[4]

Although all his visiting, travel, and military duty in the fall of 1783 had worn Wayne down physically, he immediately entered the roiling politics of his native state. It was one thing to write his friend Rush in December 1782 that he had no interest in such things, quite another to avoid their temptation once he reached Philadelphia, and his friends were delighted that he would join them in their struggles against the Yellow Whigs and the Constitution of 1776. As Wayne told Francis Johnston in September, "I had long determined in my own mind, never to put it into the power of the public to Insult me more" by running for office. Yet, he recognized that there existed "a Crisis in which the future happiness, or Misery of the Citizens of this State stands suspended." Hence, he was willing to offer himself as a candidate for the Council of Censors, a group whose purpose it was to preserve the constitution inviolate or suggest needed revisions.[5]

The Pennsylvania political campaigns of October 1783 were bitter, rancorous affairs, pitting as they did the growing power of the anti-constitution conservatives — or Republicans, as they styled themselves — against the more democratic supporters of the basic law. That the Republican party, to which Wayne naturally belonged, now had more strength than before was due to the fact that a large number of army officers had joined its ranks and that the demobilized soldiers were expected to vote for these men, both because the officers were more sympathetic to their demands for equity in demobilization and because they respected their former commanders. After a campaign full of personal abuse on all sides, on election day Wayne, though still unwell, arose from his bed to "organize" the soldiers' vote in Philadelphia. His tactics, blunt but effective, were simply to corral all the troops he could find on the streets and march them to the State House to vote en masse. The election judges found this procedure highly irregular and demanded that Wayne receive a ruling from Pennsylvania's Chief Justice Thomas McKean on whether it was legal before they would allow his compatriots to cast their ballots. Since McKean was out of town, and since Attorney General William Bradford refused to venture a judgment on the matter, the soldiers became restive, and some of their officers began to curse the judges. At that point, "Wayne declared that his men would vote," and the judges, a bit frightened, relented, allowing all the soldiers to cast their ballots ahead of citizens who had queued up at the polling place in the meantime.[6]

Whether Wayne's getting out the soldiers' vote was crucial to the outcome of the election is not clear, but the Republicans did win a majority of the Assembly seats, as well as places on the Council of Censors. To the latter body Wayne was elected, along with St. Clair, Irvine, Frederick Muhlenberg, Thomas FitzSimmons, and other leaders of "respectability," but the radicals also elected John Whitehall, John Smiley, William Findley, and similar competent people. Thus, while the membership of the Council gave Wayne and the anticonstitution men a majority, they did not have the two-thirds needed to conduct business to their liking, and before long it would become apparent to the frustrated conservatives that though they were tantalizingly close to extirpating the existing constitution of Pennsylvania, they still had a bruising political battle ahead to carry out their design.[7]

On November 10, the Council of Censors, with Wayne present, met in Philadelphia and commenced its work. The Republican majority immediately flexed its muscles by electing one of its own, Muhlenberg, to preside over the meetings and then began appointing committees to examine certain problems with which it must deal. The most important of these committees, as far as the Republicans were concerned, was one empowered to study whether the constitution needed revisions. Wayne was appointed to this committee on the nineteenth along with a majority of Republican colleagues, and over the next six weeks he met with his fellow conservatives (except when he was too ill to drag himself from bed) to hammer out recommendations on how to alter the constitution. At last, on January 2, 1784, the committee concluded its work and requested the whole Council vote in favor of recommending its work to the Assembly. The members' work had indeed been prodigious and their proposed constitutional changes vast, for they were calling for a more powerful chief executive, a two-house legislature, an independent judiciary, and many other things that if incorporated would transform the basic law and the government that operated under its aegis into instrumentalities considerably less amenable to democratic influence.[8]

Wayne was delighted with the results of his committee's work, as were his friends Rush, St. Clair, Delany, Irvine, and all other conservatives both in and out of government. The general was even more pleased when the full Council voted by twelve to ten to "recommend" that the Assembly amemd the basic document in all the ways the Republicans wished. The proconstitution minority of Censors, however, protested vehemently against these proceedings, asserting that they were illegal because they did not have the sanction of two-thirds of the membership, as the present constitution required. To the minority argument, the Republicans only replied piously that they were giving the Assembly information to allow it "to judge upon a matter, you and we, and all our posterity are so deeply interested in." After all, as they noted, when the old constitution was written, five thousand citizens were absent, serving in the army, and their sage counsel was sorely missed. Furthermore, "let it not be said, that the constitution has carried us triumphantly through a parlous war; this is far from being the case." The *people* had supported the army, *despite* the constitution, and the *people* now, represented by the Assembly, could exercise their sovereignty to rewrite the state's basic law. "Nothing," declared the anticonstitutionalists, "can be obligatory on you which is contrary to your inclinations." (Thus did the Republicans of Pennsylvania propound in 1784 a theory of popular sovereignty in support of constitutional change that later was echoed powerfully in arguments for altering the Articles of Confederation.)[9]

In private, Wayne was not optimistic about Republican chances for effecting constitutional reform. In February 1784, he wrote, "We have been laboriously engaged in framing a Constitution for this State upon the Principles of the Bill of Rights in which we meet with such opposition from *Caitiffs* of such obscure origin that even their very names were never known in Pennsa. until within this year or two then only as the Insignificant tools of party — but with all their Insignificance their Sullen *NO* will probably (by the absurdity of our Constitution) prevent the calling of a Convention. . . . I am tired of it & all Civil Politicks." Wayne's forebodings were justified, for the Assembly refused to act upon the report of the Censors. Moreover, by July 1784, his party, because of a series of unrelated personnel changes, had become a minority on the Council, and George Bryan, leader of the proconstitution Censors, managed to garner a vote of fifteen to four *against* any changes in the basic law. An apoplectic Wayne fumed after this vote, "if after all this time, we are to be *shackled* with a Constitution, that must from Its nature Degenerate into a *tyranny* — In vain have we *fought* — in vain have we *bled*." Fortunately for him, given his present state of mind, the general did not know that Bryan's brilliant political maneuvers against him and the other Republicans had in fact assured that the Constitution of 1776 would survive for another seven years.[10]

While the pro- and anticonstitution factions battled each other in the Council of Censors about the basic charter of the state, they also carped at each other about whether one clique or the other had been legally voted into office. In December 1783, it was the proconstitution people who protested, declaring that Wayne was guilty of illegal election practices. Irvine wrote to Wayne, who was abed at Waynesborough with the gout, "The Election business is under examination. There is no danger of finishing it too soon," and Wayne ought to hurry to Philadelphia. Delany also sent a similar letter, noting that Wayne should be in the Council to defend himself when the matter came to a head. But Wayne was in no hurry, for as he wrote Irvine on December 9, he would only be well enough to "*hobble* into Council on this day week," and meantime Irvine, who was now a "Senator," must procrastinate, like a good politician, until the general was able to appear. Irvine, declared Wayne, should get out of his soldierly manner of doing things directly, for, after all, "False insinuations" made by a "disappointed junto" were nothing to cause one to rush about. In any case, when he did arrive, he could "elucidate the business" to everyone's satisfaction.[11]

Wayne's confidence in the outcome of the investigation was based upon two things, a certainty that he was innocent and an equal certainty that the then-existent Republican majority on the Council would vindicate him. Consequently, when the case was finally settled on February 28, 1784, he was not surprised to learn that the Censors could find no evidence to warrant his opponents' charges and that all their assertions were therefore considered groundless. But these proceedings, despite their almost inevitable outcome, had damaged Wayne's reputation and, to a degree, the Republican cause. Hence, it behooved the conservatives to go on the offensive and charge their proconstitution opponents with illegalities at the ballot box in order to take the heat off themselves. "Persons of vile and profligate character," declared the Republicans righteously, had imposed themselves "upon the people" by abusing Pennsylvania's election laws, and they insisted upon a full-blown hearing before the Council of Censors upon the matter. Their case was heard, but not before the Council had fallen under the overwhelming domination of the radicals, including Bryan. The decision, therefore, went against Wayne and his conservative friends — as they no doubt expected that it would.[12]

By 1784, factionalism within the Council of Censors affected another important issue, the way the Pennsylvania Assembly was handling the Wyoming Valley case. The Wyoming Valley of western Pennsylvania, originally settled by people from Connecticut under auspices of the Susquehannah Company, was until 1782 claimed by both Pennsylvania and Connecticut, but in that year a federal court had ruled that the territory belonged to Pennsylvania. At the same time, however, the court ruled that all Connecticut settlers living on the land must be confirmed in possession of their property titles. The Pennsylvania legislature, ignoring the latter part of the ruling (in some measure because Assembly members had land claims there), ordered state militia into the valley to drive the Connecticut settlers away. When the Susquehannah Company militarily supported the colonists, a civil war resulted, and the whole incident threatened to cause Connecticut to renew her claims to the region. The Council of Censors, now under the control of Bryan and indignant at the Assembly for its "lack of wisdom & foresight" in handling the Wyoming Valley problem, voted fourteen to seven to censure that body and to insist that it act with due regard for national law. On the same day, the Council also demanded by about the same vote that the Assembly send it forthwith certain documents it needed in order to learn more about how the affair was being handled.[13]

Wayne and the Republicans refused their assent to both these measures, declaring that the Council majority was giving unmerited censure to the government's handling of the federal ruling. Besides, they noted gratuitously, the Assembly's bad law would not have been enacted anyway had not the constitution been written to allow a minority of the people to rule. Explicating his own position, Wayne declared in a letter to William Irvine that the Council of Censors was acting in a disgusting manner, harping constantly at the legislature but saying nothing about the weakness of the executive or the way taxes were collected. His

Republican minority of Censors, he noted virtuously, had already declared the proconstitution majority to be violators of the constitution and unfaithful guardians of the people's rights. Now they were also going to hold them up as repudiators of the Articles of Confederation and perpetrators of civil war with Connecticut. (That both these charges were *precisely* what the majority of Censors had justly accused the Assembly of doing seemed to have escaped Wayne entirely.) Finally, said the general, his Censor colleagues' majority actions, especially their "sending a *mandamus* to [the Assembly] Demanding in the name and by the Authority of the *People* of *Pennsylvania*" certain documents "without delay equivocation or excuse," had effected a permanent rupture with the poorly used Assemblymen. But the peremptory demand, he noted with vicious satisfaction, had been thrown under the table by the legislators, who recognized the document for what it was, mere campaign propaganda for the upcoming election.[14]

Wayne by late 1784 had become so embroiled in angry confrontation with his radical political enemies on the Council that he had entirely lost sight of justice and, most likely, the opinions of a majority of Pennsylvanians. For the citizenry was angry with the Assembly for the way it was handling the Wyoming affair and supported the Council majority. As for Wayne himself, he began to perceive that his seat on the Council of Censors was giving him no leverage in politics to carry out his cherished desire to efface the constitution of its democratic heresies. In fact, his constant bickering with the majority—especially on matters in which that majority acted according to the will of the polity—was only undermining his chances of achieving any other of his political aims. Therefore, in late 1784, he gave up on the Council and turned his attention toward the Assembly itself, where he hoped a broader field of activity might present itself, even if he were in a minority and hated the government's structure under the Constitution of 1776. In October, he presented himself as a candidate for the Assembly in Chester County and was returned without difficulty to that body, where he served two one-year terms with some distinction.[15]

One issue that had exercised General Wayne's attention since before the Pennsylvania line had left the South in 1783 and one he doggedly pursued as a legislator, was making sure that the soldiers received justice for their hard service from the Yellow Whigs in the Assembly. From Governor John Dickinson in January 1783, he had received a warm expression of regard for the Pennsylvania line and a request that Wayne advise him on how the state could assist the army during the demobilization. In April, Wayne had replied to this message with gratitude and relief, for he was uneasy that the Assembly might give the army short shrift now that it was not needed — especially since he felt the legislators had not supported the line when it was fighting proximate enemy armies. Then in May, Dickinson had assured Wayne that the state fully intended to show its soldiers that it "was worthy of being. . .Serv'd and Saved," and Wayne began to relax into a quiet assurance that dislike of the military was on the ebb in his native state. At that point, however, civil-military tensions were reenlivened because of a mutiny among unpaid Pennsylvania soldiers at Lancaster, which so cowed the Congress (as St. Clair informed Wayne later) that it had fled to Princeton.[16]

Therefore, when Wayne entered civil politics in the fall of 1783, he found in many circles of Pennsylvania society a greater chill toward the military than had ever before existed. The poor soldiers, who had sacrificed more than any other segment of the population in the fight against Britain, were mustered out of the service with one-tenth the money that was due them (two shillings instead of the twenty they were owed). As for the officers, they had trouble holding the state to its legal obligation of half-pay, which was enacted in March 1779, and on September 2, with Wayne's support, they sent the Assembly a petition demanding their just reward for services rendered. When no action was forthcoming on this memorial, Wayne wrote George Gray, speaker of the Assembly in February 1784, prodding the recalcitrant legislators to do justice for Pennsylvania's officers. But the legislature, though dominated by a Republican majority, remained somnolent upon this matter during the next few months.[17]

More galling by far to Wayne and his officer friends than the lack of financial reward from the state was the continuing feeling among many of their fellow citizens that the soldiery within their own state was a greater danger to society than external enemies and must be gotten rid of root and branch. This attitude especially angered the soldiers — not least because it now also infected more moderate politicians — for from their perspective they were the sole repository of virtue and justice — those very ideals for which the Revolutionary War was fought — and the other Whigs were Janus-faced hypocrites when they blathered about the "dangers" of a "standing army." At best, the politicians were merely using their silly rhetoric as an excuse to get out of their obligations, and at worst many of them were antirepublican demagogues bent on using the army as a foil to increase their own political stranglehold on the government by preserving intact the "monstrous" Constitution of 1776. It was in this tense atmosphere that quarrels broke out in Pennsylvania directly after the war over the aims of army officers in organizing the Society of the Cincinnati, a fraternity of military men created to preserve the high ideals of the Revolution and to pass on these ideals to their male heirs. General Wayne, who in October 1783 was elected vice-president of the Pennsylvania chapter (St. Clair was president), was in the midst of these rhetorical battles.[18]

To his old colleague, William Irvine, Wayne in May 1784 unleashed a torrent of indignation against those perpetrators of self-serving animus toward the army (as he saw it) that had caused him and his colleagues to suffer such grievous psychic wounds over the past few years. "The revolution in America," he said "is an event, that will fill the brightest pages of history to the end of time; & the conduct of her Officers & Soldiers will be handed down to the latest ages as a model of Virtue, perseverance & bravery — the smallness of their numbers, & the unparalled [*sic*] hardships & excess of difficulties & dangers that they have encountered in the defence of their Country, from her *coldest* to her *hotest Sun*: — places them in a point of view hurtful to the eyes of the leaders of *faction* & *party*, who possessed neither the virtue nor fortitude to meet the enemy in the field." Because the people yet paid "involuntary deference. . .to their protectors & Deliverers," continued Wayne, the envious politicians "seize with audacity every pretext, to deprecate the merits of those who have filled the breach & bled at every pore. . .The Hottentots hold that after killing a good man, the *Assassin* possesses his soul — if the leaders of faction have adopted this Idea I could almost forgive them for their own are D——n bad." The republics of Greece and Rome, he asserted, "furnish precedent innumerable for them to go upon, & the Order of *Cincinnati* was a favorable opening for them to enter" and to prejudice the minds of a people who "have been put in possession of *extreme* of liberty at too cheap a rate." Therefore, declared Wayne, these same citizens were now about "to *wipe* off the large debt due to the army, with a *Sponge* — an attempt to strike off the commutation was made at the last *Sessions*. . .by the Land Office bill." Wayne thus saw the military citizen of Pennsylvania being treated in the immediate postwar period, and even three years later he still bitterly complained that his state was "as devoid of *Justice*, as she is of *Gratitude*."[19]

When he entered the Assembly in October 1784, Wayne continued to argue in favor of the soldiers, but with little success. As time went on, he turned to other matters, and it was not long before he was speaking out loudly in opposition to Pennsylvania's continuing disenfranchisement of citizens who had declined during the war to take a test oath in support of the state against Great Britain. These oaths, which had been refused not only by loyalists but also by Quakers, neutrals, and pacifists of various political shadings, effectively kept one-half of the entire population from exercising the franchise. It was the philosophical view of Wayne and some other Republicans that these people had been punished enough for their refusal to support the war against Britain and ought to be reincorporated into the polity. That as a practical matter the disenfranchised could be expected to lend their political support to the conservative cause was also a consideration in Wayne's thinking. Therefore, in December 1784, he introduced in the Assembly a resolution "admitting all persons as Citizens who have not been active or criminal in opposition to the liberties of the State."[20]

This bill, Wayne's first major attempt at drafting legislation in a parliamentary body, went down to overwhelming defeat at the hands of the radicals, who in the elections of October 1784 had retaken control of the Assembly. In reaction, the general petulantly introduced another bill in January 1785, that would free these disenfranchised persons from paying taxes, but that one, too, was repudiated. Then, in a more serious mood, Wayne two months later collected his wits and his conservative constituency to introduce legislation setting up a committee to examine the justice of denying jury duty for those who had not sworn a test oath. Although this measure was enacted, the committee that was appointed to study the matter was dominated by radicals, who declared that the state had every right to deny jury duty to those who refused the oath and who successfully recommended to the Assembly that the law remain as it was written. A tenacious Wayne hung on to this issue, and in November 1786 he reintroduced his original legislation, asking that presently disenfranchised Pennsylvanians be freed from all political strictures and incorporated as full-fledged citizens into the body politic. With the support this time of Benjamin Franklin and other powerful statesmen, his legislation was enacted on December 13, despite continuing radical opposition, and all men of the state who had not voluntarily sided with Britain during the war were once more given full rights of citizenship.[21]

Next to the struggle over the elimination of test oaths, Wayne's remaining service in the Assembly paled into insignificance, although he was active in some other areas. One matter of legislative politics in October 1785, which was pleasant for him but did not succeed, was Robert Morris's attempt to secure his election as speaker of the Assembly. Undaunted by this inevitable defeat in a body dominated by political and ideological opponents, Wayne in November proposed to his colleagues — and got accepted — the appointment of a committee to study the possibility of declaring the Susquehanna and other rivers to be public highways and improving them at state expense. Also, he proposed that the same committee look into the possibility of building a canal, in cooperation with Maryland and Delaware, between Chesapeake Bay and the Delaware River. Eleven days later, the committee reported favorably on both these measures, and the Assembly empowered the Executive Council to begin carrying them into execution. However, another proposal of Wayne's, that a ban on the theater in Philadelphia be lifted, ran into serious trouble. "We are endeavouring to Introduce the tolerance of a theatre," he wrote, "But in this we have fail'd," for the Quakers and radicals "joined force against us, & by their sullen No dismissed the Bill." Although Wayne made what he thought was a potent argument in favor of the measure — that "if we have plays in Philadelphia, it may induce Congress to return to this city" (that body was still in Princeton) — his strictures to the Assemblymen were greeted, according to some observers, with jeers and raucous laughter from the galleries.[22]

While Wayne labored in Philadelphia with his various political projects, he did not neglect his social life. Although he found it difficult to adjust to the coldness of Philadelphia's winters after the "warmth of the climate in Georgia," he had "taken time by the forelock" and toasted his city's "winter amusements," visiting "the Ladies at all hours" and going to "routs Balls Assemblies & ca. & ca," so that "the body & mind are kept in such a whirl of pleasure dissipation & Intoxication as almost to preclude every serious Idea." Mused Wayne, "was it not for the habitual abstinence, fortitude & virtue which. . .I possess — I really believe I might be in danger, as the politeness of the *Ministers* Citizens & ca. afford me but too fine an access to their fascinating amusements, for the benefit of my health." Yet not all his free time was taken up with frivolity, for he occasionally visited Polly, his children, and his relatives at Easttown. Additionally, he had serious moments for recollection of old friendships, such as when he and the Pennsylvania officers, in August 1784, paid their respects to Lafayette, who stayed for a time in

Philadelphia while on a visit to America, and in November 1785, when he wrote his old colleague, Von Steuben, a warm letter of remembrance.[23]

As Wayne worked and played in Pennsylvania through the years 1784 and 1785, he also kept a constant eye upon important family and business affairs. That his and Polly's standard of living was comfortable if not extravagant during these years is attested by the general's business records, which show that he received income from his farm, from interest on the military certificates, from one or two rental properties in Philadelphia, and from a lease upon his Georgia estate (from the Nova Scotia lands he drew no profit). When it suited his pleasure, he dabbled in farming Waynesborough from time to time, but he did not need to in order to make a living and therefore (wisely) usually left that pursuit to his much more successful wife and various overseers. His primary personal expenses during these years were for clothes, lodging, travel expenses, and fine horses; he also had to pay sizable sums in taxes upon his numerous properties. All in all, Wayne's economic affairs in the three years directly after the war were sound and orderly, with expenditures never exceeding income, and with no apparent reason why this pleasant situation should not endure throughout the years of life that yet remained to him and Polly Wayne.[24]

The agreeable scene, however, was not to endure, for Wayne was tempted during the last half of the 1780s into business speculations in Georgia on such a vast scale that he was thrown deeply into debt and came near to being completely ruined financially. His estate on the Savannah River, Richmond, to which he secured clear title in August 1786, contained 1,300 acres of prime rice swamps, capable of producing in a good year of full operation about 800–1,000 barrels of high-grade rice, worth 2,400 to 3,000 guineas. He now intended to put this farm into full operation. But to make the estate profitable, the general must spend enormous sums of money to procure slaves for working the labor-intensive crop, to repair dikes, and to make other improvements in order to get the farm into operation. Since Wayne had already learned that slaves were in short supply after the war and that the prices he must pay to procure them would be vast, he must needs secure large sums of capital to finance the commencement of rice growing at Richmond. His first attempts at borrowing money, in 1783, had come to nought, for the American economy directly after the Revolution was in a blighted condition, and not only Wayne but everyone else found it extremely difficult to secure venture capital.[25]

In 1784, Wayne's mind was fertile with ideas about how he might lay his hands on money without too much risk, that he might join the planter aristocracy of Georgia and escape from a climate which he said was harsh enough during the winter to freeze ink in his pen before he could write a sentence. His first idea, as he told a Georgia friend, Roger P. Saunders, was to "dispose of part of my real property in this State [Pennsylvania] in order to Settle *that* upon the Savannah River." When that expedient failed, for the simple reason that no one would offer to buy Waynesborough at a price he considered reasonable, Wayne was compelled to try once more to borrow money. Still cautious about, risking too much upon the prospects of rice growing, he hesitated to offer as collateral either his farm in Chester County or his Georgia estate (the Nova Scotia lands were nowhere near valuable enough to offer as collateral on a large loan). Thus he was left with only one large item of valuable property to offer, the land certificates given him by the state of Pennsylvania for his wartime services. Although he tried to borrow money from his friend and neighbor, George Emlen, by using these depreciated certificates as surety, Emlen rejected Wayne's terms by noting that the certificates, while worth $16,000 on their face, were at that time selling at a ninety percent discount.[26]

Thus was Wayne finally forced into accepting a mortgage on one of his properties in order to secure capital — if he could find anyone with money to loan even on the strength of this collateral. It was at this point that he learned (probably from his friend Robert Morris) that he might be able to negotiate a loan with a firm of Dutch merchants, Messrs. Willem and Jan Willink, in Amsterdam, for these men, who had bought large numbers of American securities during the war, were still speculating in this country and might be interested in taking one more risk by advancing money to Wayne. As a consequence, Wayne prevailed upon Peter John Van Berkle, minister of the Netherlands to the United States, to assist him in negotiating with the Willinks, and with Van Berkle's backing — plus Robert Morris's hearty endorsement — wrote the Dutch merchants in January 1785, requesting a loan of 50,000 florins (which in English currency was about equal to 5,000 guineas), at the same time sending them the deed to Waynesborough as collateral. Even before he received a reply to this request, he optimistically assumed that the Dutch loan was as good as secured and upon that basis began preparations for the following year's rice planting by writing Saunders, Fishbourn, and William Gibbons, Jr., to ask that they purchase slaves for him and "stock" Richmond with other necessities for farming.[27]

Throughout the early months of 1785, Wayne awaited news from Amsterdam about the certification of his loan and made plans to visit Georgia for a few months to settle his business affairs in the South. Although his departure from the Delaware was delayed during January and February because his ship froze in ice on the river, at last in March he made his escape from friends and family and sailed for Charleston. After a short visit in that town, he booked passage on the Georgia packet, and with ample supplies of ham, cider, and other foodstuffs that he had accumulated for future consumption before going aboard, moved on to Savannah. There he was welcomed by numerous acquaintances, such as Fishbourn, who on July 4, 1785, threw a gala party for him and former army officers, where occurred "every demonstration of joy befitting the sons of freedom"; Catherine and Nathanael Greene, now settled on their splendid estate, Mulberry Grove, where the transplanted Rhode Island Quaker grew rice and corn in pleasant quietude; and all the merchant crowd with whom Wayne was soon to have such extensive — and often unpleasant — business dealings.[28]

At Richmond, Wayne found much work in progress, for overseers employed by Saunders were directing forty-seven Negroes in repairing banks, ditches, and canals to send water where it was needed. Saunders had purchased these workers the previous winter through Edward Penman, a broker in Charleston, who had arranged a deal with their owner, Samuel Potts of Southampton Plantation in Georgia. The total cost of the slaves had come to £3,307.10s, £1,000 of this to be paid in cash and the remainder in five yearly installments, with interest, and Wayne considered the deal reasonable. To cover the costs of these "servants," Wayne had notified the Willinks while in Charleston that he was writing three bills against them, amounting to 5,500 florins, payable to Penman's agent, Philip Jacob Cohen of Charleston. But the farm was in such wretched repair after years of neglect that even forty-seven workers were too few to get the fields ready for a crop in 1785, and Wayne wrote Delany an imploring letter to hire a good ditcher for him in Pennsylvania and to send on twenty-four ditching shovels. Delany responded to these instructions in August by notifying Wayne that it would be late fall before most of the tools could be procured and shipped. Wayne, therefore, twiddled his fingers in enforced idleness at Richmond while anxiously watching his bills mount and his only potential source of income to pay them off — a rice crop — recede farther into the future. One consolation for him, however, was a chatty letter from Margaretta, containing a request that he procure for her "a negro girl"; "I think," said the fifteen-year-old that "7 is a very proper age," and would he be so obliging as to bring her this helpmeet when he returned to Pennsylvania. (He did not.)[29]

Anthony Wayne was nothing if not an optimist, for even while the Richmond venture was far from flourishing, he expanded his landhold-ings in Georgia. Some time during the previous months, he had learned that a thousand-acre tract of land, named the Hazzard Patent, in south-ern Georgia at the head of navigation on the Satilla River, was in possession of the state and might be given away to some deserving patriot. Through careful manipulation of his political friendships in the state, he managed to convince the legislature that he was the man, and consequently that body granted him clear title to the property, which in July 1785 he visited. Charmed by his new property, Wayne in a letter to Delany pronounced it "second to none," but as he had discovered on his trip, it was being "nibbled at" by surveyors, and he indignantly wrote Governor Samuel Elbert to request that the government put a halt to this piracy. Apparently, the Assembly acted favorably to his plea, for the following summer he resurveyed the land and afterwards, until his death, retained this vast tract inviolate of debt — and of workman's boot.[30]

In August 1785, Wayne concluded that he could do no more at Richmond for the moment, and after giving management of his south-ern affairs into the hands of a friend, James Moore, he sailed northward to Pennsylvania. By this time, he had reduced his financial situation to such utter chaos that the blunders of the summer of 1785 would hound him for years to come. The source of his problem was not hard to find, and was entirely of his own making, for in spite of the fact that he had done nothing more than apply to Willem and Jan Willink for a loan, and that the Dutch merchants had written him in March that they had not yet approved his application because of unsettled politics in Europe and because they were not convinced that his loan was worth the risk, *he began to draw upon them as though they had*. The previous June, he had billed the Willinks for 5,500 florins, and in August and September, *after the merchants had written him again in July warning him that the loan had still not been approved*, he blithely informed them that he was drawing upon them again for three more bills, worth 14,088 florins in all, to be accounted to William Harris, James Penman (Edward Penman's cousin, who was pushing Edward for repayment of obligations and thereby creating problems for Wayne), and Cohen. Wayne was asking Cohen this time for money from the Willinks for payment of a debt to Adam Tunno, another man from whom he had recently purchased more slaves.[31]

When Wayne arrived in Philadelphia, he continued to struggle with his growing (self-imposed) financial difficulties. Although he continued to assure the Penmans, Potts, Cohen, and Tunno that their money soon would be forthcoming from the Willinks, his creditors began to get suspicious of Wayne's financial solvency when their "bills from Amsterdam" against the Dutch merchants began to bounce. Wayne, trying once more with the same fruitless result as the year before to borrow money from his neighbor, Emlen, on the strength of his certificates, then pleaded desperately, but futilely, with Samuel Howell to buy the certificates, so he could (as he gamely said), "dispose of a few debts." (Few indeed; only about 2,500 guineas, as he estimated to Delany nine months later.) Then he attempted to negotiate a loan with Thomas Willing, a prominent Philadelphian, for £3,000, using the same certificates as collateral but with equally bootless results. And as if these setbacks were not bad enough, he received word in the late fall of 1785 from Willem and Jan Willink that they had as yet made no final decision on whether to grant him a loan but that until they did they would continue to refuse his drafts.[32]

Wayne was now enmeshed in a frightful web of economic disaster. Owed huge sums by Pennsylvania for his wartime services, owner of vast, rich rice lands in Georgia, which if he could farm adequately would make him rich within a decade, he could not get his hands on a single shilling of capital to finance the operations necessary to extricate him from penury and "establish a permanent support for my family." The many slaves he had purchased from Potts and Tunno upon the strength of the Dutch "loan," even if that deal had stood, were not enough to work the soil to its full potential, and he had already lost one whole crop simply in trying to repair Richmond and get it ready for sowing in 1786. Now he faced the danger that his creditors would demand their money for the slaves and when it was not forthcoming, attach Richmond or Waynesborough or both, rather then merely reclaiming their "property." Sure enough, Philip Jacob Cohen, Edward Penman, and other creditors were soon informing him that he must take measures immediately to cover the debts for which the Willinks refused to reimburse them. Wayne wrote soothing letters to these men, assuring them that while there were a few technical snags holding up completion of his loan in Amsterdam, he was certain that they would have the drafts accepted in due time. Meanwhile, he said, he appreciated their patience and promised to pay the interest punctually.[33]

Actually, Wayne was not sanguine at all, by December 1785, that he could ever get a loan from the Willinks, and his promises to creditors were nothing more than a diversionary tactic to gain time. While his bargaining position with the creditors may have appeared weak under superficial analysis, he did in fact hold one trump card in the fact that both he and they knew that a foreclosure on his estate, given the present economic climate, would be as much a disaster for creditor as for debtor. Land was so cheap in those years that it could hardly be given away, much less sold, and the men who had taken Wayne's word that the Dutch loan was secure — when in fact it was not — could only wait to see if the untrustworthy general could make money in the future and get them all successfully out of a dreary economic mess. Wayne now wrote the Willinks a scathing letter, falsely accusing them of base business practices and demanding that they return the deed to Waynesborough, which he said they had deliberately held "after determining to protest my Bills" in order to make his economic problem work "doubly hard against me! " The fact was, as the merchants told Wayne in reply, they had not returned the deed because they were still trying to decide whether to grant him a loan. But his letter had certainly removed from their minds any remaining doubts as to the wisdom of granting his request, and consequently they were returning all his documents, including the deed and the applications he had sent them the year before. In July 1786, Wayne's lawyers in Philadelphia received the deed to Waynesborough, and since by then the general had returned to Georgia, they put it in safekeeping until he or a representative could retrieve it.[34]

While it was true that Wayne's stay in Philadelphia and Waynesborough during the winter of 1785–86 was troubled by financial crisis, he managed to divert his attention from his misfortunes by attending parties, talking with Mary Vining, and renewing old associations. In January 1786, he had the honor of being elected for a second time to the American Philosophical Society (the first had been during the Revolutionary War), and a month later he attended to some old business by having the musket ball that he had acquired during the Yorktown campaign of 1781 removed from his thigh, in hopes that this procedure would alleviate rheumatic symptoms in his leg. Feeling hale if not particularly hardy in April 1786, Wayne tried to forget his economic woes long enough to prepare for a return to Georgia, where he planned to spend as much time as he needed to get his finances in some order. He wrote his Waynesborough overseer, Henry Fox, detailed instructions for running that farm in the coming year, gave Delany his power of attorney to conduct his business affairs in Pennsylvania (especially those that pertained to his childrens' education), and departed once again for the South.[35]

Wayne's voyage to Savannah, as he later told Polly and Delany, took thirty tempestuous days, during which his "Capitol riding horse went over board in a Storm" and the entire ship almost went to the ocean's floor. When finally he did arrive at his destination, he had been ashore only fifteen minutes "When my faithful *white* Groom was drowned" in an accident, and his "Fixations of mind, & pains of body" had thrown him into a period where he "was scarcely capable of either writing or thinking." By June 18, his health and spirits had mended enough for him to instruct Delany to talk with friend Morris about the possibility of selling Waynesborough to clear his debts, and to inform Polly that she should visit with his mother from time to time and fill her in on what her son was doing. Also, he resumed his visits with the Greenes at Mulberry Grove, and rumors began to spread in the closeknit society of Georgia that Wayne's interest there was more with the witty, vivacious Catherine than his old military colleague. The stories were untrue, for tempted as Wayne might be by the flashing eyes and volatile liveliness of Mrs. Greene, he was not so lost to honor as to cuckold his closest friend — even had the lady cooperated, which she did not.[36]

Through many of his financial troubles of the past few years, Wayne had always taken comfort in the knowledge that, whatever evil may befall him, he could still take his leisure in company with his closest neighbor, grave and decent Nathanael Greene. It was with a dreadful shock, therefore, that he received news on the evening of June 19 that Greene was dying at Mulberry Grove. Hurrying to his friend's bedside, Wayne learned from Catherine Greene that she and her husband had been riding back from Savannah that afternoon in a carriage when Greene complained of a headache. Upon reaching home, she immediately put him to bed, and when his condition did not improve, she called in a physician, whose ministrations of blistering and bleeding did not help. Soon Greene's forehead swelled and he lapsed into a coma, and it was in this condition that Wayne found him. Stricken with grief, the Pennsylvanian sat by his friend's bedside until the end, and after Greene had breathed his last rose to compose a letter to Colonel Jackson in Savannah, asking him to take care of funeral arrangements. After Greene was buried, Wayne wrote his daughter about "the death of my long tried nearest & dearest friend & Neighbour, Major General Greene. It was in the society of yourself, Mrs. Greene & this great & good man," he told Margaretta (who had earlier expressed an interest in visiting Richmond), "that I had flattered myself with passing happy days on the banks of the Savannah." But no more could he look forward to these pleasant scenes, and their absence seemed to rob him of any further real ambition to become a rice planter. Although he bravely declared to his daughter that "brighter prospects are in view," he was fast losing interest in the vexing disorder surrounding his feeble attempts to attain the status of a landed southern gentleman.[37]

Throughout the summer of 1786 Wayne labored long and hard at making Richmond pay, and he diligently sought more capital, the item that was his key to success. From Delany, whom Wayne had empowered to take possession of the deed to Waynesborough, came news that inflation was so rampant in Pennsylvania that business confidence was shattered and he could secure no loan in that quarter. Wayne thereupon sent a memorial to the Georgia legislature, asking that it convey to him the remainder of the 4,000 guineas it had voted him in May 1782, to purchase an estate, since Richmond had not cost that entire amount. The solons treated this petition with a pointed silence, and soon Wayne was reduced to considering seriously a suggestion by his old friend Lafayette that he might join with John McQueen and Greene's son in dealing with lumber contracts. Wayne finally did not plunge into this venture, for by late summer of 1786, his economic prospects at Richmond seemed to be brightening. His rice crop was coming along, his overseer was competent, and he expected to make enough money that season to cover interest on the Penman-Potts-Tunno debts and to send Delany what he needed to pay for his children's education. As he told Delany without exaggeration two months later, if he could but get a loan of £4,000 he could quadruple the size of his crop and be entirely free of debt in only three years.[38]

Interspersed with his business of rice growing in 1786, General Wayne occasionally turned his attention to matters more or less interesting or important. In November, he was delighted to welcome into

Georgia society General Chevalier Dupleissis, a rich Frenchman who had fought with America in the Revolution, and who now had purchased an estate worth 10,000 guineas on the Savannah River near Richmond. The general, noted Wayne, had two "*very pretty*" daughters and "a *profusion* of the best choice of wines & *liqueres*," requisites enough, as far as Wayne was concerned, to bind him in fast friendship with the Marquis. On a more serious note, he watched with keen anxiety as Catherine Greene departed Georgia after her husband's death for a visit with relatives in New York. Writing her later about the "torpidity" into which he had been thrown by her leaving, he expressed sentiments bordering on love, even declaring that he had "petitioned involuntarily the supreme Governor of the Universe" to care for her. If his affection for Catherine Greene was strong, however, it was not because she encouraged him to expect from her more than a deep and abiding friendship, and as soon as he realized this fact, he kept their relationship, as it had been before Greene's death, upon that plane.[39]

As fall, then winter, came on during Wayne's long sojourn in Georgia, his rosy outlook of the previous August about his chances of success as a planter became progressively gloomier. First, he ran into delays in getting his small harvest ready for market because of the "Negro business [raids against maroon colonies of runaway slaves on the Savannah River] which consumed a week" and the sudden resignation of his overseer. Quickly he advertised in the *Georgia Gazette* for a new farm manager, and soon he had one, but meantime his bills piled up. Second, he promised Edward Penman payment of interest on his debts as soon as he could get rice ready for market, and he guaranteed to Houstoun thirty barrels to cover that man's claims, but neither creditor was placated, for each was agent for clients who in their own turn hounded Penman and Houstoun for financial satisfaction, and each insisted on seizing Wayne's *entire* crop. Pushed beyond endurance by these men, Wayne in late 1786 was threatening to abandon Richmond to his creditors. He lamented to Houstoun, "I wish to God that it had been in my power to have paid [you] fully, for rest assured, that I would make almost any sacrifice to be relieved from the *torture* of a debtor." This was, he groaned, "a Situation I never experienced until I set my foot in Georgia, & after the unfortunate contract with [Penman and Potts], which I have had abundant reason to wish had never taken place." Touching as this rendition was, noted Houstoun drily after receiving Wayne's tale of woe, it made no mention of the general's paying what he owed or of making any future arrangements to do so.[40] It was under these circumstances that General Wayne observed the end of his first full year as a rice planter, certainly not one of the more memorable seasons in a life which had seen many vicissitudes in fortune.

CHAPTER *X*

Redemption
1787–1792

BY EARLY 1787, it was at last plain to General Wayne that he could not make a success of rice planting at Richmond and that he must try to release himself of obligations to Penman, Potts, and Tunno by putting that estate into their hands on sacrificial terms. Therefore, he offered Potts a deal which he said no reasonable businessman could refuse, Richmond for 7,500 guineas, with Potts paying him the difference between what the farm was valued at and what Wayne still owed on the original debt in slaves at fifty guineas per head. If Potts would accept this arrangement, Wayne could still aspire to being a Georgia rice planter, for he could pay off Tunno for the slaves he had purchased from that man, move all his work force to his Hazzard Patent farm on the Satilla River and have labor adequate to the task of decent rice cultivation. Potts, as well as agent Penman, only scoffed at this offer, declaring that the last thing in the world they needed at that point was another piece of worthless Georgia land which they could not dispose of for their own debts. And when Wayne in June wrote them that the only other possible way he could dispose of the debt was through giving into their hands "a *paper* Certificate" from Pennsylvania, supposedly worth $16,000 on its face (but not, to be sure, as valuable as "Specie"), they were at the end of their patience with the general and began to consider legal action.[1]

In July 1787, Wayne decided that his presence in Georgia was no longer a necessity, and he returned to Philadelphia. This was a serious legal blunder, for by doing so he had laid himself open to a lawsuit by Penman, Potts, and Tunno for the sum of £3,600, their valuation of the remaining unpaid part of the original debt. To Penman, to his Georgia lawyer Aedanus Burke, and to Jasper Moylan, the creditors' attorney in Philadelphia, Wayne raged in August about "cruel" warrants and "extortionate" and "insidious" cormorants like Penman, Potts, and Tunno, but to no avail. As Moylan coolly told him, it would be a good idea for him to calm down and hire himself a competent lawyer such as his friend William Lewis. The general, on reflection, decided that Moylan was correct, and soon he and Lewis were probing for ways to get around the Penman-Potts-Tunno lawsuit without Wayne having to lose his Pennsylvania property under that state's debtor laws.[2]

These men's fertile minds were soon seething with possible stratagems and ruses. First, they said, Wayne should put Richmond up for public sale for a pittance of £2,000 or £3,000, which perhaps could be accomplished even in a depressed market because it would be such a fantastic bargain. Second, Wayne must buy time in the lawsuit by pointing out to the judge of the Philadelphia County courts, in which the creditors had sued, that Wayne was a resident of Chester County, thereby getting the case dismissed. These things were quickly accomplished, and Wayne made preparations in the fall to return to the South to attend to legal business in that quarter as well.[3]

However badly Wayne may have desired to get on with his lawyers' schemes to extricate himself from his financial difficulties, he was detained in Philadelphia during November by momentous political events. Throughout the previous summer, Wayne had met and talked with numerous delegates that had come together in the Quaker City in a convention to revise the Articles of Confederation. From the inception of their deliberations, which they confided to Wayne in quiet tavern conversations and at the numerous parties which occupied their leisure hours, the general was wholeheartedly with those "nationalists" who favored scrapping the Articles and writing a new constitution to create a stronger central government. He especially favored the idea of a powerful, independent executive, a bicameral legislature, and a judiciary that would be set apart from partisan squabbling. He also liked the proposals of those who advocated a taxing power for the national government, and he supported all provisions that might strengthen the ability of government to raise, arm, and officer a permanent military establishment for the United States. In the area of commercial and financial matters, Wayne expressed no particular opinion except to note to George Handley, Inspector General of Georgia, that it would provide *"Justice"* by giving creditors certain reasonable powers of contract while at the same time not oppressing the debtor. Ironically enough, given Wayne's own indebtedness during the 1780s, the general had consistently sided with his conservative friends against debtor-controlled legislatures, such as the "scandalous" recent one in Rhode Island, that enacted anti-creditor laws and seemed generally to be attempting to "level" society.[4]

When in September 1787 Wayne at last saw the Constitutional Convention's handiwork published in its entirety, with a provision that it take effect upon ratification of nine states, he was exultant. The acceptance of this document, he declared to Handley, would be "an event that promises stability, & greatness to the *Empire of America*" — if it could be gotten successfully through the requisite nine-state ratification process. Wayne's hopes for Pennsylvania's ratification were high, for the Republicans were in a temporary majority in the Assembly, and since to a man they favored the constitution, it was expected that they would push strongly for a quick election of delegates to attend a ratifying convention. Yet, they must work fast, before opposition to the new basic law could be organized by the likes of George Bryan, who declared that the new document was supported only by "monied men, and particularly the stockholders in the bank." Thus, with what some Pennsylvanians like David Reddick thought unseemly haste, the legislature secured a copy of the constitution even before it had been accepted by Congress, and on September 28 enacted a bill calling for a convention to be held in November, less than six weeks later. When some of the opponents of the legislation attempted to boycott this particular Assembly session and prevent a quorum, a mob of proconstitutionalists forced them to take their seats, that the legislation might be passed.[5]

When delegates to the Pennsylvania ratifying convention were chosen, Anthony Wayne was among the majority of conservatives selected to attend, and in late November, when it met in Philadelphia, he took his seat among the Federalist faction. Although it was a foregone conclusion that the Constitution of 1787 would be ratified in Pennsylvania (as Wayne told Burke) "by a decided majority," nonetheless the debates upon the document dragged on for some weeks. Wayne contributed nothing to this discussion, only taking an occasional note and trying to focus his attention on arguments that for him were entirely moot. Finally, when the last vote was cast in mid-December, Wayne stood up for the constitution, along with forty-five other of the sixty-nine delegates, then celebrated the Federalist-Republican victory in

Pennsylvania by writing his old friend Lafayette a paean for "this rising Empire" America. The United States, he told his Gallic comrade, was soon to be fixed "upon so broad & solid a basis as to insure her a conspicuous Name, among the Nations," and her prosperity was even more assured in that George Washington was certain to be her first president. Closing his letter, Wayne mused disingenuously (for he was a republican, despite his rantings against too-weak radical constitutions), "I wish he had a Son." His political work now completed in his native state, Wayne left for Georgia in the middle of December, with Antifederalist accusations still ringing in his ears that he, Washington, Franklin, and the entire proconstitution crowd were monarchists, conspirators, and villains.[6]

In Savannah, Wayne found that both his own and the state's affairs were in a muddle. Although he was advertising Richmond for sale, an Indian uprising upon the frontier of Georgia had thrown the state's economy into a tailspin and destroyed his chances of disposing of the property any time soon. The only good effect of the Indian war, he noted, was that it made most men in Georgia see the necessity of a strong federal government to help the state protect itself, and therefore cause the Constitution of 1787 to be ratified unanimously by the state's convention, despite the efforts of an "antifederal Junto" that wished otherwise. He continued to urge Delany to sell Waynesborough, but the good doctor sensed that his friend's heart was not in this desperate measure, and little progress was made during the first half of 1788 upon the venture. Meantime, Wayne planted a rice crop, bemoaned his fate to Catherine Greene in a long, maudlin letter, wherein he complained of being "*robbed* & *negelected* by a Country from which I merited better treatment," suffered from recurring gout attacks and sundry malarial agues, and instructed Lewis and Delany to do everything within their power in the Chester County courts to fend off the Penman-Potts-Tunno "harpies" for as long as they could from bringing judgment against Waynesborough.[7]

Wayne especially despised the thought of losing at this late date his ancestral seat in Pennsylvania, and he and Burke had concocted a new scheme that was almost guaranteed to wrench this property forever from the grasping hands of his creditors. If this plan worked, Wayne's creditors would have no recourse for settlement of their debt but to accept his terms on the Georgia property, Richmond, which still remained unsold. The idea was to have Wayne's mother, Elizabeth

Iddings Wayne, and Polly's mother, Mrs. Bartholomew Penrose, sue Wayne for retention of dower rights in the Pennsylvania farm. Whatever Burke may have thought of his client's sense of propriety in this affair, he thought it legal and counseled him to use any elegible method in law to extract himself from his immediate financial mess. The relevant legal point, as Burke told Wayne, was that the claims of Mrs. Wayne and Mrs. Penrose, being prior to those of the southern businessmen under Pennsylvania's statutes, would take precedence, and the general would be free of "the most unheard Villainous attempts of *Penman* and *Tonno*" to seize his Pennsylvania property.[8]

With instructions from Wayne and Burke to guide them, faithful Delany and lawyer Lewis in September 1788 plunged into the labyrinth of trying to clarify to "the two old *Ladies*" measures which might have baffled reasonably well educated lawyers. The two men did not have much luck, and throughout the next several months, Delany corresponded copiously with Wayne about the ins and outs of trying to settle all these affairs. The worst problem, he said, was that Elizabeth Wayne — to the general's mortification — was being wooed by opposition lawyers into refusing to go along with Wayne's scheme. By July 1789, Delany was trying to induce "the old Lady. . .to do as she ought," but Mrs. Wayne and the creditors' solicitors (Wayne called them "*blood hounds*") continued to drag their feet. Disgustedly, Wayne concluded that it was the intention of both his mother and his financial enemies to destroy him. Whatever happened, he told his wife gamely, it behooved her and the children to hold their heads proudly and bear these present difficulties with "proper fortitude." Wayne was determined that Penman, Potts, "Mr. Tonno & his Jew broker P. J. Cohen" would yet find that he had "a choice of one," even though he had made a grave error in not originally "disposing of every species of property that I possessed in Pennsylvania" while a chance existed in 1783.[9]

While Wayne's financial affairs in late 1788 continued to grind his spirits to shreds, the general turned with a vengeance toward trying to secure some office in the new federal government. Even before he departed Pennsylvania (and despite the possibility that he would be accused of trying to worm out of his financial responsibilities by doing so), he had attempted to stir enthusiasm for his candidacy for the new Congress, but a quickly rising Antifederalist sentiment in the state (partly as a reaction against the haste with which the Federalists the year before had pushed through ratification of the constitution) dashed his chances there. Consequently, he began an active campaign in Georgia to gain favor for election to one of the state's new Senate seats. When opponents suggested that he was not even a citizen, he heaped scorn upon them, accused them of being Tories, and pointed out, as for example in a letter to Congressman Edward Telfair in November 1788, that he had lived and farmed at Richmond for three years. In fact, he declared, "I feel a Georgian both in principal and Interest," and he hoped it was not arrogance on his part to aspire to that noble office. When others charged him with having given too-lenient terms to loyalists after seizing Savannah in 1782, he declared that their accusations were "an act of Cruelty and a crime of the deepest die," for Governor Martin, the legislature, *and* the Continental Congress all had supported and approved of his handling of the "disaffected."[10]

As Wayne canvassed the state's leading citizens, he discovered that many persons supported his candidacy in spite of "false" charges by his detractors. Benjamin Fishbourn, John Baker, Aedanus Burke, Elihu Lyman, and others reported that they had sounded sentiment for Wayne in their regions of Georgia and found it strong; only John Burnett of Fredonia reported any real opposition. It was with considerable optimism, therefore, that Wayne went before the legislature to campaign, presenting a platform that advocated reducing state taxes by getting the federal authorities to assume responsibility for Georgia's frontiers, which were being raided by Indians and Florida-based Tories. That he was peculiarly well equipped to accomplish these purposes, he boasted, was due to the "habits of friendly intimacy in which I have lived with most of the leading characters of America" and the confidence that Washington had always reposed in him. Hence, his opinions must "naturally" carry "additional weight. . .in the grand National Council where duty, inclination and interest will stimulate me to exert every influence in behalf of the state of Georgia." In the end, however, Wayne's arguments were not strong enough to overcome the feeling on the part of many Georgians that he was an alien usurper, and he lost the election to William Few and James Gunn, men whom he thereafter referred to as "things" and with whom he refused to conduct business.[11]

Undaunted by this setback, Wayne immediately launched another campaign for federal office, this time by seeking to create the position he would occupy. As he and all Georgians had long been aware, Indian depredations on the state's frontiers, aided by loyalist support from East Florida, had been creating enormous financial difficulties for this border province. Wayne's own property on the Satilla River near the southern boundary of Georgia had been raided and burned, and his tenants made prisoner by Tories in Florida with the collusion of that colony's Spanish masters. Therefore, Wayne began a campaign of restoring old relations with men in high places and cultivating new friendships by recommending various persons to federal offices in order to put them in the correct frame of mind to receive his ideas on how to best to rectify Georgia's multitude of problems. He wrote a letter to Washington congratulating the Virginian upon his ascending to the president's chair and to Alexander Hamilton he transcribed a polite note to introduce his friend James Jackson, but mostly to remind that gentleman that Anthony Wayne was still alive. Once these preliminaries had been gotten aside, Wayne began in mid-1789 to push earnestly for his new idea.[12]

Wayne's proposal, as he explained it to Congressman James Madison in June 1789, was "to make an Establishment in the *Southern District* [the public domain between Georgia's borders and the Mississippi River] similar to that wh. Genl. St. Clair presides over" in the Northwest. His purpose was to open the territory for "*National Speculation*" by projecting federal authority into the area to curb there the rapaciousness of hostile Indians, Florida loyalists, Maroons, and Spanish grandees. As Wayne envisioned it, once the Southwest Territory was organized, a governor-general would be appointed by Congress to manage the region in the national interest by exercising both civil and military authority. Since the territory was so wild and the defenseless boundaries of Georgia and South Carolina were so open to the ravages of Indian and Tory attacks, it behooved President Washington and Congress to intervene there with powerful military forces, commanded by a person whose predilection and training was military. And who just happened to be on the very scene whence military operations must originate and with the precise qualifications which Wayne had outlined? Why, himself, of course. As the general told Washington in May 1789, "should your *Excellency* be of opinion that my *tried* and *past services* added to the knowledge I have of the country" made him eligible for the job, then he would be happy to take it on.[13]

Campaigning strenuously for his proposal, Wayne throughout 1789 and into 1790 wrote numerous persons to exert influence in trying to get the Southwest Territory organized. Included in the list, in addition to Washington and Madison, were Henry Knox, secretary of war, Senators Pierce Butler and Ralph Izard of South Carolina, Congressman

James Jackson, Robert Morris, Sharp Delany, Aedanus Burke, and the entire congressional delegation of the state of Pennsylvania. Most officials were lukewarm or noncommittal in their responses to Wayne's proposal, and Knox raised a serious objection. The secretary of war pointed out to Wayne that just the year before the state of Georgia had sold ten million acres of the territories in question to the South Carolina, Virginia, and Tennessee Yazoo Companies, thereby creating insurmountable administrative difficulties for Federalists who wished to organize said lands into a territory. Wayne protested that most Georgians opposed the Yazoo sales and that it was unfair of the Congress as a consequence of them to withhold "the troops and protection of the General Government from us."[14]

Despite much effort on Wayne's part to see his project accepted by Congress, it was ultimately rejected, because the Washington administration considered it to be too controversial. In the end, not even the military aspects of the measure got past the Antifederalists. When Washington's Military Bill of 1790 came before the Senate, opponents posed the possibility of a war with the Creeks in Georgia and noted that if such a conflict broke out the administration must raise an army of 5,000 men, at an expense of $1,000,000 per annum, and build forts along the entire southern frontier. At this point William Maclay of Pennsylvania accused the administration of "ministerial management" to scare the Senate into supporting a larger army on the basis of testimony from Georgians like Wayne, which vastly overrated the "frightful. . .dangers and distress" of the state's frontier districts. Finally, the Senate would accept the addition of only four hundred men to the regular army, and no more general officers, so Wayne's hopes for any kind of military command in the South died an untimely death.[15]

Even as Wayne struggled with financial problems and economic hardships during the years 1789 and 1790, he had other things to divert his mind and give him some relief from disappointments. Since he had been advised by Aedanus Burke, his lawyer, not to stir from Georgia while legal proceedings against him continued in Pennsylvania, he paid strict attention to growing rice at Richmond. For two years, his crops were good and his profits high enough to allow him to pay off a number of small debts, even though the large ones remained — as he was constantly being reminded by Edward Penman and Adam Tunno. His correspondence with Catherine Greene was personally rewarding, for with it he not only kept up a warm friendship but also gave the lady assistance with all the means at his disposal to have Congress free her from responsibility for public debts contracted by her husband at Charleston in 1783. He also took time off from other duties to allow John Trumbull "to take my *Phiz*" for an oil portrait, and he gratefully received from President Washington in 1790 the gold medal he had been awarded by Congress for storming Stony Point eleven years before.[16]

Among the numerous disadvantages that Wayne must suffer because of his legal inability to leave Georgia, none was more heartbreaking than his separation from his children, Margaretta and Isaac. Although he was grateful that his ever-loyal friend, Sharp Delany, was caring for their economic needs and even acting at times as a surrogate father, the general felt a little guilty for neglecting them, even going so far in early 1789 as to apologize to Margaretta for being away so long. The young lady wrote in return, "How can my Dear Papa presume to ask a pardon where it is not due. . .I have often droped the Sympathetick *tear* for my Dear Parents Misfortunes in this life." Wayne's real concern however, was not for Peggy, who appeared to be a level-headed teenager, but for Isaac, who according to Delany was at Princeton University shirking his studies — as he had been doing for some six years past. It was Delany's advice to Wayne that Isaac be taken from college and apprenticed to a lawyer in Philadelphia. And although Margaretta felt that her brother's conduct had been "painted" to her father "in the darkest colours," Wayne in 1789 decided to leave the matter in Delany's hands, to resolve as he saw fit.[17]

The affairs of Wayne's children were soon settled, while the general, as usual, observed from a distance. Isaac, Delany determined, would be allowed to graduate from Princeton in 1790 and then be apprenticed to a lawyer; this procedure was followed, and soon Delany was reporting to Wayne that the young man was settled into the law office of Wayne's attorney William Lewis. Margaretta, meantime, much to Wayne's shock, had fallen in love with William Atlee, son of Colonel Samuel Atlee (whose promotion Wayne had protested in 1779 during the Revolutionary War). In June 1789, young Atlee wrote Wayne a six-page letter asking for his daughter's hand in marriage, only to receive from the general a disconcerting silence. Over the next few months, Delany periodically reported to his friend about the progress of Atlee's courtship of Margaretta, but Wayne never said a word about it in return. Finally, Delany was forced to query Wayne about Atlee's proposal, for Peggy, he said, was taking her father's silence to mean disapproval of her plans. Only then did Wayne finally write Delany — not Margaretta or Atlee — that the union had his blessing. In fact, he wrote not a single word to Margaretta about her engagement or impending marriage, nor did he mention to her the reason for his not being able to attend the wedding. Only to Delany did he allude to his enforced stay in the South by noting that the Georgia chapter of the Society of the Cincinnati had appointed him to represent the state in a general convention at Philadelphia in May 1790, but that he must not go there because his creditors might have him arrested if he did.[18]

Wayne had sunk so low in spirit by 1790 that he was even allowing his property taxes on Richmond to go unpaid and having this fact advertised in the *Georgia Gazette*. That spring, his despondency worsened when Penman, Potts, and Tunno finally pushed their long-impending Chester County lawsuit to a conclusion and got a judgment against Waynesborough. With the county sheriff quite literally knocking on the door of his Easttown house with orders to seize his lands and hold a sale, Wayne made one last desperate plea to his mother in June 1790 to join Mrs. Penrose in a suit against him and scotch the "cormorants' " plans. At the same time he composed a maudlin *apologia* to Polly for the state of his business affairs, which had its intended effect, for when Polly Wayne read the letter to Mrs. Wayne, the ill-used old lady relented (as Delany happily told Wayne in August), and at the very last second saved Waynesborough from the Georgia creditors.[19]

With Wayne's Pennsylvania property now beyond their reach, Penman, Potts, and Tunno were at the end of their legal tether, faced with a settlement of their disastrous economic venture with the general on his own terms or not at all. Therefore, after years of haggling about his obligations, yet with remarkable ease considering all the problems that his debts had caused, Wayne on April 2, 1791, cleared his indebtedness to Penman and Potts by signing over Richmond to Potts for £5,000. He and Penman fourteen days later settled for the Negroes remaining at Richmond, Wayne then paid Tunno what he was owed from money that Potts had put on account to him after they had settled for Potts's slaves, and the general, free of debt but also of his Richmond estate, came out of these transactions with Potts still obligated to him for £800 sterling.[20]

Delighted that he was now free from creditors for the first time in years, Wayne in April 1791 wrote his friend Delany a lighthearted letter explaining his latest transactions. "You'l perhaps ask," crowed Wayne, "how I brought them to those terms — I will answer you in the language of Major Flacherty — *by force my honey*." Thus, all that remained to be done, he noted to his friend, was to have his mother and mother-in-law sign a "relinquishment of dower," that he might return to full possession of Waynesborough. This matter was so trifling, he felt, that it ought not occupy Delany for more than a pleasant afternoon's visit to Waynesborough, and then all his financial problems would be finished. But, lo and behold, the two elderly women refused to budge in this matter, rather liking for a change to be in a position to dictate financial terms to Wayne, whom they considered to be an untrustworthy provider and a fiscal profligate. In a rage at this turn of events, Wayne threatened to Delany that he would "most certainly order the Sheriff to sell Waynesborough," and he felt sure his conduct would "be such as to Justify me in the eyes of the World & in the Opinion of all men of feeling, honor & sentiment." He wrote much the same thing to Polly Wayne, only adding that it would be a tragedy at this late date to have his financial affairs demolished "at the suit of our two Mothers! "[21]

That Wayne was fiercely determined to carry out his threat to sell Waynesborough was not lost on his mother and Mrs. Penrose, for they knew how headstrong Wayne could be. And if he actually did dispose of his Pennsylvania property through forced sale, then Polly Wayne would lose her home, while they would gain nothing but a few dollars that they really had no need of. Therefore, in mid-1791, they consented to Wayne's demand that they cease and desist in their lawsuit for dower claims to the estate at Easttown, and the property reverted completely into the general's hands, free of all debts and encumbrances. The depth of Wayne's gratitude to them for acquiescing in this matter was shown by the fact that he never so much as thanked them, much less paid his mother the annuity that he had legally bound himself to in 1775.[22]

In the late spring and early summer of 1791, Wayne basked in the sunlight of Savannah, where he now temporarily resided, and savored his newfound economic freedom. Listing his assets, he found that even with the loss of Richmond he was still well off financially. Besides his Chester County properties, which alone he valued at £3,812, he also possessed the Hazzard Tract of 1,500 acres in southern Georgia. Additionally, he owned 1,500 acres of "donation lands" on the Ohio River — given him by Congress for his military service in the Revolutionary War — rental properties in Philadelphia and Harrisburg, and a tract of 1,000 acres of land in Nova Scotia. Besides all this real estate, much of it improved and producing income, Wayne also possessed the certificates given him by Pennsylvania for his wartime services, worth $16,000 and yielding a small annual interest. While his income from all this real and personal property was nowhere close to being what he had dreamed of making as a Georgia rice planter, still he and Polly Wayne were better off than he could have dared dream of a few months earlier.

Wayne's buoyant and confident mood in 1791 was due not only to his recent triumphs in the field of personal finance but also to a political triumph. When in the previous fall he had failed in his attempts to influence Congress to organize a Southwest Territory and appoint him governor-general there, he turned his attention resourcefully to securing another place in government. Consequently, he and a dexterous lawyer friend Thomas Gibbon decided that he should run for a congressional seat in Georgia's First District, and Gibbon, a consummate political manipulator acted as his campaign manager and secured his success. Although Wayne regretted that he was forced in this process to unseat his friend, the incumbent James Jackson, nonetheless he was delighted with his election and assured Governor Edward Telfair "that no influence or exertions shall be wanting upon my part, to secure & perpetuate the individual rights of Georgia from being blended in the great and General mass of political Consolidation."[23]

In March, Wayne reflected upon the impact that his recent economic and political successes might have upon President Washington's attitude toward him and his chances for securing a more permanent federal position. Perhaps, he told Delany, when the president "finds that I am not totally ruined & depressed he may think me worthy of some Notice — but I don't deem it prudent to give up a Certainty for an uncertainty," and so he fully intended to hang on to his congressional seat as long as possible. In any case, he now could afford to be more choosy and would accept no "appointment at this late hour but such as I think my Services merit." As it happened, Wayne had not long to wait before coming into the great man's presence, for Washington in the spring of 1791 was on an extended southern tour and was soon to arrive in Georgia. As a member of a local arrangements committee, Wayne helped to plan the gala celebrations that Savannah would sponsor in honor of the president. When the time came on Thursday morning, May 12, for the president to appear, Wayne joined with a small committee of his fellow citizens in welcoming Washington to Georgia at Purysburgh and then accompanying him, his entourage, and other

Georgia notables "down the river" on a boat toward Savannah. Ten miles from the city, this party was met by several boatloads of "gentlemen," plus a band and a choir giving a rendition of "He Comes, the Hero Comes," and the entire cavalcade then made its way downriver to Savannah, between banks lined with cheering crowds.[24]

Wayne enjoyed these daylong festivities as only one could who had just been released from long years of worry and then honored by his fellow citizens, as he was, by election to political office. The president, after being formàlly received by Senator Gunn, Congressman Jackson, and the mayor and aldermen of Savannah, was given a twenty-six gun salute and carried by procession, in Wayne's company, to Brown's Coffee House for a civil banquet, followed by a ball attended by ninety-six "elegantly dressed" ladies. Next day, Washington rested, but on Saturday, the fourteenth "in Company with Genl. [Lachlan] McIntosh, Genl. Wayne, the Mayor and many others," he toured the city, examined the defensive works that had been built in 1779, and attended another dinner "in an elegant Bower. . .on the Bank of the River." After watching what he called "a Tolerable good display of fireworks," he retired for the evening, and on Sunday, May 15, after attending services in Christ Church, set out for Augusta with Wayne and other notables in escort. At Spring Hill, the president's party was met by a corps of dragoons and escorted to Mulberry Grove, where on the seventeenth Wayne took his leave of Washington and returned to Savannah. Noted Wayne to Gibbon the next day, the president was "extremely pleased with the marked attention (to use his own expression) which he received in this City." The visit had been a great success.[25]

It was not so clear that Wayne's own personal fortunes had been advanced by being in Washington's presence, for new difficulties soon were plaguing him and blighting even further his already somewhat tarnished public reputation. For Jackson, with good reason, was charging in the summer of 1791 that Wayne's campaign manager, Gibbon, had employed numerous corrupt practices in Camden and Effingham counties in order to guarantee his client's election. Among other things, asserted Jackson, Gibbon had arranged for his own friends to act in these counties as election judges in place of duly charged magistrates, had reported more votes for Wayne in one precinct than there were elegible voters, and had suppressed and falsified voting lists in another precinct. To make matters worse, fumed Jackson, Judge Henry Osborne, sitting on the bench of the Superior Court, had assisted

Gibbon in throwing the election to Wayne by knowingly certifying as valid what was a specious return. For Wayne himself, these frauds were a serious threat, in the short term to his seat in the House of Representatives and in the long term to his reputation for public honesty. "Both Federalists and Anti-Federalists," he declared publicly upon hearing of Jackson's charges, must hear all the evidence "in the Halls of Congress, that after the fullest investigation" of his character it might stand "pure and unsullied as a soldier's ought to be."[26]

In private, however, Wayne was anything but statesmanlike in his comments about Jackson or that man's charges against Gibbon and Osborne. He expressed to a number of friends what appeared to be a genuine surprise at his old military comrade's complaints, and there is no evidence that he had been involved in the frauds. But he was relentless in his abuse of Jackson, whom he now disparagingly referred to as "*the Little General*," and his outlook was not improved in July by a bout with the fever, "which reduced me very low." In August, he growled to Richard Wayne, "I can at present draw no conclusion, than that he has taken the advantage of a few deluded inebriated individuals to subscribe to such matter as he chose to dictate — which I believe will not redound to his Credit." A month later, Wayne believed he had discerned the true reasons for Jackson's "malicious attacks" against Gibbon, and indirectly himself: jealousy among the "Old Georgians," whose political futures he had restored in 1782 by toppling the monarchical tyranny of the royal governor Sir James Wright but who had accused him of having been too lenient toward loyalists in his proclamations to Savannah merchants in 1783. "It is my object," he declared to Matthew McAllister, "to defeat [their] notorious machinations," as well as those of "their Little General, with their own weakness."[27]

What "weakness" Wayne had in mind was not clear, for he made no effort to organize a defense against Jackson's charges in the few months remaining to him before he must sail to Philadelphia and answer the opening roll call of Congress in November 1791. Perhaps he was simply too ill of the fever to do much in September and October, for once again he was suffering badly during this time from agues and gout. In any case, once he reached Philadelphia, he began to devise numerous schemes to head off attempts by Jackson to unseat him. But pressing as these matters were for Wayne, they did not override the more important one of his celebrating a long-delayed homecoming to his native state.

For he was glad to see his family and friends, to renew long-neglected relationships with numerous other persons (not excluding Mary Vining, whom he now referred to as "my favorite fair"),[28] and personally to express his gratitude to his irreplaceable, closest comrade, Sharp Delany, for the latter's assistance over the past few years in so many ways. Although neither he nor his numerous acquaintances could have been cognizant of this fact in late 1791, he had also just ended his career as a rice planter in Georgia and had said his final farewells (as he would have put it) to "that part of the world."

As a congressman, Wayne's career was not distinguished, partly because he was a junior member of the House and therefore possessed little political seniority or clout, partly because he was crippled by Jackson's challenge to his seat, and partly because he would only be a member for six months. He did, however, attempt to focus on some important debates. For one thing, he supported a bill introduced into Congress by Senator Ralph Izard and others which successfully indemnified the estate of the late General Greene for public obligations the man had taken on in Charleston in 1783. Also, he encouraged his friend, Secretary of War Henry Knox, to send four more companies of infantry to Georgia to do battle there against the Creeks on the frontier. And he lobbied President Washington, usually without much success, to compensate Georgians for their losses in Creek Indian raids.[29]

However, Wayne's primary contribution in the House of Representatives was in lending his weight to the administration's attempts to expand the size of the United States Army in the face of Arthur St. Clair's resounding defeat by an Indian army north of the Ohio River in November 1791. He helped this proposal along largely by making speeches allaying fears of a "standing army" to republican government. In this stand, he adhered strictly to the viewpoint he had maintained since 1776, that large, regular military forces, rather than militia, presented the most eligible means to fight wars — and this was motive enough for him to support the army bill. But another reason for his unstinting aid was that someone close to the president (perhaps Wayne's friend Knox) had secretly informed him that he was a leading contender to command the army, now that St. Clair had been humiliated. Wayne, while professing public chagrin that his old nemesis had been thus rudely handled by the Northwest Indians (as Josiah Harmar had been in 1790), was privately delighted, not only because he believed this military debacle had given him an opening to lead the army but also because he still thought his fellow Pennsylvanian was an arrogant ass (due to their misunderstandings during the Revolutionary War a decade earlier). If he favored Washington's army bill, however, he still was critical of the president and Knox for their poor prosecution of the Indian wars thus far. As he growled to his son, Isaac, had St. Clair been provided with "a competent body of cavalry," the disaster might not have happened, but the damage was now being repaired by the organization of "a *proper* Legionary corps," and the "disgrace" to American arms would soon be eradicated.[30]

Although his was a powerful voice in Congress for the administration's war measures, Wayne came near to being denied the right to use the weight of his military authority in support of Washington's army reorganization, for Jackson was in full cry against his House seat. Only by arriving in Philadelphia a week after Congress had begun to conduct business did Jackson miss the opportunity to ask the House not to seat Wayne. And only a fortnight after the session began, the Georgia general went before the Representatives to contest formally the procedure whereby Gibbon had conducted Wayne's election. Despite numerous procedural dodges on the part of Wayne, the business was finally referred to a committee, where it languished until November 23. That day, Jackson's protest was put on the calendar and Wayne (using evidence sent him by Matthew McAllister) rose to give a lengthy speech against the petition. Vigorously arguing that Jackson really had only ex parte evidence, that he was using time-consuming maneuvers to draw out the matter and give the Georgia legislature time to muster in his favor, that witnesses against Gibbon had perjured themselves by signing affidavits they could not even read, Wayne finally got the business indefinitely delayed. Thereupon, both Jackson and Wayne began a vigorous campaign to have their friends in Georgia sweep the First District for every crumb of information that might bear in their favor the next time the contested election came to the floor of the House.[31]

Finally, on March 12, 1792, after Jackson had gone before the House of Representatives a fortnight earlier to protest any more delays in hearing his case, the matter came to judgment. Wayne had prepared as best he could, having collected from his friends all the evidence he could muster, but as he well knew the whole was very weak. Nonetheless, he wrote his lawyer William Lewis to be ready for the hearing, where he hoped "the little man" Jackson would "be irritated & mortified." Bluster as he may, Wayne's case was so shaky that when the proceedings began in the House he and Lewis lamely and without truth declared that key evidence in their case had not arrived from Savannah and begged for delay. After two hours of debate on this point, the petition was denied, and Jackson at last got to make his case. Issue by issue, he laid bare the devastating proof that Gibbon, "whose soul is faction, and whose life has been a scene of political corruption," had stolen the election. All the while, however, he avoided implicating Wayne in these sordid affairs, consistently pointing out that there was not a scintilla of evidence to show that his old comrade had done, or known of, anything that was mean or illegal. (Throughout his entire unpleasant confrontation with Wayne, in fact, General Jackson both publicly and privately came off as a more generous, humane, and forgiving man than did his counterpart.)[32]

There were various consequences to these proceedings, none of them particularly pleasant for any of the parties concerned. For Wayne, as he had expected, the upshot was that on March 16 the House of Representatives unanimously approved a resolution that he was not a duly elected member. Although he managed by another parliamentary ploy to have this matter delayed for another week, his non-certification was confirmed, and the House called for a new election to fill his empty chair. (Since Wayne was very soon to have new employment, and since Jackson refused to run again, the office finally was filled by John Milledge.) As for Jackson, he was called upon by Gibbon for a duel because of his attacks on that man's character in the House, but in the subsequent shooting neither of them was hurt. Jackson went on to become a United States Senator, governor of Georgia, and a popular fighter against the Yazoo land bill, which had led to massive political corruption in the state during the 1790s. The career of Judge Henry Osborne, meanwhile, had fallen into ruins, for not only had he been removed from the Superior Court and denied access to office for thirty years but also had been disbarred by the legislature from practicing law and fined $600.[33]

From this shambles of damaged reputation, charge and counter-charge, General Wayne emerged with his prestige and dignity intact. Incredibly enough, just as his career seemed at its lowest point, he secured from President Washington the one appointment that he coveted most in the entire world but had not dared expect to gain: command of the American army in the Northwest Territory with the rank of major general. Ironically, this was the position for which he had campaigned least with Washington, seeking instead to be named Surveyor General or Adjutant General. But Washington, faced in early March 1792 with the necessity to replace St. Clair, had prepared a list of possible commanders and discussed each one with his cabinet. His best prospect was Henry Lee, governor of Virginia, but this former cavalry officer was only a colonel when the Revolutionary War ended, and the president feared more mature commanders in the army might refuse to serve under him. Turning to Wayne, Washington recognized that the Pennsylvanian was a frequenter of taverns and a convivial host who did not stint in his consumption of alcohol. Therefore, even though the president remembered Wayne's good services in the war against Britain, he declared that the man was "Open to flattery; vain; easily imposed upon; liable to be drawn into scrapes;" perhaps "addicted to the bottle." Thomas Jefferson agreed. "Brave and nothing else," he said of Wayne, a man who might "run his head agt. a wall where success was both impossible and useless."[34]

These assessments of Wayne by his fellow compatriots Washington and Jefferson were unfair, because they simply were not true. Wayne was no drunkard, and his military record in the Revolutionary War refuted rather than confirmed the severe opinions of the president and secretary of state. The general had shown himself to be a competent, careful leader of men, anything but impetuous or thick-skulled in warfare (with, perhaps, the exception of the Battle of Green Spring Farm in 1781). In fact, his storming of Stony Point in 1779 proved him a master of careful planning and skillful execution — the two most important requisites of any military officer. Hence, Wayne gave the administration no real cause to be concerned with his appointment. When Washington finally did commission Wayne, he put the best face upon it, declaring that the general possessed "many good points as an Officer, and it is to be hoped, that time, reflection, good advice, and above all, a due sense of the importance of trust which is committed to him will correct his foibles." Wayne's appointment also caused quite a ruction outside administration circles — especially in Virginia, where James Monroe growled that the news was greeted with "extreme disgust." In the Senate, Monroe conducted a vigorous campaign against Wayne's appointment and in favor of Lee's, but in the end Washington's wishes carried the day, even if, as James Madison noted, "rather against the bristles."[35]

Thus pompous, gouty, acerbic Anthony Wayne, charmer of friends and implacable opponent of foes, assumed the most important American military command of his time. Notified of his appointment by Secretary Knox on April 12, 1792 he immediately accepted, declaring modestly that he would be wanting in duty and gratitude to President Washington were he to decline, and underlining that he took his new post only with the understanding that he had the full confidence and support of the administration. Thus began a remarkable cooperation between him and Knox, lasting over a period of two years and characterized from beginning to end by harmony and good will. That the secretary and Washington had made a good choice in appointing Wayne commander of the American army was underlined by George Hammond, British minister to the United States, in a letter to John Graves Simcoe, governor of Upper Canada and commander of British troops at Detroit and Niagara. Declared Hammond, "General Wayne is unquestionably the most active, vigilant, and enterprizing Officer in the American Service," even though "his talents. . .are understood to be *purely* Military, and abstracted from that profession, not to be either brilliant or solid." Hammond's statement of bias against the "military mind" was misapplied in the case of Wayne, for there was substantially more to the man than the popinjay martinet that he appeared to be in society and in most of his letters.[36]

Immediately after receiving his appointment and commission, Wayne set about putting his affairs in order before leaving Philadelphia and proceeding by command of the president to Pittsburgh, where he would make his headquarters, organize his new army, and prepare for a rapid push on to Fort Washington, near the town of Cincinnati. For the next few weeks, he made himself a nuisance with everyone who had any familiarity with the western part of the United States, as he dragged from them every ounce of information they could provide about his new area of command. He also studied the ideas of Washington and Knox on how the new 5,000-man army would be arranged, for it had been decided at Von Steuben's suggestion that regimental structure would be discarded in favor of a legionary organization, in order to ease the rigors of campaigning in wilderness areas. What all the reordering meant was that the army, instead of having separate infantry, artillery, and cavalry branches, would integrate all these elements into four Sub-Legions, each theoretically to be commanded by a brigadier general. The Sub-Legions, consisting of four companies of riflemen (despite Wayne's asssertion to Knox that rifles were "a very improper arm for an Army"), eight companies of musket-armed infantry, a troop of dragoons, and a company of artillery, would number 1,280 men each. Wayne himself, as the sole major general of the American army, would have overall command of this Legion of the United States, as it was grandly called, and everyone hoped that it would prove flexible and efficient enough for the kind of warfare it would be conducting in the Northwest Territory. General Wayne found this arrangement entirely satisfactory, both from the fact that he had successfully commanded such a force in Georgia during the Revolutionary War and because it provided him with a flexible cavalry arm, which he had noted was St. Clair's greatest weakness the year before.[37]

Wayne also paid attention to his private affairs by preparing for a long absence from home, or perhaps death, for as he cheerily told his wife Polly, one never knew on a military campaign when one might have an *"accident."* Therefore, he wrote Delany, giving detailed instructions on how his small outstanding debts were to be handled, what to do about rentals on his numerous properties, and outlining arrangements he had made with Polly for the running of his farm at Easttown. As for Isaac, he should be encouraged to keep up his studies of the law in solicitor Lewis's office, while maintaining only modest lodgings and cultivating spartan eating and drinking habits. The young man, declared Wayne to his friend, must be cognizant of the necessity for economy in living, "as my circumstances will not admit of idle [waste]." Although he groaned to Polly that he was detained in Philadelphia, and away from Easttown, by his multiple responsibilities, he was in fact spending considerable time in the gay society of the city, moving from one party to another, usually in company with his "favorite fair," Mary Vining. The handsome, forty-seven-year-old general cut quite a figure, and although a few refined ladies thought him a "coarse soldier," everyone agreed that he was indeed "brave, wonderful brave." Miss Vining, too, still made an impression — but not quite as favorably as she had with the Venezuelan Miranda in 1783. Hamilton Rowan, an Anglo-Irish refugee, who saw her at about this time, declared, "And now for Miss V. — eternally gabbling French; She is never happy unless when talking of the Compte de Lucerne, the Duc de Baron, and other French nobles who were here during the Revolution. She wears rouge from her chin to her head, I believe, and is about fifty."[38] General Wayne thus spent his last hours in eastern Pennsylvania, before taking the field against America's foes in the Northwest Territory.

CHAPTER *XI*

Commander of the Legion

1792–1793

IN EARLY JUNE 1792, General Wayne tore himself away from the pleasant company of Mary Vining and the society people of Philadelphia and made his way westward. After a pleasant trip through the gorgeous countryside of his native state, during which men on all sides assailed him with arguments against the Washington administration's recently imposed excise tax on whiskey, he arrived at his destination on June 14. Pittsburgh, Wayne discovered, was a town that contrasted jarringly with sedate, relatively clean Philadelphia. The unpaved streets were mud holes during rainy weather, dust pits when dry, and pigs roamed freely, eating garbage thrown from houses and business establishments. As for the buildings, they were mostly log hovels, and many sheltered liquor salesmen and whores. The citizens were a rough lot, and their politics tended to be too antifederalist to suit Wayne. Nonetheless, immediately upon his arrival, he put distance between himself and Washington's government on the issue of whiskey excise taxes by letting it be known that as an army commander he had no intention of using the Legion Army to enforce the collection of these revenues, for his task was "to protect the people and not oppress them." With that judicious policy, he freed himself of suspicion that he was an "agent" of the central government, sent amongst the frontiersmen to bring them to heel, and he won the wholehearted cooperation of the populace in his efforts to prepare the army for service against the Northwest Indians.[1]

Making his headquarters at newly constructed Fort Fayette, a quarter of a mile up the Allegheny River from the Forks of the Ohio, Wayne immediately plunged into the business of organizing and training his "army." In fact, his entire force on the fifteenth of June consisted of a mere forty recruits under Captain Thomas Hughes, plus the "Corporal's command of dragoons" that had accompanied him across the state. So he encouraged Knox to send forward recruits as quickly as possible, "for I realy feel awkwardly Situated, a General without Troops is something Similar to a fish out of Water." He also wrote Brigadier General James Wilkinson, who was in charge of a garrison at Fort Washington, near Cincinnati, and whom Wayne had known and liked during the Revolutionary War, to let this man, his second in command, be aware that he had arrived and to express his "singular pleasure, in having with me, a Gentleman who I have always esteemed as a friend, and who I know to be a brave and an experienced Officer." Meanwhile, he was writing to commanders of state militias up and down the frontiers instructions on how to dispose their men to guard against Indian attack and to protect public stores. He wrote to Delany a description of the primitive living conditions in his new camp and asked that a weekly "parcel" of personal goods be sent from home by way of the War Office.[2]

From the inception of his tenure as commander in chief of the Legion Army in the American West, General Wayne's military problems were multiplied by the diplomatic policies of the Washington administration. For while Wayne was under orders to bring an army into being, that he might project American power against hostile Indians in the Northwest Territory (and if need be against their allies, the British and Spanish, both of whom encroached upon territory ceded to the United States in the Treaty of Paris in 1783), at the same time he was constrained by an ongoing cease fire and truce from using that army because the president was conducting treaty negotiations with the Indians in hopes of effecting a peaceful settlement of the problem. Therefore, while he ordered frontier militiamen to defend American citizens, he also carefully instructed them to avoid incidents that might break the truce and interrupt the work of the peace commissioners, first Rufus Putnam, then Timothy Pickering, Benjamin Lincoln, and Beverly Randolph who dickered in Detroit during 1792 and most of 1793. Worse for Wayne than the restraints put upon his freedom as a military commander was that Washington's pacific overtures to the Indians convinced civilians in the East that peace was at hand and that they need not enlist in the army. Thus recruiting was hampered.[3]

While these problems would only grow worse for Wayne over the

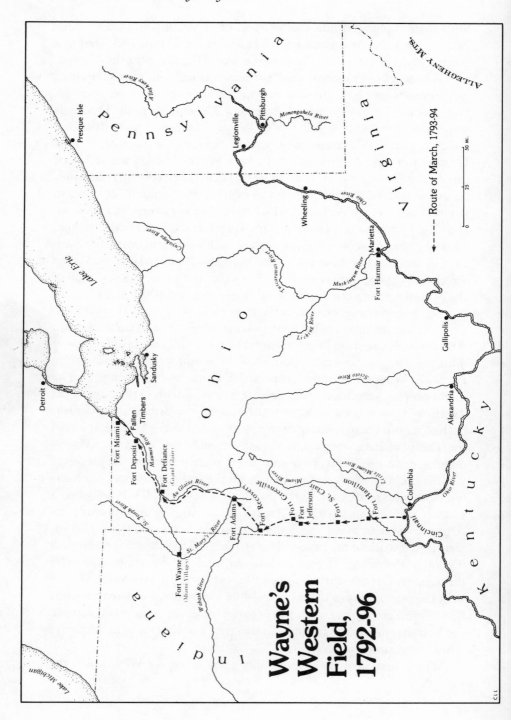

Wayne's
Western
Field,
1792-96

next few months, the general had little control over them, and he tried not to fret about the inevitable. Hence, throughout the summer months of 1792, Wayne used most of his abundant energies to turn the recruits that Knox sent him into a well-trained and highly disciplined force. "It is an established maxim," he told Wilkinson in July, "that in Order to *Secure* an Honorable peace, we ought to be *well* provided for War." Consequently, he gave strict orders to his subordinates to discipline the troops according to the strictures of the Baron Von Steuben's "Blue Book" of 1779, and to drill them in marching, executing maneuvers, and firing their respective weapons. Because Wayne had considerable trouble keeping his officers at their tasks — they, like the soldiers, loved to loiter in the taprooms of Pittsburgh — he made slow progress in forming his raw recruits into an army of regulars. When smallpox broke out in one regiment during July, he quickly isolated that unit and began a program of inoculation for his entire army. By the first of August, Wayne had under his command at Pittsburgh about 1,100 men, and more recruits, though only slowly collected in the East, continued to dribble in.[4]

Although he had problems with discipline because of the proximity of that "Gomorrah," Pittsburgh, Wayne nonetheless worked very hard to maintain what he considered adequate attention by his soldiers to their duty and the regularity of the army. That his punishments were harsh and immediate soon became well known throughout his command, and with many of his men he gained a reputation as a cruel martinet. The general was entirely unsympathetic to these complaints, declaring that when "conceited & refractory" soldiers sniveled to him about too-harsh punishments in the Legion, he "*comforted* them by an Assurance that [they] will not be lessen'd but rather increased." Therefore, he consistently meted out sentences of flogging with one hundred lashes for crimes of desertion, "intention to desert," "bad conduct" (including drunkenness), sleeping on guard duty, stealing, and being away from camp without leave. In about ten percent of these cases, he punished the guilty party with death by hanging or before a firing squad, and although Washington and Knox approved of the general's emphasis upon disciplining the soldiers ("Every thing," said Knox, "depends on that pivot. The public interest, the national Character and your personal reputation"), nonetheless they hoped that soon "there may be less call for the punishment of death." Although acceding to this advice, Wayne continued to keep his men on their toes with strict

attention to their personal appearance, daily target practices for the
riflemen and regular infantry, and full-scale drills in which the Legion
marched through the forest and threw up fortified camps in the evening.
At the same time, he also built morale among his soldiers by paying
attention to their rations, clothing, and pay (which he insisted must be
distributed monthly), and he worked to build strong loyalties among the
men to their regiment or company by emphasizing unit colors, flags,
and other paraphernalia.[5]

Although Wayne realized in August that his Legion Army was still
far from ready to conduct warfare against the Northwest Indians, he
was chafing under the strictures of the Washington administration's
continuing diplomatic overtures through the emissary Rufus Putnam.
Wayne in August and September wrote to Knox and Delany long,
detailed plans of operations for his army, which he suggested should be
implemented early the following spring, for the Indians, he said, were
ignoring the so-called truce on the frontier, and things could only get
worse. In these letters, the general outlined in broad detail the program
he would eventually put in operation against his foes, and it showed the
influence of long thought and planning. During the fall and winter, he
said, all America could do was *try* to protect the frontiers with the
regulars he now had, and perhaps send out one or two "desultory
Expeditions" of mounted volunteers, while the Legion Army was being
brought up to full strength. Militia forces, he believed, were useless for
these operations, for as he sarcastically noted, citizen soldiers were good
for nothing except to drain the public stores without corresponding
benefit. Once the Legion Army was made "*superior to insult*," and once
its supply could be guaranteed, then it should move down the Ohio
River to Fort Washington, establish north of there a strong and permanent base of operations, and proceed on into enemy territory.

The time to strike the Indians, declared Wayne, was in the spring,
when the grass was adequate for forage but before the natives had
recovered from the ravages of winter. "I consider the Indian — an
enemy," said Wayne, "formidable only when he has a choice of time &
ground: — in the *fall* of the year he's strong ferocious & full of spirits —
corn in plenty & Venison and other game every where to be met with."
But in spring, "he is half starved Weak and dispirited." Then was the
time to hit him, first with diversionary raids against the Sandusky and
St. Joseph's River settlements, then with the Legion itself. As the main
Legion force moved forward upon these tasks, it would erect small,

intermediate forts at convenient distances between Fort Washington and a place intended for the establishment of a strong and permanent post. "I wou'd," said Wayne, "make it an invariable rule to halt early each day & secure my camp before evening with small temporary breast works & Abbatis such as to cover the troops." Now, if the administration would accept this plan for the coming year, Wayne was prepared to move the Legion to Fort Washington in the spring, establish a forward post about twenty miles north of the Ohio — or perhaps even on St. Clair's battlefield — and be ready to campaign the following summer.[6]

Secretary of War Knox was not willing in September 1792 to give General Wayne this kind of freedom, for even though Knox believed the administration's peace overtures toward the Indian tribes in the Northwest were pretty much a waste of time, nonetheless he insisted upon upholding Washington's policy of giving diplomacy a try. After all, as he told Wayne, the people insisted upon it. Nevertheless, the general attempted in October once more to get the administration to alter its policy, declaring, "I hope that by this time every Idea of peace is done away — & that more efficient measures will be adopted to Complete the Legion." While Knox certainly agreed that the army ought to be put in a state of military readiness during the coming winter — and in fact was promising Wayne that it would reach a strength of 2,500 well-equipped soldiers with a full complement of artillery before spring of 1793 — he continued to insist that every possible peace proposal must be followed to the end. "We shall always possess the power of rejecting all unreasonable propositions," he told Wayne persuasively. "But the sentiments of the great mass of the Citizens of the United States are adverse in the extreme to an Indian War and although these sentiments would not be considered as sufficient cause for the Government to conclude an infamous peace, yet they are of such a nature as to render it advisable to embrace every expedient which may honorably terminate the conflict." Moreover, noted Knox, "the favorable opinion and pity of the world is easily excited in favor of the oppressed. The Indians are considered in a great degree of this description — If our modes of population and War destroy the tribes the disinterested part of mankind and posterity will be apt to class the effects of our Conduct and that of the Spaniards in Mexico and Peru together."[7]

Despite Knox's best efforts to persuade Wayne that the administration's peace overtures were absolutely necessary, the general found a great part of the secretary's arguments to be nonsensical, separated as he was from the forces of public opinion that buffeted Washington and his cabinet in Philadelphia. On the frontier, where he continued daily to hear of Indian outrages against American patrols and flags of truce, he felt certain that nothing would come of the seemingly endless negotiations that consumed so much of the diplomats' time and energies. However, orders were orders, and he continued to adhere manfully to his instructions from Knox, recognizing, as the secretary of war continued to remind him, that even were negotiations not going on with the Indians, Wayne could do little more than what he was doing in any case — preparing for war in the spring of 1793, should the necessity arise. So he pursued the business at hand in late 1792, moving his Legion away from the allurements of the flesh at Pittsburgh to a new site that he reconnoitered in late October, about twenty-two miles downstream on the Ohio River from his present location. Naming this place Legionville, he finally began shifting his troops to his new camp in late November, and by the early part of December he had his soldiers hutted for the winter in a healthful, defensible location where it was easier than it had been at Pittsburgh to enforce discipline upon his sometimes recalcitrant troopers. When Washington received news of the founding of Legionville, he was piqued that Wayne had not moved on to Fort Washington. When these views were transmitted to Wayne by Knox in late November, the surprised general replied with a polite argument that supply problems had dictated his taking post at Legionville for the winter.[8]

As Wayne worked through the summer and fall of 1792 "to make an army from the rawest heterogeneity of materials, that were ever collected together" (as he told Wilkinson in December), he also kept up with personal affairs in eastern Pennsylvania. His friend Delany was having trouble getting Edward Penman to honor Wayne's bills upon the £800 that the Charleston merchant owed him, and the general, turning the tables on Penman, threatened to sue him. This business was settled amicably — or so everyone thought — between Delany and Penman's representatives in Philadelphia, but matters of a political nature arose in the Quaker City to threaten Wayne's peace of mind. As Delany put it, "Your Conduct Dr. General will be well watched — you may have Enemies — you have many Friends." These comments, so cryptic that they set Wayne's nerves on edge, caused him immediately to query his friend about who his "enemies" were and why they had suddenly emerged, but he never received a reply. Family concerns also were on

Wayne's mind, especially news from his son-in-law, William R. Atlee, that the young man had been charged with extortion and compelled to undergo a lengthy trial before being cleared of the indictment. Rushing to the defense of his daughter's husband, Wayne declared to Atlee that there was no doubt in his own mind that he was innocent of the charges — a position that meant a great deal to both his son-in-law and Margaretta. With his brother-in-law, William Hayman, and his old friend, Thomas Hartley, Wayne also corresponded, discussing business affairs relating to Waynesborough and remembering the good times they had enjoyed during the previous winter.[9]

Problems with his health continued in 1792 to plague Wayne, but he did not allow them to interfere with his professional responsibilities. In September, he complained to Delany that he was suffering a "cruel fit of vomiting. . ., so as almost to incapacitate me," but he soon recovered. Then in December, just before the Christmas holidays, he fell ill with a "serious and alarming attack of the most violent flux & bilious vomiting that I ever experienced." For three days, Wayne told Delany, he was "prepared for an awful change," because his "Monitor" warned him that he was near death, and it was not until he "threw up a green seated Jelly" from his stomach that he felt better. But, he declared, he was still "weak & low," suffering from a continuing "flux," which no medicine — not even laudanum, the bark, or tartar emetic — would touch. At that time, he could only ride a horse for two hours per day, and he could only hope that his condition would soon improve. Not long afterwards, his "monster" (as he called the disease) did begin to relax its grip, for the general soon was being described by Captain William Eaton of the Fourth Sub-Legion as "firm in constitution [and] in resolution; industrious; indefatigable, determined and persevering; fixed in opinion, and unbiassed in judgment." In fact, said Captain Eaton, Wayne was enduring "fatigue and hardship with a fortitude uncommon for a man of his years. I have seen him. . .sleep on the ground, like his fellow soldiers, and walk around the camp at four in the morning, with the vigilance of a sentinel."[10]

Wayne's attempts to restore his physical vigor in late 1792 were not helped by the news he received from various quarters about the course of public affairs in America. During the latter part of December he learned for certain what he had expected was the case since the previous October — that the Indians of the Northwest would settle for nothing less in peace negotiations with the United States than the Ohio River as a southern boundary to their territory. The "insolent propositions from the *friendly* Indians," he fumed to Knox in late December, "carries such strong features of B——h policy and Influence that I shou'd be induced to conclude there will not be single member in either house of Congress who will not see thru' this cobweb [of] insidious state intrigue." To underscore his evidence, he was sending Cornplanter and other Six Nations' chiefs to Philadelphia, so that they could confirm their demands to the president in person. Three weeks later the Indians appeared in Philadelphia, made their arguments, and persuaded the administration that hopes of a peaceful settlement of Indian claims in the Northwest Territory were dim indeed. Hence, Knox, on March 5, 1793, wrote Wayne a letter amending his earlier statements regarding the government's policies toward the Indians, at least to the extent of informing Wayne that he could expect war to begin some time in 1793. Meantime, however, he was constrained from conducting any military operations, save frontier patrolling against the Indians, while he continued to prepare his Legion for almost inevitable conflict.[11]

Another problem that concerned Wayne as he sat in his gloomy camp at Legionville during the winter of 1792–93 was an attempt by some members of Congress partially to disband the Legion that he had so manfully struggled to embody as a fighting force. On December 20, the general learned that Congressman John Steele of North Carolina had introduced a resolution in the House of Representatives calling for the army to be reduced in strength to only two regiments, that the government might save money and at the same time effectively use good, sturdy militiamen to cover the frontiers. Over the next two weeks, Washington and the Federalists strongly resisted this bill, arguing that the administration's bargaining position with the Indians would be destroyed by this reduction and noting that regulars were indispensable in warfare in the West. Into the midst of this struggle, Wayne innocently dropped a bombshell when he sent in a petition from his officers to Knox on the inadequacy of the soldiers' diet, to which he gave his own endorsement. Angrily replying to this petition and to Wayne's letter approving it, Knox wrote the general privately that both he and the president looked upon the petition as being an "extremely improper measure," which could only play into the hands of the antimilitaristic opponents of the regular army. Fortunately, the petition had no ill effects, and Steele's motion was defeated on January 5, 1793, by sixteen votes.[12]

As for Wayne, he was only perplexed by Washington's chastisement of him and never admitted to Knox that his sending in the petition at that awkward time might have caused serious damage to the cause of the army. He did, however, assert on January 15, that the congressional attempt to reduce his Legion had injured morale among his officers, for they "conceive that they hold their Commissions, on a very precarious tenor, ie upon the whim or caprice of a restless juncto." Fumed Wayne to Delany, "There is certainly a strong spice of the old Antifederal leaven in the present Congress but I hope and trust that they will not carry their point — by provoking any part of Government, or its meritorious officers to resign their places — which appears to be the principal object that these restless Members have in View."[13]

Throughout the early months of 1793, Wayne was occupied with Indian affairs. In February, he was informed by one Joseph Collins, a trader in the Illinois country, that the Northwest Indians, while professing peaceful intentions toward the United States, were preparing for hostilities. Wayne immediately sent this news on to Knox, but he received in reply instructions that he was not to provoke the Indians by building up "Stores or Magazines. . .at the head of your line and particularly. . .any considerable accumulation of troops at your advanced posts." The reason for this order, Wayne learned, was that the administration in April intended to send Pickering, Lincoln, and Randolph to negotiate some more with the Indians and did not want the Legion army to give the natives the slightest excuse for belligerence against these men. In addition, Wayne was told by Knox to treat Cornplanter and other chiefs, who were returning to their people, with dignity and respect when they arrived in his camp. Wayne carried out these orders to the letter, conducting with the natives long talks in mid-March and forwarding the substance of these discussions on to Knox. The general could not resist, however, pointing out to Secretary Knox that Cornplanter had attempted to get him to promise that his army would remain at Legionville until after negotiations between the American peace commissioners and the Northwest Indians had begun at Sandusky. The effect of such an agreement, he said, would be to immobilize the army for the summer, for the Ohio River would soon be too low to carry barge traffic. A short time later, he reported to Knox a precise return on all soldiers in existing American garrisons north of Fort Washington — a total number of 346 — in case the Indians later accused him of slipping in more troops than were actually there.[14]

Private affairs, some pleasant, others painful, often diverted Wayne in early 1793 from military business in his camp at Legionville. He struck up a happy correspondence with Hugh Henry Brackenridge, author and jurist, who in 1793 was writing "a work, entitled Captain Farago" (later to be known to the world as *American Chivalry*), the third volume of which he sent the general for his "Amusement." From Delany came good news that Isaac Wayne was studying hard, although the young man was slightly miffed at his father for being denied the right to control his own finances. Wayne, meantime, was writing Catherine Greene one of his long, sentimental missives, complaining that her "*cold* indifference" in not keeping in touch with him had "added a *chill* to the frozen aspect round me whilst barely existing under a *thin* Marquee, surrounded with snow & ice 'which does not bite so keen as kindness past forgot.' " But the most important personal events for Wayne were the failing health of his wife and mother, which he learned about from Margaretta, who suggested that he perhaps should write his old parent. Stung by this comment, perhaps because of a guilty conscience, he read into it an implication that he was not paying enough attention to his family, and he strongly rejected the aspersion. "You [and Isaac] were both Infants," he said to his daughter, "when I was first called upon by my Country — to defend her rights & Liberties," and from this cause had "an affectionate & indulgent parent — been lost, and almost estranged to his children & family. This therefore may account for my *seeming* neglect."[15] Margaretta, however, might easily have pointed out to her father that his oversights stemmed not from public duty but purely avoidable slights.

That Wayne was soon to reap the bitter harvest of his neglect of family was seen in the last letter that his wife Polly wrote before she gasped her final breath as a result of some unspecified illness. The poor woman, long ignored and shabbily treated by her husband, responded in late 1792 to a letter that her son had written her about his recent conversion to the ethic of hard work and serious purpose. Gratefully, Polly replied to the young man that he could thank God for "not being as Carless as your Earthly father has bean (on account of absence) of your morals." But, she mused, "I sincerely. . .believe [his being gone was] to take the matter in it Tru Light a Great deal more advantage to you than a Disadvantage." Concluding this critique of her husband's worth as an example for her son, the sick, despondent woman wished Isaac "all the happyness this unsartain World Can a ford you" and on the evening of

April 19, 1793, after much suffering, died at Waynesborough, surrounded by her friends and family. As usual in cases of crisis in the Wayne family at Easttown, good and loyal Sharp Delany took care of all arrangements, including Mary Wayne's funeral and the settling of her estate. To the general, he and William R. Atlee broke the news of his wife's death, Delany in a kind and gentle way, the son-in-law in a cold, formal note that only covered the barest details of the sad news.[16]

On April 28, the general finally received word from Atlee that Mary Wayne had died — and at last showed remorse. His mind, he told Knox on the twenty-ninth, was "in such a state of torture for the recent loss of my long loved & very esteemed *Maria*" that he could only with difficulty continue to administer the Legion Army. And if Wayne had behaved badly toward Polly while she was alive, he now recouped some of his tarnished humanity by the dignified and generous way that he acted toward his relatives in the next month. He pleaded to Margaret Penrose, Mary Wayne's sister, that she live at, and enjoy, Waynesborough, as had "my ever lamented *Polly*." When she accepted the offer, Wayne thanked her and admonished her always to keep the house open to his sister, Ann Hayman, and her husband William. He expressed to this latter gentleman profound gratitude on May 28 for the way in which Hayman was caring for Waynesborough's farming operations, and he noted a concern that his "good old Mother" might also soon pay "the last debt of Nature." Her departure, he said, "is naturally to be expected from her very advanced age, but my poor Polly might have been spared longer." Whether his thoughts about Elizabeth Wayne were a presentiment or whether he had received earlier word that she was near death is not clear, but in any case they proved all too true. Wayne's mother died on May 5, only seventeen days after Polly had passed away, and Delany and Hayman relayed this sad news to the general not long thereafter.[17]

Wayne's sorrow at the loss of Polly Wayne and his mother was a momentary pang and had no lingering effects upon the general's life. That he had been estranged from both for many years was a well-known fact among his family and acquaintances, and no one tried to pretend to him that they did not understand this point. If anything was different with Wayne now, it was probably the awareness that at long last he was free to pursue even more openly his smoldering affair with Mary Vining, but that it, like everything else in mid-1793, must take second place to the general's consuming interest in things military. So his life quickly returned to its old track, and he threw all his energies into his immediate project of pushing the American army forward from Legion-ville to Fort Washington.

To expedite these plans, General Wayne returned temporarily to Pittsburgh in the spring, in order to speed up the flow of military stores from that place and to correspond with the War Office in Philadelphia. The news he was receiving from the East, through Secretary Knox, was not encouraging, for the Washington administration was now informing him that for the summer of 1793 he could expect the army's strength to reach only 3,000 men. It was true, said Knox sadly to the general, that Congress had authorized a force of 5,000 soldiers, but recruiting throughout the nation was lagging so badly that the War Department would never be able in the next few months to fill the entire quota. Therefore, Wayne must augment his army with 1,000 mounted volunteers from Kentucky. Since the general despised all non-regular soldiers and was exasperated by the very thought that he must depend upon these proud Kentuckians, his impending departure for Fort Washington was not as happy an occasion as it might have been. Not even an official statement of respect from the citizens of Pittsburgh for his conduct as commander of the Legion while at that place did much to brighten his outlook on the eve of his great adventure.[18]

Depart, nonetheless, Wayne did, with a ringing paean to Knox that he intended with "honest Zeal to serve my Country" by moving forward against its Indian and British foes. Upon reaching Legionville, he made his headquarters temporarily aboard a barge that he named *The Federal*, then moved downriver with the Legion through the timbered country of America's rugged frontier, occasionally passing a small settlement like Wheeling or Marietta. But Wayne continued in a sour mood, even refusing, according to one observer, to allow "his Officers the privilege of setting their feet on shore until they arrived at French station." Moreover, he gave his soldiers strict orders that they were not to fire at targets on shore, lest roving Indians believe that they were targets and retaliate. At Fort Harmar, just below Marietta, he paused for a time, but soon he pushed the Legion on past Gallipolis, Alexandria, and Colum-bia. Finally, on the fifth of May, Wayne's flotilla reached Cincinnati, near Fort Washington, where he has hailed by the town's eleven hun-dred inhabitants and a Sub-Legion that he has sent on earlier in the year. After greetings from Arthur St. Clair, governor of the Northwest Territory, Brigadier General James Wilkinson, who had commanded American troops in the Northwest Territory until Wayne's arrival, and

Federal Judge John Cleves Symmes, Wayne and his officers were entertained at a gala banquet.[19]

General Wayne, who during his lifetime had seen and done much that might shock persons of more tender sensibilities and who himself lived by no genteel code of behavior, was amazed at the openness of the city of Cincinnati. He agreed with a sergeant in his command, who noted that "a man possessed of the least tincture of morality must wish his stay here as short as possible." The village, declared Wayne to Knox, was "filled with ardent *poison* & Caitiff wretches to dispose of it." Therefore, he quickly marched his men a mile farther down the river and took post at the only eligible campsite within a reasonable distance of Fort Washington and the Ohio River, which he named Hobson's Choice. He reported all these activities to Knox on May 9, at the same time praising Wilkinson, whose command, he said, "bespakes the Officer, & merits my highest approbation." He also told the secretary of war that he needed more clothing for his men, although he admitted that the Legion troops were less wasteful of that article than any he ever commanded "during the late War." "I am also endeavouring," he noted to Knox, "to make the riflemen believe in that arm, the Infantry in heavy buck shot & the bayonet, the Dragoons in the sword, & the Legion in their United Prowess."[20]

Before long, General Wayne was sadly perplexed as to how he should conduct himself as commander of the United States Army in his anomalous situation at Hobson's Choice in the summer of 1793. "I really feel my situation awkward, unpleasant & embarassing! " he told Knox on the twenty-seventh of May; "to make efficient arrangements for an active Campaign, will involve a heavy debt upon the Nation, — and I may probably be censured for having acted without positive (altho' implied) orders, shou'd peace eventually take place." Yet, on the other hand, "were I to omit this essential business, until the moment of Operations (shou'd the war progress) it wou'd then be too late to make the heavy & necessary deposits at the advanced posts! & I shou'd be defaulted for not having made those deposits in time." The general's solution to this dilemma was to make "*a provisional arrangement*," by ordering the quartermaster general into Kentucky to "increase transport," but not as much as Wayne really wanted — at least "*for the present*." He had also ordered Colonel David Strong to open a road northward between Forts Hamilton, St. Clair, and Jefferson, on the same model as one Wilkinson had already made from Fort Washington to Fort Hamilton. As for yet receiving any military stores of consequence to send over the new road on the newly collected transport, he could only inform Knox that "not a partical" of these expected supplies had yet arrived at Hobson's Choice. The army's contractors, Robert Elliot and Eli Williams, who had agreed to furnish his Legion with 250,000 rations, were not yet forthcoming with any of the vital food-stuffs they were supposed to deliver.[21]

Not the least of Wayne's anxieties at his new encampment in mid-1793 involved his inability to make adequate preparations for war because of the administration's Indian policy. In addition, he must muster enthusiasm to ask the Kentuckians to organize a mounted volunteer corps to join his army for the upcoming campaign, even though the very thought of irregular troops turned his stomach. Hence, he wrote Governor Isaac Shelby of Kentucky three times during May and June, asking him to embody a force of 1,000 to 1,500 men by the middle of July to join his Legion and campaign against the common foe. Shelby immediately complied with Wayne's requisition, having been warned beforehand by Knox to expect it, by writing Major Generals Charles Scott and Benjamin Logan, two veterans with "considerable experience in Indian Wars," to call for a muster of the state's militia. Wayne supplemented the governor's correspondence by appealing to these men himself, and although Logan thought the entire idea not to be "consistent with good policy," General Scott agreed to go along — if the mounted militia could act *independently* of Wayne's Legion Army.[22]

General Wayne found this idea abhorrent, and he reacted vehemently against it. "Nothing," he fumed to Knox on June 20, "shall induce me to commit the honor & dignity of Government nor to expose the Legion (unnecessarily) to the whole Combined force of the enemy — whilst *two thousand* mounted Volunteers under the Governor & all the Militia Generals & Subordinate Officers of the State of Kentucky (in pay of the United States) were stealing a March very wide from the Army — in order to burn a few Wigwams & to capture a few women & Children & in which (a business that might as well be effected by two Hundred) — they cou'd not meet with any Opposition, until they returned *triumphantly & safe* to their respective homes — leaving the Legion to contend with the difficulty & danger." He hoped that the Kentuckians would see in the end that they must be subordinate to his orders, and he had so written the governor, Scott, and Logan. Finally, they acceded to Wayne's insistence that the Kentucky militia follow his leadership, and the relieved general on July 1 commissioned Scott, a veteran of the Revolutionary War, as an officer in the United States Army. Before long, General Scott sent Wayne word from Lexington that the Mounted Volunteer Corps was mustered and ready to ride at a moment's notice.[23]

Through July and much of August 1793, Anthony Wayne waited in "anxious suspense" that was "almost intolerable" for news about the course of America's peace negotiations with the Indians. He wrote to Knox on July 2 that he was doing what was "absolutely necessary" at the "head of the line" to prepare for a forward movement of the Legion Army, should word arrive that the treaty talks were unsuccessfully concluded. The Northwest Indians took these measures as a defiance of the truce, and they protested vehemently to the American peace negotiators and to Washington about Wayne's "belligerence." Although the general warned the administration that these charges were silly and merely Governor Simcoe's way of "trifling" with the American peace commissioners, Knox on July 20 wrote the general a strongly worded note of caution about violating *in any way* his standing orders not to reinforce his northermost position at Fort Jefferson, the "head of the line," under command of General Wilkinson. Disgustedly, Wayne explained to Knox that all he was doing was supplying troops already at that post, and he fumed that the Indians were merely jealous because they saw a guard protecting cattle "which they were *prevented from stealing*." Grudgingly, he acceded to the necessity of withdrawing 187 men from Wilkinson's force, even though his coercion came from "reports of idle savages." He grumbled to Knox, "I had presumed that as Commander in Chief of the Legion of the United States, some *confidence* ought to have been placed in my *honor* as well as *Conduct*." Knox's only reply to Wayne's grousing was to insist that in order to secure the safety of the commissioners and guarantee the good faith of the United States, the president's orders "must be rigidly observed."[24]

But General Wayne's period of frustration was near an end, for on August 25, the commander received news from the commissioners, Pickering, Lincoln, and Randolph (who had just arrived at Fort Erie on the Lakes), that the Indians refused to bargain and that war would soon commence. Immediately, Wayne began drafting orders for war, going into detailed instructions with his officers on how to organize the Legion for a march northward. And within a few days he had his troops conducting intricate training maneuvers to prepare for conflict with the Indians. To Elliot and Williams, who had still not come close to providing the rations they had contracted for, he wrote letters prodding them to fulfill their obligations by getting the foodstuffs to Fort Jefferson by October. He also began to send Wilkinson letters, encouraging his second in command to prepare for conflict, and with that officer he got into a minor (or so it seemed at the time) altercation over Wilkinson's confusing the terms "light companies" and "elite corps" when discussing the arrangement of the Legion.[25]

Although Wayne, in his flurry of military preparations in early September 1793, seemed on the verge of marching the Legion northward along the Miami River, he actually spent the rest of the month in careful preparation for this maneuver. As he told Knox in a letter that underlined his wise caution at this time, "Knowing the critical situation of our Infant Nation & feeling for the honor & reputation of Government — (which I will support with my latest breath:) you may rest assured that I will not commit the Legion Unnecessarily & unless more powerfully supported than I at present have reason to expect." His only plan for the rest of the winter, he informed Knox, was to take an advanced post at or near Fort Jefferson, forty or fifty miles north of Cincinnati, hurl defiance at the Indians in hopes that they might change their mind about war, and continue preparations to move in strength against his foes in the following spring. Working within these guidelines, he wrote a letter to General Scott, who was now at Georgetown, Kentucky, with the mounted volunteers, asking the general to march those troops forward and help guard his Legion in its advance.[26]

To his utter astonishment, Wayne learned from Scott on the twenty-second of September that only 200 Kentucky volunteers still remained embodied at Georgetown, and that the Legion commander could expect few more than that number eventually to come forward. Wayne growled to Scott in late September, "This is not a common or little predatory war made by a few tribes of Indians; it is a confederated war forming a chain of circumvallation around the frontiers of America . . .and unless the fire kindled at the *Miamis of the Lake* [where the confederation had been born] is extinguished by the blood of the *Hydra* (now a little way in our front) it will inevitably spread along the frontiers of Pennsylvania, Virginia, Kentucky, the Territory S.W. of the Ohio, South Carolina and Georgia inclusive." Then he pleaded to the Kentuckian, "One United & Gallant effort of the Legion and Mounted Volunteers will save the lives of many, very many thousands of helpless women & Children." After this exhortation, Scott did collect 1,500 of the Kentuckians for Wayne's fall campaign, but of this number most joined the Legion army only *after* it had reached its winter quarters.[27]

By late September, General Wayne had completed preparations for his northward march with his proud Legion Army. His provisions were collected and loaded on wagons that had been painstakingly gathered together at Hobson's Choice over the past few weeks, his men were ready to go into motion, and his letters from old friends David Jones and Sharp Delany, wishing him God's protection, were read and safely tucked away in his luggage. Then trouble struck the Legion Army, in the form of an influenza epidemic, and General Wayne, along with a large number of his troops, were laid low for days on end with fever, chills, vomiting, and aches. Finally, however, despite agues, influenzas, or any other impediment, Wayne declared to Wilkinson that he intended to move northward, and on October 7 he finally set out from Hobson's Choice, in weather described by St. Clair as the "finest. . .one ever saw." Following the wide roads that he and Wilkinson had caused to be opened in preparation for the advance, Wayne moved carefully toward Fort Hamilton, the first station on the "line" from the Ohio River to Fort Jefferson, as he followed his own carefully laid plan of march that he had outlined to Knox and Delany in the summer of 1792. Always, day or night, the general had far in advance of his army and on its flanks strong dragoon patrols searching for Indian raiding parties, and never in the evening did he encamp without securing his position with "small temporary breast works & Abatis such as to cover the troops." It was not his intention to be surprised, as the American generals sent earlier against the Northwest Indians had been; shrewd caution was to be the hallmark of Anthony Wayne's methodical assault on America's enemies north of the Ohio River.[28]

After only a short stay at Fort Hamilton, Wayne pushed his army on toward Fort St. Clair and then Fort Jefferson. With every day that passed, he expected and almost hoped to meet the Indians in a pitched battle and end his campaign in glorious victory. But the Indians remained hidden from view. So, without incident, six days after he had departed Hobson's Choice, he reached the "end of the line," half a dozen miles north of Fort Jefferson, where his good, wide road came to an abrupt terminus. Then, for a moment on the fifteenth of October, it looked as though Wayne might get his battle, because that day some Legion dragoons ran into a strong Indian party, not far from his camp on the southwest branch of the Miami River. The Indians turned out to be a detached raiding party, and therefore no large battle developed on Wayne's front. Despite the smallness of enemy numbers, however, the dragoons retreated in confusion from this unpleasant confrontation and threw their general into a pet. To a man, he had the squad placed under arrest and given a court martial, at the same time ordering that the grave of the commanding officer be dug in anticipation of the court's verdict. Sure enough, the leader of the retreat was found guilty and ordered shot, but at the last moment Wayne pardoned the condemned man, then used the occasion of the Legion's parade for this spectacle to harangue the troops for half an hour on the horrors of cowardice.[29]

Although Wayne had now progressed as far as he had originally intended to before taking winter quarters with his Legion Army, he began to grumble to Knox and Wilkinson that he wanted to go even farther north, but for the shortage of supplies at Fort Jefferson. The problem, he fumed, was that the contractors Elliot and Williams, rather than fulfilling his explicit orders to rush forward 250,000 rations, had supplied only 70,000, with 12,000 more on the way. These, he told Senator John Edwards and Secretary Knox in separate letters during late October, were quite adequate to support his troops where they were, but too few to feed an army on the march — and he was beginning to get suspicious that Antifederalist pressures, rather than simple inefficiency, were behind the contractors' foot dragging. Wayne hinted darkly to St. Clair that "in the failure or *defect* on the part of the Contractors respecting the deposits of provisions & the additional means of transport order.d," there had been "something like a many headed Monster" designed "to reduce me to a retreat." Therefore, he began writing periodic letters to Elliot and Williams (which he continued throughout the winter), berating them for their dereliction of duty in not fulfilling their obligations. Also, he finally concluded that the supply situation was such that he must stay put for the winter — certainly not withdraw from "an inch of land we have occupied" — and work on procedures to protect supply convoys and camps from a "desperate & determined" enemy. His men were in constant danger from ambush, as he emphasized to Edwards and Knox with a report about a convoy protected by 90 troopers under command of Lieutenant John Lowry, which was fired upon the morning of the seventeenth of October near Fort St. Clair. Consequently, he said, he was strengthening the escorts for convoys and hoped to avoid another incident "along the line."[30]

With his mind already made up to winter on the site his army now occupied, General Wayne on October 31 belatedly called his generals, Wilkinson, Scott, Robert Todd, Thomas Barbee, and Thomas Posey to a council of war to assess their opinions about what his immediate course of action should be. Since none of these officers questioned the commander in chief's decision to stay put for the season, Wayne's plan of operations was confirmed. Scott did want the general to detach the Kentucky Mounted Volunteers for a "desultory expedition against the Indian Villages at Au Glaize," but Wayne felt that the proposed expedition was too hazardous and as a substitute offered to let Scott ride against a small Delaware town to the southwest of the new Legion camp. As it turned out, Wayne did not even get to launch this minor foray, for to his utter disgust one-third of Scott's men — through no fault of the Kentucky general — simply decamped in mid-November without orders and lit out for home. This unconscionable desertion, snapped Wayne to Knox, "will show whether that prejudice" he had earlier shown against militia troops "was well founded or not. . . . Let the Legion be completed, & I wish no *further or other force*" to defeat the "haughty savages" in the ensuing spring and summer. Since the remaining Kentucky militianmen were now too few in number to serve any good military purpose, the commander dismissed them as well, but he admonished General Scott to be ready in the spring of 1974 to have his men take the field once more.[31]

Since the Legion was to remain where it was for the next few months, Wayne in mid-November put his troops to building a permanent military installation. Soon fatigue details were laboring upon a stockade to enclose an area of about fifty acres, with strong bastions on the corners for the mounting of the army's howitzers. Along with huts for his men, Wayne also had officers' quarters, mess halls, storage rooms and other buildings erected, and soon the place was snug and secure for the winter. The new post General Wayne named Fort Greeneville, in honor of his friend and colleague, General Nathanael Greene, and as he described the site to Catherine Greene in December, it must have been imposing indeed. The fort, he noted, was located on high, commanding ground, almost surrounded by a beautiful, extensive prairie that was broken in places by islands of trees. All this territory appeared to be a favorite hunting ground of the "hostiles," which he believed were assembling about eight miles in his front to contest for control of the land. In any case, the Legion had no worry, for it was ensconced in an unassailable post, and unless "Fortune, a Capricious female, with whom I may no longer be a favorite," intervened against him, Wayne had every hope of eventually destroying the power of the Northwest Indians.[32]

CHAPTER *XII*

Fallen Timbers
1793–1794

ALTHOUGH WAYNE in letters to friends made his situation at Fort Greeneville sound idyllic, conditions were far from serene in the Legion's encampment in late 1793. For one thing, as Wayne told Wilkinson, the contractors Elliot and Williams continued to fall short on their contractual obligations, sending to the army in mid-December "700 scrawny cattle" and no salt with which to cure the meat. In addition, Wayne by Christmas was once more abed with the "Caitiff" fever, and although he wanted to have dinner on the 25th with Wilkinson, he was incapable of riding to Fort Jefferson, where his second in command held sway, for the occasion. Worse than these matters were growing murmurs in the Legion Army against Wayne's severe discipline and against what some of his officers termed his "petulant" behavior toward them. He had allowed this situation to get so bad by late December that even a few of his friends were congratulating colleagues who had managed to secure furloughs and escape the "abject servitude" of having to live under Wayne's authoritarian ways. Declared another officer, "there is no calculating on anything but insult and opression" from the suspicious, dark-browed General Wayne, who stalked the confines of Fort Greeneville like a caged tiger, ever ready to lash out against real or imaginary personal insults or challenges to his authority.[1]

Part of Wayne's difficulties were self induced — a truth that the general found difficult to admit. It was a fact, however, that his regimen toward his fellow officers was strict to the point of harshness and that, perhaps worse, he played favorites with them. As a case in point,

249

Captain Edward Butler (youngest brother of Wayne's old friend Richard Butler of Revolutionary War days and a favorite of the general) was accused by superior officers, such as Major Thomas Cushing, of being incompetent in his job as deputy adjutant general. Wayne, instead of intervening in this matter on Cushing's side, actually had the major arrested for insubordination and paid not the slightest attention to the charges against Butler. Then, when another officer, Captain Isaac Guion, stood up for Cushing, Wayne charged the captain with unmilitary behavior and disobedience of orders. Finally, Colonel John Hamtramck, commanding officer of the First Sub-Legion, insisted to Wayne that Butler, who had disobeyed general orders, must not be screened from censure by his position as a member of the general's headquarters "family." Indignantly, Wayne lashed out at Hamtramck, whose loyalty to his commander in chief had never been in doubt, reminding him to attend to his own affairs and insultingly chiding the colonel about the "disrespectful" comment that Wayne was protecting officers who did not do their duty. Quietly Hamtramck swallowed the unfair reprimand, but it did not alter the point that Wayne was guilty of *precisely* what the colonel had accused him. It was not surprising that Hamtramck, in response to this churlish behavior on the part of Wayne, concluded that "There is no doubt about it; the old man is really mad."[2]

In truth, Wayne was no more "mad" in 1793 than when he was given his undescriptive sobriquet years before in the war for American independence. While part of his surliness and his short-tempered mishandling of personal relations was due to his physical discomfort because of lingering illness, and while part was merely his manifestation of a basic attitude about the necessity to maintain tight discipline in his command, much more was due to Wayne's lucid, and entirely correct, belief that he had real political enemies in the officer corps of the Legion. Wayne declared to Delany on January 1, 1794, that many of his subordinates constantly resented his authority, thwarted his orders, and spread untrue stories about him in both the army and eastern society, because they suffered the "same baneful leaven" that motivated Antifederalists to attack not only President Washington, "the most worthy and immaculate character of this or any other age," but also the "confidential officers of his government."[3]

The source of most of Wayne's problems in the Legion in late 1793 — although he did not know this fact — was Brigadier General James Wilkinson, whose continuous underhanded attempts to erode the commander's authority, both within and without the army, were beginning to bear fruit. Wilkinson, a man who throughout his lifetime was motivated almost exclusively by considerations of personal advantage and who had reentered the American army in 1791 because of ambition, had been promoted brigadier general a year later and fully expected to replace St. Clair as commander of the Legion Army when the latter officer was defeated in the same year. The Washington administration, though, was aware that Wilkinson had earlier been part of a scheme to entice Kentucky to declare independence from the United States and form an alliance with Spanish Louisiana, and the president did not consider the man trustworthy enough to hold the supreme military position in the American army. (This distrust was not misplaced, for strong evidence would be unearthed within the next four years by the Washington administration and by Wayne himself, that the Kentuckian was still an agent of the Spanish in New Orleans.)

Bitterly disappointed when command of the Legion devolved upon Wayne, Wilkinson began acting as though his position at Fort Washington was independent of the commander's and he corresponded with Secretary of War Knox upon this basis. General Wayne, of course, could not tolerate this state of affairs, and he subsequently clarified the situation in a friendly manner with both Knox and Wilkinson and compelled his second in command to subordinate himself within the army hierarchy. While overtly complying with this arrangement, Wilkinson continued over the next few months to erode Wayne's authority in whatever ways he could. He practically forced Wayne's friend, Captain John Armstrong, from the service in early 1793, apparently for no other reason than that the man admired the Legion commander. And although Wayne subsequently appointed Armstrong to lead a special corps of mounted volunteers, the captain never forgot Wilkinson's persecution. Later, as sheriff of Cincinnati, he high-handedly abused pro-Wilkinson men (such as Captain Guion) by arresting them on trumped-up charges. Wilkinson also cultivated friendly relations with antiadministration politicians, even going so far as to supply them with confidential military information and to write letters critical of Wayne's strategic plans. But most seriously of all for General Wayne, Wilkinson began to turn officers in the Legion against their commander, by disparaging Wayne's abilities and railing against his "ruthless," authoritarian discipline.[4]

Thus, by early 1794, Wayne was faced with a situation at Fort

Greeneville in which the officer corps was split into "two distinct Parties," with the Wilkinson people openly arrayed against him. One supporter of Wilkinson accused Wayne (not to his face) of being "Rude, Ungentlemanly, and Unjust." Wayne still suspected nothing regarding Wilkinson and continued to remain partial to his second in command, as he had from the first moment he reached Pittsburgh in 1792. At that time, Wayne had expressed great pleasure that Wilkinson, his "friend," was his lieutenant, and shortly afterwards, he went out of his way to assist Wilkinson's wife in making a trip eastward toward Philadelphia. Before long, however, Wilkinson — who of all officers in the Legion had least reason to complain about Wayne's attitude toward him — began to carp and pick at relatively minor "slights" from Wayne, such as the commander's correcting him in a letter a few months before on the meaning of the term "light company." In October 1793, Wilkinson wrote a friend, Harry Innes, "My General treats me with great civility, and with much professed Friendship, yet I am an O, for he conceals his intentions from me, never asks my opinion, & when sense of Duty forces me to give it, he acts against it." Wayne, he declared, was a "blockhead." Because Wayne was still unaware of his plans, Wilkinson as late as the spring of 1794, still overtly reciprocated Wayne's professions of respect. But already he was planning, as soon as may be, to break publicly with Wayne and attempt in ways other than surreptitious to destroy the reputation and career of the one man that he believed stood in the way of his towering ambition to command the Legion Army.[5]

Even though personal and martial discontents continued into the early months of 1794 to disturb the repose of Legion Officers at Fort Greeneville, General Wayne continued his methodical program of applying pressure against the Northwest Indians, to force them to sue for peace on terms acceptable to President Washington. Early in January, he announced to Knox that a Legion expedition of eight companies and some detached artillery under Major Henry Burbeck had taken possession of St. Clair's old battlefield of 1791, twenty miles to the north of Fort Greeneville, and had erected a small fort there, which he named Recovery. After reinforcing this post and making it impregnable to Indian assault, he then impelled small military units even farther northward toward Indian towns on the Auglaize River. One of these patrols, he told Knox, had had a brush with the Indians, in which three privates and five natives had been killed, but Wayne, unrelenting in his attacks despite this loss, sent Captain William Eaton out for another bout with the enemy. Meantime, he wrote Governor Isaac Shelby of Kentucky, ordering that mounted volunteers from that state, still embodied between Georgetown and Lexington, be immediately put under his command, to be used in case a rumored French military expedition, said by Knox possibly to be organizing in Kentucky for attacks on Spanish possessions in the Mississippi Valley, should actually be launched. Assured by Shelby in early February that no such scheme was afoot, the relieved commander rescinded his order and turned his attention full time to contending with Indians to the northward.[6]

General Wayne's powerful thrust to St. Clair's old battlefield and his building of Fort Recovery, both intended to overawe his native foes with the power of the Legion to the point that they would sue for peace without a fight, seemed in mid-January, 1794, to have had its hoped-for effect. A Delaware Indian named George White Eyes came forward to Fort Greeneville under flag of truce to parley with Wayne about the possibility of a peaceful settlement of their differences. The general welcomed his antagonist with great ceremony but made clear immediately that he must talk not only with the chiefs of the Delawares but representatives of other Indian tribes as well. If the Indians truly wanted peace, he told George White Eyes, they must agree to release all white prisoners now in their control and arrange for a full-scale treaty by the next full moon (February 14). In the interim, Wayne agreed with the Indians to have the Legion Army and the native warriors observe a cease-fire in place.[7]

As he told Knox, Wayne understood that he was taking risks by adhering to this course of action, for it was entirely possible that the Indians might use peace negotiations to buy time to remove their women and children out of the way of impending destruction while securing winter provisions and reconnoitering Legion strength. Perhaps, he said, he would come to regret the loss of this present "Golden favorable Opportunity" to advance against his enemies over frozen swamps and lakes and prove to the "Haughty savages" that not even inclement weather or distance were "security against the effect of the Bayonet Espontoon & fire of the American Legion." But he felt sure, and so he told General Posey on January 21, that the Indians would sue for peace and confirm that Wayne had made the right decision by delaying military operations while seeking immediate peace.[8]

For the next month, Wayne waited uneasily for a response from the

Indians to his call for a peace parley. Writing to his friend, Delany, he complained that "this is a cold & dreary wilderness at this season of the year without any other cover than a thin & worn our *Marquee* with scarcely any of the *Necessities* & few or none of the *Comforts* of life." He would have been unhappier than he was had he known that his Indian foes — Buckongahelas, a Delaware chieftain, Blue Jacket, a Shawnee war leader, and Little Turtle, chief of the Miami — meeting in grand council, were rejecting his call for peace. Part of their obstinancy, he would learn, was based upon promises from Guy Carleton, Lord Dorchester, British governor of Lower Canada, that the English probably would be at war with America within a year and that if so the Indians could expect fully to recover all lands they had lost since 1783. Another cause for the Indians' decision for war was their belief that Wayne was untrustworthy, a notion that received a powerful boost when on the twenty-third of January Big Tree, a Seneca chieftain, suddenly became deranged at Fort Greeneville and killed himself. Unfortunately, Wayne tried to claim that the man's Indian enemies had put something in his food to make him depressed, and this ham-handed attempt at psychological warfare backfired when all the chiefs rejected the story as ludicrous, instead listening to Dorchester's British agents, who argued that Big Tree's death may have been caused by Wayne himself. Thereafter, nothing that General Wayne could say (and he tried many times, even into late March, to persuade the Indians to sue for peace) had the slightest effect in changing their minds. It became a growing certainty that the Legion, reinforced by Kentucky Mounted Volunteers must fight the Indians — and perhaps the British in Detroit — for supremacy in the Northwest Territory.[9]

Consequently, Wayne immediately began to put his army in final order for a culminating drive northward into Indian territory. He wrote Secretary Knox, advising the administration that his men needed new clothing after their long winter at Fort Greeneville and complaining that Congress was not giving him enough support in his attempts to expand the size of his army beyond its present number of 2,000 effectives, over and above the garrisons he must keep in his fortified base camps. But after being informed by Knox on March 31 that the Legion was already as large as it would be for the upcoming campaign, Wayne did not appear greatly chagrined at his prospects for destroying Indian power in the ensuing months. Meantime, he proceeded to order Major Thomas Doyle of the First Sub-Legion to occupy Fort Massac on the north bank of the Ohio River, about ten miles below the mouth of the Tennessee River, in order to implement Knox's wish to head off angry Kentuckians from making "hostile inroads into the dominions of Spain" because the Spanish authorities were threatening their trade on the Mississippi River. He also favorably responded to Kentucky governor Isaac Shelby's request to provide pay for state militiamen who were patrolling along the Ohio River to defend against Indian raids into the Commonwealth.[10]

In the midst of his military preparations, Wayne was shocked in early May to receive a letter from Issac Wayne, informing him of the contents of Elizabeth Iddings Wayne's last will and testament. His mother, it appeared, had taken revenge upon her undutiful son for his neglect in paying her annuity, for most of her estate of more than £1,000 had gone to the children of his sister, Ann Hayman. Moreover, the Haymans were designated executors of the will. Wayne himself had been left with only £5, and his children, Margaretta and Isaac, had received £165 each; even these funds were to be drawn from monies that Mrs. Wayne decreed were still owed her estate from Wayne's unpaid annuities. The general, in a letter to Isaac on May 9, 1794, declared his astonishment at these stipulations, but was certain that they stemmed from some sort of derangement that possessed the old lady shortly before her death. The matter, he was sure, could be "amicably resolved" with the Haymans, should he live to return home. "In the meantime," he exhorted his son, "I must request you to keep on good terms with Captain Hayman and all your relations as far as possible and treat them with polite civility; at least, it costs nothing; add to this, it is prudent."[11]

As the campaigning season approached, James Wilkinson, Wayne's bitter but still sub-rosa enemy, became more actively involved in opposing his commander. In fact, it appears that Wilkinson was even going to the extraordinary length of prevailing upon Elliot and Williams to slow deliveries of provisions to the Legion, that Wayne be compelled to delay mounting a campaign until it was too late in the season for it to succeed and that Wilkinson's hand be strengthened in his machinations to secure command of the Legion Army. Wayne a few months before had come to suspect that someone was meddling with the contractors' attempts to supply his army, but he still attributed his troubles to a generalized Antifederalist intrigue rather than to his ambitious subordinate. "The same Nefarious faction which continues to convulse the grand Council of the Nation," he told Knox on May 30, had thrown snares in their path, but he was moving vigorously to stamp out the opposition. To Elliot and Williams he roared, "I will no longer be imposed upon or trifled with, nor shall the army be starved, nor shall the Interest, Honor and Dignity of the Nation suffer through your neglect and non-compliance with positive and repeated Demands." With these and similar admonitions from Wayne ringing in their ears, the contractors busied themselves in forwarding provisions to the Legion at Fort Greeneville, and Wilkinson's scheme to delay the army's advance by starving it was thwarted.[12]

With Wayne succeeding, in spite of all his subordinate's machinations thus far, to prepare the Legion for an immediate campaign against the Indians, Wilkinson now wrote, or had written, an anonymous newspaper assault against the commander. This article, which was widely printed, accused General Wayne of every grossly incompetent thing that it was remotely possible for an army commander to be guilty of. Among other things, Wilkinson, or his stooge, charged Wayne with wastefulness, stupidity, incompetence, stealing, drunkeness, favoritism toward "his pimps and parasites," and a refusal to pay attention to Indian peace proposals. With this publication, signed "Army Wretched," Wilkinson intended to create such restlessness in Congress and the Legion against Wayne that the Washington administration would be compelled to relieve its controversial commander, even if the president and Knox — who of all men were in a situation to know that the essay was malicious — did not believe any of the charges. Wilkinson's scheme failed. President Washington, bolstered by private support in Philadelphia from General Charles Scott, who declared in a letter to Knox that Wayne was conducting his affairs with "great Sobriety & extream attention to the duty of the Army," stood by General Wayne during this period of political turmoil. At the behest of Washington, Knox wrote Wayne, reiterating the administration's continued backing of him, pointing out that the protests came from "disorganizers," whose "imbecillity" destroyed their own credibility, and declaring that the secretary of war would do all within his power to defend Wayne "against all misrepresentations" in Congress.[13]

Wilkinson was disgusted, to say the least, at this turn of events. Not a little of his anger was directed against General Scott, whom he called privately "a fool, a scoundrel and a poltroon," and whom he feared might be appointed to command the Legion Army should Wayne be incapacitated or lose the position for any other reason. Hence, he now made formal charges against Wayne to Knox in the War Department, including all of the matters he had already stated publicly or anonymously in the newspapers, and he demanded of both General Wayne and the administration a court of inquiry in order to scotch the spread of "rumors" that he had made attempts to ruin the Legion's system of supply as a way of embarrassing his commander. When Knox received Wilkinson's request, he merely ignored it, claiming that since it had been made in a private letter the general was not serious about the contents. Knowing that Wilkinson's sole purpose in this affair was to ruin General Wayne, Knox did not mention Wilkinson's letter to the Legion's commander. Meanwhile, Secretary Knox and the president arranged to have a Federalist organ, the *Gazette of the U.S.*, publicly counteract antagonistic newspaper assaults on the performance of their Legion commander by using General Scott's favorable letter about Wayne as a basis for much of their defense.[14]

Even with the evidence mounting that Wilkinson was after his scalp, General Wayne refused to respond in kind and continued, as he had been doing for months, to soothe Wilkinson and attempt to woo him into a more cooperative frame of mind. So, while he rejected Wilkinson's demand for an inquiry as "ideal" under the circumstances of time and place, nonetheless he expressed a "wish" that the officer would travel up to Fort Greeneville and examine all the facts relative to the commander's difficulties in trying to run the army under adverse circumstances. Wilkinson's "advice & cordial assistance upon the present momentous occasion," declared Wayne in this conciliatory letter, would be most welcome. At the same time, Wayne admitted to Wilkinson that as far as he was concerned, General Scott ought to inherit command of the Legion, should Wayne for any reason lose his ability to do the job, for the procedure conformed to "military etiquette." Wilkinson, reduced to temporary impotency by Knox's refusal to support him against Wayne, could do no more than ignore his commander's overtures of friendship, attack Wayne in private correspondence to friends, and await a more propitious moment to mount another public assault against Wayne's character and credibility.[15]

With Wilkinson momentarily silenced, General Wayne turned his attention to preparing for the summer campaign against the Indian tribes. By May 26, he was receiving disquieting intelligence that the British in Canada under Lord Dorchester and Simcoe were intervening directly on the side of their Indian allies by refurbishing an old army post named Fort Miami, near Roche de Bout on the Maumee River. Into this fort, Wayne was told, the British were throwing a garrison of 400 men and a number of heavy cannon to protect the Indians, 2,000 in number, who had gathered at that place to halt the American army's advance into lands they claimed by treaty and by right of ancient occupation. Immediately, Wayne wrote Governor Shelby of Kentucky, asking that 1,000 mounted volunteers be sent to the Legion Army at Fort Greeneville, for the commander now determined that he would launch an expedition against the enemy on or about the first of July. He complained to Knox that British occupation of Fort Miami made his situation "delicate & disagreeable," for were he to be forced into assaulting the Royal troops in that post, America might be accused of aggression and get into a war with the British nation. Yet, declared the Legion's commander to Governor Shelby, if the administration gave him the signal to attack the Indians, he would proceed to close the eighty-mile gap between Fort Greeneville and Roche de Bout and destroy the "savage barbarity" of Simcoe's "red Myrmidons" in the Maumee River Valley.[16]

For Knox and the administration, Dorchester's blatant violation of American territorial sovereignty was, to say the least, embarrassing. In April 1794, President Washington had sent an emissary, John Jay, to London with instructions to hammer out agreements with Britain on posts in the Northwest Territory, and other matters. Should Wayne be compelled to attack English troops while these delicate negotiations were going forward, the United States might find itself forced either to recall Jay or to commence a full-fledged war against Great Britain. In this situation, President Washington did not flinch. He gave orders to Knox that if it became necessary in the course of Wayne's operations against the Indians, the general was to "dislodge the party at the rapids of the Miami." Thus, Knox told Wayne, "You are hereby authorized in the name of the President of the United States to do it." General Wayne was delighted with these instructions for they showed that Washington was willing to repose confidence in his ability to handle this delicate affair to the honor and credit of the nation, and they removed his last impediment to action. He was, to be sure, somewhat sobered by intelligence that his Indian foes might receive support not only from the English garrison at Fort Miami but also 1,500 militiamen who were collecting at Detroit. Still, not the least daunted, he continued with aplomb throughout the remainder of June to make final preparations for advancing his Legion Army northward in a massive push against his enemies.[17]

The general's program was interrupted on June 30 by events that he believed at the time had only slowed his invasion but which in fact ultimately assured his triumph over the Indians by weakening their power. Early that day, about 2,000 Indians — practically the entire warrior force of the confederacy — surrounded Fort Recovery after destroying a 360-horse pack train and killing more than 100 Legion soldiers that guarded it. Subsequently, the Indians, led by Blue Jacket, Little Turtle, and Simon Girty, laid siege to the fort, which was garrisoned by eight companies of infantry and a new commandant, Captain Alexander Gibson. Finally, on the following day, the besiegers had to admit that their fighting strength had been perilously sapped by losses and at midday were compelled to withdraw northward toward home. Leaving the field where (as Wayne crowed) "they had upon a former Occasion been proudly Victorious," the mortally stricken Indian army suffered a final ignominy in seeing Gibson's small garrison sally forth and taunt them to return and fight.[18]

In early July 1794, on the verge of the most important military campaign of his career, General Wayne's thoughts turned to his family, friends, and mortality. He wrote to Delany on July 10, "As this may possibly be the last letter that fate will permit me to trouble you with, I have to request as my last favor that you will continue to be the friend & Guardian of my Orphan Children." Four days later, he drafted a will, bequeathing to his son Isaac Waynesborough, a lot in Harrisburg, 1,500 acres of his federal lands, and the estate in Georgia "called Hazzard's Cowpen." Upon Margaretta Atlee he bestowed the remainder of the estate, which comprised a house and lot in Philadelphia and 1,500 acres of Pennsylvania land grants, with the exception of "my large landed estate in the province of Nova Scotia," which was to be divided equally between Wayne's children after part of it had been sold to settle Wayne's "just debts." Concluding his legal business, Wayne the same day wrote for Delany a statement of his accounts, in order that his friend might settle obligations against the estate, should it become necessary to do so.[19]

General Wayne then turned his attention to composing what he believed might be his final letter to Issac (at the same time ignoring his daughter Margaretta). Anticipating an "interview" with the "largest number of savages" ever collected on the continent of North America, he told his son, he expected that he would be killed. Therefore, he was appointing Isaac co-executor of his estate, along with Delany and William Lewis, and was enclosing to him a copy of his financial statement to Delany and his will, to be executed "after a 'certain event.' " One purpose of the general's letter was to instruct Isaac on how to dispose of his personal papers, "which are very voluminous and rather promiscuously tyed together in bundles, and deposited in trunks, some at Waynesborough, some at Fort Washington, and some at this place." Among these papers, noted Wayne, were "many miscellaneous idle and juvenile letters that I fully intended to destroy, together with such as were no longer useful or necessary, and which I must solemnly enjoin you to perform immediately after my decease." The general also wanted his son to make sure that the "chain of title" to Waynesborough was secure, so that if the general fell during "that solemn appeal to arms, against superior numbers," Isaac would be assured ownership of the Wayne family's ancestral acres. Concluded Wayne, "If I am doomed to fall, — I hope and trust that my conduct will be such, as never to cause a blush upon the face of my children, or to require the kind paliation of a friend. Under these impressions, and with those sentiments I am only left to implore the omnipotent Governor of the Universe, to bestow his choicest blessings on, and to take into his protection, my only son & daughter. Adieu my dear friend, give your amiable and lovely sister a last embrace from your affectionate father."[20]

Last preliminaries for a march from Fort Greeneville were completed by Wayne during the next two weeks. On the sixteenth of July, 1,500 mounted volunteers from Kentucky began arriving at his command, and he set the army to hewing a wide road into the wilderness along his intended route of march toward the Auglaize River. Drawing up an order of march for his army, which now consisted of 2,169 soldiers, he instructed his men to advance in double column with dragoons protecting them on all sides and with scouts ranging far in front in order to reduce the risk of ambush. The Kentucky Mounted Volunteers, he said, would be stationed in the rear of the Legion Army to guard its communications and at the same time to stay within supporting distance of the main force. During the march, enjoined Wayne, the army must exercise the same caution that it had during its advance to Fort Greeneville, by building each night a square, fortified camp with breastworks of logs and an abatis all around. Artillery must be parked in the center of these seventy-five-acre sites, to be employed in case of an enemy assault. But Wayne's primary emphasis now, as it always had been during the training period, was having the soldiers rely on offensive spirit and highly disciplined bayonet charges. These plans made and all in readiness, Wayne wrote Secretary Knox on July 27, "Our advance will be as rapid and as secret as the nature of the case will admit and before the enemy can be informed."[21]

Next day, July 28, 1794, General Wayne gave the order for the Legion to march, and his soldiers swung out of the gates at Fort Greeneville with spirit and optimism. This well-trained force, prepared by Wayne with great care over a period of two years for the duty it was now undertaking, stepped smartly through the heat and humidity toward Fort Recovery. At noon the following day, the Legion proudly moved past that garrison, which a few days before had withstood the full might of the Indian army's assault, and from within the fort it received the salutes of cannon that had earlier been salvaged from the wreckage of St. Clair's defeat. Moving on beyond Fort Recovery, the army plunged into the wilderness at the end of the prepared road, and began fighting through "Thickets almost impervious, thru Marassies, Defiles & beads of Nettles more than waist high & miles in length." At last, three days later, after crossing seemingly innumerable streams, some of which were deep enough to require bridges, the army burst out of the forest onto open prairie near the St. Mary's River. There, Wayne on August 1 halted his men, built a strong camp, sent out scouts to probe for signs of the Indians, and began erecting a blockhouse which he later named Fort Adams. While hurrying his men along with their construction work, Wayne on the second of August was almost "deprived of life," as he told Isaac Wayne later, "by the falling of a tree. . .& was only preserved by an old trunk near where I was struck down — which supported the body of the tree from crushing me to attoms." Declared William Clark, a lieutenant in the Fourth Sub-Legion and a close friend of Wilkinson, had the tree been but a little more accurate in its fall it "had certainly deprived certain individuals of their A.W. & Particular persons of their concequence."[22]

Although Wayne survived this close call with death, he was nevertheless mentally shaken by the experience, his body was "much bruised," and his already none-too-stable health was undermined even more. Although he could still lead the army, it was only at the expense of much pain that he did so, for as he informed his son, "I find that I have been injured inwardly, from the frequent discharges of blood and by an almost total loss of appetite." More than a month later, he was "still weak and languid, nor can I expect to be restored to health until I experience a relaxation from anxiety and fatigue." Meantime, he was making "free use of bark and a partial state of rest" to maintain his health, at least well enough that he could keep command of the army. With his strength partially restored, and with the completed fort put under charge of a sick officer and forty equally sick troopers, Wayne on August 4 set the Legion in motion once more toward his waiting enemies on the Maumee River near Lake Erie.[23]

The route of march that General Wayne chose from that point was different from the one Josiah Harmar had used in 1790 or the one St. Clair had intended to follow a year later. Instead of descending the St. Mary's River into the heart of Indian power at the Miami villages on the Maumee River and then following the Maumee eastward toward Roche de Bout and British-occupied Fort Miami, he followed the Auglaize River directly northward toward Grand Glaize. Although the British in Canada and their Indian allies soon became aware of Wayne's direction of march, they were caught off guard, as were his own officers, whom he had not informed of his plans. The Indians had expected Wayne to advance against the Miami villages first and had prepared to meet the Legion Army on ground of their own choosing by shifting their strength in that direction. Additionally, both the Indians and the British were thrown into uncertainty by rumors, which Wayne had shrewdly allowed to circulate, that the American army intended to bend its line of march northeastward, directly toward Fort Miami. Before Wayne's enemies could decide where his forces would debouch into the Maumee Valley, he and the Legion Army on August 8 arrived at the recently abandoned village of Grand Glaize, which had been alerted only hours before by an American deserter. In any case, Wayne's army was now successfully interposed between enemy forces to the west (at the head-waters of the Maumee River), and to the east (at Roche de Bout and Fort Miami), and in a position, according to Lieutenant John Boyer, to defy "the English, Indians, and all the devils in hell."[24]

For a week, Wayne remained at Grand Glaize, making last-minute preparations for a push down the Maumee toward Lake Erie. Immediately, the general set his men to building a stronghold to command the confluence of the Auglaize and the Maumee rivers, which he named Fort Defiance. This powerful bastion he intended as a shield against enemies in the rear of his Legion as it pushed eastward, and also as a strongpoint to fall back on should he be forced to retreat. As the fort was being constructed, Wayne spent his time collecting food and forage for his army from fields and prairies nearby. He also sent numerous scouting parties to reconnoiter in all directions for signs of a gathering Indian army. Attempting one last time to lure the Indians into negotiations for peace without a battle, Wayne on August 13 — against the advice of Wilkinson — sent out an appeal for a parley with the chiefs. Since the Indians' response was merely to call for more time to discuss the matter, Wayne reluctantly accepted the fact that his enemies were stalling for time in hopes of using up the campaigning season in idle palaver. Consequently, he refused their offer and only awaited construction of Fort Defiance before putting his army once more in motion toward his foes.[25]

On August 15, with the stronghold nearing completion, Wayne ordered his army to advance eastward along the river's northern bank. Although he was convinced that the Indians would not offer battle, Wayne still had no intention at this late date of letting down his guard. Hence, on August 18, when he had maneuvered to within ten miles of the British stronghold of Fort Miami, he paused to throw up a rude stockade (which he named Fort Deposit) for all military stores and equipment not needed in battle with the Indians. By the evening of the nineteenth, the "citadel," as he called it, was about three-fourths completed, and Wayne determined that early the next day he would leave 200 men behind to work on Fort Deposit, while the remainder of his Legion, stripped of all baggage and other unnecessary encumbrances, would drive on toward Fort Miami.[26]

The morning of August 20, 1794, dawned hot and clear, and as General Wayne struggled out of bed that day, he realized that within the next few hours, some sort of climax to his military operations of the past two years would likely have been reached and passed. Either his Legion Army would clash with the Indians, who showed signs of preparation for an imminent battle with his forces, or he would confront the British commandant of Fort Miami, Major William Campbell, and perhaps precipitate a war between the United States and Great Britain. Secure in the knowledge that whatever he had to do he operated with the full approbation of President Washington and key cabinet members in Philadelphia, Wayne confidently prepared for his duties as a commander in battle. Much worse for him than any anxiety of mind on that hot morning of the twentieth of August was the physical agony of an

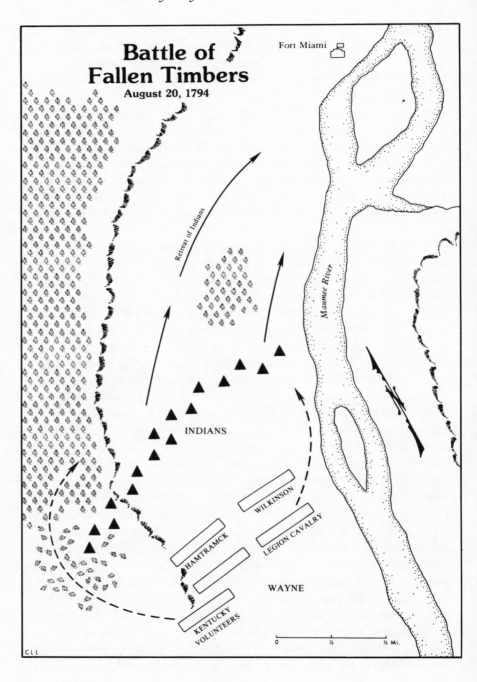

**Battle of
Fallen Timbers**
August 20, 1794

Fort Miami

Retreat of Indians

Maumee River

INDIANS

WILKINSON

LEGION CAVALRY

HAMTRAMCK

WAYNE

KENTUCKY
VOLUNTEERS

0   ¼   ½ Mi.

CLL

attack of gout, which he overcame only by swathing his arms and legs in flannel bandages before donning his uniform and swinging with difficulty into the saddle to lead his troops. But bodily infirmities or no, Wayne adjusted himself as best he could upon his mount, gave the order for the army to march, and at eight o'clock rode forward to his destiny. The Legion soldiers of his right wing he placed under the command of James Wilkinson, those on the left of Hamtramck. The extreme left flank of the army Wayne ordered to be protected by a brigade of Kentucky Mounted Volunteers under Brigadier General Robert Todd, while the right he intended to be anchored upon the Maumee River by the Legion cavalry, in charge of Captain Robert Mis Campbell. To bring up the rear of his army, Wayne disposed another force of mounted volunteers under Brigadier General Joshua Barbee, and at a considerable distance in front of the Legion he stationed a "select Battalion commanded by Major William Price with orders to warn the Commander should contact with the enemy be made."[27]

As Wayne rode forward with his troops over the next five miles, Major Price probed forward with his vanguard — and suddenly ran into an Indian army that was hidden in the woods and grasslands in the Americans' front, between the Legion and Fort Miami. Reeling back from the fire of the warriors, Price's corps became intermingled with Wilkinson's light infantry, and the brigadier general was forced to order all those troops to the rear for reforming. As Wayne listened to the musket fire from his advanced guards' initial brush with the Indians, he realized that the long-awaited battle with the natives had at last begun. Quickly, he rode forward with the remainder of his Legion Army to determine the strength of his foes and to reconnoiter the ground that his troops occupied. Although he could not determine the exact number of warriors facing him, he estimated (correctly) that there were about 1,000; what he did not know was that in addition there were probably some 60 Canadian militiamen. In any case, as Wayne viewed the dispositions of his enemies, it was clear to him that they had chosen their site of battle with care, for they occupied an area that had once been in the path of a tornado and was covered with a tangle of uprooted trees and underbrush which, as the general later noted to Knox, made it difficult "for cavalry to act" and afforded the enemy "a most favorable covert for their savage mode of warfare."[28]

Wayne also quickly noted that the Indians' plan appeared to be to attack his army's left wing, and he began arranging his troops to halt this movement with a thrust of his infantry into the enemy's center and with at least spoiling cavalry charges against both the enemy's flanks. By this time, Wilkinson had arrayed one part of the Legion Army into line of battle to face the Indians, and Wayne now ordered deployment of a second line, behind the first and in support, while he directed General Scott to ride with his Kentuckians "by a circuitous route" around the left of the American line and fall upon the native army in a cavalry charge from the rear. Meanwhile, his front line of infantrymen was immediately to assault the Indians, rouse them "from their coverts at the point of the bayonet," and deliver upon their backs as they retreated "a close & well directed fire," so as to deny them the chance to reload their muskets. Finally, Captain Campbell and the Legion cavalry were to advance with the rest of the army against the Indians as best they could on the American right flank near the Maumee River, penetrate the enemy's line, and roll it up.

All these orders, said General Wayne later in describing the battle to Knox, "were obeyed with spirit & promptitude." The front line of infantry, with arms trailed and deadly bayonets gleaming in the sunlight, charged with impetuosity against the Indians' positions, and after nearing their lines halted to deliver a deadly aimed fire at the warriors, who were ensconced behind their cover of logs and trees. Then, before the Indians could recover from the shock of the Legion's volley, the Americans rushed forward in a bayonet charge, howling at the top of their lungs. Under the weight of this unrelenting and highly disciplined advance, the Indians broke and ran. "We were driven," said one warrior chieftain, "by the sharp ends of the guns of the Long Knives, and we threw away our guns and fought with our knives and tomahawks. . . . But the Great Spirit was in the clouds, and weeping over the folly of his red children," who had "refused to smoke in the lodge of the great chief, Chenoten [Wayne]." Therefore, the Indians were routed from their concealed positions and pushed back more than two miles over the next hour through thickets and swamps, finally losing their great leader, Turkey Foot, of the Ottawas, who while attempting to rally them was cut down by a soldier's bullet.[29]

So total was Wayne's triumph over the Indians on the morning of August 20, 1794, in what was to become known as the Battle of Fallen Timbers, that General Scott and his Kentucky horsemen never even managed to get into the fight. The Indians simply fell back faster than Scott's mounted troops could plunge through the thick underbrush on the American left wing to get within striking distance of the enemy's right flank. Campbell's Legion cavalry, however, did turn the Indians' left flank, near the Maumee River, and his troopers rode at full gallop among the fleeing warriors, who had been forced from their cover by the American infantrymen using the terrible "sharp ends" of their guns. Gleaming cavalry broadswords now swished through the air, hewing down the nearly defenseless Indians, as the entire mob of intermingled cavalrymen and braves swirled past the tightly shut gates of Fort Miami. At last the Legion horsemen broke off their chase and returned to the victorious main body of General Wayne's exulting American army. Special praise, declared Wayne to Knox when he reported the results of this triumph, accrued to Wilkinson, Hamtramck, DeButts, and others, "whose brave example inspired the troops." (Wilkinson reciprocated his commander's generous gesture by declaring to Senator John Brown of Kentucky and Congressman Harry Innes that Wayne in the battle lacked resolution and enterprise, covered his ignorance of warfare by gasconade, neglected the wounded after the fighting ceased, sent his soldiers into battle without adequate equipment, and was generally indifferent to public expense; Wilkinson said the same results that Wayne achieved at Fallen Timbers with a costly regular army could have been accomplished with 1,500 volunteers in only thirty days' campaigning.)[30]

Following the short but violent battle with his Indian foes on the banks of the Maumee River, General Wayne assessed his losses and examined his strategic position. At a cost of 33 dead and 100 wounded troopers, Wayne's army had put his enemies to total flight, and although he could not know this fact at the time, had also destroyed their will further to resist his mighty veteran army. "The enemy," he crowed, "are. . .at length taught to *dread* — & our soldiery to *believe* in the Bayonet." His immediate problem now was the British fort in his front, for its garrison remained snugly protected behind closed gates and its commander, Major Campbell, showed every intention of fulfilling his orders to hold the post. For six days after his triumph over the Indians, Wayne remained near Fort Miami, destroying for miles about the helpless natives' crops and villages and trying to goad Campbell into a belligerent act. But nothing the general did — from provocative military maneuvers with his army in full view of the fort's garrison to a blustering, acrimonious exchange of notes with Campbell — had the slightest effect.[31] Finally, Wayne (not willing to take upon himself responsibility for starting a war between the United States and Britain) reluctantly concluded that he must leave Fort Miami intact and concentrate upon the major purpose of his campaign, which was the utter desolation of Indian power in the Upper Maumee Valley. Therefore, on August 26, he abandoned Roche de Bout to Major Campbell's domination and marched his soldiers westward toward more powerful centers of Indian civilization.

CHAPTER *XIII*

Peace in the Northwest
1794–1795

IMMEDIATELY UPON the arrival of Wayne's triumphant Legion Army at Grand Glaize, the site of Fort Defiance, the general put his men to work improving the defenses of that post, leveling ground to widen his cannons' fields of fire, digging deep trenches to guard against surprise attack, and setting up longer and stronger stockade fences. While carrying out these tasks, he also continued to destroy Indian corn and villages within a fifty-mile distance of the Maumee River on both sides. Wayne was convinced that these measures were necessary, for he was certain that his enemies intended one more desperate military effort against the Legion Army. Constantly receiving intelligence that the Indians around Fort Miami were being reinforced from Niagara for that purpose, he declared, "This is a business rather to be wished for than dreaded whilst the army remain in force," for the American triumph in the present Indian campaign would "only be more complete and decisive" if such an attack were to occur. The Indians, meantime, continued to vent their impotent rage against Wayne's ravaging army by keeping his sentries awake at night, "making most Dreadful yells, Howling like wolves, & crying like owls." But they never attempted any significant attack against the now-dreaded Legion Army, and Wayne's more immediate problem in early September was that supplies were beginning to run low at Fort Defiance. While he verbally lashed the contractors, Elliot and Williams, to improve their performance in delivering goods to the army, he also pressed General Scott's proud — and disgusted — Kentucky Mounted Volunteers into service for a time as pack horsemen to assist the quartermaster corps in bringing up vital stores of food.[1]

Although Wayne's duties at Fort Defiance in the first half of September were not as demanding as they had been for the past few weeks, he found little time to relax, for business, both public and personal, continued to consume his time and energies. On September 12 he sent his Indian foes an invitation for a general peace parley, only to have his message received with a stony silence. In the meantime, he also wrote his son, Isaac Wayne, filling the young man in on the details of his campaign to that time and thanking him for sending on certain scurrilous newspaper attacks that had appeared in the eastern press against the general. The "assassins" who wrote these pieces, he growled, were mere "catspaws of a Democratic or rather Demoncratic party both in & out of Congress," whose mischief reached even to the town of Cincinnati, where they had gained control of the sheriff. He was sure, however, that his own rectitude would protect him from these attacks, and that when the "Caitiffs" were unmasked (he still did not know that Wilkinson was behind much of the anti-Wayne propaganda) they would be held up to the light of the public ridicule which they so richly deserved.[2]

Indian parties, meantime, continued to harass the fringes of Wayne's Legion Army, cutting off small groups, ambushing patrols, moving rapidly and with stealth. To put an end to these aggravating nuisance attacks, Wayne decided to march his army westward to the Miami villages, the site of Josiah Harmar's defeat in 1790, and show the natives once and for all that their hegemony was broken, by seizing their most vital lands and constructing a permanent military post upon them. In this manner he also intended to destroy their warlike spirit and compel them to come to terms with American might in the Northwest Territory. Leaving a powerful garrison at Fort Defiance, the American commander set out on September 15 to effect what he hoped would be his last, and ultimately most successful, military maneuver of the campaign of 1794.[3]

Arriving unmolested at the Miami villages on the seventeenth, General Wayne immediately put his men to cutting timber for a new fort. A month later, he had the edifice completed and christened (according to the commander, "by the will of the Legion") Fort Wayne. The general declared this bastion to be the most important post between the St. Lawrence and the Gulf of Mexico, and absolutely vital for America to keep well-garrisoned, if the nation wished to see Indian power permanently suppressed in the region of the United States between the Ohio River and the Great Lakes. In a letter to Secretary Knox on October 17, he hammered home this point, for he was receiving from the East disquieting rumors that Congress again seemed on the verge of reducing the regular army by not completing its enlistments or replacing those soldiers whose terms of service were about to expire. Should the national legislature not enlist a full complement of regulars, declared Wayne, "We have fought bled & conquered in vain, the fertile Country that we are now in possession of will again become a range for the Hostile Indians of the West."[4]

Since the government's military policy was out of his hands, Wayne had to let others resolve the standing-army issue in Philadelphia, while he turned his attention to problems closer to hand. In October, he received a note from Lord Dorchester, informing him that John Jay and the British ministry had agreed to leave matters in the American Northwest "in statu quo" while negotiations went on between them, except that he and Wayne were to conduct an exchange of prisoners and effect a restoration of property that might have been seized by either side. Meantime, Wayne dismissed the Kentucky Mounted Volunteers on October 13, congratulating them on their contributions to the campaign and sending Governor Shelby a letter giving the volunteers credit for his triumph in battle. This militia force, declared Wayne to Knox, had proved to be the best that he had ever seen, especially in its willingness to remain in the field for a long period of duty.[5]

It had been General Wayne's intention all along to tarry only a short while at the Miami villages before marching southward to Fort Greeneville for the winter, and so in late October he prepared to depart Fort Wayne with part of his Legion. After appointing Colonel Hamtramck commandant of the post, he marched away from the fort that bore his name in the center of Indian power in the Northwest Territory. On the second of November, he arrived at Fort Greeneville, amidst cannon salutes and pompous ceremonials of welcome, with the "*Skeleton* of the Legion" — as he put it to Secretary Knox a few days later — but boasting that his army had now concluded "an ardous & very fatiguing, but a Glorious tour of Ninety seven days," in which it had marched and countermarched over 300 miles of territory, hewing a wide wagon road over much of the distance and constructing two fine, powerful, and permanent military posts to dominate the newly conquered lands. He reiterated to Knox, as well as to his son, Isaac Wayne, and his friend Delany, his earlier warning that all these exertions would go for naught should Congress refuse to keep a standing army embodied to garrison the posts and overawe the defeated Indians.[6]

In early November, Wayne at last received from the Indian leaders a favorable response to his calls for a peace conference. He congratulated them for finally coming to their senses and urged them to shut their ears to blandishments of "evil men" — British Governor Simcoe and the Indian agent Alexander McKee — to delay conclusion of a treaty. But in mid-December, despite his rising hopes that the "Indian business" would soon be settled, Wayne was compelled to report to Knox that the native leaders still hesitated to come to terms, apparently because they hoped that the Legion Army would be dissolved by Congress during the winter.[7]

While Wayne on the frontier prodded the Indians toward a peace settlement, his reputation in the East was under severe assault by opponents of Washington's Federalist administration. On Wednesday, December 3, 1794, a motion was made in the House of Representatives that the legislators offer three resolutions of thanks for the army's victory at Fallen Timbers, one to General Wayne personally, one to the regular troops, and one to Scott and the Kentucky Mounted Volunteers. Instantly there was a cry from the Antifederalists that these resolutions were dangerous in principle, that they set a bad precedent in honoring a mere general and an army, both of whom had done nothing more than earn their pay. After lengthy debate, it was decided by the solons that perhaps nothing would be amiss in their thanking the regulars and Scott's militiamen, but they refused to accord to Major General Anthony Wayne the same honor. Hence, they deleted any mention of the commander's name in the final resolution, a slight which Secretary Knox pointedly overlooked when he sent the resolution on to Wayne and the army. "It is with great satisfaction," said Knox, "the President of the United States directs the communication of the unanimous thanks of the House of Representatives to you, your army and the Kentucky Volunteers." General Wayne, upon receiving this resolution, also ignored the omission of his name, only noting silently that it was a curious way for the (supposedly) grateful representatives of a (supposedly) grateful people to treat a general whose military genius had done so much to advance the nation's welfare and future prosperity.[8]

Congressional debates, Indian intrigues, the weakening of the Legion Army by soldiers ending their terms of enlistment — all these problems, vital as they may have been for General Wayne during the winter of 1794–95, were overridden by the Pennsylvanian's "discovery" in December 1794 that James Wilkinson was attempting to strike a deal with the British in Canada to aid America's foes in combining the Northwest Territory with a part of Upper Canada in an independent nation. At least so the evidence indicated, although it was likely that Wayne, coming suddenly to believe the worst about his erstwhile friend, may have jumped to conclusions about Wilkinson's willingness to sell himself and a significant portion of United States territory to the British. Wayne asserted to Secretary Knox, "I have a strong ground to believe that this man is a principal agent, set up by the British & *Democrats* of Kentucky to dismember the Union," and he declared that "Was a peace once Established with the Indians no consideration wou'd induce me to remain a single hour longer in the service shou'd that worst of all bad men belong to it."[9] Obviously, the commander had been abruptly converted from his previous friendship with his subordinate in the Legion Army, and if his charges were true they raised the now-reciprocal Wayne-Wilkinson altercation far beyond the realm of a mere personal clash to the plane of vital American national interest.

What were the bases of Wayne's charges and the causes for his radical change of heart toward the brigadier? There were many, and they had been accumulating for some years. Even in the time before the commander had assumed his present post in 1792 (as Wayne had been apprised by Knox) Wilkinson was involved in a plot by some Kentuckians to get that territory to declare independence from the United States and ally itself with Spain. During the next two years, Wayne had suspected, but could never prove, that Wilkinson was interfering with the army contractors in supplying his Legion, that Wayne might fail in his mission to destroy Indian power in the Northwest and allow the brigadier to supersede him. Also, when the Washington administration was faced with the Whiskey Rebellion in 1794 in western Pennsylvania, General Wayne had heard disquieting rumors that there was more to that matter than a mere rebellion against excise taxes, that it was in fact a deliberately induced attempt by the British in Canada — with the assistance of their creature Wilkinson — to weaken the political unity of the United States.

All these matters, despite the weight of suspicion against Wilkinson, were for Wayne no more than hearsay and innuendo — until December 1794. At that time there came to Wayne's attention, through news from Chaplain David Jones, one Robert Newman, a former Kentucky schoolteacher, who was being held in the guardhouse at Fort Greeneville awaiting execution as a deserter from the American army. Declared Newman to Jones (who immediately passed the information to Wayne), he had direct and positive proof that Wilkinson was involved in a plot with British leaders in Canada to separate Kentucky and the Northwest Territory from the United States and — apparently — combine it with an Upper Canada that would also declare independence from Britain. Immediately, Wayne promised Newman clemency if he would make a full, written confession of these matters, and Newman was only too happy to comply. Thus appeared a written deposition from Newman that was at once bizarre and fascinating. In it he declared that Wilkinson and James Hawkins, a Kentucky land speculator, had hired him as a courier between the brigadier and Alexander McKee, British Indian agent, to deliver detailed written plans from Wilkinson to certain British officials in Detroit about Wayne's forthcoming military operations in 1794. Not all officials in Detroit were in on the scheme, and so when Governor Simcoe (who was not) learned that Newman had deserted the American army and turned up in Canada, he presumed the Kentuckian was an enemy agent and expelled him. While making his way back to the Legion, Newman was arrested in Pittsburgh as an army deserter and arrived back at Wayne's headquarters in irons.[10]

Despite the suspicious fuzziness of much of Newman's long monologue (Wayne himself declared that the man's "answers are rather mysterious negative & equivocal"), they corroborated many of Wayne's suspicions about Wilkinson. The general wrote to Knox on December 14, 1794, that Newman's story certainly justified the severity with which President Washington had suppressed the Whiskey rebels, for there was "no doubt in my mind but that there was & is a premeditated plan forward for the dismemberment of the Union thro' the machinations & intrigues of the British Agent [Wilkinson]." It also explained why there was a curious paucity of supplies for the Legion Army during the previous military campaign and why the Indians and British on the Maumee River in mid-August 1794 were alerted to his coming, thus denying him the ability to put an American garrison into "a certain post at the foot of the rapids of the Miamis of the Lake."[11]

As to Newman's veracity and trustworthiness as a source of intelligence, Wayne was "at a loss as to how to proceed" with the man. Certainly all he had said was not true; perhaps he was saying many things only because he suspected that Wayne wanted to hear them and by this means intended to save himself from the hangman's noose. Yet, his evidence, said Wayne, did tend "to shew that there is 'something rotten in the State of Denmark' & which ought to be guarded against." At the least, the general was persuaded by January 1795 that Wilkinson was a paid agent of some British citizens in Canada and that should the brigadier secure command of the Legion Army American interests in both Kentucky and the Northwest Territory would be fatally compromised. Knox and the administration fully sympathized with these sentiments, and their determination to support General Wayne to avert such a "disaster" was only hardened by these latest revelations. Wayne in the meantime put out orders to Captain John Pierce, commandant of Fort Washington, instantly to arrest James Hawkins should he appear in Cincinnati, and to seize all his personal papers. As the general noted to Knox on February 21, "if it does no good, it can do no harm."[12]

With General Wayne's sudden discovery of Wilkinson's supposed intrigues with Canadians in the winter of 1794–95, the Washington administration decided that it would serve no good purpose to keep Wayne in the dark any longer about the brigadier's charges of the previous June and July. In any case, Wilkinson since then had continued to keep up a steady drumbeat of criticism to Judge Harry Innes and others. "The whole operation" of Wayne's army in 1794, declared Wilkinson, "presents us a tissue of improvidence, disarray, precipitancy, Error & Ignorance, of thoughtless Temerity, unseasonable Cautions, and shameful omissions, which I may safely pronounce, was never before presented to the view of mankind." Declared Wilkinson to Innes in December 1794, Wayne was "a liar, a drunkard, a Fool, the associate of the lowest order of Society, & the companion of their vices, of desperate Fortune, my rancorous enemy, a coward, a Hypocrite, and the contempt of every man of sense and virtue."[13]

With these new slanders of Wilkinson's beating about their heads, President Washington and his cabinet quickly sent off to their army commander copies of his subordinate's letters of the previous June 30 and July 18, containing all Wilkinson's charges. Both Washington and Knox felt it was absolutely necessary to silence Wilkinson, for his rantings against Wayne endangered the future of the Legion Army in Congress (a bill extending the standing army's life for three more years was at that precise time being taken under consideration by Congress, and Antifederalists wanted only an excuse such as Wilkinson's charges to use against it). At the same time, Knox pleaded with both Wayne and

Wilkinson to settle this matter in private, for the good of the service and all concerned. Knox also laid down to Wilkinson the challenge that he either be forthcoming with specific evidence to bolster his complaints against the commander or let the matter drop.[14]

When in early 1795 Wayne received Knox's revelations about these doings of his second in command, he was genuinely surprised to learn that Wilkinson had made such pointed and unfair comments about him to the secretary of war. But he was also confirmed in his opinion that Wilkinson was a despicable enemy of his own country, who would stoop to any chicanery in order to forward the interests of his foreign masters, and himself. On January 25, 1795, in an eleven-page letter to the secretary of war, written in a white hot fury, Wayne declared that Wilkinson's "Charges accusations & imputations against me: were as unexpected as they are groundless: & as *false*, as they are base & insidious." The "vile invidious man," he fumed, had continued to treat him "with attention politeness & delicacy" while at the same time "*impiously*" working behind his back to destroy him. It was true, admitted Wayne, "that his Opinions & mine did not always quadrate," but that was primarily due to the fact that Wilkinson's ideas "were seldom founded in judgment, but generally the spurious production of a capricious moment." Resoundingly denying that Wilkinson's charges against him had any validity whatsoever, Wayne asserted that "On the contrary — I always indulged the Brigadier, in all that he wished or requested, except when those wishes or requests were incompatible with established rules & etiquette, & with the benefit of the Service — or when opposed to arrangements made for bringing the war, to a speedy, happy, & honorable issue." In sum, declared Wayne, Wilkinson was "as devoid of *principle* as he is of *honor* or *fortune*."[15]

The fury of Wayne's response to Knox's request for a reconciliation was not matched by Wilkinson. On the contrary, the brigadier, in writing Knox a "public letter" on Janury 1, 1795, declared, "My Lips are now Sealed, my Pen is dismissed from depicting well founded grievances, and I implore Heaven that the painful office may never be forced upon me." This maneuver was only a necessary tactical retreat, for he now saw clearly that the Washington administration would support General Wayne in any open quarrel between the two officers. Privately, however, he continued to demean Wayne, reiterating to Knox on the second of January all the charges he had laid against him previously and adding a new one, that Wayne's official battle report for

Fallen Timbers was so inaccurate that it could just as well be describing "the battle of the Kegs." He now began to cultivate opposition members of Congress as potential allies in helping him grasp power and bided his time until these persons — for their own political and ideological reasons — could strike at Wayne and the Federalist administration and elevate him, their favorite, to command of the Legion Army.[16]

Meantime, the fame of General Wayne had spread throughout the East, as the repercussions of his victory at Fallen Timbers began to be felt. When word of the general's triumph reached President Washington in the fall of 1794, it immediately became clear to him — and even to some of his political foes in Congress — that Wayne's point of view had been correct all along: Military power, manifesting itself in the form of a powerful regular army, in this case at least, could resolve for the United States what diplomacy was unable to accomplish.[17] Quickly, Secretary Knox, with the president's blessing, began using Wayne's victory and his letters advocating the continuation of the Legion to encourage Congress to extend the life of the standing army at least until a general peace treaty was concluded with the Indians. The Republicans were not impressed by Knox's arguments, preferring instead to quote Wilkinson's viewpoint that the same job could have been done by militiamen at infinitely less cost, and by early 1795 there was a full-scale whispering campaign going on against Wayne in Philadelphia because of his alleged tyranny and stupidity as an army commander. For instance, Cornelius Sedam of Philadelphia was writing in March 1795, "By many Genl. Wayne has been Sensured," but "Saying here and Saying there has no Effect. He has Done the Business and that Settles the Dispute. The President it Seems is highly Pleased with his Conduct and so are the members of Congress in General." Sedam was right, for the Congress of the United States on March 3 voted to extend the life of the Legion Army for three more years — much to the joy of General Wayne and the administration he served.[18]

Although General Wayne in late 1794 and early 1795 was preoccupied with scotching the devious plans of James Wilkinson, he yet found time to keep in touch with family and friends in the East. He confessed to Delany on the twenty-third of December that his physical strength was near an end, what with the many months of fighting the British "Hydra" and the rottenness in his own army. Yet he dare not "commit the Administration" of the Legion "into *Other* hands," so he must stay with the army rather than coming home to rest for a season. He also found time to commiserate with his son Isaac, who was discouraged at the pace with which his law studies proceeded. "Rise superior to every difficulty," urged Wayne, for "your learning will prepare you for the first posts in the nation. Let integrity, industry & probity be your constant goals." And if Isaac wished, as he had earlier requested, to take over management of Waynesborough, that was fine with the general — as long as it did not conflict with his law studies.[19]

News from his daughter, Margaretta Atlee, also attracted Wayne's attention during this time. In September 1794, William R. Atlee, the general's son-in-law, wrote that his wife was terribly despondent about the double losses of her mother and an infant child in only a short time of each other. Isaac Wayne had visited them, he said, and that helped some, but Margaretta was still very low in spirits. Not until February 1795 did Wayne reply to Atlee's letter, at which time he noted that Isaac had already informed him of his daughter's pain and sorrow, to which he saw no reason to add by writing her. Such memories as Margaretta cultivated, he mused, "are of no avail, but often prove injurious if not fatal to those who cherish them to an extravagant or weak excess." Still, "her happiness & prosperity has always lay near my heart in every Vicissitude of fortune, & if there shou'd be an apparent neglect in point of correspondence, rest assured that it did not proceed from want of sincere friendship & affection for you but from a pressure of business."[20]

Before this letter reached the Atlees, Margaretta sat down to write her father, from whom she had received no letter in almost three years. An affectionate heart, she began, felt the silence of a parent who had been gone all that time without writing, especially when this apparent neglect was added to her losses. "I have Buried one of the fines't little Boy's perhaps in the world," she said; "He liv'd 5 months. . .I must forget if I am to live." Meantime, she pointed out, her husband had written Wayne often but received no replies, while "My Brother frequently has Letters, & generally informes me." The Atlees had moved to the country, she said, and now resided in Chester County, near Waynesborough, where they visited regularly. Grandmother Penrose and Aunt Margaret were well, and this latter woman, said Margaretta, could not be too much praised for her care of Polly Wayne in her last illness. "Her sufferings indeed demanded it of us two that we be always at her bedside," and "her great sufferings wou'd have moved a stranger. . . . I hope & wish never to experience what I have within these two Years pass'd."[21] The general did not reply.

In the depth of winter, during the early months of 1795, the Indian tribes with whom General Wayne was trying to negotiate a treaty found themselves starving because of the destruction of their crops the previous summer by the Legion Army. Hence, some of them came in early January under flag of truce to Fort Greeneville as supplicants, having learned from sad experience that promises from their erstwhile friends, Governor Simcoe and Indian agent McKee, were not worth the breath it took to make them. Entering the presence of splendidly uniformed General Wayne in the council house of the fort, they could not help noticing the vast contrast between the well-dressed, well-fed Americans and their own tattered and bedraggled selves. Instantly, they were informed that under no circumstances could negotiations for peace take place on any other terms than the Americans' best offer, that the Ohio River would never be considered as a boundary line between Indian and United States territory. In any case, Wayne peremptorily announced to the few Indian leaders present, the only way binding talks could occur would be if the chieftains of the Wyandots, Chippewa, Ottawa, Potawatomi, Delawares, Miami, and other Indian tribes were willing to negotiate within six months at Fort Greeneville.[22]

Reluctantly, but inevitably, Wayne's Indian visitors agreed to these terms, and leaving hostages as a guarantee of their keeping the cease-fire that now went into effect, they retired from Fort Greeneville with an agreement to come again with their fellow chieftains on June 15, 1795, and hammer out a permanent peace treaty. As they departed they carried with them a preliminary draft of a treaty with which Wayne had provided them and a copy of which the general sent to Secretary Knox in Philadelphia. The object of peace now within his sights, General Wayne jocularly told Knox, on the twelfth of February, that "the bayonet is the most proper instrument, for removing the Film from the Eyes — & for opening the Ears of the Savages, that has ever been discover'd — it has also an other powerful quality! its glitter instantly dispeled the darkness, & let in the light."[23]

When Secretary of War Henry Knox departed Washington's cabinet in the spring of 1795, Wayne lost a staunch supporter in the East. But the new secretary, Timothy Pickering, proved to be just as loyal to the general, and that loyalty was reciprocated by Wayne. Therefore, the two men, after writing effusive letters of mutual respect to each other on Pickering's assumption of his new tasks, went on with business as usual. In April, the war secretary informed Wayne that he was forwarding to Fort Greeneville $25,000 worth of gifts for the

Indians who would be coming to the treaty negotiations in June, but he warned the general not to distribute any presents unless negotiations were successful. Additionally, he empowered the commander to promise the Indian leaders an annual subsidy of $10,000 per year for the land they relinquished. In a private note, he thanked Wayne for exposing the "conspiracy" that had threatened to dismember the nation and noted that "*all confidence*" in "a certain character" had been destroyed by Wayne's revelations.[24]

On May 15, Pickering sent Wayne a detailed set of instructions on the limitations the general must adhere to in his negotiations with the Indians. The boundary line to be drawn between American and Indian territory, he said, should conform to that proffered in the treaty of Fort Harmar, written in 1789. It was not the aim of the United States to gain more territory than was its due, but only to ensure peace. Nevertheless, Wayne must press for the right of America to maintain whatever military posts within its own domain that it deemed appropriate. To reinforce the administration's intentions vis à vis the desired treaty terms, Secretary Pickering sent along with his letter a detailed, twelve-page model for General Wayne to follow. The commander approved most of these terms but noted to Pickering that the proposed boundary line left American and Indian settlements uncomfortably close to each other. Why not, he suggested, set up a buffer zone for the indefinite future between the two sides, "a kind of consecrated ground," upon which neither side must infringe? Pickering found this idea impracticable, and the general did not include it in the final treaty.[25]

In April 1795, General Wayne was confronted with a problem in the guise of his old nemesis, Arthur St. Clair. The latter, it seemed, as federal governor of the Northwest Territory at Cincinnati, was upset because Wayne was not informing him about the progress of negotiations with the Indian tribes. Not until late April did St. Clair learn that Wayne had put in place a cease-fire with the Indians, and then only because Pickering told him. Thus, when General Wayne wrote him on June 5 to encourage the civil government to assist the army in keeping the peace while negotiations proceeded, the governor frostily replied, "As I have never, sir, had any information on the subject of the armistice," and as in any case he had doubts that an agreement struck by a military man was binding on civilians, and as the citizenry had yet "no notice of it, that I know of," he was somehow at a loss as to how he could cooperate with Wayne, although to do so "would give me pleasure, sir."

After receiving this letter, the general quickly mended his oversight, and St. Clair began to receive regular reports from Fort Greeneville about treaty proceedings. In addition, Wayne was only too happy to provide the governor in August with an escort of dragoons to accompany him on a trip of inspection into the "western Counties" of the territory.[26]

In two other civil-military incidents during 1795, Wayne clearly showed his continuing belief that in a military organization — even one supported, as in the United States, by a government founded on strong notions of personal liberty — the individual, and society at large, must subordinate this freedom to the necessity of military discipline within the army itself. One problem began when Colonel Hamtramck at Fort Wayne arrested Captain William Preston for what the commandant called a refusal to obey orders. When the captain appealed to Wayne for redress in the case, the general refused to intervene. As Wayne noted to Hamtramck, the young officer clearly was guilty, and "you were right in supporting your orders. . . . He is a very young officer — with rather too high an idea of *Equality* — those ideas are well enough in Civil Life — but dangerous in an army." Another case occurred when a "bad man" named Timothy Haley was thrown into jail by army authority at Fort Greeneville and the civil judges of the territory demanded his release "as a subject of civil law." To this request, Wayne issued a polite but firm refusal, citing as authority for his peremptory action certain sections of the Articles of War which had been "recognized by five successive acts of Congress passed under the present Constitution."[27]

During all this time, Wayne's dealings with the Indians proceeded apace. In late May, he was informed by Pickering that certain emissaries from the Quakers, with Washington's approval, were going among the tribes to promote peace. What the general thought about this piece of arrant nonsense he did not say, but he knew in any case that it could do no harm to ongoing negotiations. More worrisome were continuing violations of the cease-fire by both sides, for as Wayne told Pickering these would be magnified by the British in Canada as proof that a treaty was unworkable. As the mid-June date for commencement of the parley approached, Wayne expanded his works at Fort Greeneville to accommodate the Indians as they arrived, but shrewdly constructed his redoubts in such a way as to allow his cannon to point directly into the midst of the natives, in case they should attempt an uprising, as Pontiac had done years before at Detroit. Soon the many tribes began to collect at the fort, led by their venerable chiefs Little Turtle, Blue Jacket, White Pigeon, Buckongahelas, and others. The total number of Indians at the post finally numbered 1,130 before the treaty had been completely hammered out.[28]

Not until July 15, exactly one month later than they had originally been slated to begin, did General Wayne formally commence the negotiations for the treaty with the Indians. Assisting the commander were William Henry Harrison, Thomas Lewis, Henry DeButts, James O'Hara, and Chaplain David Jones. Arrayed against the Americans were the major chieftains, led (more or less) by Little Turtle. General Wayne, resplendently arrayed in his full dress uniform, opened the proceedings after some days of preliminaries by addressing the Indian leaders, through French-Canadian interpreters, reminding them that they had violated the treaty of Fort Harmar, signed in 1789. Two days later, Little Turtle replied that the treaty had been unfairly obtained and that it had given away too much of the Indians' sacred tribal hunting grounds. Wayne on the twenty-fourth retorted that the Indians must have come to that realization late, as they had already ceded away to the British and French vast areas of their territory. But, said Wayne, as a representative of his nation, he wished to be fair, and although America had already twice purchased the land under dispute, he would do so again if necessary.[29]

It was the close of Wayne's speech, however, that really sealed the fate of the Indian chieftains. The general had received information from Secretary of War Pickering, written on July 4, that the Senate of the United States had just ratified the Jay Treaty. The crucial part of this pact, for Wayne's immediate purposes, was that Britain had agreed to withdraw royal forces in the following year from all forts and garrisons on the American side of the international boundary line drawn by the Treaty of Paris in 1783. When the general made this startling revelation to the chieftains, it was brought home to them even more forcefully than it had been the previous winter that they could no longer depend upon Britain for aid and that they had no alternative but to agree to Wayne's terms. Consequently, on August 3, 1795, a treaty was concluded between them and General Wayne, in which they reluctantly ceded to the United States a vast tract of land to the south and east of a line encompassing much of Ohio and part of Indiana. Additionally, all hostilities were to cease, prisoners to be exchanged, and the United States to indemnify the Indian tribes by immediate grants of money as well as annual tributes of goods in future.[30] From his perspective and from the perspective of most Americans, Anthony Wayne, in hammering out the treaty at Fort Greeneville, had performed admirably and could be proud of his prowess as a diplomat. Negotiation of this pact was the culmination of his service as commander of the American army in the Northwest Territory.

CHAPTER *XIV*

Good Soldier's Reward
1795–1796

ALTHOUGH BY midsummer General Wayne had performed admirably both his military and diplomatic tasks in the Northwest Territory, he was not to escape the odium that was heaped upon the Washington administration by its political detractors in the rancorous months of in-fighting over the Jay Treaty and other matters. That agreement, which had been crucial for Wayne in his negotiations with the Indians, was looked upon by some Americans as a despicable capitulation to British power. Even Pickering admitted to Wayne that the document was no more than the best bargain the United States could get under the circumstances, but he still hated the fact that it had been taken up by Antifederalist, pro-French "Jacobins" as a useful bludgeon against Washington and all those who labored in the president's administration.

Declared Pickering to Wayne, the Antifederalists' problem was that they seemed determined to align the United States behind France, even if it meant putting the nation into a posture of belligerence with Britain. "Prudent, thinking men," he observed, could "rejoice in the successes of the French against the combined tyrants who would have overwhelmed them" and still be "on good terms with all other Nations" — especially the British, "who have it so much in their power to hurt us." But when President Washington attempted to stabilize American relations with Britain through negotiation of the Jay Treaty, he was vilified by "two or three Jacobin Newspapers," which were so biased in their reporting that "a stranger would suppose the president a haughty tyrant, and that we were on the eve of a revolution." Pickering was desperately afraid that the raging of the "Demoncrats" would anger the British and cause them to drag their feet about withdrawing from United States territory in the Northwest, a consideration that Wayne echoed on August 9. Should that happen, warned Wayne, it was entirely possible that the Indians would renege on the treaty he had just negotiated and revive their war against the United States. But much to his — and Pickering's — relief, the people seemed to be swinging in favor of the Jay Treaty, and there was reason to hope that it would be executed and that the British would evacuate their posts on American soil as scheduled.[1]

Given the circumstances in which the United States found itself vis-à-vis the British in the Northwest Territory during the fall of 1795, Wayne strongly believed that now was no time for the army to let down its guard or be withdrawn from its posts north of Fort Washington. On the contrary, he was informing Pickering on September 14 that he was setting out on an expedition toward the St. Mary's and Auglaize rivers to reconnoiter sites for the construction of additional posts, in order more firmly to secure American control in the region. Pickering, however, speaking for the administration, wished for Wayne to consider reducing the expensively maintained garrisons already in place, especially the one at Fort Greeneville. This was not to be considered an order, for only the general on the scene could know where and how much military might was needed in order to overawe the Indians and keep distant posts reinforced. Nor did Wayne accept Pickering's suggestion, for a retrograde motion of the army, he told the secretary on November 9, after arriving back at Fort Greeneville from his trip, would only reinforce British arguments — which were already being "sported" about to Indians in Detroit — that Britain and America would be at war over the Jay Treaty in the spring and that the Indians could then break their recent agreement with the United States and join in the fighting against their foes. In any case, supplies for the army's winter garrisons had already been brought forward and would cost more to move back to Fort Washington than the government could possibly save by a withdrawal.[2]

A continuing perplexity for General Wayne, one which consumed more and more of his time in late 1795, was the apparent meddling of the Spanish authorities at New Orleans, New Madrid, and other posts on the Mississippi River with the trade of Kentuckians on that stream. Already the year before, Wayne had been compelled, at Secretary Knox's suggestion, to send Major Thomas Doyle and the First Sub-

Legion to garrison Fort Massac on the Ohio below the mouth of the Tennessee River in order to deter angry Kentucky militiamen from attacking Spanish garrisons along the Mississippi.[3] Since the governor of Kentucky either could not or would not intervene in this matter to calm his angry citizenry, Wayne as commander of the military district must assume this policeman's role along with his many other duties. Throughout the intervening months, General Wayne had encouraged Major Doyle in the latter's thankless duty and supported him when he had arrested some Spaniards for the murder of American citizens on United States territory.

By September 1795, Wayne's difficulties with the Spanish authorities were mounting. As he informed Pickering, rumors were filtering back to him that Señor Manuel Gayoso de Lemos, governor of a region which the Spaniards grandly referred to as the "District of Natchez," was constructing a fort at Chickasaw Bluffs, near the town of Memphis, on the American side of the Mississippi River. Immediately, Wayne reinforced his garrison at Fort Massac and ordered Lieutenant William Clark to reconnoiter down the Ohio and Mississippi rivers by barge under flag of truce to discover the truth of these reports. He sent with Clark a strongly worded message to the "Commander of the Spanish troops at Chickasaw Bluffs" that if he were infringing on United States territory he must desist and withdraw at once. When Clark returned, he brought word that not only were the Spanish building the suspected illegal fort but also another one, about seven and a half miles below the mouth of the Ohio River. Meanwhile, the Spanish governor wrote General Wayne, declaring that Spanish activities in that region were perfectly legal, based as they were on a treaty cession by the Chickasaw Indians to the Spanish crown.[4]

When Pickering and the administration heard of these proceedings, they strongly supported Wayne's investigation of alleged Spanish encroachments but hinted on November 7 that outstanding differences between the two nations were shortly to be adjusted by treaty to America's satisfaction. Therefore, Wayne must not precipitate a disturbance that might imperil negotiations then going on in Europe between Charles Cotesworth Pinckney and Spanish diplomats. (At the time Pickering wrote, Pinckney had already signed with Spain on October 27 the Treaty of San Lorenzo, which among other things guaranteed Americans free navigation of the Mississippi and the withdrawal of all Spanish garrisons on American soil.) Wayne, however, was not in a conciliatory mood, and on the twentieth of November blasted his Excellency, Manuel Gayoso de Lemos for his behavior, which was "a new & Extraordinary mode of demonstrating the wishes and intentions of the Spanish Government to preserve Harmony & friendship with the United States of America."[5] The governor did not respond to this intemperate letter.

Meanwhile, Wayne, who had applied earlier to Secretary Pickering for a winter leave of absence to visit Philadelphia (after more than three years' absence), learned that the leave had been granted. The problem that had restrained him from suggesting an earlier leave was that Wilkinson would assume command during his absence — a state of affairs which pleased no one but Wilkinson. Finally, it had been decided by Pickering that this "delicate subject" could be resolved by Wayne's making "*all* arrangements proper to be observed in your absence" and Wilkinson being "enjoined *not to make any the least alteration*" in them unless hostilities should make it absolutely necessary. Wayne followed this procedure, much to Wilkinson's discomfiture, by ordering the latter from his winter quarters at Fort Washington to Fort Greeneville and then presenting him with a cold, formal and minutely precise list of instructions to follow while Wayne was *in absentia*. Then, after arranging with army contractors in Cincinnati for delivery of supplies to his Legion the following year, after receiving an uncharacteristically complimentary message of good bye from Governor St. Clair, and after publishing a touching proclamation in general orders to the men of the Legion Army, he departed Fort Greeneville in mid-December.[6]

The general's progress of a thousand miles across America during January 1796, was uneventful but for bouts of pain from gout. He was rewarded for his travails by the reception he received from his home town, his family, and his close friends. Through his entire career, Anthony Wayne, the swashbuckling military romanticist, thirsted for public adulation, and no matter how many times he may have denied this fact, it was nonetheless a powerful force in his character. Therefore, he reveled in the attention he now received from everyone, both high and low in society, for his triumph over the Indians in the Northwest Territory. As he approached Philadelphia in the late afternoon of Saturday, February 6, he was met four miles outside the town by three troops of Philadelphia Light Horse and escorted into the center of the city. As he crossed the Schuylkill River, he received a salute of fifteen cannon fired by artillerists in Center Square. All along his route, he was met by the ringing of bells and shouts of joy from thousands of citizens, who lined the muddy streets and jostled each other to see and welcome General Wayne, their hero of the moment.[7]

The general's parade through the city ended at the City Tavern, where he dismounted from his horse and scanned the neat city that held so many memories for him. He was delighted to note in the surrounding crowds many veterans of his old Revolutionary War battalions, wearing their uniforms in honor of their former commander. He was also pleased that evening to view a display of fireworks over Philadelphia, "in celebration of the Peace lately concluded [by General Wayne] with the Western Indians." Although he was finally allowed that night to get some rest after his long and arduous journey, during the next few days he was feted by the rich and famous of Philadelphia. On February 12, he was entertained at a party which Vice President John Adams also attended. The following day, Adams noted to Abigail Adams, "General Wayne was there in glory. This man's feelings must be worth a guinea a minute. The Pennsylvanians claim him as theirs, and show him a marked respect." Then, on February 18 and 25, two great dinners were held by military men in Philadelphia at Richardet's and Weed's taverns to honor Wayne; in attendance on these auspicious occasions were all officers of the United States Army in the city at the time and also the famous old general, Daniel Morgan.[8]

In the midst of all these festivities, General Wayne found time to visit a number of government officials and private acquaintances. One of the first calls he made was at the home of President Washington, to inform him personally of events in the West. Wayne also spent much time in conversation with the new secretary of war, James McHenry, about military affairs. As soon as was humanly possible, the general ducked from public gaze long enough to drop in on his oldest and best friend, Sharp Delany, whom he found recovering from a long illness. He also hastened to see his son, Isaac, upon whom he had lavished so much attention over the past few years while neglecting his daughter, Margaretta. The young man, Wayne was delighted to learn, was doing well as a law student in the office of William Lewis. It was not until two weeks later that he finally betook himself to rural Chester County to visit the Atlees. Margaretta, hurt by this neglect, later wrote him, "I thought I was forgotten by a Father whom I tenderly & affectionately love & respect."[9]

Poor Margaretta's observation was not far from the truth, for her famous father was being beguiled again by Mary Vining, and he could not give his attention to less important matters such as visiting a daughter. To the theater, to lavish entertainments at the homes of Philadelphia's wealthiest citizens, General Wayne was soon escorting Miss Vining, until rumors began to fly that they were engaged to be married. At least one person (and perhaps others as well) was shocked by this news. Mrs. Williamina Cadwalader, widow of General John Cadwalader, wrote to a friend, Ann Ridgely, "Such a weather-beaten, vulgar, affected old soldier, I should have thought, would not have suited her refinement." Yet Mrs. Cadwalader had heard the news of their engagement from a direct source, Mrs. Elizabeth Graeme Ferguson (another lady with whom Wayne had flirted at an earlier age), who was told the rumor by a person on quite friendly terms with Miss Vining. Besides, "since then I have had a confirmation." If the stories about an impending liaison between Wayne and Mary Vining had any truth to them, neither the general nor the lady ever breathed a word about their truthfulness. Certainly they continued to be seen together, on shopping trips through the streets of Philadelphia, or at the fireside of John Vining's home, where Miss Vining now resided. Perhaps they planned to delay news of their engagement until Wayne had completed his tour of duty in the West (the general intended to return to the Legion Army in the spring, in order to carry out the occupation of Detroit and to fulfill other provisions of the Jay Treaty). In any case, as Mrs. Cadwalader noted, "This is a strange affair of Miss Vining's, though 'none but the brave deserve the fair' and that he was brave is undoubted."[10]

Wayne's engrossment in affairs of the heart in early 1796 did not keep him from involvement in political and military activities while he remained in the East. Even before his arrival in Philadelphia, his name had been put forward by his friend DeButts and other well-wishers as a candidate for the position of secretary of war. When Pickering had been appointed secretary of state in January, the position had been thrown open, and a number of men, including Henry Lee of Virginia and Wayne, had been proposed to fill the office. Wayne's candidacy did not get very far, however, for as one excitable opponent of the general declared, "Terror has seized the public mind from the apprehension that we should be reduced to a state of insolvency" if the Pennsylvanian should win the appointment. Therefore, this same worthy had put forward the name of James McHenry "as an alternative & many seem glad to get out of the danger! " Apparently so, for McHenry won the position, and General Wayne, perhaps because he had been nudged out of the race by this Irishman, never warmed to the new secretary as he had to Knox and Pickering. In any case, the charges of profligacy laid against him by his enemies were nonsense and probably politically motivated, for he was (as anyone knew who wished to take the time to find out) always extremely careful with public property. Nevertheless, the slander worked to keep him from becoming secretary of war.[11]

Other gentlemen, especially from the interior of the state, made a fainthearted attempt to push Wayne as a candidate for governor of Pennsylvania in the race of 1796. The general was tempted by this idea, for it appealed not only to his egotistical desire for public acclaim but also to his sincere wish to serve the state, which now operated under a much more conservative constitution than the one he had fought against during and after the Revolutionary War. But when Wayne sampled opinions of prescient political observers in Pennsylvania about the chances of a Federalist candidate in 1796, he quickly learned that he would not be elected under that party's banner. The problem, he found, was that his old friend Thomas Mifflin was the overwhelming choice of Federalist and Republican alike, and his heart simply was not in making a race against someone he admired, and who would surely defeat him in any case. Thus, he did not campaign, and on election day he was buried at the polls by a vote of 30,020 to 193.[12]

If he had no success in gaining political office, General Wayne did come out a winner in certain matters before the United States Congress that bore directly on his reputation. Within days after he arrived in Philadelphia, the Senate took up the question of approving the treaty that he had negotiated with the Northwest Indians, and much to his delight it was ratified with ease. Another issue that was near and dear to his heart was not, for during this time a battle developed between the Federalists and their opponents over whether to reduce the size of the Legion. The strongest argument of the Antifederalists against the army's present size was that Wayne's forces no longer confronted any enemy that necessitated the number of troopers he commanded. President Washington and members of his cabinet, on the other hand, insisted that the Indians must still be overawed and that Britain and Spain must be compelled to abide by their agreements to abandon posts on American soil.[13]

In March, Wayne became involved in this debate, when a Republican-dominated committee of the House of Representatives called him to give testimony about the army. Along with McHenry, whom Wayne had already briefed about the needs of the Legion, the general strongly recommended that "the safest course is to leave the establishment as it stands for the present." The committee totally disagreed and on March 25 recommended to the House that Wayne's forces be reduced by sixty percent, to 2,000 men. But it did not stop there. In a measure that amply repaid General Wilkinson's cultivation of opposition members of Congress, it also recommended that the reduced army be led by a brigadier general instead of a major general and that this officer be allowed no aides — a proposal designed not only to save money but also to induce a disgusted General Wayne to resign, so that the Antifederalists' darling, the devious Wilkinson, might take over.[14]

Anxiously, Wayne watched the debate in the House of Representatives on this proposal, after it had been sent up by the committee for approval. And although his good friend, Representative Thomas Hartley, argued strenuously against it on the floor, it was accepted by a wide margin when it came to a vote. The entire measure, complained Chauncey Goodrich, was nothing more or less than an Antifederalist scheme "to get rid of Genl Wayne and place the army in the hands of a Jacobin and what is worse a western incendiary." Yet, no supporter of General Wayne, or Wayne himself, was completely devastated by this course of events, for everyone felt sure that the administration's position was stronger in the Senate. They were right, for in May, the senators, while acceding a reduction in the size of the Legion, refused to embarrass President Washington, or his commander, by accepting the House's elimination of the rank of major general. Although the opposition thundered in its newspapers that the entire matter was a gigantic Federalist coverup of Wayne's malfeasance in the West, the Antifederalists were compelled in May to accept a law that would extend General Wayne's command of the Legion Army for at least nine more months — at which time the matter might be reopened.[15]

With the power of his position thus precariously supported by the Congress of the United States, General Wayne in May 1796 began final preparations for a return to his wilderness command. Just prior to his departure, however, General Wayne went into conclave with Secretary McHenry to discuss the implications for national security of Brigadier General James Wilkinson's scheming in the West. It was now strongly suspected by the administration, and so McHenry informed Wayne, that this man was in addition to all his other faults a *paid agent of the*

Spanish, working for the interests of that power rather than for his own country's security. Bad enough had been the suspicion that Wilkinson had earlier plotted with Kentuckians to get that state to break away from the union and declare independence in league with the Spanish Empire. Bad enough had been Wayne's (apparently exaggerated) belief the year before that the brigadier was conspiring with certain British officials in Canada against the best interests of the United States. But this situation was potentially worse than any of the others, for if it were true, it might implicate Wilkinson in treasonous activities. Therefore, it required not much imagination on the part of Wayne, the president, or any Federalist cognizant of Wilkinson's activities and plans to discern how dangerous to America's western interests such a scheme might be.[16]

Wayne had become suspicious the year before that Wilkinson was mixed up in some business or other with Spanish colonial officials in Louisiana and had attempted to interdict secret messages between Wilkinson and the Spanish in New Orleans. First, he had ordered Lieutenant Clark, whom he sent to check upon Spanish activities at Chickasaw Bluffs, to take no one with him except his barge crew and to accept no letters or packets to anyone in Spanish territory. Second, the general had sent Captain Zebulon Pike to replace Major Thomas Doyle as commander of Fort Massac, under the strictest orders to stop and search all vessels on the Ohio River for suspicious bundles or letters (which might, of course, turn out to be correspondence between Wilkinson and Spanish colonial officials). Wayne was now interested to learn, in late May 1796, that the Washington administration also had suspicions about Wilkinson's "Spanish connection," and he was fascinated to discover that McHenry and other cabinet members had been conducting a quiet investigation into whether the man had anyone assisting him in the business of selling out to a foreign power. As McHenry told Wayne, the name of Dr. Thomas Power, long suspected of being another agent receiving Spanish gold, had turned up. For the activities of this man, and for his relationship to Wilkinson, noted McHenry to Wayne, the general must be constantly on the alert in the coming months.

But the revelations about Wilkinson and Power were not the only ones that Secretary McHenry had to divulge to Wayne about enemy agents in the West. He also informed the general that Washington's cabinet had become aware not long before that the French minister in Philadelphia had dispatched to the Ohio and Mississippi River valleys two French officers, Victor Collot and Joseph Warin, both of whom were skilled mapmakers, with orders to gather information about the region. These men were especially interested in fortifications, both American and Spanish, for France hoped soon to repossess the western lands that it had lost by treaty to Britain in 1763. McHenry told Wayne that the president and his cabinet were especially desirous of finding some pretext to seize the pair's papers, so if the general could devise a way to block their passage of the Ohio river and effect this capital aim, it would be much to the benefit of the United States. Consequently, Wayne immediately wrote Captain Pike at Fort Massac a top-secret message, ordering him both to arrest Power and to seize the French spies' documents, should any of these persons attempt to transport themselves or their luggage through the West by way of the Ohio River.[17]

With Secretary McHenry's revelations still echoing in his mind, General Wayne in early June 1796 took leave of President Washington, family members, friends, and Miss Vining, and rode westward to recommence his duties as army commander in the Northwest Territory. Despite the fact that he could expect Wilkinson to continue underhanded intrigues and personal attacks against him, Wayne still expected his upcoming months of service to be relatively easy. His primary missions, after all, were merely to take possession of British and Spanish posts on United States soil as they were evacuated by the respective armies, and to keep the Indians pacified in the process. On June 24, he reached Pittsburgh, where he found a letter awaiting him from Colonel Hamtramck at Fort Wayne, with news that the Chippewas seemed on the verge of reneging on their treaty agreements. Wayne discounted Hamtramck's fears but decided that he would push on rapidly toward Fort Greeneville just in case they were true.[18]

More importantly, Wayne upon his arrival at Pittsburgh talked with certain gentlemen, such as Hugh Henry Brackenridge, and learned that the Spanish agent Power really was intriguing in the West to forward Spain's advantage. His continuing purpose, as well as that of Wilkinson and others, was to separate these lands from the American union and declare an independent nation in alliance with Spain (or with France, should Louisiana in the future revert back to control of that country). Supposedly, Wayne informed McHenry, Power had visited Pittsburgh with this news, while he was on his way to see General Wilkinson, who had ridden down to Fort Washington to meet him. Power was de-

lighted, reported Wayne, that the brigadier was then in command of the
Legion Army, if only temporarily, and looked forward to the time when
Wilkinson's position would be permanent.[19]

In mid-July, General Wayne reached his headquarters at Fort
Greeneville and immediately relieved Wilkinson of command. His first
order of business was to push forward with plans to have Captain Pike at
Fort Massac intercept Dr. Power, or the Frenchmen, and seize their
papers. To his distress, he now learned from Pike that the latter had
earlier stopped Collot and Warin on a barge flying the flag of Spain —
before he knew they were specifically targeted for arrest — and had let
them proceed with their business. The only result of that episode was
that Spanish officials protested to Secretary of State Pickering about
American soldiers insulting their nation's flag and caused the general
and Pike considerable embarrassment.[20]

After this fiasco, General Wayne realized that the French officers
had probably eluded his grasp, but he was not about to give up his
scheme to seize evidence against Dr. Power. In fact, that gentleman had
quite recently departed downriver, supposedly on a trading mission to
New Madrid, with a bargeload of bacon. And since he had only days
before been in contact with Wilkinson, there was hardly any doubt that
he carried documents from the brigadier to Spanish authorities in New
Orleans. Therefore, Wayne dispatched to Captain Pike urgent orders
that he be on the lookout for Power's boat and seize it if he could. Pike,
however, did not espy the transport, only noting to Wayne on July 28
that it might have gotten by Fort Massac before he received the general's
orders, or slipped by his post under cover of darkness. The captain did
have one piece of important news, that Judge Benjamin Sebastian of
Kentucky had joined the conspiracy and bore watching.[21]

Disheartened that his prey had eluded his trap, Wayne nevertheless
determined to make one last try at seizing evindence against Wilkinson
and his partners, when Power made his way back upriver later in the
summer from his supposed trading mission. The general was absolutely
sure, and so informed McHenry on the twenty-eighth of July, that the
agent intended to return not only with documents for Wilkinson and
Judge Sebastian but also a "royal chest" of money from the Spanish
governor for payment to these men for services rendered. Wayne's plan
to seize evidence came within a whisker of succeeding, for on August 8
Lieutenant John Steele did stop a barge about half way between the falls
of the Ohio and Fort Massac, which had on board Dr. Power and a cargo

consisting of many barrels of coffee, sugar, rice, and tobacco. After a thorough search of the vessel — but without smashing open any of the sealed casks of produce — Lieutenant Steele reluctantly allowed Power and his goods to proceed upriver (although, as he told Wayne later, he was suspicious that the two men were not regular traders because of the oddness of their cargo).[22]

When General Wayne received this news, he was devastated, for he was certain that Power had with him on that barge all the proof he needed to destroy the secessionist conspiracy as well as the malignant "worst of all bad men," James Wilkinson. As he told Captain Pike and Secretary McHenry, it was obvious that the agent had stashed incriminating documents as well as a large sum of money, probably around $10,000 from the Spanish governor, in one or more of the barrels. Their hauling tobacco to Kentucky, snorted Wayne, was an obvious proof that they were not real merchants, for that was like "taking coals to New Castle." Although he was convinced that Wilkinson and Sebastian had been bankrolled to continue their criminal activities, he had no way to prove his suspicions, for now that his purpose was "discovered" by his enemies he must terminate the watch on the Ohio at Fort Massac.[23]

In any case, Wayne's attention by that time had been diverted from destroying Wilkinson's reputation to defending his own against the brigadier's attacks in the East. As soon as Wayne had reassumed command of the Legion Army at Fort Greeneville, Wilkinson hied himself to Philadelphia, where among his Antifederalist legislative allies he brought his scheming at last into broad daylight by demanding a formal court-martial against Wayne. Considerably embarrassed by the brigadier's latest performance, Washington and his cabinet tried to put the man off by noting that the Articles of War contained no provision for proceeding in such a fashion against an army commander. But when Wilkinson, in a shrewd political maneuver, threatened to take his case directly to Congress and have opposition legislators launch an investigation of Wayne in the full glare of public opinion and partisan politics, Washington's attorney general, Charles Lee, quickly reexamined the Articles of War and "discovered" there certain nuances (which previously had escaped his learned eye) allowing the president as commander in chief of the armed forces to order judicial proceedings against Wayne after all.[24]

The commander of the Legion Army was kept abreast of these

activities by Secretary McHenry and Captain Thomas Lewis. From the secretary on the ninth of July came a warning that Wayne would directly be receiving a copy of all Wilkinson's charges, to allow the general to "meet them if necessary." And from Lewis came a note that "Your friend W. is here industriously engaged to bring forward show charges which he has trumpt up at different times." Wayne, of course, knew what was afoot in all these schemes. "The fact is," he wrote McHenry, "my presence with the army is very inconvenient, to the nefarious machinations of the Enemies of Government & may eventually prevent them from dissolving the Union."[25] But incapable of doing more personally to ward off Wilkinson's attacks on his conduct, Wayne had to content himself with depending upon his supporters in Washington's cabinet to defend his reputation.

Meanwhile, General Wayne continued the business of running the army. On the twenty-third of July, he reported to the secretary that Captain Henry DeButts had occupied Detroit ten days earlier and that he was planning to move his headquarters to that town in August. In the early part of that month, he proceeded from Fort Greeneville through the wilderness toward his new post, all the while reminding his subordinates to reciprocate any politeness on the part of British officers who were retiring from forts on American soil. When he reached Fort Miami by river barge on August 10, he declared to McHenry that English officers, as they departed their positions, had been extremely accommodating toward United States troops, and the Washington administration should give this fact due weight in later relations between the United States and Great Britain.[26]

At last, on August 13, 1796, General Wayne arrived at the town of Detroit, the place toward which he had bent much of his attention during the past three years. His reception there, which he later described to his son, was a remarkable event. First, he was surrounded at some distance from the settlement "by the Chiefs & Warriors of numerous tribes of Indians — who welcomed their *Father* by repeated volleys delivered from their Rifles ear pearching Yells — & friendly shakes by the hand & other demonstrations of joy agreeable to the custom & usage of those brave & hardy sons of the Wilderness of the West." Then, as he entered the town itself, he was presented with "a federal salute of artillery Music & c.," a formal military review by the garrison and Colonel Hamtramck, who had earlier been ordered from Fort Wayne to Detroit, and a document signed by the Legion officers at the post declaring their delight once more to be serving under him.[27]

The physical appearance of Detroit in 1796 made a favorable impression upon the new commandant. The town, he noted to Secretary McHenry and Isaac Wayne, was "beautifully situate" upon the west bank of the Detroit River, in a strategic location between Lakes Erie and Huron. The buildings were constructed of wood and crowded together, but many of them were well furnished by their wealthy merchant owners and their "well-bred. . .elegant & sensible" womenfolk. Through the town ran a "main street. . .parallel with the river," which had "a Gate at each end defended by a block house erected over it." Surrounding the whole were "high pickets & Bastions at proper distances which are endowed with Artillery," and inside the walls was "a kind of Citadel which serves for barracks for part of the troops." Entrance to the post was gained only through one of the two gates on Main Street, and these were closed each evening at sunset after the town had been cleared of Indians — a practice which Wayne believed had been instituted after Pontiac's Rebellion in 1763, at which time that chieftain had tried to destroy the garrison at night. About 1,200 Indians were then in attendance at Detroit, noted the commander, living off American largesse, "in the day time. . .appear[ing] perfectly domesticated," but nevertheless required to withdraw during the hours of darkness.[28]

Settling into his comfortable new headquarters, General Wayne quickly fell into the normal routine of army business that ever consumed his time and energy, no matter where he was located. In late September, he told McHenry that these affairs, although mostly routine, had detained him at Detroit longer that he intended and that it was now impossible for him to visit Michilimackinac as he had planned to do earlier in the summer. He was working to improve the flow of supplies to his army and to survey, as *per* McHenry's instructions of the twenty-second of July, all government-owned stores of any kind in the hands of American troops in his jurisdiction. In late September, he learned by confidential letter from McHenry that President Washington intended to retire from public life at the end of his second term of office. The president's policies, Wayne declared, had ever been "founded in wisdom & patriotism. . ., for which he is so universally & justly celebrated (a few *Demoncrats* excepted — & even they in their hearts must acknowledge his worth)." Therefore, the man would be sorely missed, not the least by Wayne, who as an Army officer in the Revolutionary War and as commander of the Legion Army, had received steadfast support from the man.[29]

As he dealt with military matters, General Wayne also assisted the

Washington Administration in establishing civil government in those parts of the Northwest Territory that had previously been under the control of the British. The commander had taken with him to Detroit the secretary of the Territory to establish a civilian authority there, because Governor St. Clair himself had been unable to make the trip. Since Wayne was by no means certain that he had acted within his authority, he immediately wrote Secretary of State Pickering, informing him of this action and citing as warrant for it the absolute necessity of quickly locating a governmental presence in the region. To aid even more the process of fixing civil authority within his military jurisdiction, he followed up in August a request by Oliver Wolcott, Jr., Comptroller of the Treasury, that he collect information helpful for establishing procedures in the Northwest Territory to collect federal revenues. In all these matters, Wayne made clear his continuing and fixed principle that the supremacy of civilian government over the military must be asserted and supported by American army officers of all ranks.[30]

The affairs of General Wayne proceeded with unaccustomed serenity in the fall of 1796, for unlike his previous tours of duty, this one did not burden him in mind and body with a multiplicity of serious problems. His repose was shattered, however, in a painful and dramatic way in early October when his old and (supposedly) faithful friend, Reverend David Jones, arrived in Detroit. When the latter presented himself at headquarters after a long and arduous journey from Philadelphia, he was frostily dismissed by Wayne and told he could go right back home again. Confused and hurt by his friend's harsh greeting, Jones inquired with certain persons as to why Wayne was acting so curiously. The answer was that Wayne suspected him of having leaked to James Wilkinson, many months before, confidential information that Robert Newman was Wayne's source of information about Wilkinson being an "agent" of the British. Jones, declared the general, had been "taken in, deceived, & betrayed, by those with whom you expected to obtain favor & interest." Now aware of the problem, the reverend explained to Wayne the muddled series of coincidences that had led him to his conclusion; Jones insisted that he was totally innocent. At last it became clear to Wayne that he was wrong in suspecting his old friend of betrayal, and Jones agreed to remain with the general at his headquarters.[31]

Although General Wayne's responsibilities in the summer and fall of

1796 were less onerous than they had been in previous years, he was nonetheless suffering a recurrence of the gout, which had plagued him mostly during or immediately after times of severe mental and physical hardship. He wrote to a Philadelphia physician, Dr. Nicholas Wray, in early September that a "slow lingering fever" had plagued him for days, and "altho I have made free use of the peruvian bark," it still continued. Despite his illness, the general maintained a steady regimen of work and put forward a bold front, for on the twenty-eighth of September an observer noted, "The commander in chief is in good health & much beloved." Nevertheless, Wayne himself knew that his strength was waning and that he could possibly be facing a physical crisis as severe as some he had suffered in the past, in which he had been near death. Although he was only a relatively youthful 51, he had already abused his health with such rigorous military service and such high living in peacetime that his body had deteriorated under the strain.[32]

Having never tried before to conserve his strength when duty — or pleasure — called, Wayne did not do so now. For some weeks, he had been mulling over the possibility of moving his headquarters from Detroit to a place nearer Philadelphia, where he could remain in closer communication with the War Office. His present remoteness from the seat of government, he noted to Secretary McHenry on November 12, could only become worse during winter, after the rivers and lakes froze over, so he had determined to set out soon by way of Presque Isle, on Lake Erie, for Pittsburgh, where he could establish headquarters in "a central place." Consequently, in mid-November, after appointing Hamtramck commandant of Detroit, and after receiving from the inhabitants of the town a memorial of gratitude for the gracious manner in which he had conducted himself while doing duty there, he boarded the sloop *Detroit*, in company with his aides, including Henry DeButts, plus some other traveling companions, and departed the post.[33]

Although General Wayne promised McHenry in his last letter before leaving Detroit that he would correspond further with the War Office from Presque Isle about future military plans, he did not write again. When he reached his destination on November 18, he was extremely ill with the gout and had to be removed very gingerly from his quarters aboard the ship to warm and comfortable lodgings in a blockhouse there. Under the watchful ministrations of Captain Russell Bissell, commandant of the Presque Isle blockhouse, Wayne in the next week or so began to rally from this latest bout of a disease that had plagued him for years, and by the latter part of November Bissell was informing Major Isaac Craig, deputy quartermaster general at Pittsburgh, that the general was recovering nicely and would be on his way within a few days toward his new headquarters.[34]

A week later, however, General Wayne's condition had taken a serious turn for the worse and deteriorated rapidly to the point that he was obviously in danger of dying. Immediately Captain Bissell dispatched couriers to ride like the wind for Detroit in order to summon medical assistance for the general, who was in agony because the gout had settled in his stomach and had sent his temperature soaring. By the fourteenth of December, Wayne had been in excruciating torment for a week and was quite literally burning up with fever; "how long he can continue to suffer such torture," wrote the grieving DeButts to Major Craig on that day, "is hard to say." Shortly after DeButts penned these words, Dr. George Balfour, a surgeon with the army at Detroit, rode into the fort and quickly examined his patient — only to declare that the man was too far gone for medical assistance. Finally, at ten minutes past two o'clock on the morning of December 15, 1796, Major General Anthony Wayne was relieved of his agony by a death that under the circumstances could only be considered a blessing.[35]

The following day, with simple ceremony, Wayne was buried in a plain oak coffin at the foot of the flagstaff of the blockhouse, attended by the loyal DeButts, Captain Bissell, and the members of his command, and most of the populace of Presque Isle. According to his wish, Wayne was clad in his best uniform, a fitting attire for a man who had devoted the best part of his life to military affairs. Not long after these formalities were complete, Captain Bissell caused to be erected over the general's frozen grave a simple stone monument, etched with the initials, "A. W." and around the burial site he placed a plain wooden railing.[36] At peace beside the quiet waters of Lake Erie, removed from the stormy blasts of tempest that had roiled his life, Anthony Wayne slept with all humankind that had gone before him.

Even after his death, however, General Wayne continued to exert a powerful influence upon many persons whose quietude he had interrupted while alive. His nemesis, James Wilkinson, was the most directly affected, for this marplot at last seized the coveted prize of command of the United States Army. No one in President Washington's administration wanted this to be so, neither did they have any way of avoiding it without causing more political problems than they solved.

Therefore, the Congress of the United States allowed the rank of major general to lapse, and Wayne's former position of command devolved, more or less by *fiat*, upon Brigadier General Wilkinson.[37]

Family and friends were also affected, especially Sharp Delany and Wayne's son, Isaac. Delany noted with heartfelt grief that his "esteemed Friend's death" was "most distressing intelligence," and Isaac Wayne was similarly distraught. On a more practical level, these two men over the next few months tried to unravel Wayne's financial affairs, and they found the task next to impossible. Issac Wayne had to travel southward to Charleston and confront Edward Penman in order to get a settlement of money still owed General Wayne's estate from the deal struck between the two men in 1791. In the meantime, the executors followed Wayne's last will and testament of 1795 in resolving other matters pertaining to the distribution of the general's property, and when they had finished this wearisome task congratulated themselves upon resolving amicably all issues pertaining to the Wayne estate. But many years later, Isaac Wayne was rudely surprised when the United States Treasury Department informed him that the general's estate supposedly owed the government $5,000 for an obligation that was outstanding at the time of Wayne's death. Thereupon, Isaac Wayne interposed a counterclaim against the federal government, declaring that the Treasury owed Wayne's estate the amount of $5,870.84. Not until January 1811 was this matter finally settled when Congress, at Isaac's behest, enacted special legislation granting him the sum he was owed — which he immediately applied against the claim charged by the government against his father.[38]

Thirteen years after Wayne's death, his repose at Presque Isle (now named Erie) was interrupted when the pride of relatives and civic-minded citizens of Chester County moved them to bring the general's body home. In an address to the Pennsylvania Assembly in late 1808, Thomas McKean lamented the sad fact that his home state ignored the graves and life histories of a number of notable Pennsylvania revolutionaries, including Anthony Wayne. This sudden rekindling of interest in their late father's memory led Isaac Wayne and Margaretta Atlee to determine upon reinterring Wayne's body in the family's burial plot at St. David's Church, Radnor Township, near Waynesborough. Seeking information on what physical condition the general's remains might be in by that time, Isaac Wayne queried old Dr. Benjamin Rush, who informed him that in all likelihood Wayne had long ago turned to dust.

Consequently, the general's bones could easily be "taken up. . ., put in a box in their natural order," and surrounded by sawdust or wood shavings for shipment home. "I rejoice," declared Rush, "that public honor is at last to be done to one of the heroes of the American Revolution — I love his name — he was a sincere patriot, a brave soldier, and what is more, — an honest man."[39]

Thus assured that the project of moving General Wayne's body was feasible, Isaac Wayne traveled to Erie in August 1809 to effect the task. Unable himself to bear the emotional strain of presiding over the disinterring of his father's remains, he commissioned Dr. J. C. Wallace, a friend of the general's, to do the work. But when Wallace opened the grave, he found, much to his dismay, that Wayne was remarkable well preserved, having suffered decay in only the lower part of one leg. Since it was impossible to transport the remains in this state (embalming being out of the question), Wallace, with Isaac Wayne's approval, dissected the body and boiled the parts in a large iron kettle to render the flesh from the bones. Thereupon, the skeleton was cleaned, arranged in order in a new casket, and shipped home in that fashion. As for the contents of the kettle, as well as the surgeon's knives used in the "operation," they were ceremoniously returned to Wayne's old coffin and reburied in the original grave, which years later was obliterated, after the blockhouse burned and the parade ground was graded level.[40]

When after a tiresome journey of 850 miles Isaac Wayne arrived in Easttown with his father's bones on October 3, 1809, his entourage was met by an honor guard of Pennsylvania militiamen drawn up to escort the general to Waynesborough for a final time. The following day, in company with the same military guard, Wayne's coffin was taken in solemn processional through roads lined with friends and relatives to St. David's Church. "At 11 o'clock," wrote Isaac Wayne later to his father's old comrade in arms, Colonel Francis Johnston, "my worthy Ancestor & the Friend of Man" was interred within the cemetery, after which the Reverend David Jones "delivered a lengthy & an appropriate discourse."[41] (According to unattested legend, there was among the throngs of people come to pay their last respects on that day the aging society belle, Mary Vining, who for the first time since the general's death had left the self-imposed seclusion of her Wilmington home.) Finally, over the general's grave a stone monument in his honor was erected by the Society of the Cincinnati and the Philadelphia, Chester County, and Delaware County militia companies. Then at last, in the hushed and beautiful setting of the churchyard at St. David's, Major General Anthony Wayne rested in an utter quietude that he had rarely known during his extremely active life.

NOTES

Chapter I Genesis of a Soldier, 1745–1776

1. James McHenry to Nathanael Greene, June 20, 1781, cited in Louis Gottschalk, *Lafayette and the Close of the American Revolution* (Chicago, 1942), 252–53; Greene to McHenry, July 24, 1781, Bernard C. Steiner, *The Life and Correspondence of James McHenry: Secretary of War Under Washington and Adams* (Cleveland, 1907), 38; George Washington's "Opinion of the General Officers," March 9, 1792, John C. Fitzpatrick, ed., *The Writings of George Washington from the Original Manuscripts, 1745–1799* (30 vols., Washington, D.C., 1931–44), XXXI, 509–15; Douglas Southall Freeman, *George Washington: A Biography* (7 vols., New York, 1947–57), IV, 461A, V, 479; *John R. Alden, A History of the American Revolution* (New York, 1969), 254.

2. Ebenezer Elmer, "Journal Kept During An Expedition to Canada in 1776," New Jersey Historical Society, *Proceedings*, 1st Ser., III (1849), 55; Charles Royster, *A Revolutionary People at War: The Continental Army and American Character, 1775–1783* (Chapel Hill, N.C., 1979), 76.

3. Greene to McHenry, July 24, 1781, Steiner, *McHenry*, 38; Marquis de Chastellux, *Travels in North America in the Years* 1780, 1781 and 1782, Howard C. Rice, tr. (2 vols., Chapel Hill, 1963), I, 11–12; Alexander Graydon, *Memoir of a Life, Chiefly Passed in Pennsylvania, Within the Last Sixty Years*. . .(Harrisburg, Pa., 1811), 277.

4. Anthony Wayne to Washington, July 4, 1779, Anthony Wayne Papers, Vol. VII, Historical Society of Pennsylvania, hereafter Wayne Papers, HSP; Wayne's General Orders, July 7, 1776, Samuel Hazard, et al., eds., *Pennsylvania Archives* (138 vols. to date, Philadelphia and Harrisburg, 1664–   ), Ser. 2, X, 119; "Orderly Book of the Second Pennsylvania Continental Line, Col. Henry Becker," *Pennsylvania Magazine of History and Biography*, XXXV (1911), 474–75, XXXVI (1912), 249, hereafter cited as *PMHB*; Graydon, *Memoir*, 127.

5. Mary Wayne to Isaac Wayne, [1792], Anthony Wayne Papers, William L. Clements Library, hereafter Wayne Papers, WLCL.

6. Isaac Wayne (son), "Biographical Memoir of Major General Anthony Wayne, *The Casket: Flowers of Literature, Wit and Sentiment*, [IV], 193; John W. Jordan, ed., *Colonial and Revolutionary Families of Pennsylvania: Genealogical and Personal Memoirs* (3 vols., New York and Chicago, 1911), III, 1321.

7. Records of Wayne Family [undated], Wayne Papers, I, HSP; Isaac Wayne, "Biographical Memoir," *Casket*, [IV], 193; Jordan, *Families*, III, 1321–22.

8. Isaac Wayne, "Biographical Memoir," *Casket*, [IV], 193.

9. Ibid., 193–94.

10. Ibid., 194; Edward Potts Cheyney, *History of the University of Pennsylvania, 1740–1940* (Philadelphia, 1940), 119.

11. Isaac Wayne, "Biographical Memoir," *Casket*, [IV], 194–95.

12. Wayne to John Hughes, April 10, 1765, John Hughes Papers, Historical Society of Pennsylvania, hereafter Hughes Papers, HSP; William Otis Sawtelle, "Acadia: The Pre-Loyalist Migration and the Philadelphia Plantation," *PMHB*, LI (1927), 273–76.

13. Wayne to Hughes, April 10, 1765, Hughes Papers, HSP; Beamish Murdock, *A History of Nova-Scotia, or Acadie*. . .(3 vols., Halifax, 1865–67), II, 454.

14. Wayne to Hughes, May 30, 1765, Wayne Papers, I, HSP; Wayne to Hughes, July 9, August 5, 1765, Hughes Papers, HSP; Hughes to Wayne, June 3, 1765, cited in Sawtelle, "Acadia," *PMHB*, LI, 273–76.

15. Wayne to Hughes, October 7, 1765, and Copies of Land Grants of October 31, 1765, Wayne Papers, I, HSP; Hughes' Copy of Land Grants, dated November 1, 1765, Hughes Papers, HSP; Wayne's Agreement with Alexander McNutt for surveying lands, October 30, 1765, and Account by William Nesbitt of Fees Paid in Nova Scotia on Land Owned by Alexander McNutt, etc., November 28, 1765, both in St. John's River Society Papers, Nos. 4 and 6, American Philosophical Society Library; Sawtelle, "Acadia," *PMHB*, LI, 273–76.

16. Isaac Wayne, "Biographical Memoir," *Casket* [IV], 195, says the year was 1767; Charles Janeway Stillé, *Major-General Anthony Wayne and the Pennsylvania Line in the Continental Army* (Philadelphia, 1893), 10, says May 1766; Stillé is probably accurate.

17. Wayne to Amesbury and Bond, December 19, 1766, Wayne Papers, WLCL; Wayne to Thomas Proctor, June 5, 1767, Anthony Wayne Papers, Detroit Public Library; Isaac Wayne, "Biographical Memoir," *Casket*, [IV], 194.

18. Isaac Wayne to Wayne, May 6, 1774, Wayne to Messrs. Nourse & Lowell, December 24, 1774, Wayne to John Hunter of Barbados, September 7, 1775, Wayne Papers, WLCL; Deed, Isaac Wayne and Elizabeth Iddings Wayne, May 10, 1774, Wayne to Messrs. Harper & Dick, September 7, 1775, Wayne Papers, I, HSP; Indenture of Isaac Wayne and Elizabeth Iddings Wayne, December 3, 1774, in the Orrin June Collection, Waynesborough.

19. Wayne's comments in speech as he stood for the Provincial Assembly in Chester County, August 13, 1774, Wayne Papers, I, HSP.

20. Subscription for Relief of Poor of Boston, August 13, 1774, Wayne Papers, I, HSP; Isaac Wayne, "Biographical Memoir," *Casket*, [IV], 194.

21. Draft of Proclamation, [1774], and Draft of Speech, [1774], Wayne Papers, I, HSP.

22. *Votes and Proceedings of the House of Representatives of the Province of Pennsylvania, 1682–1776*, Gertrude MacKinney, ed., in *Pennsylvania Archives*, Ser. 8, V–IX (Harrisburg, 1931–35), VIII, 7211–12; Theodore Thayer, *Pennsylvania Politics and the Growth of Democracy, 1740–1776* (Harrisburg, 1953), 163; Richard Alan Ryerson, *The Revolution is Now Begun: The Radical Committees of Philadelphia, 1765–1776* (Philadelphia, 1976), 101–02.

23. *Votes and Proceedings*, VII, 7238–45; *Minutes of the Council [i.e., Committee] of Safety of the Province of Pennsylvania*, Vol. X, of *Colonial Records of Pennsylvania, 1683–1790* (16 vols., Harrisburg, 1852–53), 280; Ryerson, *Revolution*, 119n, 121n.

24. *Minutes, Council of Safety*, 285–341; *Votes and Proceedings*, VIII, 7351, 7358, 7380, 7382; Thayer, *Pennsylvania Politics*, 172; J. Paul Selsam, *The Pennsylvania Constitution of 1776: A Study in Revolutionary Democracy* (Philadelphia, 1936), 84–85.

25. Isaac Wayne, "Biographical Memoir," *Casket*, [IV], 195.

26. *Minutes, Council of Safety*, 373–74, passim; *Pennsylvania Gazette*, September 27, 1775; *Pennsylvania Packet*, October 2, 1775; Selsam, *Pennsylvania Constitution*, 83; Ryerson, *Revolution*, 152; Thayer, *Pennsylvania Politics*, 175. Ryerson asserts (*Revolution*, 137n) that Wayne lost the election to a Quaker. Apparently he was incorrect on this point, for there is strong evidence that Wayne was in the Assembly after October 1775.

Italicized words in direct quotations throughout the book are Wayne's emphasis.

27. Jno. Bartholomew and Lewis Gronow to Wayne, December 15, 1775, Francis Johnston to Wayne, December 18, 1775, General Order #1, January 1, 1776, Wayne Papers, I, HSP; Worthington C. Ford, ed., *Journals of the Continental Congress, 1774–1789* (34 vols., Washington, D.C., 1904–37), IV, 24; *Minutes, Council of Safety*, 442.

28. William H. Smith, ed., *The St. Clair Papers* (2 vols., Cincinnati, 1882), I, 107–08, 108n, 365n.

29. Ford, ed., *Journals of Congress*, IV, 29, 108, 118, 129, 134; Wayne to Captain Persifer Frazer, January 26, 1776, *PMHB*, XXXI (1907), 137–38; Francis Johnston to Wayne, February 26, 1776, Wayne Papers, I, HSP; Wayne to John Morton, February 8, 1776, Peter Force, ed., *American Archives: A Documentary History of the Origin and Progress of the North American Colonies* (9 vols., Washington, D.C., 1837–53), Ser. 4, IV, 958; Wayne to John Hancock, February 17, 1776, Letters of Brig. Gen. Anthony Wayne, Papers of the Continental Congress, No. 161, Vol. I, 187, hereafter cited as Wayne Letters, PCC, 161, I; "Orderly Book, Marcus Hook," March 28, 1776, *PMHB*, XXIX (1905), 472–73.

30. "Memorandum Book of the Committee and Council of Safety, 1776–77," *Pennsylvania Archives*, Ser. 2, I, 471; "A Remonstrance from the Committee of Inspection and Observation of Chester County to the Assembly," February 12, 1776, *Pennsylvania Packet*, March 4, 1776; David Freeman Hawke, *In the Midst of a Revolution* (Philadelphia, 1961), 148–49.

31. "Return of 4th Bn., Pennsylvania Regulars, Anthony Wayne, Colonel," February 17, 1776, Wayne Letters, PCC, 161, I, 192; Johnston to Wayne, February 26, 1776, Wayne Papers, I, HSP; Graydon, *Memoir*, 108, 122–23; "Orderly Books, Marcus Hook," March 9, 1776, *PMHB*, XXXIX, 472; Hawke, *Midst*, 148–49.

32. Wayne to Sharp Delany, April 22, 1776, Wayne Papers, I, HSP.

33. Ford, ed., *Journals of Congress*, IV, 163, 167, 187–88; Edmund C. Burnett, ed., *Letters of Members of the Continental Congress* (8 vols., Washington, D.C., 1921–36), I, 357.

34. Wayne to "My Dear Captain," April 11, 1776, Wayne Papers, I, HSP; Mary Wayne to Wayne, January 29, 1776, Wayne Papers, WLCL; Force, ed., *American Archives*, Ser. 4, V, 726.

35. Ford, ed., *Journals of Congress*, IV, 300; Wayne to Mary Wayne, April 22, 1776, and to Sharp Delany, April 22, 1776, Wayne Papers, I, HSP; Wayne to Congress, April 26, 1776, Wayne Letters, PCC, 161, I, 194.

36. Francis Johnston to Wayne, April 25, 1776, Wayne Papers, I, HSP; Washington's General Orders, April 27, 1776, George Washington Papers, Library of Congress, hereafter cited as Washington Papers, LC; Wayne to Mary Wayne, April 28, 1776, Wayne Papers, Detroit Public Library; Mary Wayne to Wayne, April 29, May 6, 1776, Wayne Papers, WLCL.

37. Wayne to Johnston, May 6, 1776, to Mary Wayne, May 10, 1776, Sally Robinson to Wayne, May 8, 1776, Wayne Papers, I, HSP.

Chapter II   Canada and Ticonderoga, 1776–1777

1. Wayne to Thomas Robinson, May 26, 1776, Wayne Papers, I, HSP.

2. Wayne to Johnston, May 14, 18, 1776, to Robinson, May 26, 1776, Wayne Papers, I, HSP; Wayne to George Washington, May 14, 1776, Washington Papers, LC.

3. John Sullivan to Washington, May 18, 1776, Washington Papers, LC; Wayne to Robinson, May 26, 1776, Wayne Papers, I, HSP; Sullivan to Congress,

June 1, 1776, Otis G. Hammond, ed., *Letters and Papers of Major General John Sullivan, Continental Army*, New Hampshire Historical Society, *Collections* XIII – XIV (Concord, N.H., 1930–31), I, 212; John Trumbull, *Autobiography, Reminiscences, and Letters, 1756–1841* (New York, 1841), 30; John Lacey, "Memoirs. . .," *PMHB*, XXV (1901), 192–97, 343–44, 347–51, 500; Charles P. Whittemore, *A General of the Revolution: John Sullivan of New Hampshire* (New York, 1961), 26–27.

4. Sullivan to Washington, June 5, 6, 1776, to William Thompson, June 6, 1776, Hammond, ed., *Sullivan Papers*, I, 218–19, 222.

5. Wayne to Benjamin Franklin, et al., June 13, 1776, Wayne to Delany, June 13, 1776, Wayne Papers, I, HSP; Thomas Hartley to Jasper Yeatts, June 12, 1776, *Pennsylvania Archives*, Ser. 2, X, 71–74.

6. Ibid.; *Pennsylvania Register*, June 13, 1829.

7. Ibid.

8. Ibid.; Howard H. Peckham, ed., *The Toll of Independence: Engagements & Battle Casualties of the American Revolution* (Chicago, 1974), 18.

9. Wayne to Franklin, et al., June 13, 1776, and to Mary Wayne, June 13, 1776, Wayne Papers, I, HSP; Hartley to Yeatts, June 12, 1776, *Pennsylvania Archives*, Ser. 2, X, 74; Sullivan to Phillip Schuyler, June 19, 1776, Hammond, ed., *Sullivan Papers*, I, 250; Wayne's General Orders, June 11, 1776, *Pennsylvania Archives*, Ser. 2, X, 118; Paul David Nelson, "Guy Carleton versus Benedict Arnold: The Campaign of 1776 in Canada and on Lake Champlain," *New York History*, LVII (1976), 343–44; Richard J. Hargrove, *General John Burgoyne* (Newark: University of Delaware Press, 1983), 93.

10. Guy Carleton to Lord George Germain, June 20, August 10, 1776, Colonial Office Papers, Class 42, Vol. 35, pp. 60–61, 122–23, Public Records Office (Microfilm Copy, Public Archives of Canada); Sullivan to Washington, June 12, 1776, Hammond, ed., *Sullivan Papers*, I, 230; Lacey, "Memoirs" *PMHB*, XXV, 202; James Wilkinson, *Memoirs of My Own Times* (3 vols., Philadelphia, 1816), I, 51; Nelson, "Carleton versus Arnold," *New York History*, LVII, 344–45; A. L. Burt, "The Quarrel Between Carleton and Germain: An Inverted Story," *Canadian Historical Review*, XI (1930), 211; Hargrove, *Burgoyne*, 94.

11. Wilkinson, *Memoirs*, I, 51-54.

12. Ibid.

13. Ibid., 54–55.

14. Sullivan to Schuyler, June 19, 1776, to Washington, June 24, 1776, Hammond ed., *Sullivan Papers*, I, 253, 263; Lacey, "Memoirs," *PMHB*, XXV, 203–04; Whittemore, *Sullivan*, 29–30; Nelson, "Carleton Versus Arnold," *New York History*, LVII, 346–49; Hargrove, *Burgoyne*, 94.

15. Sullivan to Schuyler, June 22, 1776, Hammond, ed., *Sullivan Papers*, I, 258–59; Elizabeth Iddings Wayne to Wayne, June 30, 1776, Mary Wayne to Wayne, July 6, 1776, Wayne Papers, WLCL.

16. John Trumbull to Horatio Gates, July 12, 1776, Trumbull, *Autobiography*, 302; Field Officers to Sullivan, July 8, 1776, Hammond, ed., *Sullivan Papers*, I, 282–83; Ford, ed., *Journals of Congress*, V, 488; Paul David Nelson, *General Horatio Gates: A Biography* (Baton Rouge, 1976), 56–61; Whittemore, *Sullivan*, 30–31.

17. "Minutes of Council of War," July 7, 1776, Force, ed., *American Archives*, Ser. 5, I, 233; Gates to Washington, July 29, 1776, Horatio Gates Papers, Box 19, New-York Historical Society; Wayne to Benjamin Franklin, July 31, 1776, Benjamin Franklin Papers, IV, 98, American Philosophical Society Library; *Pennsyl-*

vania Archives, Ser. 2, X, 78; Nelson "Carleton versus Arnold," *New York History*, LVII, 63–66.

18. Wayne to Mary Wayne, August 12, 1776, to Joseph Penrose, August 23, to Benjamin Franklin, et al., September 1, 1776, to Benjamin Rush, September 10, 1776, Franklin to Wayne, August 28, 1776, Penrose to Wayne, September 3, 1776, Wayne Papers, I, HSP.

19. Wayne to Mary Wayne, October 14, 1776, to Rush, October 18, 1776, Wayne Papers, I, HSP; Hargrove, *Burgoyne*, 95.

20. Wayne to Rush, November 5, 1776, to Delany, October 25, November 5, 1776, to Benjamin Franklin, November 15, 1776, Wayne Papers, I, HSP; Wayne to Rush, November 24, 1776, Wayne Papers, Detroit Public Library.

21. "General Orders, Northern Army," November 18, 1776, Force, ed., *American Archives*, Ser. 5, III, 878; Wayne to Gates, November 20, 1776, Wayne Papers, II, HSP; Richard Varick to Schuyler, November 20, 1776, Philip Schuyler Papers, New York Public Library; Schuyler to Wayne, November 23, 1776, New-York Historical Society, *Collections*, XI, (New York, 1880), 41–42; Jonathan Gregory Rossie, *The Politics of Command in the American Revolution* (Syracuse, 1975), 215–18.

22. Varick to Schuyler, November 18, 1776, Schuyler Papers, New York Public Library.

23. Wayne to Franklin, July 29, 1776, Wayne Papers, I, HSP; Wayne to Gates, December 1, 1776, Gates Papers, IV, New-York Historical Society.

24. Wayne to Schuyler, December 18, 1776, January 6, 1777, Schuyler to Wayne, December 23, 1776, January 23, 1777, Wayne Papers, II, HSP.

25. Wayne to Pennsylvania Committee of Safety, December 4, 1776, to Schuyler, November 24, December 2, 1776, to Congress, December 2, 1776, to George Clymer, December 15, 1776, Schuyler to Wayne, December 10, 1776, Wayne Papers, I, II, HSP; Wayne to Gates, December 1, 1776, Gates Papers, IV, New-York Historical Society.

26. Wayne to Peters, November 12, 1776, to Johnston, November 12, 1776, to Hartley, December 20, 1776, Wayne Papers, I, II, HSP; Wayne to Gates, December 1, 1776, Gates Papers, IV, New-York Historical Society.

27. Benedict Arnold to Wayne, November 25, 1776, Anthony Wayne Letters, Greene Library, West Chester State College; Wayne to Mary Wayne, January 3, 1777, Wayne Papers, II, HSP.

28. Wayne to Delany, December 15, 1776, to James Moore, January 1, 1777, to R. Stockton, January 3, 1777, Wayne Papers, II, HSP.

29. Wayne to Schuyler, January 2, 22, 1777, to Varick, March 11, 1777, Wayne Papers, II, III, HSP.

30. Schuyler to Wayne, December 29, 1776, January 6, 1777, Wayne to Schuyler, January 2, 1777, Wayne Papers, II, HSP.

31. Schuyler to Wayne, January 27, February 7, 1776, Wayne to Schuyler, February 2, 1776, Wayne Papers, II, HSP.

32. Wayne to Schuyler, January 22, 26, February 12, 1777, Wayne to Measom, January 25, 1777, Wayne Papers, II, HSP.

33. Wayne to Schuyler, February 12, 24, 1777, to Delany, February 20, 1777, Schuyler to Wayne, February 16, 19, 1777, Wayne Papers, II, HSP.

34. For Lee's attitude toward discipline and training, see John Shy, "Charles Lee: The Soldier as Radical," in George A. Billias, ed., *George Washington's Generals* (New York, 1964), 34, 37, 41. Some other officers' views are examined in Paul

David Nelson, "Citizen Soldiers or Regulars: The Views of American General Officers on the Military Establishment," *Military Affairs*, LXIII (1979), 126–32.

35. Wayne to Delany, December 15, 1776, to R. Stockton, January 3, 1777, to George Measom, February 23, 1777, Wayne Papers, II, HSP.

36. Wayne to Captain North, December 11, 1776, Wayne Papers, II, HSP; Ford, ed., *Journals of Congress*, V, 762–63, 788; Articles of War, ibid., VI, 1125.

37. Wayne to Congress, January 2, 1777, to Schuyler, February 8, 13, 1777, Wayne Papers, II, HSP; Wayne to Schuyler, February 4, 1777, Wayne Papers, Society Collection, Historical Society of Pennsylvania, hereafter cited as Society Collection, HSP; Wayne to Congress, February 2, 1777, Smith, ed., *St. Clair Papers*, I, 384–85; Wayne to Gates, February 5, 1777, to Congress, March 2, 1777, Wayne Letters, PCC, 161, I, 197–98, 201–02; Ford, ed., *Journals of Congress*, VI, 1040, VII, 49, 134, 180.

38. James Bowdoin to Wayne, February 10, 1777, Wayne to Colonel Joseph Wood, March 2, 1777, to Schuyler, March 11, 1777, Wayne Papers, II, III, HSP.

39. Wayne to Sally Robinson Peters and Hetty Griffits, February 16, 1777, *Book Prices Current* (1967), 1232; Wayne to Delany, February 20, 1777, to Elizabeth Iddings Wayne, March 2, 1777, to Mary Wayne, April 1, 1777, Wayne Papers, II, III, HSP.

40. Gates to Wayne, March 18, 1777, Wayne Letters, Greene Library, West Chester State College; Washington to Wayne, April 12, 1777, Wayne Papers, III, HSP; Ford, ed., *Journals of Congress*, VII, 141.

Chapter III   Trials in Pennsylvania, 1777

1. Washington to Heath, April 18, 1777, *Heath Papers*, Massachusetts Historical Society, *Collections*, Ser.5, IV (1878), 48.

2. Washington's General Orders, May 22, 1777, Washington Papers, LC; Ford, ed., *Journals of Congress*, V, 762–63, 788.

3. Wayne to Mary Wayne, August 26, 1777, to John Paterson, May 8, 1777, Wayne Papers, III, HSP.

4. Washington to Wayne, May 20, 26, 1777, Washington Papers, LC; Wayne to Benjamin Rush, June 2, 1777, Benjamin Rush Papers, Josiah Trent Collection, Duke University Medical Center Library; Wayne to Board of War, June 3, 1777, to Delany, June 7, 1777, to Mary Wayne, June 7, 1777, to Peters, June 17, 1777, Wayne Papers, III, HSP; Graydon, *Memoir*, 127; Thayer, *Greene*, 171.

5. Washington to Wayne, June 16, 1777, Wayne to Delany, misdated June 20, written some time after June 22, 1777, Wayne Papers, III, HSP; Wayne to Benjamin Lincoln, June 16, 1777, Lloyd W. Smith Collection, Morristown National Historical Park; Washington to Congress, June 22, 1777, Washington Papers, LC; Washington to Jonathan Trumbull, June 23, 1777, *Trumbull Papers*, Massachusetts Historical Society, *Collections*, Ser. 5, X (1885), 73; Don Higginbotham, *Daniel Morgan: Revolutionary Rifleman* (Chapel Hill, N.C., 1961), 59; North Callahan, *Daniel Morgan: Ranger of the Revolution* (New York, 1961), 124; Thayer, *Greene*, 174.

6. John Morton to Wayne, August 16, 1776, *PMHB*, XXXIX (1915), 373; Rush to Wayne, September 24, 1776, Wayne Papers, I, HSP.

7. Wayne to Franklin, October 3, 1776, Benjamin Franklin Papers, I, 23, Charles Patterson Van Pelt Library, University of Pennsylvania; Peters to Wayne, October 16, 1776, May 27, 1777, Rush to Wayne, May 19, 1776, *PMHB*, XXX

(1906), 113–14; Rush to Wayne, April 2, 1777, Rush Papers, Josiah Trent Collection, Duke University Medical Center Library.

8. Wayne to Rush, June 7, 1777, Rush to Wayne, May 19, June 5, 1777, Wayne Papers, III, HSP.

9. Washington to Wayne, July 24, 1777, Washington Papers, LC.

10. Wayne to Mary Wayne, June 7, 1777, Wayne Papers, III, HSP; Elizabeth Iddings Wayne to Wayne, July 13, 1777, Wayne Papers, WLCL.

11. Washington to Wayne, August 19, 1777, Washington's General Orders, August 22, 1777, Washington Papers, LC; Wayne to Elizabeth Graeme Fergusson, September 14, 1777, Wayne Papers, IV, HSP; Ford, ed., *Journals of Congress*, IX, 882n; Worthington C. Ford, "Defenses of Philadelphia in 1777," *PMHB*, XVIII (1894), 163.

12. Council of War, August 21, 1777, Fitzpatrick, ed., *Writings of Washington*, IX, 109–10, 110n; Graydon, *Memoir*, 291; Freeman, *Washington*, IV, 462–64.

13. Wayne to Mary Wayne, August 26, 1777 (2), Wayne Papers, III, HSP.

14. Wayne to Washington, September 2, 1777, Wayne Papers, IV, HSP.

15. On the army's dispositions, and the battle, see George Weedon to John Page, September 11, 1777, George Weedon Papers, Chicago Historical Society.

16. Washington to Congress, September 11, 1777, Washington Papers, LC.

17. Sullivan to Congress, October 6, 1777, Hammond, ed., *Sullivan Papers*, I, 475–76; Weedon to Page, September 11, 1777, Weedon Papers, Chicago Historical Society; Washington to Congress, September 11, 1777, Washington Papers, LC.

18. Washington to Congress, September 11, 1777, Washington Papers, LC; Wayne to Thomas Mifflin, September 15, 1777, Wayne Papers, IV, HSP; "Candidus" [Sullivan] to Messrs. Powers & Willis, n.d., Hammond, ed., *Sullivan Papers*, I, 473; John André, *Major André's Journal: Operations of the British Army Under Lieutenant Generals Sir William Howe and Sir Henry Clinton, June, 1776 to November, 1778* (Tarrytown, N.Y., 1930), 88.

19. Washington to Congress, September 11, 1777, Washington Papers, LC; Washington to Wayne, September 18, 1777, John Fitzgerald to Wayne, September 18, Wayne Papers, IV, HSP; Peckham, *Toll*, 40.

20. Wayne to Washington September 19, 1777 (2), Washington to Wayne, September 19, 1777, Washington Papers, LC.

21. Wayne's Court Martial Defense, October 25, 1777, Wayne Papers, IV, HSP; Frank Moore, ed., *Diary of the American Revolution* (2 vols., New York, 1860), I, 498–99.

22. Wayne to Washington, September 21, 1777, Wayne's Court Martial Defense, October 25, 1777, Wayne Papers, IV, HSP.

23. Ibid.

24. Wayne to Mary Wayne, September 22, 1777, Abner Robinson to Wayne, September 22, Washington to Wayne, September 23, 1777, Wayne Papers, IV, HSP; Peckham, *Toll*, 41.

25. Lyman H. Butterfield, ed., *Diary and Autobiography of John Adams* (4 vols., Cambridge, 1961), II, 267; Wayne to Washington, September 27, 1777, Washington Papers, LC; Tench Tilghman to Wayne, September 27, 1777, Wayne Papers, IV, HSP.

26. Minutes of Council of War, September 28, 1777, Washington Papers, LC; Wayne to Mary Wayne, September 30, 1777, Wayne Papers, IV, HSP.

27. Wayne to Mary Wayne, October 3, 1777, Wayne Papers, IV, HSP.

28. This paragraph and subsequent ones on the battle of Germantown are based upon Wayne to Mary Wayne, October 6, 1777, Wayne Papers, IV, HSP; Sullivan to Mesech Weare, October 25, 1777, Hammond, ed., *Sullivan Papers*, I, 542–47, Washington to Congress, October 5, 1777, Washington Papers, LC; Lord Stirling to ———, October 5, 1777, William Alexander, Lord Stirling Papers, New York Public Library; and Henry Knox to Lucy Knox, October 6, 1777, Henry Knox Papers, Massachussetts Historical Society.

29. William Howe to Henry Clinton, October 8, 1777, Sir Henry Clinton Papers, William L. Clements Library; Stillé, *Wayne*, 98.

30. Wayne to Washington, October 6 [misdated October 4], 1777, Wayne to Mary Wayne, October 6, 1777, Wayne Papers, IV, HSP; Peckham, *Toll*, 42.

31. Washington's General Orders, October 11, 1777, Washington Papers, LC; Wayne to Washington, October 11, 17, 1777, Minutes of Court of Inquiry, Lord Stirling, Chairman, October 13–15, 1777, Wayne Papers, IV, HSP.

32. Wayne to Washington, October 22, 1777, Wayne Papers, IV, HSP.

33. Washington's General Orders, October 24, November 1, 1777, Washington Papers, LC; Wayne's Court Martial Defense, October 25, 1777, Wayne Papers, IV, HSP.

Chapter IV   Valley Forge and Monmouth, 1777–1779

1. Council of War, November 8, 1777, Washington to Congress, November 17, 1777, Washington Papers, LC; Wayne to Peters, November 18, 1777, Wayne Papers, IV, HSP.

2. Wayne to Peters, November 18, 1777, Wayne Papers, IV, HSP.

3. Wayne to Mifflin, November 10, 1777, Gates Papers, VIII, New-York Historical Society. James Thomas Flexner characterizes Wayne (incorrectly) as being "violently critical" of Washington (*George Washington in the American Revolution, 1775–1783* [Boston and Toronto, 1967], 342). For arguments casting doubt on the existence of the "Conway Cabal," see Bernhard Knollenberg, *Washington and the Revolution, a Reappraisal: Gates, Conway, and the Continental Congress* (New York, 1940), and Nelson, *Gates*, 157–77.

4. Washington to Wayne, October 26, December 3, 1777, Wayne to Washington, October 27, 1777, Wayne Papers, IV, HSP; Councils of War, November 8, 24, 1777, Wayne to Washington, November 25, December 4, 1777, Washington Papers, LC.

5. Council of War, November 30, 1777, Washington Papers, LC; Wayne to Peters, December 19, 31, 1777, Wayne Papers, IV, HSP.

6. Ann Wayne Hayman to Wayne, November 11, 1777, Elizabeth Iddings Wayne to Wayne, June 15, 1778, Wayne Papers, WLCL; Peters to Wayne, December 16, 1777, Wayne to Peters, December 19, 30, 1777, to Mary Wayne, February 7, 1778, Sally Robinson Peters, May 17, 1778, Wayne Papers, IV, V, HSP.

7. Sullivan, Maxwell, and Wayne to Washington, November 23, 1777, Wayne to Washington, December 26, 1777, Washington Papers, LC; Washington to Wayne, December 27, 1777, Wayne Papers, IV, HSP; Wayne to Gates, January 26, 1778, Gates Papers, IX, New-York Historical Society.

8. Ford, ed., *Journals of Congress*, V, 762–63; Royster, *Revolutionary People*, 313.

9. "A Remonstrance from the Committee of Inspection and Observation of Chester County to the Assembly," February 12, 1776, *Pennsylvania Packet*, March 4, 1776; Wayne to Thomas Wharton, November 22, 1777, Wayne Papers, WLCL.

10. Wharton to Wayne, December 12, 1777, Wayne to Recruiting Officers, February 10, 1778, *Pennsylvania Archives*, Ser. 1, VI, 86–87, 248; Wayne to Wharton, February 10, 1778, Wayne Papers, WLCL; Wayne to Wharton, February 18, 1777, to John Bayard, May 13, 1778, Wharton to Wayne, April 2, 1778, Wayne Papers, IV, V, HSP.

11. Wayne to Wharton, November 22, 1777, Wayne Papers, WLCL; Wharton to Wayne, December 12, 1777, *Pennsylvania Archives*, Ser. 1, VI, 86–87; Lord Stirling to Wayne, January 26, 1778, Wayne to Stirling, February 11, 1778, to Peters, May 13, 1778, Wayne Papers, IV, HSP.

12. Wayne to Wharton, April 1, 1778, *Pennsylvania Archives*, Ser. 1, VI, 408–09; Wayne to Gouverneur Morris, May 16, 1778, Morris to Wayne, May 21, 1778, Wayne Papers, V, HSP.

13. Entry of June 2, 1778, in Edward H. Tatum, ed., *The American Journal of Ambrose Serle, Secretary to Lord Howe, 1776–1778* (San Marino, 1940), 302; Oath of Allegiance, 1778, Miscellaneous Manuscripts Collections, American Philosophical Society Library.

14. Wayne to Peters, February 8, 1778, to Will. Henry, May 14, 1778, Peters to Wayne, February 18, 1778, Wayne Papers, IV, V, HSP.

15. Wayne to Washington, February 25, 1778, Washington Papers, LC.

16. Wayne to James Livingston, February 26, 1778, to Count Pulaski, February 27, 1778, to Washington, March 4, 1778, Pulaski to Wayne, February 7, 28, 1778, Wayne Papers, IV, HSP; Washington to Wayne, February 28, March 2, 1778, Washington Papers, LC.

17. Wayne to Washington, March 4, 1778, Wayne Papers, IV, HSP; Miecislaus Haiman, *Poland and the American Revolutionary War* (Chicago, 1932), 29.

18. Wayne to Washington, March 14, 1778, Washington to Wayne, March 15, 1778, Washington Papers, LC.

19. Wayne to Wharton, March 27, 1778, Wayne Papers, IV, HSP.

20. Washington to General Officers, April 20, 1778, Wayne to Washington, April 21, 23, 1778, Washington Papers, LC; Baron deKalb to Comte deBroglie, May 5–7, 1778, B. F. Stevens, ed., *Facsimiles of Manuscripts in European Archives Relating to America, 1773–1783* (25 vols., London, 1889–95), VIII, 821; Freeman, *Washington*, V, 1–2.

21. Wayne to Congress, May 13, 16, 1778, Wayne Letters, PCC, 161, I, 211, 215–16; Wayne to Delany, May 21, 1778, John Laurens to Wayne, May 22, 1778, Wayne Papers, V, HSP; Wayne to Irvine, April 27, 1778, William Irvine Papers, I, Historical Society of Pennsylvania, hereafter Irvine Papers, HSP; Ford, ed., *Journals of Congress*, XI, 516, 519.

22. Council of War, June 17, 1778, Wayne to Washington, June 18, 1778, Washington Papers, LC; John R. Alden, *General Charles Lee: Traitor or Patriot?* (Baton Rouge, 1951), 205–06.

23. Washington to Wayne, June 18, 1778, Council of War, June 24, 1778, Wayne to Washington, June 24, 1778, Washington Papers, LC; Flexner, *Washington in the Revolution*, 298; Freeman, *Washington*, V, 16–18; Alden, *Lee*, 208–09.

24. Alexander Hamilton to Washington, June 26, 1778, Lafayette to Washington, June 26, 1778, Jared Sparks, ed., *Correspondence of the American Revolution* (4 vols., Boston, 1853), II, 145, 147; *Lee Papers*, New-York Historical Society, *Collections*, IV–VII (1871–75), II, 424, hereafter *Lee Papers*; Washington to Lafayette, June 26, 1778, to Charles Lee, June 27, 1778, Fitzpatrick, ed., *Writings of Washington*, XII, 122, 142.

25. *Lee Papers*, III, 3–5; Wayne and Charles Scott to Washington, June 30, 1778, Sparks, ed., *Correspondence*, II, 150–52; Alden, *Lee*, 216.

26. Wayne and Scott to Washington, June 30, 1778, Sparks, ed., *Correspondence*, II, 150–52; Wayne to Mary Wayne, July 1, 1778, Wayne Papers, V, HSP; Lee to Robert Morris, July 3, 1778, *Lee Papers*, II, 458.

27. Wayne and Scott to Washington, June 30, 1778, Sparks, ed., *Correspondence*, II, 150–52; Lee to Morris, July 3, 1778, *Lee Papers*, II, 458; Wayne to Mary Wayne, July 1, 1778, Wayne Papers, V, HSP; Freeman, *Washington*, V, 28–29; Alden, *Lee*, 218–19, 224.

28. Wayne to Mary Wayne, July 1, 1778, Wayne Papers, V, HSP; Freeman, *Washington*, V, 30.

29. John Laurens to Henry Laurens, June 20, 1778, Washington to Congress, July 1, 1778, Lee to Morris, July 3, 1778, Hamilton to Elias Boudinot, July 5, 1778, *Lee Papers*, II, 434, 444–45, 458, 470; Freeman, *Washington*, V, 30; Peckham, *Toll*, 52.

30. Lee to Washington, June 28, 30 (2) [misdated July 1], and Charges, June 30, 1778, *Lee Papers*, II, 435–36, 438, III, 2; Wayne and Scott to Washington, June 30, 1778, Sparks, *Correspondence*, II, 150–52; Was..ington to Lee, June 30, 1778, Fitzpatrick, ed., *Writings of Washington*, XII, 133; Alden, *Lee*, 231.

31. *Lee Papers*, III, 3–5; Wayne to Mary Wayne, July 14, 1778, to Greene, July 14, 1778, to Delany, July 20, 1778, to Henry Lee, July 20, 1778, Wayne Papers, V, HSP; Alden, *Lee*, 235.

32. Lee Papers, III, 195; George W. Corner, ed., *The Autobiography of Benjamin Rush* (Princeton, N.J., 1948), 156.

33. Wayne to Peters, May 13, August 5, 1778, to Abner Robinson, August 15, 1778, Wayne Papers, V, HSP; Council of War, September 1, 1778, Wayne to Washington, September 2, 1778, Washington Papers, LC.

34. Wayne to Sullivan, July 29, 1778, John Sullivan Papers, New Hampshire Historical Society; Sullivan to Wayne, November 8, 1778, Chester County Historical Society; Wayne to Congress, September 8, 1778, Wayne Letters, PCC, 161, I, 233–34; Elizabeth Iddings Wayne to Wayne, August 24, 29, 1778, Mary Wayne to Wayne, September 7, 1778, Wayne Papers, WLCL; Ford, ed., *Journals of Congress*, XII, 908; St. Clair's Trial: New-York Historical Society, *Collections*, XII (1880), 3 — 171, and Smith, ed., *St. Clair Papers*, I, 447–457n; Schuyler's Trial: New-York Historical Society, *Collections*, XI (1879), 7–24.

35. Wayne to Morris, January 24, 1779, to Peters, October 5, 1778, to Pennsylvania Assembly, October 26, 1778, to Joseph Reed, December 28, 1778, January 5, 1779, Morris to Wayne, September 8, 1778, Reed to Wayne, January 14, 23, 1778, Wayne Papers, V, VI, HSP.

36. Wayne to Peters, October 5, 1778, to Reed, October 6, 13, November 10, 1778, Wayne's Personal Notes, October 14, 1778, Reed to Wayne, October 25, 1778, Wayne Papers, V, VI, HSP.

37. Washington to Wayne, October 2, November 11, 1778, Washington Papers, LC; Washington to Wayne, December 4, 1778, Wayne to Irvine, December 28, 1778, to Washington, January 2, 1779, to Charles Lee, January 7, 1779 (2), Lee to Wayne, January 9, 1779, Wayne Papers, VI, HSP; Alden, *Lee*, 265, 350n.

38. Walter Stewart to Wayne, November 29, 1778, Wayne Papers, VI, HSP; Frederick D. Stone, "Philadelphia Society One Hundred Years Ago," *PMHB*, III (1879), 361–94.

39. Wayne to Delany, May 21, 1778, to Washington, February 10, 1779, Wayne Papers, V, VI, HSP; Ford, ed., *Journals of Congress*, XI, 495–96, 502; Royster, *Revolutionary People*, 313.

40. Wayne to Peters, October 21, 1778, Dreer Collection: Revolutionary Generals, Historical Society of Pennsylvania; Burton Alva Konkle, *George Bryan and the Constitution of Pennsylvania, 1731–1791* (Philadelphia, 1922), 162.

41. Wayne to Irvine, November 12, December 28, 1778, to Mifflin, et al., November 23, 1778, to Stewart, November 29, 1778, to Pennsylvania Assembly, March 13, 1779, Irvine to Wayne, October 27, 1778, Thomas Robinson to Wayne, November 11, 1778, Wayne Papers, VI, HSP.

42. Wayne to Pennsylvania Assembly, March 10, 1779, *Book Prices Current* (1935), 672; Wayne to Committee of Field Officers of the Pennsylvania Line, March 14, 1779, Wayne Papers, VI, HSP.

43. Wayne to John Henderson, et al., October 10, 1778, Wayne Papers, V, HSP.

44. Washington to Wayne, March 16, 1779, enclosing extract of William Livingston to Washington, March 9, 1779, Wayne to Washington, March 23, 1779, Washington Papers, LC.

45. Wayne to Washington, February 10, 1779, Washington Papers, LC; Washington to Wayne, February 16, May 18, 1779, James Chambers, et al., to Wayne, March 27, 1779, Wayne to Washington, February 28, 1779, Wayne Papers, VI, HSP; John Wright, "The Corps of Light Infantry in the Continental Army," *American Historical Review*, XXXI (1926), 455; Higginbotham, *Morgan*, 95.

46. Wayne to Morris, October 5, 1778, to John Armstrong, April 21, 1779, Wayne Papers, V, VI, HSP; Washington to Wayne, March 7, 1779, Washington Papers, LC; Ford, ed., *Journals of Congress*, XIV, 575–76.

47. Wayne to Washington, April 16, 1779, Dreer Collection: Revolutionary Generals, Historical Society of Pennsylvania; Wayne to Washington, May 18, 1779, Washington Papers, LC; Wayne to Mary Wayne, March 3, 1779, to Irvine, June 7, 1779, to Richard Butler, June 7, 1779, to Stewart, June 7, 1779, to Henry Archer, June 11, 1779, Wayne Papers, VI, HSP.

Chapter V Stony Point and Stormy Politics, 1779–1780

1. Wayne to Stewart, June 7, 1779, to Mary Wayne, June 24, 1779, Washington to Wayne, June 21, July 1, 1779, Wayne Papers, VI, VII, HSP.

2. Wayne to Washington, July 3, 1779, Washington to Wayne, July 4, 1779, Wayne Papers, VII, HSP; Washington to Wayne, July 9, 1779, Washington Papers, LC.

3. Wayne to Washington, July 9, 10, 1779, Washington to Wayne, July 5, 1779, Wayne Papers, VII, HSP; Washington's General Orders, July 8, 1779, Fitzpatrick, ed., *Writings of Washington*, XV, 380–81.

4. Washington to Wayne, July 10, 1779, Wayne Papers, VII, HSP.

5. Washington to Wayne, July 10, 1779, Wayne Papers, VII, HSP; Washington to Wayne, July 9, 1779, Wayne to Washington, July 15 , 1779, Washington Papers, LC.

6. Wayne to Washington, July 14, 17, 1779, Washington to Wayne, July 14, 1779, Battle Orders, July 15, 1779, Wayne Papers, VII, HSP.

7. Wayne to Delany, July 15, 1779, Wayne Papers, VII, HSP. Standard studies of the battle of Stony Point are Henry B. Dawson, *The Assault on Stony Point*,

by *General Anthony Wayne, July 16, 1779* (Morrisania, N.Y., 1863), and Henry P. Johnston, *The Storming of Stony Point on the Hudson, Midnight, July 15, 1779* (New York, 1900).

8. Wayne to Washington, July 17, 1779, Wayne Papers, Society Collection, HSP.

9. Wayne to Washington, July 16, 1779, Washington Papers, LC; Johnston, *Stony Point*, 81–84.

10. Wayne to Washington, July 16, 1779, Washington Papers, LC; Wayne to Washington, July 17, 1779, Wayne Papers, Society Collection, HSP; Wayne's General Orders, July 16, 1779, cited in Johnston, *Stony Point*, 86; Ford, ed., *Journals of Congress*, XIV, 890; Peckham, *Toll*, 62.

11. Washington to Congress, July 21, 1779, Washington Papers, LC; St. Clair to Wayne, July 27, 1779, Washington to Wayne, July 19, August 15, 1779, Schuyler to Wayne, July 30, 1779, Adam Stephen to Wayne, August 10, 1779, John Armstrong to Wayne, September 15, 1779, Delany to Wayne, July 27, 1779, Lafayette to Wayne, October 7, 1779, Reed to Wayne, July 20, October 25, 1779 (enclosing Assembly Resolution of October 10, 1779), Rush to Wayne, August 6, 1779, Charles Lee to Wayne, August 11, 1779, Wayne Papers, VII, VIII, Society Collection, HSP; Henry Clinton, *The American Rebellion. . .*, William B. Willcox, ed. (New Haven, Conn., 1954), 133; Wayne to Congress, August 10, 1779, Wayne Letters, PCC, 161, I, 220–23; Ford, ed., *Journals of Congress*, XIX, 356, 886, 890.

12. Thomas Posey to Wayne, August 10, 28, 1779, Isaac Sherman to Wayne, August 22, 24, 1779, Return Meigs to Wayne, August 22, 1779, William Hull to Wayne, August 25, 1779, Wayne to Meigs, August 23, 1779, to Posey, August 28, 1779, Wayne Papers, VII, HSP; Wayne to Congress, August 10, 1779, Wayne Letters, PCC, 161, I, 220–23.

13. Washington to Wayne, October 9, 15, 22, 26, 1779, Wayne to Washington, October 9, 14, 24, December 18, 1779, Wayne Papers, VII, VIII, IX, HSP; Wayne to Washington, October 22, 1779, Washington Papers, LC.

14. Washington to Wayne, December 28, 1779, Wayne Papers, VIII, HSP; Wayne to Irvine, December 14, 1779, Irvine Papers, II, HSP.

15. Washington to Wayne, December 28, 1779, Captain Pendleton to Wayne, December 31, 1779, R. Putnam, et al., to Wayne [December 31, 1779], Wayne to Officers of Light Corps, January 12, 1780, to Washington, January 12, 1780, Wayne Papers, IX, X, HSP.

16. *Pennsylvania Packet*, January 27, 1780.

17. Wayne to Robert Magaw, March 12, 1780, Wayne Papers, IX, HSP.

18. William Spence Robertson, ed., *The Diary of Francisco de Miranda, Tour of the United States, 1783–1784* (New York, 1928), 32; Mrs. Henry G. Banning, "Miss Vining, A Revolutionary Belle," *American Historical Register*, (July, 1895), 1194–1205; John A. Munroe, "The Philadelawareans: A Study in the Relations Between Philadelphia and Delaware in the Late Eighteenth Century," *PMHB*, LXIX (1945), 137–38; Elizabeth Montgomery, *Reminiscences of Wilmington, in Familiar Village Tales, Ancient and New* (2nd. ed., Wilmington, Del., 1872), 133–34; Edward Robins, *Romances of Early America* (Philadelphia, 1902), 87–100.

19. Reed to Wayne, December 9, 1779, Wayne to Johnston, March 25, 1780, Wayne Papers, IX, X, HSP; Wayne to Irvine, March 10, 1780, *Historical Magazine*, VI (1862), 322–23.

20. *Pennsylvania Packet*, April 8, 1780; Royster, *Revolutionary People*, 312.

21. Reed to Wayne, June 13, 1781, cited in John F. Roche, *Joseph Reed: A Moderate in the American Revolution* (New York, 1957), 187.

22. Wayne to Washington, May 11, 1780, to Colonel Blair, May 27, 1780, Wayne Papers, X, HSP; Washington to Wayne, May 18, 1780, Washington Papers, LC; Wayne to Johnston, May 18, 1780, Sol Feinstone Collection, American Philosophical Society Library.

23. Wayne to Washington, February 4, May 11, July 10, 1780, Wayne Papers, IX, X, HSP; Washington to Wayne, May 11, 1780, Washington's General Orders, June 14, 1780, Washington Papers, LC.

24. Wayne to Washington, June 23, 1780, Washington to Wayne, June 23, 1780, Washington Papers, LC; Wayne to Margaretta Wayne, June 29, 1780, *Book Prices Current*, (1971), 1185, (1973), 1143.

25. Wayne to Washington, July 19, 1780, Wayne Papers, X, HSP.

26. Washington to Wayne, July 20, 1780, Washington Papers, LC; Clinton, *American Rebellion*, 200.

27. Wayne to Washington, July 22, 1780, Washington Papers, LC; Clinton, *American Rebellion*, 200.

28. Wayne to Reed, July 26, 1780, Wayne Papers, X, HSP; Zebulon Pike to Wayne, July 21, 1780, Charles B. Pike Collection, Chicago Historical Society.

29. Wayne to Washington, July 22, 1780, Washington Papers, LC; Wayne to Reed, July 26, 1780, Reed to Wayne, August 4, 1780, Wayne Papers, X, HSP; Peckham, *Toll*, 73.

30. *Royal Gazette*, August 16, 30, September 30, 1780; Winthrop Sargent, *The Life of Major John André* (New York, 1871), 234–49; Carl Van Doren, *Secret History of the American Revolution* (New York, 1941), 321.

31. Wayne and Irvine to Washington, August 10, 1780, Wayne to Washington, September 3, 1780, Washington to Wayne, September 6, 1780, Washington Papers, LC; Washington to Wayne, August 11, 1780, Cadwalader Papers, Maryland Historical Society; William McPherson to Wayne, August 12, 1780, Wayne Papers X, HSP.

32. Wayne and Irvine to Field Officers of Pennsylvania Line, August 12, 1780, Wayne to Reed, September 3, 1780, Wayne Papers, X, HSP; Smith, ed., *St. Clair Papers*, I, 107–08.

33. St. Clair to Wayne, September 4, 1780, Wayne to Washington, September 13, 1780, Wayne Papers, X, HSP; Memorial of General Officers, July 11, 1780 and General Officers to Alexander McDougall, July 11, 1780, Alexander McDougall Papers, IV, New-York Historical Society; Roger J. Champagne, *Alexander McDougall and the American Revolution in New York* (Schenectady, 1975), 160.

34. Washington to Wayne, September 26, 1780, Fitzpatrick, ed., *Writings of Washington*, XXXVI, 551; Wayne to Washington, September 27, 1780, to Hugh Sheel, October 2, 1780, Wayne Papers, X, HSP.

35. Wayne to Johnston, September 29, 1780, to Delany, October 2, 1780, Wayne Papers, X, HSP; Wayne to Robinson, October 1, 1780, Wayne Papers, Detroit Public Library; Willard M. Wallace, *Traitorous Hero: The Life and Fortunes of Benedict Arnold* (New York, 1954), 269; Freeman, *Washington*, V, 213n.

Chapter VI Mutiny, 1780–1781

1. Wayne to Board of War, October 13, 1780, Wayne Papers, X, HSP; Wayne to Irvine, September 30, November 7, 1780, *Historical Magazine*, VI (1862), 323, 336–37.

2. Washington to Wayne, October 6, 1780, Peters to Wayne, November 8, 1780, Wayne to Washington, October 11, 1780, to Daniel Brodhead, November 2, 1780, to Johnston, November 25, 1780, Wayne Papers, X, HSP; Wayne to Congress, Wayne Letters, PCC, 161, I, 225–27; Return of Pennsylvania Troops, December 11, 1780, *Pennsylvania Archives*, Ser. 1, VIII, 647.

3. Wayne to Reed, September 26, 1780, to A. Dunham, December 7, 1780, to John Moylan, December 30, 1780, Reed to Wayne, August 4, December — , 1780, Wayne Papers, X, XI, HSP; Wayne to Reed, October 17, 25, 1780, *Pennsylvania Archives*, Ser. 1, VIII, 587–88, 593; Wayne to Pennsylvania Assembly, October 9, 1780, *Book Prices Current* (1935), 673; Wayne to Reed, November 7, 1780, William Bradford Reed, ed., *Life and Correspondence of Joseph Reed* (2 vols., Philadelphia, 1847), II, 313–15.

4. Johnston to Wayne, October 31, November 6, 1780, Wayne to Johnston, November 7, 1780, to Irvine, November 22, 1780, Wayne Papers, X, XI, HSP; Robert L. Brunhouse, *The Counter-Revolution in Pennsylvania, 1776–1790* (Harrisburg, 1942), 92.

5. Wayne to Irvine, December 6, 1780, to Reed, December 16, 1780, to Johnston, December 16, 1780, Johnston to Wayne, December 7, 18, 1780, Evan Edwards to Wayne, December 10, 1780, Richard Humpton to Wayne, December 17,1780, Wayne Papers, XI, HSP; *The Statutes at Large of Pennsylvania, from 1682 to 1801*, James T. Mitchell and Henry Flanders, comps. (14 vols., Harrisburg, 1896–1909), December 18, 1780, Ch. 920, X, 223–28; *Journals of the House of Representatives of the Commonwealth of Pennsylvania. . .*(Philadelphia, 1782), November 11, 1780, 522–23, December 8, 12–14, 16, 1780, 547, 551–52, 555; Brunhouse, *Counter-Revolution*, 92.

6. Wayne to Reed, December 16, 1780, Washington to Wayne, November 21, 1780, Wayne Papers, X, XI, HSP; Washington to Wayne, November 27, 1780, Washington Papers, LC; Washington to Wayne, November 14, December 28, 1780, Sol Feinstone Collection, American Philosophical Society Library; Wayne to Washington, December 25, 1780, *Book Prices Current* (1935), 673; Chastellux, *Travels*, I, 111–12, 185.

7. Wayne to Johnston, December 16, 1780, Wayne Papers, XI, HSP.

8. Delany to Wayne, December 21, 1780, Wayne Papers, XI, HSP.

9. Wayne to Washington, January 2, 1781, Wayne's General Orders, January 2, 1781, Wayne Papers, XI, HSP. An excellent account of the army unrest during this time is Carl Van Doren, *Mutiny in January: The Story of a Crisis in the Continental Army. . .*(New York, 1943).

10. Washington to Wayne, January 3, 1781, Wayne, Butler & Stewart to Washington, January 4, 1781, Wayne to Reed, January 4, 1781, Wayne Papers, XI, XII, HSP.

11. Wayne to Sergeants, January 4, 1781, to Reed, January 6, 1781, Sergeants to Wayne, January 4, 1781, Reed to Wayne, January — , 1781 Wayne Papers, XI, XII, HSP.

12. British Proposal to Pennsylvania Troops, n.d., Wayne to Washington, January 8, 1781, Wayne Papers, XI, HSP; Reed, ed., *Reed*, II, 331; Clinton, *Rebellion*, 241–42.

13. Reed to Wayne, January 7, 1781, Reed, ed., *Reed*, II, 324–25; Wayne to Washington, January 8, 1781, to Congress, January 8, 1871, to Reed, January 8, 1781, Washington to Wayne, January 8, 1781, Wayne Papers, XI, XII,HSP; Ford, ed., *Journals of Congress*, XIV, 41.

14. Copy of Agreement, [January 8, 1781], Wayne to Washington, January 12, 1781, Wayne Papers, XI, XII, HSP; Court Martial Proceedings, January 11, 1781, Smith, ed., *St. Clair Papers*, I, 538n.

15. Washington to New York and New England governors, January 20, 1781, Washington Papers, LC.

16. Wayne to Pennsylvania Executive Council, January 15, 1781 (2), to Washington, January 21, 1781, Stewart to Wayne, January 22, 1781, Wayne Papers, XI, XII, HSP.

17. Wayne to Washington, January 28, 29, 1781, Washington to Wayne, January 27, February 2, 1781, Wayne Papers, XI, XII, HSP; Ford, ed., *Journals of Congress*, XIX, 79.

18. Wayne to Irvine, February 5, 1781, *Historical Magazine*, VI (1862) 337.

19. St. Clair to Wayne, March 7, 1781, Isaac B. Dunn to Wayne, March 9, 1781, Wayne to Craig, May 11, 1781, to St. Clair, March 7, 1781, Wayne Papers, XII, HSP.

20. Washington to Wayne, February 26, April 8, 1781, Lafayette to Wayne, March 4, 7, 13, 1781, Wayne Papers, XII, HSP; Lafayette to Wayne, March 9, 1781, Wayne Letters, Greene Library, West Chester State College; Ford, ed., *Journals of Congress*, XIX, 177.

21. Wayne to Lafayette, March 7, 1781, to Irvine, March 10, 1781, to Butler, March 10, 1781, to Washington, March 19, 1781, Wayne Papers, XII, HSP; Washington to Wayne, April 8, 1781, Washington Papers, LC; Lafayette to Washington, March 7, 1781, Louis Gottschalk, ed., *The Letters of Lafayette to Washington, 1777–1799* (New York, 1944), 155; Reed to Wayne, March 17, 1781, Wayne Letters, PCC, 161, I, 229–31; Ford, ed., *Journals of Congress*, XIX, 255.

22. Wayne to Irvine, March 25, 1781, Irvine Papers, IV, HSP; Wayne to Irvine, April 10, 1781, to Reed, April 13, 1781, Wayne Papers, XII, HSP.

23. Richard Butler to Wayne, April 28, 1781, St. Clair to Wayne, May 2, 1781, Reed to Wayne, May 11, 21, 1781, Jacob Morgan (for Reed) to Wayne, May 21, 1781, Wayne Papers, XII, HSP.

24. Wayne to Reed, May 16, 1781, to Board of War, May 20, 1781, Board of War to Wayne, Ma6 18, 1781, Wayne Papers, XII, HSP; Ford, ed., *Journals of Congress*, XX, 516.

25. Wayne to Lafayette, May 19, 20, 1781, to Mary Wayne, May 25, 1781, Wayne Papers, XII, HSP; Wayne to Washington, May 26, 1781, enclosing Court Martial Proceedings, May 20, 22, 1781, Washington Papers, LC; Van Doren, *Mutiny*, 234–35, 250–56.

26. Wayne to Fishbourn, May 25, 1781, to Mary Wayne, May 25, 1781, Wayne Papers, XII, HSP.

27. Wayne to ——, June 16, 1781, Wayne Papers, XIII, HSP; William Smith Livingston to Samuel B. Webb, May 28, 1781, Worthington C. Ford, ed., *Correspondence and Journals of Samuel Blachley Webb* (3 vols., Lancaster, Pa., 1893), II, 341.

28. Livingston to Webb, May 28, 1781, Ford, ed., *Webb Correspondence*, II, 341; Wayne to ——, June 26, 1781, Wayne Papers, XIII, HSP. Two eyewitness accounts of events at York in mid-May, 1781, by Samuel Dewees and Ebenezer Denny, I have discounted because they were written so long after the events described (John Smith Hanna, comp., *A History of the Life and Services of Captain Samuel Dewees* [Baltimore, 1844], 228–32; William H. Denny, ed., *Military Journal of Major Ebenezer Denny* [Philadelphia, 1860], 237–38). Carl Van Doren (*Mutiny in January*, 250–51) called Dewees's account "a hash of memory and melodrama,"

while Denny, in a typical example of inaccuracy, dates the mutiny on May 1. In writing my account of these events, I found Van Doren's analysis useful, but I believe Professor Van Doren missed a crucial point that all other narrators also overlook. It was Van Doren's contention that Livingston's description of events was just as inaccurate as Dewees's (he did not mention Denny's, or Wayne's of June 26, 1781), because it did not dovetail with court martial records of May 20, and May 22. But if there was (as I am convinced and so describe in my account) a *second* mutiny on May 25, wholly separate from the one that took place earlier, then the Wayne and Livingston letters make sense, for they describe events that actually occurred — no matter how much their stories may diverge in details.

29. The Articles of War are in Ford, ed., *Journals of Congress*, II, 111–22. General Washington approved of Wayne's repression of the mutinous spirit at York. Washington to Wayne, June 29, 1781, Washington Papers, LC.

30. Wayne to Washington, May 26, 1781, Washington Papers, LC; Wayne to Board of War, May 26, 1781, to St. Clair, May 26, 1781, to ——, June 16, 1781, Wayne Papers, XIII, HSP; Wayne to Reed, May 26, 1781, Dreer Collection: Revolutionary Generals, Historical Society of Pennsylvania.

Chapter VII   The Virginia Adventure, 1781

1. Lafayette to Wayne, May 3, 7, 15, 1781, Wayne Papers, XII, HSP; Sir James Wright to Lord George Germain, January 26, 1781, Georgia Historical Society, *Collections*, III (1842), 332–33.

2. Lafayette to Wayne, May 27, 28, 29, 31, June 2, 5, 7, 1781, Wayne Papers, XII, XIII, HSP; Charlemagne Tower, *The Marquis de Lafayette in the American Revolution* (2 vols., Philadelphia, 1901), II, 310–11, 321–22, 326; Benjamin Franklin Stevens, ed., *The Campaign in Virginia, 1781: An Exact Reprint of Six Rare Pamphlets on the Clinton-Cornwallis Controversy*, [2 vols., London, 1888], I, 477, 488.

3. Clinton to Cornwallis, June 11, 1781, Stevens, ed., *Clinton-Cornwallis Controversy*, II, 18–20.

4. Wayne to Lafayette, May 31, 1781 (2), June 1, 4, 6, 7, 1781, to Greene, June 4, 1781, John Hendrick to Wayne, June 1, 1781, Wayne Papers, XIII, HSP; Authorization for John Bryan to Impress Flour, Meat, etc., June 6, 1781, West Jersey Manuscripts, New Jersey Historical Society; John Davis, "The Yorktown Campaign. . .," *PMHB*, V (1881), 292.

5. Richard Henry Lee to Washington, June 12, 1781, Sparks, ed., *Correspondence*, III, 335; Lee to Virginia Delegates to Congress, June 12, 1781, Julian Boyd, ed., *The Papers of Thomas Jefferson* (21 vols. to date, Princeton, 1950–), VI, 92; — Robinson to ——, June 13, 1781, Wayne Papers, XIII, HSP.

6. Wayne to Delany, June 9, 1781, to Lafayette, June 22, 25, 30, July 2, 1781, Lafayette to Wayne, June 21, 22, 25, 26, 30, 1781, Wayne Papers, XIII, HSP.

7. Accounts of the battle of Green Spring Farm are in Wayne to Washington, July 8, 1781, Washington Papers, LC; Wayne to Peters, July 8, 1781, Lafayette to Congress, July 8, 1781, Wayne Papers, XIII, HSP; Wayne to Robert Morris, July 12, 1781, E. James Ferguson, et al., eds., *The Papers of Robert Morris, 1781–1784* (3 vols. to date, Pittsburgh, 1973–), I, 178–79; Franklin and Mary Wickwire, *Cornwallis: The American Adventure* (Boston, 1970), 342–46; Steven E. Kagle, ed., *The Diary of Josiah Athens* (New York, 1975), 39–40.

8. Lafayette's General Orders, July 8, 1781, *Pennsylvania Gazette*, August 1, 1781; Lafayette to Congress, July 9, 1781, The Marquis de Lafayette Letters, PCC,

156, 174–75; Washington to Wayne, July 30, 1781, Washington Papers, LC; Greene to Wayne, July 24, 1781, Wayne Papers, XIII, HSP; Gottschalk, *Lafayette and the Close of the Revolution*, 267; Freeman, *Washington*, V, 304n; Hugh F. Rankin, *The American Revolution* (New York, 1964), 315–17; Peckham, *Toll*, 87. Not even in the privacy of his diary was Washington critical of Wayne's performance at Green Spring Farm. See Donald Jackson and Dorothy Twohig, eds., *Diaries of George Washington* [6 vols., Charlottesville, Va., 1976–80], III, 401.

9. Wayne to Mary Wayne, July 11, 1781, to Reed, July 16, 1781, Lafayette to Wayne, July 13, 1781, Wayne Papers, XIII, HSP; Wayne to Irvine, July 16, 1781, *Historical Magazine*, VI (1862), 339–40; Kagle, ed., *Josiah Athens*, 40; Royster, *Revolutionary People*, 230.

10. Wayne to Washington, July 16, 1781, Washington Papers, LC; Wayne to Reed, July 16, 1781, to St. Clair, July 16, 1781, to Lafayette, July 22, 1781, to Thomas Nelson, July 23, 1781, Lafayette to Wayne, July 15, 1781, Wayne Papers, XIII, HSP; Wayne to Irvine, July 16, 1781, *Historical Magazine*, VI (1862), 339–40; Wayne to Nelson, July 22, 1781, Dreer Collection: Revolutionary Generals, Historical Society of Pennsylvania.

11. Lafayette to Wayne, July 21, 23, 24, 27, 31, August 3, 4, 6, 1781, Wayne to Nelson, July 24, 1781, to Lafayette, July 24, August 2, 5, 7, 10, 1781, Wayne Papers, XIII, XIV, HSP.

12. Wayne to Irvine, July 29, 1781, to Daniel Morgan, July 29, 1781, to William Davies, August 6, 1781, Lafayette to Wayne, August 6, 1781, enclosing Nelson to Lafayette, August 3, 1781, Davies to Wayne, August 6, 1781 (2), Wayne Papers, XIII, XIV, HSP.

13. Wayne to Lafayette, August 9, 1781, to Nelson, August 19, 1781 (2), Reed to Wayne, August 24, 1781, Wayne Papers, XIV, HSP; Wayne to Irvine, August 14, 1781, *Historical Magazine*, VI (1862), 340; Wayne to Reed, August 14, 1781, *Pennsylvania Archives*, Ser. 1, XIX, 358–59.

14. Irvine to Wayne, July 6, 1781, Irvine Papers, IV, HSP; *Statutes at Large*, June 25, 1781, Ch. 946, X, 346, September 29, 1781, Ch. 951, X, 364–66; Brunhouse, *Counter-Revolution*, 93.

15. Wayne to Washington, July 27, 1781, *The Collector* (1980), 19; Wayne to Morgan, July 27, 1781, to Irvine, August 14, 1781, Wayne Papers, XIII, HSP.

16. Lafayette to Wayne, August 22, 25, 31, 1781, Wayne to Lafayette, August 23, 28, 31, 1781, Wayne Papers, XIV, HSP; Freeman, *Washington*, V, 311; John R. Alden, *The South in the Revolution, 1763–1789* (Baton Rouge, La., 1957), 295.

17. Lafayette to Wayne, September 1, 1781, Wayne to Lafayette, September 2, 1781, to Mary Wayne, September 12, 1781, to Morris, September 14, 1781, Wayne Papers, XIV, HSP.

18. Wayne to Mary Wayne, September 12, 1781, to Margaretta Wayne, September 12, 1781, to Peters, September 12, 1781, to Lafayette, September 18, 1781, Wayne Papers, XIV, HSP; Freeman, *Washington*, V, 331–32.

19. Wayne to ——, October 1, 1781, to ——, October 20, 1781, enclosing "Journal," September 1–October 19, 1781, Wayne Papers, XIV, HSP; Wayne to Reed, October 3, 1781, *Pennsylvania Archives*, Ser. 1, XIX, 430; Alden, *South in the Revolution*, 298.

20. Wayne to ——, October 20, 1781, Wayne Papers, XIV, HSP; Wayne to Burke, September 3, 1781, Wayne Papers, Miscellaneous Manuscripts, Library of Congress.

21. Wayne to Morris, October 26, 1781, Rush to Wayne, October 30, 1781, Wayne Papers, XIV, HSP.

22. Stewart to Wayne, December 24, 1781, David Jones to Wayne, December 28, February 7, 1782, Wayne Papers, XIV, XV, HSP.

23. Burke to Wayne, August 30, 1781, Greene to Wayne, September 29, 1781, Rush to Wayne, October 30, 1781, Wayne Papers, XV, HSP.

24. Wayne to John Irwin, November 7, 1781, Wayne Papers, XIV, HSP.

25. Wayne to Washington, November 4, 1781 (2), Washington to Wayne, November 4 (2), Washington Papers, LC.

Chapter VIII   Southern Triumph, 1781–1783

1. *Diary of General David Cobb*, Massachusetts Historical Society, *Proceedings*, Ser. 1, XIX (1881–82), 71; Wayne to Theodorick Bland, November 18, 1781, to Margaretta Wayne, November 18, 1781, Wayne Papers, XIV, HSP; Wayne to Greene, November 30, 1781, Nathanael Greene Papers, William L. Clements Library, hereafter cited as Greene Papers, WLCL.

2. Wayne to St. Clair, December 6, 20, 1781, to Henry Archer, December 14, 1781, Wayne Papers, XIV, HSP; Wayne to Greene, December 24, 1781, Greene Papers, WLCL.

3. Greene to Wayne, January 9, 1782, Wayne Papers, XIV, HSP; Kenneth Coleman, *The American Revolution in Georgia, 1763–1789* (Athens, Ga., 1958), 141; Charles C. Jones, *The History of Georgia* (2 vols., New York, 1883), II, 505.

4. Wayne to John Martin, January 14, 17, 1782, to John Eustace, January 14, 1781, to Lee, January 17, 1782, William Wayne to Wayne, January 18, 1782, Wayne Papers, XIV, XV, HSP; Wayne to Greene, January 17, 1782, to Martin, January 19, 1782, Greene Papers, WLCL; Alexander Leslie to Lord George Germain, January 3, 1782, Historical Manuscripts Commission, *Report of American Manuscripts in the Royal Institution of Great Britain* (4 vols., London, 1904–09), II, 379; Jones, *Georgia*, II, 505.

5. Greene to Wayne, January 22, 29, February 4, 1782, Martin to Wayne, February 3, 1782, Joseph Habersham to Wayne, February 8, 1782, Wayne to Greene, January 23, 26, February 1, 1782, to Habersham, January 30, 1782, Wayne Papers, XV, HSP; Wayne to Greene, January 26, February 1, 6, 11, 1782, Greene Papers, WLCL; Martin to Wayne, January 29, John Martin Papers, Georgia Historical Society.

6. Wayne to Martin, January 14, February 13, 1782, Copies of Proclamations, February 14, 1782, to Mary Wayne, March 2, 1782, Wayne Papers, XIV, XV, HSP; Wayne to Martin, February 19, 1782, Joseph Valence Beven Papers, Georgia Historical Society; Wayne to Greene, March 11, 1782, Greene Papers, WLCL; Sir James Wright to Undersecretary Knox, February 23, 1782, Georgia Historical Society, *Collections*, III (1842), 372–75; Alexander Leslie to Clinton, March 12, 1782, Sir Alured Clarke to Leslie, April 11, 1782, Hist. MSS. Comm., *Royal Institution*, II, 418, 447–48; A. D. Candler, ed., *Revolutionary Records of Georgia, 1769–1784* (3 vols., Atlanta, Ga., 1908), II, 320.

7. Wayne to Greene, February 11, 22, 28, 1782, Greene Papers, WLCL; Wayne to Irvine, February 24, 1782, to Stewart, February 25, 1782, Wayne Papers, XV, HSP.

8. Wayne to Greene, March 4, 1782, Greene Papers, WLCL; Greene to Wayne, March 6, 1782, Wayne Papers, XV HSP.

9. Wayne to Mary Wayne, March 2, 1782, to Peters, March 6, 1782, to Martin, March 9, 26, 31, 1782, to Thomas Posey, April 4, 1782, Greene to Wayne, March 23, 1782, Martin to Wayne, March 16, 23, 1782, Posey to Wayne, April 2, 1782, Wayne Papers, XV, XVI, HSP; Wayne to Martin, March 26, 1782, Wayne Papers, Miscellaneous Manuscripts, Library of Congress; Wayne to Martin, March 15, 1782, Beven Papers, Georgia Historical Society; Wayne to Greene, March 11, 17, 25, April 1, 1782, Greene to Wayne, March 26, April 6, 1782, Greene Papers, WLCL; Greene to Wayne, March 12, April 6, 1782, Nathanael Greene Papers, Henry L. Huntington Library, hereafter cited as Greene Papers, Huntington Library; Martin to Wayne, March 14, 23, 1782, Martin Papers, Georgia Historical Society.

10. General Return of Army, March 29, 1782, Wayne to Martin, April 7, 17, 1782, to Greene, May 4, 1782, Wayne Papers, XVI, HSP; Greene to Wayne, March 7, 1782, Nathanael Greene Papers, Perkins Library, Duke University; Wayne to Greene, April 9, 18, 28, 1782, Greene to Wayne, April 29, 1782, Greene Papers, WLCL; Greene to Wayne, April 21, 1782, Greene Papers, Huntington Library; Martin to Wayne, April 10, 1782, Martin Papers, Georgia Historical Society; Candler, ed., *Revolutionary Records of Georgia*, II, 326.

11. Wayne to Greene, May 7, 1782, Greene Papers, WLCL; Wayne to Thomas Moore, May 10, 1782, Wayne Papers, XVI, HSP; Wayne to Rush, May 10, 1782, Wayne Papers, Miscellaneous Manuscripts, Library of Congress.

12. Candler, ed., *Revolutionary Records of Georgia*, I, 374, II, 108, 115, III, 171; Martin to Wayne, May 6, 1782, John Martin Papers, Perkins Library, Duke University; Savannah Unit, Georgia Writer's Project, WPA in Georgia, "Richmond-Oakgrove Plantation, Parts I-II," *Georgia Historical Quarterly*, XXIV (1940), 128–31.

13. This and subsequent paragraphs are based on Wayne to Greene, May 24, 1782, Greene Papers, WLCL; Wayne to Martin, May 26, 1782, to Delany, May 27, 1782, Wayne Papers, XVII, HSP; Wayne to Comte de Rochambeau, May 30, 1782, Greene Papers, Perkins Library, Duke University; Greene to Wayne, May 28, 1782, Greene Papers, Huntington Library; Henry Lee, *Memoirs of the War in the Southern Department of the United States*, Robert E. Lee, ed. (New York, 1869), 554–56; Jones, *Georgia*, II, 510–11.

14. Peckham, *Toll*, 95.

15. Wayne to Greene, May 13, 27, 1782, Greene Papers, WLCL; Greene to Wayne, May 21, June 1, 1782, Greene Papers, Huntington Library.

16. Alured Clarke to Wayne, May 29, 1782, Sir James Wright to Wayne, May 29, 1782, Greene to Wayne, June 5, 14, 1782, Wayne to Clarke, May 30, 1782, to Wright, May 30, 1782, Proclamation to Soldiers in Savannah, May 30, 1782, to Martin, June 1, 1782, to Greene, June 6, 1782, to Peters, June 8, 1782, Wayne Papers, XVII, HSP; Wayne to Greene, May 30, 1782, to Wright, June 14, 1782, Greene Papers, WLCL.

17. Greene to Wayne, April 10, June 6, 21, 1782, Wayne Papers, XVI, XVII, HSP; Wayne to Greene, June 13, 1782, Greene Papers, WLCL.

18. Lee, *Memoirs*, 555.

19. Ibid., 556, based upon recollections of Captain Alexander Parker, who was with Wayne during the events described.

20. Wayne to Greene, June 24, 1782, Wayne Papers, XVII, HSP.

21. Lee, *Memoirs*, 557–61, containing Posey's observations in a footnote, 558–59, written later by request of the editor, Robert E. Lee. An interesting but

inaccurate anecdote about this battle is found in Edmund Pendleton to James Madison, August 19, 1782, Massachusetts Historical Society, *Proceedings*, Ser. 2, XIX (1905), 159–60, and Alexander Garden, *Anecdotes of the Revolutionary War in America* (Charleston, S.C., 1822), 373–74.

22. Greene to Wayne, June 18, July 14, 1782, Wayne to Greene, June 30, 1782, Greene Papers, WLCL; Martin to Wayne, June 17, 1782, Wayne to Alured Clarke, June 27, 1782, Clarke to Wayne, June 28, 1782, Wayne Papers, XVII, HSP; Wayne to Greene, June 22, 1782, Greene to Martin, July 14, 1782, Greene Papers, Perkins Library, Duke University; Wayne to Patrick Carr, June 26, 1782, Sol Feinstone Collection, American Philosophical Society Library.

23. Wayne to Merchants of Savannah, June 17, 1782, Orders for Occupying Savannah, June 17, 1782, Wayne Papers, WLCL; Wayne to Martin, June 19, July 11, 1782, to Greene, June 17, July 12, 1782, Wayne Papers, XVII, XVIII, HSP; Thomas U. P. Charlton, *The Life of Major General James Jackson* (Augusta, Ga., 1809), 33, 43–44; Candler, ed., *Revolutionary Records of Georgia*, III, 123, 137; Jones, *Georgia*, II, 516–17; Coleman, *Revolution in Georgia*, 144.

24. Candler, ed., *Revolutionary Records of Georgia*, III, 137, 147.

25. Wayne to Greene, July 17, 1782, Greene Papers, WLCL; Wayne to ———, July 13, 1782, to Samuel Salton, et al., July 13, 1782, Indian Speech, n.d., Proclamation to Inhabitants of E. Florida, July 24, 1782, Greene to Wayne, August 2, 1782, Wayne Papers, XVIII, HSP.

26. Wayne to Martin, July 27, 1782, to Greene, July 31, 1782, Greene to Wayne, August 2, 1782, Wayne Papers, XVIII, HSP; Wayne to Greene, July 28, 1782, Greene Papers, Perkins Library, Duke University; Candler, ed., *Revolutionary Records of Georgia*, III, 167.

27. Wayne to Georgia Assembly, August 3, 1782, to Posey, August 5, 1782, Wayne Papers, XVIII, HSP; Wayne's Proclamation to Savannah Merchants, August 9, 1782, James Belcher Papers, Perkins Library, Duke University; Wayne to Greene, August 12, 1782, Greene Papers, WLCL; Candler, *Revolutionary Records of Georgia*, III, 179–80.

28. Wayne to Greene, August 24, 29, 1782, Greene to Wayne, August 24 (2), 29, 1782, Wayne Papers, XVIII, HSP; Wayne to Greene, August 31, 1782, Greene Papers, Perkins Library, Duke University.

29. Wayne to Morris, September 2–29, 1782, to Rush, December 24, 1782, Wayne Papers, XVIII, HSP.

30. Wayne to Martin, October 21, 1782, to Butler, December 21, 1782, to Rush, December 24, 1782, to James Moore, January 1, 1783, Wayne Papers, XVIII, XIX, HSP; Wayne to Mary Wayne, September 19, 1782, Wayne Papers, Detroit Public Library.

31. Wayne to Greene, October 5, 1782, Greene Papers, WLCL; Greene to Wayne, October 5 (2), November 2, 1782, Wayne Papers, XVIII, HSP; Thaddeus Kosciuszko to Greene, September 11, 1782, cited in Haiman, *Poland in the Revolution*, 133–34; Paul K. Walker, ed., *Engineers of Independence: A Documentary History of the Army Engineers in the American Revolution, 1775–1783* (Washington, [1982]), 292.

32. Wayne to Greene, November 2, 1782, Greene to Wayne, November 4, 1782, Wayne Papers, XVIII, HSP.

33. Wayne to Morris, September 29, 1782, to Richard Hawley, October 21, 1782, to Martin, October 21, 1782, to Butler, December 21, 1782, Greene to Wayne, November 7, 1782, Arrangement of Pennsylvania, Maryland and North Carolina Line, November 9, 1782, Wayne Papers, XVIII, HSP.

34. Wayne to Mary Wayne, September 29, 1782, Wayne Papers, Detroit Public Library; Wayne to Peters, November 12, 1782, to Rush, December 24, 1782, Rush to Wayne, September 16, 1782, Wayne Papers, XVIII, HSP.

35. Greene to Wayne, November 26, December 6, 14, 1782, Wayne to Greene, December 13, 1782, to Delany, December 17, 1782, to Moore, January 1, 1783, Wayne Papers, XVIII, XIX, HSP; James Wemyss to Maurice Simmons, December 13, 1782, Greene Papers, WLCL; Wayne to Greene, December 12, 1782, Huntington Manuscripts, Henry E. Huntington Library; Eldon Jones, "The British Withdrawal from the South, 1781–85," W. Robert Higgins, ed., *The Revolutionary War in the South: Power, Conflict, and Leadership: Essays in Honor of John Richard Alden* (Durham, N.C., 1979), 278.

36. Wayne to Washington, January 17, 1783, Washington Papers, LC; Wayne to Rush, January 20, 1783, Rush Papers, Trent Collection, Duke University Medical Center Library; Wayne to James Jackson, February 8, 1783, to Anthony White, February 8, 1783, Wayne Papers, XIX, HSP; Ford, ed., *Journals of Congress*, XXIII, 835–36, 875.

37. Wayne to Catherine Greene, February 22, 1790, Nathanael Greene Papers, Richmond, Georgia, photostats in Greene Papers, WLCL.

38. Greene to Lyman Hall, March 14, 1783, Greene Papers, Perkins Library, Duke University; Wayne to Dickinson Chaston, April 20, 1783, cited in Isaac Wayne, "Biographical Memoir," *Casket*, [V], 69; Wayne to Greene, May 23, 1783, Wayne Papers, XIX, HSP; Thayer, *Greene*, 412–13.

39. Wayne to Jonathan Penrose, March 17, 1783, to John Nesbit, March 27, 1783, to William Gibbon, June 29, 1783, Wayne Papers, WLCL; Wayne to John Dickinson, April 20, 1783, to Lyman Hall, June 29, 1783, to Gibbon, July 22, 1783, Dickinson to Wayne, May 17, 1783, Wayne Papers, XIX, HSP; Greene to Wayne, June 26, 1783, Wayne Letters, Greene Library, West Chester State College; "Richmond-Oakgrove," *Georgia Historical Quarterly*, XXIV, 130–31.

Chapter IX Politics and Debt, 1783–1786

1. Morris to Wayne, February 4, 1783, Wayne Papers, XIX, HSP.

2. Wayne to Joseph Habersham, October 1, 1783, to Jackson, October 1, 1783, Wayne Papers, XIX, HSP.

3. Wayne to Habersham, October 1, 1783, to Jackson, October 1, 1783, Habersham to Wayne, December 28, 1783, Wayne Papers, XIX, HSP; James Penman to Wayne, October 1, 1783, Wayne to Habersham, October 6, 1783, to Gibbon, May 16, 1784, Wayne Papers, WLCL; Wayne to James Budden, March 25, 1784, Sol Feinstone Collection, American Philosophical Society Library.

4. Wayne to Washington, November 1, 1783, Delany to Wayne, December 9, 1783, Washington to Wayne, December 14, 1783, Wayne Papers, XIX, HSP; Wayne to Washington, December 14, 1783, Washington Papers, LC; Wayne to Leonard Cecil, December 1, 1783, Wayne Papers, WLCL; Wayne to Cecil, March 17, 1784, Philip H. Ward Collection, University of Pennsylvania Library; Isaac Wayne, "Biographical Memoir," *Casket*, [V], 70; Freeman, *Washington*, V, 479.

5. Wayne to Johnston, September 17, 1783, Wayne Papers, XIX, HSP.

6. Thomas FitzSimons to ——, n.d., Gratz Collection, Historical Society of Pennsylvania; Brunhouse, *Counter-Revolution*, 144.

7. Smith, ed., *St. Clair Papers*, I, 116–17; Brunhouse, *Counter-Revolution*, 142–43.

8. Minutes, Council of Censors, November 10, 1783–September 1, 1784, Wayne Papers, Detroit Public Library; Frederick Muhlenberg to Wayne, December 18, 1783, Wayne Papers, XIX, HSP; *Pennsylvania Archives*, Ser. 3, X, 789–90; *Proceedings Relative to Calling the Conventions of 1776 and 1790* (Harrisburg, 1825), 68–77; Konkle, *Bryan*, 258.

9. *Proceedings Relative to Conventions of 1776 and 1790*, 80–82.

10. Wayne to Edwards, February — , 1784, Wayne Papers, Detroit Public Library; Draft of Speech by Wayne to Pennsylvania Executive Council, 1784. Sol Feinstone Collection, American Philosophical Society Library; *Proceedings Relative to Conventions of 1776 and 1790*, 83–128; Konkle, *Bryan*, 259.

11. Irvine to Wayne, December 10, 1783, Irvine Papers, VIII, HSP; Wayne to Irvine, December 9, 1783, Delany to Wayne, December 9, 1783, Wayne Papers, XIX, HSP; Brunhouse, *Counter-Revolution*, 144–45.

12. *Proceedings Relative to Conventions of 1776 and 1790*, 83–91; Brunhouse, *Counter-Revolution*, 145.

13. Julian P. Boyd and Robert J. Taylor, eds., *The Susquehannah Company Papers* (11 vols., Wilkes-Barre, Pa., Ithaca, N.Y., and London, England, 1930–71), VIII, 55–56; Merrill Jensen, *The New Nation: A History of the United States During the Confederation, 1781–1789* (New York, 1940), 335–36.

14. Wayne, Reasons for Publishing the Dissent of the Minority, upon the Wyoming Business, [1784], Wayne to Irvine, September 14, 1784, Wayne Papers, WLCL; Boyd and Taylor, eds., *Susquehannah Company Papers*, VIII, 55–56.

15. *Pennsylvania Packet*, October 16, 1784.

16. Dickinson to Wayne, January 1, May 17, 1783, Wayne to Dickinson, April 20, 1783, Wayne Papers, XIX, HSP; St. Clair to Wayne, June 15, 1783, Smith, ed., *St. Clair Papers*, I, 586. At least one zealous soldier, John Armstrong, Jr., wished in mid-1783 that "Mad Anthony" headed the mutineers, that the army might use its influence to secure what Armstrong saw as its just deserts (Armstrong to Gates, May 30, 1783, Gates Papers, XVI, New-York Historical Society; C. Edward Skeen, *John Armstrong, Jr., 1758–1843* [Syracuse, 1981], 15–16).

17. Wayne to Johnston, September 17, 1783, Wayne Papers, XIX, HSP; Wayne to George Gray, February 5, 1784, Wayne Papers, WLCL.

18. *Pennsylvania Packet*, October 7, 1783.

19. Irvine to Wayne, April 28, 1784, Wayne to Irvine, May 18, 1784, Wayne Papers, XIX, HSP; Wayne to Delany, May 24, 1784, Wayne Papers, WLCL.

20. Isaac Wayne, "Biographical Memoir," *Casket*, [V], 71.

21. *Pennsylvania Packet*, December 30, 1784, January 19, 1785; *Minutes of the. . .General Assembly of the Commonwealth of Pennsylvania. . .*(Philadelphia, 1781–90), April 8, 1785, 302–05; *Minutes. . .*, November 11, 23, 25, December 13, 1786, 38–40, 54–56, 66–70, 92–93; Brunhouse, *Counter-Revolution*, 164, 168, 179– 180.

22. Morris to Wayne, June 4, 1785, Wayne Papers, XIX, HSP; Isaac Wayne, "Biographical Memoir," *Casket*, [V], 71; *New York Packet*, December 5, 1785, February 6, 9, April 6, 10, 1786.

23. Wayne to —— Edwards, February — , 1784, Wayne Papers, Detroit Public Library; Wayne to Mary Wayne, July 22, 1784, Wayne Papers, XIX, HSP; Wayne to Von Steuben, November 16, 1785, C. E. French Papers, Massachusetts Historical Society; Louis Gottschalk, *Lafayette Between the American and the French Revolution, 1783–1789* (Chicago, 1950), 86.

24. Rental Agreement with John Young, July 25, 1785, Wayne Papers, WLCL;

Wayne to Mary Wayne, July 22, 1784, Wayne Papers, XIX, HSP; Anthony Wayne's Receipt Book, 1785–92, American Philosophical Society Library.

25. "Richmond-Oakgrove," *Georgia Historical Quarterly*, XXIV, 130–31; Wayne's Deed to Richmond, Deed Book D, 403, App. 64, Chatham County Court House, Savannah; Edward Telfair to Wayne, August 16, 1786, Edward Telfair Papers, Detroit Public Library; Wayne to P. J. Berkle, October 22, 1784, Wayne Papers, XIX, HSP.

26. Wayne to Roger P. Saunders, August 1, 1784, to George Emlen, September 29, 1784, Ward Collection, Van Pelt Library, University of Pennsylvania; Thomas Moore to Wayne, January 14, 1785, Wayne Papers, WLCL.

27. Wayne to Saunders, August 1, 1784, Ward Collection, University of Pennsylvania Library; Wayne to William Gibbons, Jr., September 22, 1784, William Gibbons Papers, Perkins Library, Duke University; Wayne to Saunders, September 22, December 19, 1784, March 3, 1785, to Fishbourn, November 5, 1784, to Willem and Jan Willink, January 1, 1785, Wayne Papers, WLCL; Wayne to Peter John Van Berkle, October 22, 1784, Wayne Papers, XIX, HSP; Theodore Thayer, *Nathanael Greene: Strategist of the American Revolution* (New York, 1960), 166.

28. Wayne to Saunders, January 11, 23, February 2, 1785, Wayne Papers, WLCL; *Georgia Gazette*, July 7, 1785; Thayer, *Greene*, 438.

29. Wayne to Saunders, December 19, 1784, to Delany, June 7, 1785, to Willem and Jan Willink, June 9, 1785, Margaretta Wayne to Wayne, July 1, 1785, Delany to Wayne, August 12, 1785, Wayne Papers, WLCL.

30. Anthony Wayne's Receipt Book, 1785–92, American Philosophical Society Library; Wayne to Delany, August 7, 1785, to Samuel Elbert, August 20, 1785, Edward Penman to Wayne, February 23, 1786, Notes on Surveying Hazzard Tract, July 13, 1786, Wayne Papers, WLCL; Wayne to Elbert, September 14, 1785, Ward Collection, Van Pelt Library, University of Pennsylvania.

31. Willem and Jan Willink to Wayne, March 26, July 29, 1785, Edward Penman to Wayne, May 21, July 30, September 29, 1785, Wayne to Willem and Jan Willink, August 12, September 28, 1785, to James Moore, August 12, 1785, Wayne Papers, WLCL.

32. Willem and Jan Willink to Wayne, October 31, 1785, Wayne to Thomas Willing, February 13, 1786, to Delany, May 24, 1787, Wayne Papers, WLCL; Wayne to George Emlen, March 1, 1786, Wayne Papers, XIX, HSP; Wayne to Samuel Howell, March 4, 1786, Orrin June Collection, Waynesborough.

33. Philip Jacob Cohen to Wayne, December 8, 1785, Willem and Jan Willink to Wayne, January 6, 1786, Wayne to Willing, February 13, 1786, to Cohen, February 5, 1786, to Penman, June 18, 1786, to Delany, May 24, 1787, Wayne Papers, WLCL.

34. Wayne to Willem and Jan Willink, December 20, 1785, Willem and Jan Willink to Wayne, March 7, 1786, Isaac Hazenhorst to Wayne, July 13, 1786, Penman to Wayne, July 24, 1786, Wayne Papers, WLCL.

35. Wayne's Certificate of Election to the American Philosophical Society, signed by Benjamin Franklin, January 20, 1786, Orrin June Collection, Waynesborough; Wayne's Instructions. . .,1786, *Collector* (1978), 5; Wayne's Power of Attorney to Delany, April 20, 1786, Wayne Papers, WLCL.

36. Wayne to Mary Wayne, June 18, 1786, Wayne Papers, Detroit Public Library; Wayne to Delany, June 18, 1786, Wayne Papers, WLCL.

37. Wayne to Margaretta Wayne, June 28, 1786, Wayne Papers, XIX, HSP; Thayer, *Greene*, 445.

38. Delany to Wayne, July 11, October 6, 1788, Wayne to Delany, November 1, 27, 1786, Wayne Papers, WLCL; Wayne's Memorial to Georgia House of Representatives, August 10, 1786, Lafayette to Wayne, December 20, 1786, Wayne Papers, XIX, HSP; W. C. Hartridge, ed., *The Letters of Don Juan McQueen to his Family, Written from Spanish East Florida, 1791–1807* (Columbia, S.C., 1943), 10–11.

39. Wayne to ——, November 20, 1786, Wayne Papers, XIX, HSP; Wayne to Catherine Greene, August 1, December 8, 1786, Greene Papers, Richmond, Georgia, photostats in Greene Papers, WLCL.

40. Wayne to Houstoun, January 6, 1787, Ward Collection, Van Pelt Library, University of Pennsylvania; Wayne to Penman, January 6, 1787, to Houstoun, March 6, 1787, Delany to Wayne, January 20, 1787, Penman to Wayne, January 29, March 3, 1787, Houstoun to Wayne, May 5, 1787, Wayne Papers, WLCL.

Chapter X Redemption, 1787–1792

1. Wayne to James and Edward Penmàn, February 10, 1787, to Edward Penman, June 13, 1787, Edward Penman to Wayne, March 3, June 20, 1787, Wayne Papers, WLCL.

2. Wayne to Aedanus Burke, August 12, 1787, Wayne Papers, XIX, HSP; Wayne to Edward Penman, August 30, 1787, Jasper Moylan to Wayne, September 3, 1787, Wayne Papers, WLCL; Wayne to John Jenkins, August 18, 1787, Ward Collection, Van Pelt Library, University of Pennsylvania.

3. Burke to Wayne, September 3, 1787, Wayne to Delany, October 23, 1787, Wayne Papers, WLCL.

4. Wayne to George Handley, May 28, 1787, Wayne Papers, WLCL; William L. Benton, "Pennsylvania Revolutionary Officers and the Federal Convention," *Pennsylvania History*, XXXI (1964), 426–27; Richard H. Kohn, *Eagle and Sword: The Federalists and the Creation of the Military Establishment in America, 1783–1802* (New York, 1975), 174.

5. Wayne to George Handley, May 28, 1788, Wayne Papers, WLCL; Jackson Turner Main, *The Antifederalists: Critics of the Constitution, 1781–1788* (Chicago, 1961), 187–92; Brunhouse, *Counter-Revolution*, 202–11.

6. Wayne's Notes Taken at Pa. Ratifying Con., November 27, 30, 1787, Wayne Papers, WLCL; Wayne to Lafayette, July 8, 1788, Wayne Papers, XIX, HSP; Benton, "Pennsylvania Revolutionary Officers," *Pennsylvania History*, XXXI, 426.

7. Wayne to Delany, February 20, May 14, July 16, 1788, to William Lewis, February 20, 1788, to Burke, May 1, 1788, Lewis to Wayne, September 9, 1788, Wayne Papers, WLCL; Wayne to Catherine Greene, April 20, 1788, Greene Papers, Richmond, photostats in Greene Papers, WLCL; Advertisement for Richmond, December, 1787, Ward Collection, Van Pelt Library, University of Pennsylvania; E. Merton Coulter, *Georgia: A Short History* (Chapel Hill, N.C., 1947), 172; Kenneth Coleman, ed., *A History of Georgia* (Athens, Ga., 1977), 95.

8. Delany to Wayne, September 8, 9, 1788, Wayne to Burke, October 10, 1788, Wayne Papers, WLCL.

9. Wayne to Burke, October 7, 1788, to Delany, October 7, 1788, April 4, 1789, February 10, 1790, Delany to Wayne, March 21, July 13, 1789, Wayne Papers, WLCL; Wayne to Mary Wayne, May 30, 1789, Wayne Papers, XIX, HSP.

10. Wayne to Telfair, November 1, 1788, Wayne Papers, WLCL; Wayne to Asa

Emanuel, December 15, 1788, Wayne, Stites, Anderson Papers, Georgia Historical Society.

11. Wayne to Emanuel, December 15, 1788, Wayne, Stites, Anderson Papers, Georgia Historical Society; Elihu Lyman to Wayne, November 3, 1788, Burke to Wayne, November 10, 1788, Fishbourn to Wayne, November 12, 1788, John Baker to Wayne, November 20, 1788, John Burnett, to Wayne, December 8, 1788, Wayne Papers, WLCL.

12. Wayne to Elijah Clark, November 1, 1788, Wayne Papers, WLCL; Wayne to Washington, April 6, 1789, Wayne Papers, XIX, HSP; Washington to Wayne, May 4, 1789, Washington Papers, LC; Wayne to Alexander Hamilton, April 6, 1789, Harold C. Syrett and Jacob E. Cooke, eds., *Papers of Alexander Hamilton* (26 vols., New York, 1961–79), V, 316.

13. Wayne to James Madison, June 15, 1789, Wayne Papers, Miscellaneous Manuscripts, Library of Congress; Wayne to Washington, May 19, 1789, Wayne Letters, PCC, 161, I, 241–44.

14. Wayne to Pierce Butler and Ralph Izard, July 4, 1789, Wister Papers, Historical Society of Pennsylvania; Wayne to Washington, August 30, 1789, Wayne Letters, PCC, 161, I, 245–48; Wayne to Delany, October 21, 1789, to Members of Senate and House of Representatives from Pennsylvania, May 19, 1790, Wayne Papers, WLCL; Wayne to Henry Knox, March 20, 1790, Knox Papers, Massachusetts Historical Society; Wayne to Washington, February 1, 1790, Washington Papers, LC; James Madison to Wayne, July 31, 1789, Knox to Wayne, August 9, 1789, April 10, 1790, Izard to Wayne, October 1, 1789, Morris to Wayne, October 23, 1789, Wayne Papers, XIX, HSP; Samuel G. McLendon, *History of the Public Domain of Georgia* (Atlanta, 1924), 35–39.

15. Edgar S. Maclay, ed., *Journal of William Maclay, United States Senator from Pennsylvania, 1789–91* (New York, 1890), 240; Kohn, *Eagle and Sword*, 100–01.

16. Wayne to Mary Wayne, November 15, 1788, to Catherine Greene, November 15, 1789, Burke to Wayne, April 29, 1789, Catherine Greene to Wayne, December 30, 1789, Wayne Papers, XIX, HSP; Wayne to Catherine Greene, March 10, 1789, February 4, 22, 1790, Greene Papers, Richmond, photostats in Greene Papers, WLCL; Wayne to Catherine Greene, February 21, 1790, Greene Papers, WLCL; Washington to Wayne, March 25, 1790, Washington Papers, LC.

17. Wayne to Delany, December 5, 1788, Wayne Papers, Society Collection, HSP; Margaretta Wayne to Wayne, March 4, 1789, Delany to Wayne, March 21, 1789, March 25, 1790, Wayne Papers, WLCL.

18. William Atlee to Wayne, June 12, 1789, Charles F. Gunther Collection, Chicago Historical Society Library; Delany to Wayne, July 13, 1789, March 25, May 4, August 11, November 6, 1790, Wayne to Delany, April 18, 1790, Wayne Papers, WLCL.

19. Wayne to Penman, February 19, 1790, to Adam Tunno, February 10, April 24, 1790, to Elizabeth Iddings Wayne, June 28, 1790, to Mary Wayne, June 28, 1790, Penman to Wayne, February 21, March 4, 21, 1789, Tunno to Wayne, November 9, 1789, March 6, 1790, Delany to Wayne, August 11, 1790, Chester County Court of Common Pleas, Judgment, May, 1790, Wayne Papers, WLCL; *Georgia Gazette*, July 9, 1789.

20. Wayne to Henry Laurens, November 19, 1790, to Tunno, December 9, 1790, April 20, May 19, June 2, 1791, to Samuel Potts, April 12, 14, 1791, to Penman, October 1, 4, 1790, to Delany, May 19, 1791, Tunno to Wayne, December 1, 1790, May 10, 26, June 12, 1791, Potts to Wayne, April 13, 1791, Agreements

between Wayne, Penman, & Potts, April 2, 16, 1791, Deed to Richmond, April 16, 1791, Wayne Papers, WLCL. That Penman and Potts were correct in their assessment that Richmond was not worth what Wayne owed them is seen in that the estate was sold in 1803 — twelve years after Wayne's debt was cleared — for a mere £2,000 ("Richmond-Oakgrove," *Georgia Historical Quarterly*, XXXIV, 132–34).

21. Wayne to Delany, April 13, May 19, 1791, Wayne Papers, WLCL; Wayne to Mary Wayne, April 13, 1791, Wayne Papers, XIX, HSP.

22. Wayne to Mary Wayne, May 19, 1791, Wayne Papers, Detroit Public Library.

23. Wayne to Gibbon, January 21, 1791, to Telfair, January 22, 1791, Houstoun to Wayne, December 30, 1790, James Seagrove to Wayne, April 4, 1791, Wayne Papers, WLCL; Wayne to Telfair, February 1, 1791, Wayne Papers, University of Georgia Library.

24. Wayne to Delany, March 1, 1791, to Gibbon, May 18, 1791, Wayne Papers, WLCL; *Georgia Gazette*, May 18, 1791.

25. Wayne to Gibbon, May 18, 1791, Wayne Papers, WLCL; Jackson and Twohig, eds., *Washington Diaries*, VI, 128; *Georgia Gazette*, May 18, 1791; Archibald Henderson, *Washington's Southern Tour, 1791* (Boston, 1923), 208; Adelaide Wilson, *Historic and Picturesque Savannah* (Boston, 1889), 91–92.

26. Matthew McAllister to Wayne, August 12, 1791, Richard Wayne to Wayne, August 12, 1791, Robert Montfort to Wayne, August 13, 1791, Wayne Papers, WLCL; Wayne to ――, April 2, 1792, Wayne Papers, XX, HSP.

27. Wayne to Richard Wayne, August 18, 1791, to McAllister, September 7, 1791, Wayne's Essay, "The Old Georgians of Charleston Analyzed" [1791], Wayne Papers, WLCL; Wayne to James Seagrove, October 9, 1791, Wayne Papers, XIX, HSP.

28. Wayne to Mrs. Bab. McLaine, June 29, 1792, Wayne Papers XX, HSP.

29. Izard to Wayne, April 14, 1792, Wayne Papers, WLCL; Kohn, *Eagle and Sword*, 126.

30. Wayne to Major John Berrier, December 5, 1791, Wayne Papers, WLCL; Wayne to Isaac Wayne, December 15, 1791, Wayne Papers, Detroit Public Library; Kohn, *Eagle and Sword*, 126; Lawrence Delbert Cress, *Citizens in Arms: The Army and the Militia in American Society to the War of 1812* (Chapel Hill, N.C., 1982), 111–13, 129–31.

31. Wayne to McAllister, November 10, 1791, to McAllister, Gibbon, Samuel Stirk, November 29, 1791, Depositions Against Wayne, January, 1793, Wayne Papers, XIX, HSP; Wayne to McAllister, November 18, 1791, to Gibbon, Stirk, and McAllister, February 10, 1792, Jackson's Petition to House of Representatives, [1791], Wayne's Notes of Testimony to House of Representatives [November 23, 1791], Robert Montfort to Wayne, December 8, 1791, Richard Wayne to Wayne, January 11, 1792, McAllister to Wayne, January 15, 1792, Wayne Papers, WLCL; Joseph Gales, comp., *The Debates and Proceedings in the Congress of the United States, 1789–1824* (42 vols., Washington, D.C., 1834–56), III, 176, 210.

32. Wayne to Lewis, February 29, 1792, Wayne Papers, WLCL; Gales, comp., *Debates of Congress*, III, 457–72.

33. Gales, comp., *Debates of Congress*, III, 472, 475–79; Charlton, *Jackson*, 83, 119–21.

34. Washington's "Opinion of the General Officers," March 9, 1792, Fitzpatrick, ed., *Writings of Washington*, XXXI, 509–15; Jefferson's Cabinet Notes, March

9, 1792, Franklin B. Sawvel, ed., *The Complete Anas of Thomas Jefferson* (New York, 1903), 61–62; Kohn, *Eagle and Sword*, 125–26.

35. Washington to Henry Lee, June 30, 1792, Fitzpatrick, ed., *Writings of Washington*, XXXII, 27–78; James Monroe to Jefferson, June 17, 1792, S. M. Hamilton, ed., *The Writings of James Monroe* (7 vols., New York, 1898–1903), I, 232; James Madison to Henry Lee, April 15, 1792, James Madison Papers, Library of Congress; Kohn, *Eagle and Sword*, 125–26.

36. Knox to Wayne, April 12, 1792, Wayne to Knox, April 13, 1792, Wayne Papers, XX, HSP; George Hammond to John Graves Simcoe, April 21, 1792, E. A. Cruikshank, ed., *The Correspondence of Lieut. Governor John Graves Simcoe. . .*(5 vols., Toronto, Ontario, 1923–31), I, 131–32; Wayne's Commission as Major General, May 10, 1792, Orrin June Collection, Waynesborough; North Callahan, *Henry Knox: General Washington's General* (New York, 1958), 321–28.

37. Wayne to Isaac Wayne, December 15, 1791, Wayne Papers, Detroit Public Library; Organization of the Army in 1792, December 17, 1792, Walter Lowrie and Matthew Clarke, eds., *American State Papers: Documents, Legislative and Executive of the Congress of the United States* (38 vols., Washington, D.C., 1832–61), Class V, *Military Affairs* (7 vols.), I, 40–41.

38. Wayne to Mary Wayne, April 24, 1792, Wayne Papers, XX, HSP; Wayne to Delany, June 2, 8, 1792, Wayne Papers, WLCL; Hamilton Rowan to Mrs. Rowan, November 1, 1796, Archibald Hamilton Rowan, *Autobiography* (Dublin, 1840), 301; Munroe, "Philadelawareans," *PMHB*, LXIX, 137–38.

Chapter XI   Commander of the Legion, 1792–1793

1. Wayne to Knox, June 15, 1792, Wayne Papers, WLCL; Leland D. Baldwin, *The Whiskey Rebels* (Pittsburgh, 1939), 85.

2. Wayne to Knox, June 15, 1792, to Delany, June 22, 1792, Wayne Papers, WLCL; Wayne to James Wilkinson, June 16, 1792, to County Lieutenants, June 23, 1792, Knox to Wayne, June 15, 20, 22, 1792, Wayne Papers, XX, HSP; Wilkinson to Wayne, June 21, 1792, Special Collections, Joseph Regenstein Library, University of Chicago.

3. Wayne to Knox, June 22, 29, 1792, Wayne Papers, WLCL.

4. Wayne to Knox, July 6, 1792, Wayne Papers, WLCL; Wayne to Wilkinson, July 7, 10, 1792, to Knox, July 13, 1792, Wayne's General Orders, July 17, 21, August 30, 1792, Knox to Wayne, July 13, 1792, Wayne Papers, XX, HSP; Baldwin, *Whiskey Rebels*, 87–88.

5. Wayne to Knox, September 14, 1792, Knox to Wayne, September 14, 1792, Wayne Papers, XXI, HSP; Richard C. Knopf, "Crime and Punishment in the Legion, 1792–1793," *Bulletin of the Historical and Philosophical Society of Ohio*, XIV (1956), 232–38.

6. Wayne to Knox, August 24, September 28, 1792, Wayne Papers, XXI, XXII, HSP; Wayne to Delany, August 24, 1792, Wayne Papers, WLCL.

7. Knox to Wayne, September 7, 21, October 5, 12, 1792, January 5, 1793, Wayne to Knox, October 19, 26, 1792, Wayne Papers, XXI, XXII, HSP.

8. Wayne to Knox, October 12, 26, November 9, 16, 23, 29, December 6, 1792, Knox to Wayne, November 9, 17, 24, 1792, Wayne Papers, XXII, XXIII, HSP; Observations of President Washington on General Wayne's Letter of the 14th Nov. 1792 to Secretary Knox, November 23, 1792, Fitzpatrick, ed., *Writings of Washington*, XXXII, 234–35.

9. Wayne to Delany, September 28, October 26, November 23, 1792, Delany to Wayne, September 21, November 10, 1792, Atlee to Wayne, November 6, 1792, March 19, 1793, Wayne Papers, WLCL; Wayne to Atlee, December 12, 1792, to Hartley, January 1, 1793, Wayne Papers, XXIII, XXIV, HSP; Wayne to William Hayman, December 28, 1792, *PMHB*, XIX (1895), 121–22.

10. Wayne to Delany, September 28, December 25, 1792, Wayne Papers, WLCL; Wayne to Hayman, December 28, 1792, Wayne Papers, XXIV, HSP; Isaac Wayne, "Biographical Memoir," *Casket*, [V], 120.

11. Wayne to Cornplanter, Red Arrow, Chiefs of Allegheny, December 25, 1792, Knox to Wayne, March 5, 1793, Wayne Papers, XXII, XXIII, XXIV, HSP; Wayne to Knox, December 21, 28, 1792, Wayne Papers, WLCL; Cress, *Citizens in Arms*, 131–32.

12. Wayne to Knox, December 12, 1792, January 4, 1793, Knox to Wayne, December 22, 1792, Wayne Papers, XXIII, XXIV, HSP; Gales, comp., *Debates of Congress*, IV, 750, 762–68, 773–802; Francis Paul Prucha, *The Sword of the Republic: The United States Army on the Frontier, 1783–1846* (New York, 1969), 33–34; Kohn, *Eagle and Sword*, 147.

13. Wayne to Knox, January 15, 1793, Wayne Papers, XXIV, HSP; Wayne to Delany, February 22, 1793, Northwest Territory Collection, Indiana Historical Society.

14. Wayne to Knox, February 16, March 4, 15, 22, 30, 1793, Knox to Wayne, March 9, 1793, Wayne Papers, XXV, HSP.

15. Hugh Henry Brackenridge to Wayne, January 1, February 20, 1793, Delany to Wayne, January 4, 1793, Wayne Papers, WLCL; Wayne to Catherine Greene, February 11, 1793, Greene Papers, Richmond, photostats in Greene Papers, WLCL; Margaretta Atlee to Wayne, January 16, 1793, Wayne Papers, Detroit Public Library; Isaac Wayne, "Biographical Memoir," *Casket*, [V], 119.

16. Mary Wayne to Isaac Wayne, [1792], Wayne Papers, WLCL; Delany to Wayne, April 19, 1793, Atlee to Wayne, April 20, 1793, Wayne Papers, XXIV, HSP.

17. Wayne to Knox, April 29, 1793, Wayne Papers, XXVI, HSP; Delany to Wayne, May 11, 1793, Hayman to Wayne, May 31, 1793, Wayne Papers, WLCL; Wayne to Margaret Penrose, May 28, 1793, Northwest Territory Collection, Indiana Historical Society; Wayne to Hayman, May 28, 1793, Maupin Family Papers, Alderman Library, University of Virginia.

18. Wayne to Knox, April 5, 13, 20, 1793, Knox to Wayne, April 13, 20, 1793, John Gibson for People of Pittsburgh to Wayne, April — , 1793, Wayne to People of Pittsburgh, [April, 1793], Wayne's General Orders, April 28, 1793, Wayne Papers, XXVI, HSP.

19. Wayne to Knox, April 27, 1793, Wayne's General Orders, May 6, 1793, Wayne Papers, XXVI, HSP; Dudley Woodbridge to ——, May 1, 1793, Woodbridge Papers, Detroit Public Library.

20. Wayne to Knox, May 9, 1793, Wayne Papers, XXVI, HSP.

21. Wayne to Knox, May 27, 1793, Wayne Papers, XXVI, HSP.

22. Knox to Wayne, May 17, 1793, Wayne to Isaac Shelby, May 18, June 14, 1793, to Charles Scott, June 14, 1793, to Benjamin Logan, June 14, 1793, Shelby to Wayne, June 24, 1793, Wayne Papers, XXVI, XXVII, HSP; Shelby to Wayne, May 27, 1793, Charles Scott Papers, Margaret I. King Library, University of Kentucky.

23. Wayne to Knox, June 20, 1793, to Scott, August 5, 1793, Scott to Wayne,

August 1, 10, 1793, Wayne Papers, XXVII, XXVIII, HSP; Wayne to Shelby, July 1, 1793, to Scott, August 13, 1793, Shane Collection, Presbyterian Historical Society; Commissions of Officers of Mounted Volunteers of Kentucky, July 1, 1793, Edward E. Ayer Collection, Newberry Library.

24. Wayne to Knox, June 20, July 2, 10, August 8, 1793, Knox to Wayne, July 20, (2), August 16, 1793, Wayne Papers, XXVII, XXVIII, HSP.

25. Benjamin Lincoln, Beverley Randolph, and Timothy Pickering to Wayne, August 23, 1793, Preston Family: Joyes Collection, Filson Club Library; Wayne's General Orders, August 25, 1793, Wayne to Wilkinson, September 7, 11, 1793, Knox to Wayne, September 3, 1793, Wilkinson to Wayne, September 9, 11, 1793, Wayne Papers, XXVIII, XXIX, HSP; Wilkinson to Wayne, September 14, 1793, Samuel Mackay Wilson Manuscript Collection, Margaret I. King Library, University of Kentucky; Wayne to Messrs. Elliot and Williams, July 18, 1793, Park Collection, Morristown National Historical Park.

26. Wayne to Knox, October 5, 1793, to Scott, October 5, 1793, Wayne Papers, XXIX, HSP.

27. Scott to Wayne, September 12, 1793, Wayne Papers, WLCL; Wayne to Scott, September 22, 1793, Hardin Family Collection, Chicago Historical Society.

28. Wayne to Knox, September 17, 1793, to Wilkinson, September 30, October 1, 5, 1793, Wayne Papers, XXIX, HSP; David Jones to Wayne, September 17, 1793, Delany to Wayne, September 20, 1793, Wayne Papers, WLCL; St. Clair to Knox, [1794], Smith, ed., *St. Clair Papers*, II, 327.

29. John H. Buell, "A Fragment from the Diary of Major John Hutchinson Buell, U.S.A.," *Journal of the Military Service Institution*, XL (1907), 105.

30. Wayne to Senator John Edwards, October 22, 1793, to Knox, October 23, 1793, to Elliot and Williams, October 16, 23, November 12, December 3, 1793, January 1, April 17, 22, 23, May 1, 6, 1794, Wayne Papers, XXX, XXXI, HSP; Wayne to St. Clair, November 7, 1793, Arthur G. Mitten Collection, Indiana Historical Society.

31. Council of War, October 31, 1793, Thomas Barbee to Wayne, November 1, 1793, Wilkinson and Posey to Wayne, November 1, 1793, Robert Todd to Wayne, November 1, 1793, Scott to Wayne, November 9, 1793, Wayne to Scott, November 2, 1793, Wayne Papers, XXX, HSP; Scott to Wayne, October 31, 1793, Scott Papers, King Library, University of Kentucky; Wayne to Knox, November 15, 1793, Knox Papers, Massachusetts Historical Society.

32. Wayne to Knox, November 15, 1793, Knox Papers, Massachusetts Historical Society; Wayne to Catherine Greene, December 17, 1793, Greene Papers, Richmond, photostats in Greene Papers, WLCL; Scott to Wayne, January 15, 1794, Scott Papers, King Library, University of Kentucky.

Chapter XII Fallen Timbers, 1793–1794

1. Wayne to Wilkinson, December 19, 22, 1793, Wayne Papers, XXXI, HSP.

2. John Hamtramck to Wayne, November 22, 1793, Wayne to Hamtramck, November 23, 1793, Wayne Papers, XXXI, HSP.

3. Wayne to Delany, January 1, 1794, Wayne Papers, XXXI, HSP.

4. Wilkinson to Wayne, September 12, 1792, Wayne to Isaac Guion, November 10, 1794, Wayne Papers, WLCL; Wilkinson to Knox, November 3, 1793, James Wilkinson Letters, Kentucky Historical Society; Wilkinson to Harry Innes, October 3, 1793, Harry Innes Papers, Library of Congress; John Armstrong to Wayne,

March 23, 1793, John Armstrong Papers, Indiana Historical Society; Wilkinson, *Memoirs*, II, 108–14. The characterization of Wilkinson is in James Ripley Jacobs, *Tarnished Warrior: Major-General James Wilkinson* (New York, 1938), 132.

5. Campbell Smith to Otho Holland Williams, November 16, 1793, Otho Holland Williams Papers, Maryland Historical Society; Thomas Cushing to Jer. Wadsworth, May 15, 1794, Joseph Trumbull Papers, Connecticut State Library; Wayne to Wilkinson, June 16, 1792, December 22, 1793, Wilkinson to Wayne, July 23, 1792, Wayne Papers, XXX, XXXI, HSP; Wilkinson to Innes, October 23, 1793, Innes Papers, Library of Congress; Kohn, *Eagle and Sword*, 179–80; Thomas Robson Hay, "Some Reflections on the Career of General James Wilkinson," *MVHR*, XXI (1935), 471–94. See also, Thomas Robson Hay and M. R. Werner, *The Admirable Trumpeter: A Biography of General James Wilkinson* (Garden City, N.Y., 1941).

6. Wayne to Shelby, January 6, 1794, to Knox, January 8, 1794, Wayne Papers, XXXII, HSP; Shelby to Wayne, February 11, 1794, Wayne Papers, WLCL.

7. Wayne to Western Indians, January 14, 1794, Cruikshank, ed., *Simcoe Papers*, II, 131–32.

8. Wayne to Knox, January 18, 1794 (2), Wayne Papers, XXXII, HSP; Wayne to Posey, January 21, 1794, Thomas Posey Collection, Indiana Historical Society.

9. Wayne to Delany, March 21, 1794, Wayne Papers, WLCL; Wayne to Knox, March 25, 1794, to Six Nations, March 26, 1794, Wayne Papers, XXXIII, HSP.

10. Wayne to Knox, March 3, 10, 20, May 7, 1794, to Wilkinson, March 24, April 14, May 13, 15, 1794, to Shelby, May 21, 1794, Knox to Wayne, March 31, 1794, Wayne Papers, XXXIII, XXXIV, XXXV, HSP; Shelby to Wayne, May 9, 1794, Wayne Papers, WLCL.

11. Wayne to Isaac Wayne, May 9, 1794, Wayne Papers, WLCL.

12. Wayne to Elliot and Williams, May 18, 24, June 1, 9, 1794, to Knox, May 30, 1794, Wayne Papers, XXXV, HSP; Hay, "Reflections," *MVHR*, XXI, 479–80.

13. Knox to Wayne, March 13, 1794, Wayne Papers, XXXIII, HSP; Wayne to Knox, April 20, 1794, Northwest Territory Collection, Indiana Historical Society; Scott to Knox, April 30, 1794, Scott Papers, King Library, University of Kentucky.

14. Knox to Wilkinson, July 12, 1794, Knox Papers, Massachusetts Historical Society; Wilkinson to Wayne, June 8, 1794, Gratz Collection, Historical Society of Pennsylvania; "A Friend to Truth," *Gazette of the U.S.*, July 19, 1794; Jacobs, *Tarnished Warrior*, 140; Kohn, *Eagle and Sword*, 181.

15. Wayne to Wilkinson, June 8, 1794, Wilkinson to Wayne, June 8, 1794, Wayne Papers, XXXV, HSP.

16. Wayne to Shelby, May 26, 1794, to Knox, May 26, 30, 1794, Wayne Papers, XXXV, HSP.

17. Knox to Wayne, June 7, 1794, Wayne to Knox, June 10, 1794, Wayne Papers, XXXV, XXXVI, HSP; Thomas A. Bailey, *A Diplomatic History of the American People*, seventh ed. (New York, 1964), 75.

18. William Gibson to Wayne, June 30, July 1, 2, 5, 1794, Wayne to Knox, July 7, 1794, Wayne Papers, XXXVI, HSP; James Ripley Jacobs, *The Beginning of the U.S. Army, 1783–1812* (Princeton, N.J., 1947), 168–70.

19. Delany to Wayne, June 14, 1794, Wayne to Delany, July 10, 14, 1794, Wayne Papers, WLCL; Wayne's Last Will and Testament, July 14, 1794, Wayne Papers, Detroit Public Library.

20. Wayne to Isaac Wayne, July 14, 1794, Wayne Papers, WLCL.

21. Wayne to Knox, July 16, 1794, Wayne Papers, WLCL; Wayne to Knox, July 27, 1794, Wayne Papers, XXXVI, HSP.

22. Wayne to Isaac Wayne, September 10, 1794, Wayne Papers, XXXVII, HSP; R.C. McGrane, ed., "William Clark's Journal of General Wayne's Campaign," *Mississippi Valley Historical Review*, I (1914), 418–44, hereafter cited as McGrane, ed., "Clark's Journal," *MVHR*, I; "Journal of Lieutenant Boyer," in John Jeremiah Jacob, *A Biographical Sketch of the Life of the Late Capt. Michael Cresap* (Cincinnati, 1866), 315–22, hereafter cited as Boyer, "Journal."

23. Wayne to Isaac Wayne, September 10, 1794, Wayne Papers, XXXVII, HSP.

24. E. A. Cruikshank, ed., "Diary of an Officer in the Indian Country-1794," *Magazine of Western History*, II, (1885), 387; Boyer, "Journal," 315–22.

25. Wilkinson to Wayne, August 12, 1794, Speech of Indians to Wayne, August 15, 1794, Wayne Papers, XXXVII, HSP; Wayne to Indian Chiefs, August 13, 1794, Cruikshank, ed., *Simcoe Papers*, II, 371–72.

26. John Cook, "General Wayne's Campaign in 1794 & 1795: Captain John Cook's Journal," *American Historical Record*, II (1873), 315, hereafter cited as Cook, "Journal," *Amer. His. Record*, II; McGrane, ed. "Clark's Journal," *MVHR*, 426–28; Richard C. Knopf, transcriber, *The West Point Orderly Books* [for the U.S. Legion, May 24, 1792–September 28, 1794] (4 vols. in one, Columbus, Ohio, 1954), I, 133.

27. Wayne to Knox, August 28, 1794; J. Porter to Thomas R. Peters, November 6, 1817, Wayne Papers, XXXVII, XLVIII, HSP.

28. Wayne to Knox, August 28, 1794, Wayne Papers, XXXVII, HSP; Jacobs, *U.S. Army*, 173.

29. Wayne to Knox, August 28, 1794, Wayne Papers, XXXVII, HSP; Dresden W.H. Howard, ed., "The Battle of Fallen Timbers, as told by Chief Kin-Jo-I-No," *Northwest Ohio Quarterly*, XX (1948), 46; Cook, "Journal," *Amer. His. Record*, II, 316; John K. Mahon, "Anglo-American Methods of Indian Warfare, 1676–1794," *Mississippi Valley Historical Review*, XLV (1958), 257; Jacobs, *U.S. Army*, 174–75; Russell F. Weigley, *The American Way of War: A History of United States Military Strategy and Policy* (New York, 1973), 67, 488, n. 17.

30. Wayne to Knox, August 28, 1794, Wayne Papers, XXXVII, HSP; Howard, ed., "Kin-Jo-I-No's Account," *N.W. Ohio Quarterly*, XX, 47–48; Wilkinson to John Brown, August 28, 1794, Wilkinson Papers, Detroit Public Library; Wilkinson to Innes, October 13, 1794, Innes Papers, Library of Congress.

31. Wayne to William Campbell, August 22, 1794 (2), Campbell to Wayne, August 21, 22 (2), 1794, Wayne Papers, XXXVII, HSP; Howard, ed., "Kin-Jo-I-No's Account," *N.W. Ohio Quarterly*, XX, 47–48; Samuel Flagg Bemis, *Jay's Treaty: A Study in Commerce and Diplomacy* (New York, 1923), 180; Arthur G. Bradley, *Sir Guy Carleton, Lord Dorchester* (Toronto, Ontario, 1907), 286–87.

Chapter XIII   Peace in the Northwest, 1794–1795

1. Wayne to Knox, August 28, 1794, September 20, 1794, to Scott, September 8, 1794, to Elliot and Williams, September 10, 1794, Wayne Papers, XXXVII, HSP; Mahon, "Methods," *MVHR*, LVIII, 271; McGrane, ed., "Clark's Journal," *MVHR*, I, 433.

2. Wayne to Western Indians, September 12, 1794, Cruikshank, ed., *Simcoe Papers*, III, 79–80; Wayne to Isaac Wayne, September 10, 1794, Wayne Papers, XXXVII, HSP.

3. Wayne to Knox, September 20, 1794, Wayne Papers, XXXVII, HSP.

4. Wayne to Knox, September 20, October 17, 1794, Wayne Papers, XXXVII, HSP.

5. Dorchester to Wayne, October 6, 1794, Wayne to Scott, October 13, 1794, to Shelby, October 13, 1794, to Knox, October 17, 1794, Wayne Papers, XXXVII, HSP; Wayne to Winthrop Sargent, October 9, 1794, Winthrop Sargent Papers, Massachusetts Historical Society.

6. Wayne to Hamtramck, October 22, 1794, Wayne Papers, WLCL; Wayne's General Orders, October 23, 1794, Cruikshank, ed., *Simcoe Papers*, II, 409–10; Wayne to Isaac Wayne, November 10, 1794, to Knox, November 12, 1794, to Delany, November 14, 1794, Wayne Papers, XXXVIII, HSP.

7. Wayne to Western Indians, November 4, 1794, January 1, 1795, to Knox, November 12, December 23, 1794, Wayne Papers, XXXVIII, XXXIX, HSP.

8. Gales, comp., *Debates of Congress*, IV, 956–66; Knox to Wayne, December 5, 1794, Wayne Papers, XXXVIII, HSP; Freeman, *Washington*, VII, 226.

9. Wayne to Knox, January 29, 1795, Wayne Papers, XXXIX, HSP.

10. Robert Newman's account: Certificate of David Jones Relating Robert Newman's Part in a Conspiracy Agt. the U.S., October 25, 1796, Wayne Papers, WLCL; *Berkeley Intelligencer*, June 18, 1808, and Newman to ——, June 8, 1797, Northwest Territory Collection, Indiana Historical Society. For confirmation that the British in Canada somehow definitely had learned Wayne's plan for campaigning after August 8, 1795, see Cruikshank, ed., "Officer's Diary-1794," *Mag. Amer. History*, II, 387.

11. Wayne to Knox, December 14, 1794, Wayne Papers, WLCL.

12. Wayne to Knox, December 23, 1794, January 29, February 13, 21, 1795, Wayne Papers, XXXVIII, XXXIX, HSP.

13. Wilkinson to Innes, November 10, December — , 1794, Innes Papers, Library of Congress.

14. Knox to Wayne, December 5, 1794, Wayne Papers, XXXVIII, HSP; Knox to Wilkinson, December 4, 5, 1794, Innes Papers, Library of Congress.

15. Wayne to Knox, January 25, 1795, Wayne Papers, WLCL.

16. Wilkinson to Innes, January 1, 1795, to Knox, January 2, 1795, Innes Papers, Library of Congress; Jacobs, *Wilkinson*, 144–46, 152–56.

17. Jackson and Twohig, eds., *Washington Diaries*, VI, 178–79.

18. Cornelius R. Sedam to — Mills, March 31, 1795, Special Collections, Regenstein Library, University of Chicago; Gales, comp., *Debates of Congress*, IV, 1515–16; Kohn, *Eagle and Sword*, 176–78; Cress, *Citizens in Arms*, 132.

19. Wayne to Isaac Wayne, November 10, December 23, 1794, to Delany, December 23, 1794, Wayne Papers, XXXVIII, HSP.

20. Atlee to Wayne, September 27, 1794, Wayne Papers, Detroit Public Library; Wayne to Atlee, February 22, 1795, Gunther Collection, Chicago Historical Society Library.

21. Margaretta Atlee to Wayne, February 29, 1795, Wayne Papers, WLCL.

22. Wayne to Tarke and Sandusky chiefs, January 1, 1795, to Chippewa, Ottawa, Potawatomi, et al., January 19, 1795, Wayne Papers, XXXIX, HSP; Jacobs, *U.S. Army*, 179.

23. Wayne to Knox, January 24, February 12, 1795, Wayne Papers, XXXIX, HSP.

24. Timothy Pickering to Wayne, April 8, 15 (2), 25, 1795, Wayne Papers, XL, HSP.

25. Pickering to Wayne, April 8, May 15, June 29, 1795, Wayne to Pickering, May 15, September 2, 1795, Wayne Papers, XL, XLII, HSP; Draft of Treaty from Pickering, May 16, 1795, Northwest Territory Collection, Indiana Historical Society.

26. St. Clair to Pickering, April 28, June 11, 30, 1795, Wayne to St. Clair, August 19, 1795, Smith, ed., *St. Clair Papers*, II, 343, 375–77, 387–88; Wayne to St. Clair, June 2, 5, 28, August 15, 1795, Wayne Papers, XLI, XLII, HSP; St. Clair to Wayne, July 31, 1795, Wayne Papers, WLCL.

27. Wayne to Captain Preston, June 25, 1795, Preston Family Papers, Filson Club Library; Wayne to Hamtramck, June 25, 1795, to Thomas Doyle, July 1, 1795, to Judge John C. Symmes, July 1, 1795, Wayne Papers, WLCL.

28. John Parrish to Wayne, May 25, 1795, Wayne Papers, WLCL; Parrish to Wayne, May 30, 1795, Wayne to Parrish, June 17, 1795, Wayne Papers, XLI, HSP.

29. Lowrie and Clarke, eds., *American State Papers*, Class II, *Indian Affairs* (2 vols.), I, 562–64; Jacobs, *U.S. Army*, 180.

30. Pickering to Wayne, July 4, 1795, Wayne to Pickering, August 9, 1795, enclosing Copy of Treaty, Wayne Papers, XLII, HSP.

Chapter XIV Good Soldier's Reward, 1795–1796

1. Pickering to Wayne, June 17, August 1, September 5, 1795, Wayne to Pickering, August 9, 1795, Wayne Papers, XLI, XLII, HSP.

2. Wayne to Pickering, September 19, November 9, 1795, Pickering to Wayne, October 3, 1795, Wayne Papers, XLII, XLIII, HSP.

3. Wayne to Doyle, April 15, 1795, Wayne Papers, XL, HSP.

4. Wayne to Pickering, September 3, 19, October 5, November 12, 1795, Wayne to William Clark, September 10, 1795, to Commander of Spanish Troops at Chickasaw Bluffs, September 10, 1795, Wayne Papers, XLII, XLIII, HSP; Wayne to Pickering, September 15, 1795, Timothy Pickering Papers, Massachusetts Historical Society.

5. Pickering to Wayne, November 7, 1795, Wayne to Manuel Gayoso de Lemos, November 20, 1795, Wayne Papers, XLIII, HSP.

6. Pickering to Wayne, October 24, 1795, Wayne to Hamtramck, November 20, December 9, 1795, to Wilkinson, November 30, December 14, 1795, to Messrs. Scott & Co., December 1, 1795, Wayne Papers, XLIII, HSP; St. Clair to Wayne, December 5, 1795, Smith, ed., *St. Clair Papers*, II, 394–95; Wayne's General Orders, December 14, 1795, Knopf, ed., *West Point Orderly Books*, IV, 3.

7. *American Daily Advertiser*, February 8, 1796; "Extracts from the Diary of Jacob Heltzheimer, 1768–1798," *PMHB*, XVI (1892), 412–22.

8. *American Daily Advertiser*, February 8, 20, 1796; John Adams to Abigail Adams, February 13, 1796, *PMHB*, XXI (1897), 33.

9. Margaretta Atlee to Wayne, February — , 1796, Wayne Papers, Society Collection, HSP.

10. Mrs. Williamina Cadwalader to Ann Ridgely, February 20, 1796, Cadwalader Collection, Historical Society of Pennsylvania.

11. Hugh Williamson to James McHenry, January 27, 1796, cited in Steiner, *McHenry*, 165; Richard C. Knopf, ed., *Anthony Wayne: A Name in Arms; Soldier, Diplomat, Defender of Expansion Westward of a Nation; the Wayne-Knox-Pickering-McHenry Correspondence* (Pittsburgh, 1960), 480.

12. Harry Martin Tinkcom, *The Republicans and Federalists in Pennsylvania, 1790–1801* (Harrisburg, 1950), 159.

13. Gales, comp., *Debates of Congress*, V, 905–13; Lowrie and Clarke, eds., *American State Papers, Military Affairs*, I, 112–13; Kohn, *Eagle and Sword*, 183; Cress, *Citizens in Arms*, 133.

14. Wayne to McHenry, February 24, 1796, Wayne Papers, XLIII, HSP; Lowrie and Clarke, eds., *American State Papers, Military Affairs*, I, 114–15.

15. Gales, comp., *Debates of Congress*, V, 102–05, 110–11, 1418–23, 1429 – 30; *Aurora*, May 19, 1796; McHenry to Wayne, May 29, 1796, Wayne Papers, XLIV, HSP; Kohn, *Eagle and Sword*, 184–85.

16. That the suspicions of the Washington administration and General Wayne were not unfounded, see Hay, "Reflections," *MVHR*, XXI, 480; Hay and Werner, *Admirable Trumpeter*, 134–62; and Jacobs, *Tarnished Warrior*, 152.

17. Wayne to William Clark, September 10, 1795, to Zebulon Pike, November 29, May 25, 1796, Northwest Territory Collection, Indiana Historical Society.

18. Wayne to McHenry, June 24, 1796, Wayne Papers, XLIV, HSP.

19. Wayne to McHenry, June 27, 1796, Wayne Papers, XLIV, HSP; Jacobs, *Wilkinson*, 150.

20. Wilkinson to Wayne, July 7, 1796, Pickering to Wayne, June 10, 1796, Wayne Papers, WLCL; Wayne to Wilkinson, July 16, 1796, Wilkinson to Wayne, July 16, 1796, Pike to Pickering, August 1, 1796, Wayne Papers, XLV, HSP; Wayne to Pickering, July 23, 1796, Wayne Papers, Society Collection, HSP.

21. Wayne to Pike, July 6, 1796, to McHenry, July 8, 1796, Pike to Wayne, August 6, 22, 1796, Northwest Territory Collection, Indiana Historical Society.

22. Wayne to McHenry, July 28, 1796, John Steele to Wayne, August 28, 1796, Wayne Papers, XLIV, XLV, HSP; Jacobs, *Wilkinson*, 151–52; Hay and Werner, *Wilkinson*, 151–52.

23. Wayne to Pike, October 12, 1796, John Steele to Wayne, August 28, 1796, Wayne Papers, XLVII, HSP.

24. Washington to McHenry, July 1, 1796, Fitzpatrick, ed., *Writings of Washington*, XXXV, 108–09; McHenry to Pickering, July 5, 1796, Memorandum of Charles Lee, November 22, 1796, James McHenry Papers, William L. Clements Library; Kohn, *Eagle and Sword*, 186–87.

25. McHenry to Wayne, July 9, 1796, Wayne Papers, XLIV, HSP; Wayne to McHenry, July 28, 1796, Thomas Lewis to Wayne, December 2, 1796, Northwest Territory Collection, Indiana Historical Society.

26. Wayne to McHenry, July 11, 23, August 10, 28, 1796, to DeButts, July 10, 1796, Wayne Papers, XLIV, XLV, HSP.

27. Wayne to Isaac Wayne, September 10, 1796, Memorial of Legion Army to Wayne, August 14, 1796, Wayne Papers, XLV, XLVI, HSP.

28. Wayne to Isaac Wayne, September 10, 1796, to McHenry, September 20, 1796, Wayne Papers, XLVI, HSP.

29. McHenry to Wayne, July 20, August 5, 19, 27, September 2, 10, October 26, 1796, Wayne to McHenry, September 5, 20, October 3, 28, November 12, 1796, Wayne Papers, XLV, XLVI, XLVII, HSP; Wayne to McHenry, August 29, 1796, McHenry Papers, William L. Clements Library; Wayne to Major B. Howe, October 8, 1796, Huntington Manuscripts, Huntington Library; Wayne to Major William Winston, September 5, 1796, Ohio Historical Society.

30. Wayne to Pickering, July 23, 1796, Caleb Swan to Wayne, September 4,

1796, Oliver Wolcott to Wayne, July 29, 1796, Wayne Papers, WLCL; Wayne to Wolcott, September 4, 1796, Wayne Papers, XLVI, HSP.

31. David Jones to Wayne, October 4, 10, 13, 1796, Wayne to Jones, October 5, 10, 14, 1796, H.G. Jones Collection, American Baptist Historical Society; Horatio Gates Jones, ed., "Extracts from the Original Manuscript Journal of the Rev. David Jones, A.M., Chaplain of the United States Legion. . .," *Michigan Pioneer and Historical Collections*, VIII (1907), 395.

32. Charles Brown to ——, September 28, 1796, Brown Papers, Detroit Public Library; Wayne to Dr. Nicholas Wray, September 5, 1796, Wayne Papers, XLVI, HSP.

33. Wayne to McHenry, November 12, 1796, to Hamtramck, November 13, 1796, Citizens of Detroit to Wayne, November 14, 1796, Wayne Papers, XLVII, HSP.

34. Wayne to McHenry, November 12, 1796, Wayne Papers, XLVII, HSP; Russell Bissell to Isaac Craig, November 29, 1796, Anthony Wayne Letters, Chester County Historical Society; Laura G. Sanford, *The History of Erie County, Pennsylvania, from its First Settlement* (New York, 1861), 90.

35. DeButts to Craig, December 14, 15, 1796, Wayne Letters, Chester County Historical Society.

36. Delany to Isaac Wayne, December 30, 1796, Wayne Papers, XLVII, HSP.

37. Lowrie and Clark, eds., *American State Papers, Military Affairs*, I, 117; Gales, comp., *Debates of Congress*, V, 1418–23, 1462, VI, 1573, 1576, 2945; Kohn, *Eagle and Sword*, 187.

38. Delany to Isaac Wayne, December 30, 1796, Bill for Relief of Heirs of General Wayne, January 19, 1811, Wayne Papers, XLVII, XLVIII, HSP; Isaac Wayne to McAllister, January 24, 1797, to Gibbons, March 4, 1797, to Delany March 12, 29, 1797, Delany to Lewis, March 20, 1797, Wayne Papers, WLCL.

39. Thomas McKean's Address to the Pennsylvania Assembly, December 8, 1808, *Pennsylvania Archives*, Ser. 4, IV, 653; Rush to Isaac Wayne, August 30, 1809, Wayne Papers, Detroit Public Library.

40. J. E. Reed, Secretary, Erie County Historical Society to Mrs. Charles Abell Murphy, June 27, 1938, Wayne Letters, Chester County Historical Society. Not until 1876 was this burial place rediscovered, whereupon three years later the legislature of Pennsylvania appropriated money to build a monument to Wayne at Erie. The committee appointed to carry out this task erected on the site a model of the blockhouse, which covered "a new stone. . .over the grave" (*The American Architect and Building News*, XXI [1889], 159).

41. Isaac Wayne to Johnston, October 27, 1809, Wayne Papers, Detroit Public Library.

SELECTED BIBLIOGRAPHY

Manuscript Collections

American Baptist Historical Society, Rochester, New York
   H. G. Jones Collection
American Philosophical Society Library, Philadelphia
   Sol Feinstone Collection
   Benjamin Franklin Papers
   Nathanael Greene Papers
   Miscellaneous Manuscripts Collection
   Zebulon M. Pike Papers
   St. Johns River Society Papers
   Anthony Wayne's Receipt Book, 1785–92
Chester County Historical Society, West Chester, Pennsylvania
   Anthony Wayne Letters
Chicago Historical Society, Chicago
   Alfred Creigh Collection
   Col. R. T. Durrett Collection
   Charles F. Gunther Collection
   Hardin Family Collection
   John Mills Collection
   Charles B. Pike Collection
   George Weedon Papers
   James Wilkinson Papers
University of Chicago, Special Collections, Joseph Regenstein Library, Chicago
Cincinnati Historical Society, Cincinnati
   Tobert Elliot Manuscripts
   Torrence Collection
   Anthony Wayne Manuscripts
Clark University, Robert Hutchings Goddard Library, Worcester, Massachusetts
William L. Clements Library, Ann Arbor, Michigan
   Clinton Papers
   Nathanael Greene Papers (including photostats of Nathanael Greene Papers, Richmond, Georgia)
   Haskell Collection
   James McHenry Papers
   Michigan Collection
   Miscellaneous Collection
   Northwest Territory Collection
   James S. Schoff Collection
   Anthony Wayne Papers
Connecticut State Library, Hartford
   Joseph Trumbull Papers
Detroit Public Library, Detroit
   Askin Papers
   Bald Papers
   Brown Papers

Burton Historical Collection
Covington Papers
"Diary of David Jones Re Journey from Pittsburgh to Detroit as Chaplain of
 Wayne's Army," July 3–November 3, 1796
Hamtramck Papers
Henley Papers
Jones Papers
"Letters from General Wayne and General Wilkinson to the Quarter Master
 General," 1796–98
"Orderly Books of Wayne's Sub-Legion," August, 1794–December 7, 1796
Rohnert Papers
Simcoe Papers
United States Archives
Anthony Wayne Papers
Wilkinson Papers
Woltz Papers
Woodbridge Papers
Duke University, Perkins Library, Durham, North Carolina
James Belcher Papers
Nathanael Greene Papers
John Martin Papers
Samuel Stirk Papers
Anthony Wayne Papers
Duke University Medical Center Library, Josiah C. Trent Collection, Durham,
 North Carolina
Benjamin Rush Papers
Filson Club, Louisville, Kentucky
Joyes Collection: Preston Family
Isaac Shelby Papers
Georgia Historical Society, Savannah
Joseph Valence Beven Papers
James Jackson Papers
John Martin Papers
William Bacon Stevens Papers
Wayne, Stites, Anderson Papers
University of Georgia Libraries, Athens
Keith Morton Read Georgia Manuscripts
Historical Society of the County of Montgomery, Norristown, Pennsylvania
Historical Society of Pennsylvania, Philadelphia
Joseph Ball Papers
Cadwalader Collection
Connaroe Autograph Collection
Dreer Collection: Revolutionary Generals
Etting Collection: Generals of the Revolution
Simon Gratz Autograph Collection
Andrew and James Hamilton Papers
John Hughes Papers
William Irvine Papers
Jenkins Family Papers
McKean Papers

Miscellaneous Materials
Jonathan Potts Papers
Provincial Delegates Betters
Society Collection
Charles Janeway Stillé Papers
Anthony Wayne Papers
Wister Papers
Henry E. Huntington Library, San Marino, California
Nathanael Greene Papers
Huntington Manuscripts
Indiana Historical Society, Indianapolis
John Armstrong Papers
Benjamin Harrison Collection
Harrison Miscellaneous Collection
Indiana Territory Collection
Arthur G. Mitten Collection
Northwest Territory Collection
Personal File-James Wilkinson
Thomas Posey Collection
William H. Smith Collection
Francis Vigo Photostats
Kentucky Historical Society, Frankfort
Field Book, Wayne's Campaign, November 29, 1794–February 5, 1795
James Wilkinson Letters
University of Kentucky, Margaret I. King Library, Lexington
Charles Scott Papers
Samuel Mackay Wilson Manuscript Collection: Miscellaneous Correspondence,
1757–1902
Library of Congress, Manuscript Division, Washington
Daniel Brodhead Papers
Peter Force Transcripts
Horatio Gates Papers
Nathanael Greene Papers
Harry Innes Papers
Miscellaneous Manuscript Collection: Anthony Wayne Papers
George Washington Papers
James Wilkinson Papers
Maryland Historical Society, Baltimore
Cadwalader Papers
Otho H. Williams Papers
Massachusetts Historical Society, Boston
C. E. French Papers
C. Guild Papers
William Heath Papers
Henry Knox Papers
Miscellaneous Papers
Norcross Collection
Timothy Pickering Papers
W. Sargent Papers
John Sullivan Papers

Morristown National Historical Park, Morristown, New Jersey
  Park Collection
  Lloyd W. Smith Collection
  Wayne Transcripts
National Archives, Washington
  Letters of Brigadier Gen. Anthony Wayne. Papers of the Continental Congress,
    No. 161
New Hampshire Historical Society, Concord
  John Sullivan Papers
New Jersey Historical Society, Newark
  Edwin A. Ely Autograph Collection
  West Jersey Manuscripts
New-York Historical Society, New York
  William Alexander, Lord Stirling Papers
  William Finnie Papers
  Horatio Gates Papers
  John Lacey Papers
  Alexander McDougall Papers
  Joseph Reed Papers
  Walter Stewart Papers
  Benjamin Van Cleve Papers
  Baron Von Steuben Papers
New York Public Library, New York
  Bancroft Transcripts
  Emmet Collection of Manuscripts
  Myers Collection
  Phillip Schuyler Papers
Newberry Library, Chicago
  Edward E. Ayer Collection
North Carolina State Department of Archives and History, Raleigh
  Johnston Collection, Hayes Library
Ohio Historical Society, Columbus
University of Pennsylvania, Charles Patterson Van Pelt Library, Philadelphia
  Benjamin Franklin Papers
  Philip H. Ward Collection
Presbyterian Historical Society, Philadelphia
  The Shane Collection
John F. Reed Collection, King of Prussia, Pennsylvania
  Valley Forge Material
  Whitemarsh Material
University of South Carolina, South Caroliniana Library, Columbia
  Ralph Izard Papers
University of Virginia, Alderman Library, Charlottesville
  Gwathmey (Cabell) Collection
  Maupin Family Papers
Waynesborough Estate, Paoli, Pennsylvania
  Orrin June Collection
West Chester State College, Greene Library, West Chester, Pennsylvania
  Letters of General Anthony Wayne
State Historical Society of Wisconsin, Madison
  The Lyman C. Draper Manuscript Collection

Printed Primary Sources

Acomb, Evelyn M., tr. and ed. *The Revolutionary Journal of Baron Ludwig Von Closen, 1780–1783.* Chapel Hill: University of North Carolina Press, 1958.

Adams, Charles Francis, ed. *Familiar Letters of John Adams and His Wife Abigail Adams, During the Revolution.* New York: Hurd and Houghton, 1876.

——. *The Life and Works of John Adams.* 10 vols. Boston: Little, Brown and Co., 1854.

American State Papers: Documents, Legislative and Executive of the Congress of the United States. Walter Lowrie and Matthew Clarke, eds. 38 vols. Washington: Gales and Seaton, 1832–61.

André, John. *Major André's Journal: Operations of the British Army Under Lieutenant Generals Sir William Howe and Sir Henry Clinton, June, 1776 to November, 1778.* Tarrytown, N.Y.: William Abbot, 1930.

Balch, Thomas, ed. *Papers Relating Chiefly to the Maryland Line During the Revolution.* Philadelphia: T. K. and P. G. Collins, 1857.

Boudinot, J. J., ed. *The Life, Public Services, Addresses, and Letters of Elias Boudinot.* 2 vols. Boston: Houghton Mifflin Co., 1896.

Boyd, Julian, ed. *The Papers of Thomas Jefferson.* 21 vols. to date. Princeton, N.J.: Princeton University Press, 1950– .

——and Robert J. Taylor, eds. *The Susquehannah Company Papers.* 11 vols. Wilkes-Barre, Pa.: Wyoming Historical and Genealogical Society, and Ithaca, N.Y.: Cornell University Press, 1930–71.

Boyer, John. "Journal of Lieutenant Boyer," in John Jeremiah Jacob. *A Biographical Sketch of the Life of the Late Capt. Michael Cresap.* Cincinnati: J. F. Uhlhorn, 1866.

Buell, John H. "A Fragment from the Diary of Major John Hutchinson Buell, U.S.A.," *Journal of the Military Service Institution,* XL (1907), 102–13, 260–68.

Burnett, Edmund C., ed., *Letters of Members of the Continental Congress.* 8 vols. Washington D.C.: Government Printing Office, 1921–36.

Burton, Clarence M. "General Wayne's Orderly Book," *Michigan Pioneer and Historical Collection,* XXXIV (1904), 341–733.

Butterfield, Lyman H., ed. *Letters of Benjamin Rush.* 2 vols. Princeton; N.J.: Princeton University Press, 1951.

——. *Diary and Autobiography of John Adams.* 4 vols. Cambridge, Mass.: Harvard University Press, 1961.

Calendar of the Pickering Papers. Massachusetts Historical Society, *Collections,* Ser. 6, VIII. Boston: The Society, 1896.

Campbell, Charles, ed. *The Bland Papers: Being a Selection from the Manuscripts of Colonel Theodoric Bland, Jr.* 2 vols. Petersburg, Va.: E. & J. Ruffin, 1840–43.

Candler, A. D., ed. *Revolutionary Records of Georgia, 1769–1784.* 3 vols. Atlanta, Ga.: Franklin-Turner Co., 1908.

Chastellux, Marquis de. *Travels in North America in the Years 1780, 1781 and 1782.* Howard C. Rice, Jr., tr. 2 vols. Chapel Hill: University of North Carolina Press, 1963.

Chinard, Gilbert, ed. *Lafayette in Virginia: Unpublished Letters from the Original Manuscripts in the Virginia State Library and the Library of Congress.* Baltimore: The Johns Hopkins Press, 1928.

Clinton, Sir Henry. *The American Rebellion. . . .* William B. Willcox, ed. New Haven, Conn.: Yale University Press, 1954.

Cook, John. "General Wayne's Campaign in 1794 and 1795: Captain John Cook's Journal," *American Historical Record,* II (1873), 311–16, 339–45.

Corner, George W., ed. *The Autobiography of Benjamin Rush*. Princeton, N.J.: Princeton University Press, 1948.

Cruikshank, E. A., ed. *The Correspondence of Lieut. Governor John Graves Simcoe, With Allied Documents Relating to His Administration of the Government of Upper Canada*. 5 vols. Toronto: Ontario Historical Society, 1923–31.

——. "Diary of an Officer in the Indian Country-1794," *Magazine of Western History*, II (1885), 387–96.

Davis, John. "The Yorktown Campaign: Journal of Captain John Davis of the Pennsylvania Line," *Pennsylvania Magazine of History and Biography*, V, (1881), 290–310.

Debates and Proceedings in the Congress of the United States, 1789–1824. Joseph Gales, comp. 42 vols. Washington, D.C.: Gales and Seaton, 1834–56.

Denny, William H., ed. *Military Journal of Major Ebenezer Denny*. Philadelphia: J. B. Lippincott, 1860.

Dewees, Samuel. *A History of the Life and Services of Captain Samuel Dewees*. . . . John Smith Hanna, comp. Baltimore: Robert Neilson, 1844.

Diary of William Dunlap, 1766–1839. New-York Historical Society, *Collections*, LXIV. New York: The Society, 1931.

Elmer, Ebenezer. "Journal Kept During an Expedition to Canada in 1776," New Jersey Historical Society, *Proceedings*, Ser. 1, III. Newark: The Society, 1849.

Ferguson, E. James, et al., eds. *The Papers of Robert Morris, 1781–1784*. 3 vols. to date. Pittsburgh: University of Pittsburgh Press, 1973– .

Fitzpatrick, John C., ed. *The Writings of George Washington from the Original Manuscripts, 1745–1799*. 39 vols. Washington, D.C.: Government Printing Office, 1931–44.

Force, Peter, ed. *American Archives: A Documentary History of the Origin and Progress of the North American Colonies*. 9 vols. Washington, D.C.: Government Printing Office, 1837–53.

Ford, Worthington C., ed. *The Writings of George Washington*. 14 vols. New York: G. P. Putnam's Sons, 1889–93.

——. *Correspondence and Journals of Samuel Blachley Webb*. 3 vols. Lancaster, Pa.: Wickersham Press, 1893.

——. *Journals of the Continental Congress, 1774–1789*. 34 vols. Washington D.C.: Government Printing Office, 1904–37.

Gottschalk, Louis, ed. *The Letters of Lafayette to Washington, 1779–1799*. New York: Privately Printed by Helen Fahenstock Hubbard, 1944.

Graydon, Alexander. *Memoir of a Life, Chiefly Passed in Pennsylvania, Within the Last Sixty Years*. . . . Harrisburg: John Wyeth, 1811.

Hamilton, Stanislaus Murray, ed. *The Writings of James Monroe*. 7 vols. New York: G.P. Putnam's Sons, 1898–1903.

Hammond, Otis G., ed. *Letters and Papers of Major General John Sullivan, Continental Army*. New Hampshire Historical Society, *Collections*, XII–XV. Concord: The Society, 1930–39.

Hartridge, W. C., ed. *The Letters of Don Juan McQueen to his Family, Written from Spanish East Florida, 1791–1807*. Columbia, S.C.: Bostick & Thornley, 1943.

Hastings, Hugh, and James A. Holden, eds. *Public Papers Of George Clinton, First Governor of New York*. 10 vols. New York: State of New York, 1899–1914.

Hazard, Samuel, et al., eds. *Pennsylvania Archives*. 138 vols. to date. Philadelphia and Harrisburg: The State, 1644– .

Hiltzheimer, Jacob. *Extracts from the Diary of Jacob Hiltzheimer, 1765–1798.* J. C. Parsons, ed. Philadelphia: William Fell & Company, 1893.

Historical Manuscripts Commission. *Report on American Manuscripts in the Royal Institution of Great Britain.* 4 vols. London: Mackie and Co., 1904–10.

Howard, Dresden W. H., ed. "The Battle of Fallen Timbers, as Told by Chief Kin-Jo-I-No," *Northwest Ohio Quarterly*, XX (1948), 37–49.

Hunt, Gaillard, ed. *Writings of James Madison.* 9 vols. New York: G. P. Putnam's Sons, 1900–10.

Idzerda, Stanley, ed. *Lafayette in the Age of the American Revolution: Selected Letters and Papers, 1776–1790.* 1 vol. to date. Ithaca, N.Y.: Cornell University Press, 1977– .

Jackson, Donald, and Dorothy Twohig, eds. *The Diaries of George Washington.* 6 vols. Charlottesville: University Press of Virginia, 1976–80.

Johnston, Henry P., ed. *The Correspondence and Public Papers of John Jay.* 4 vols. New York: G. P. Putnam's Sons, 1890–93.

Jones, Horatio Gates, ed. "Extracts from the Original Manuscript Journal of the Rev. David Jones, A.M., Chaplain of the United States Legion, Under Major-General Wayne, During the Indian Wars of 1794–5–6," *Michigan Pioneer and Historical Collections*, VIII (1907), 392–95.

Journal of the Council of Censors Convened at Philadelphia. . . .. Philadelphia: Hall and Sellers, 1783.

Journals of the House of Representatives of the Commonwealth of Pennsylvania, Beginning the Twenty-Eighth day of November, 1776, and Ending the Second Day of October, 1781. Philadelphia: John Dunlap, [1782].

Kappler, Charles J., ed. *Indian Affairs: Laws and Treaties.* 2 vols. Washington: Government Printing Office, 1904.

Kent, Donald H., and Merle H. Deardorff, eds. "John Adlum on the Allegheny: Memoirs for the Year 1794," *Pennsylvania Magazine of History and Biography*, LXXXIV (1960), 265–324, 435–80.

Knopf, Richard C., ed. *Anthony Wayne, A Name in Arms: Soldier, Diplomat, Defender of Expansion Westward of a Nation: the Wayne-Knox-Pickering-McHenry Correspondence.* Pittsburgh: University of Pittsburgh Press, 1960.

——. *The Journal of Joseph Gardner Andrews.* Columbus: Ohio Historical Society, 1958.

——. "A Precise Journal of General Wayne's Last Campaign," American Antiquarian Society, *Proceedings*, LXIV. Worcester, Mass.: The Society, 1954.

——. "Two Journals of the Kentucky Volunteers, 1793 and 1794," *Filson Club History Quarterly*, XXVII (1953), 247–81.

——. "Wayne's Western Campaign: The Wayne-Knox Correspondence, 1793 – 1794," *Pennsylvania Magazine of History and Biography*, LXXVIII (1954), 298–341, 424–55.

——, transcriber. *The West Point Orderly Books [For the U.S. Legion, May 24, 1792– September 28, 1794].* 4 vols. in one. Columbus: The Anthony Wayne Parkway Board, Ohio State Museum, 1954.

Labaree, Leonard W., and William B. Willcox, eds. *The Papers of Benjamin Franklin.* 20 vols. to date. New Haven, Conn.: Yale University Press, 1959– .

Lacey, John. "Memoirs of Brigadier-General John Lacey, of Pennsylvania," *Pennsylvania Magazine of History and Biography*, XXV (1901), 1–13, 191–207, 341–54, 498–515.

Lee, Henry. *Memoirs of the War in the Southern Department of the United States.* Robert E. Lee, ed. New York: University Publishing Co., 1869.

Lee Papers, New-York Historical Society, *Collections*, IV–VIII. New York: The Society, 1872–76.

"Letter of John Morton to Anthony Wayne, 1776," *Pennsylvania Magazine of History and Biography*, XIX (1895), 112–15.

"Letters from General Wayne and General Wilkinson to the Quartermaster General," *Michigan Pioneer and Historical Collections*, XXV (1907), 617–37.

"Letters of Gen. Wayne to Gen. Irvine, 1778–1784," *Historical Magazine*, VI (1862), 322–23, 336–42.

"Letters Relating to the Death of Major General Anthony Wayne," *Pennsylvania Magazine of History and Biography*, XIX (1895), 112–15.

Lydenberg, Harry Miller, ed. *Archibald Robertson, Lieutenant-General Royal Engineers, His Diaries and Sketches in America, 1762–1780*. New York: The New York Public Library, 1930.

Maclay, Edgar S., ed. *Journal of William Maclay, United States Senator from Pennsylvania, 1789–1791*. New York: D. Appleton and Company, 1890.

McGrane, R. C., ed. "William Clark's Journal of General Wayne's Campaign," *Mississippi Valley Historical Review*, I (1914), 418–44.

Maxwell, W. J., comp. *General Alumni Catalogue of the University of Pennsylvania*. Philadelphia: Alumni Association of the University, 1917.

Minutes of the Convention of the Commonwealth of Pennsylvania, which Commenced at Philadelphia, on Tuesday the Twenty-Fourth Day of November. . .[1789]. Philadelphia: Z. Poulson, Jun., [1790].

Minutes of the Council of Censors, 1783–1784, in *Pennsylvania Archives*, Series 3, X. Harrisburg: The State, 1896.

Minutes of the Council [i.e. Committee] of Safety of the Province of Pennsylvania, vol. X, *Colonial Records of Pennsylvania*. 16 vols. Harrisburg: The State, 1852–53.

Minutes of the. . .General Assembly of the Commonwealth of Pennsylvania. Philadelphia: The State of Pennsylvania, 1781–90.

Moore, Frank. *Diary of the American Revolution*. 2 vols. New York: Charles Scribner, 1860.

"Orderly Book, Fourth Pennsylvania Battalion, Col. Anthony Wayne, 1776," *Pennsylvania Magazine of History and Biography*, XXIX (1905), 470–78.

Peckham, Howard H., ed. *Sources of American Independence: Selected Manuscripts from the Collections of the William L. Clements Library*. 2 vols. Chicago: University of Chicago Press, 1978.

———. *Toll of Independence: Engagements and Battle Casualties of the American Revolution*. Chicago: University of Chicago Press, 1974.

Phillips, George Morris, comp. *Historic Letters from the Collection of the West Chester State Normal School*. Philadelphia: J. B. Lippincott Company, 1898.

Pickering, Octavius, ed. *The Life of Timothy Pickering*. 4 vols. Boston: Little, Brown and Co., 1867–73.

Proceedings in the House of Representatives of the United States of America, Respecting the Contested Election for the Eastern District of the State of Georgia. Philadelphia: Parry Hall, 1792.

Proceedings Relative to Calling the Conventions of 1776 and 1790. . . . Harrisburg: J. S. Wiestling, 1825.

Quaife, M. M., "General James Wilkinson's Narrative of the Fallen Timbers Campaign," *Mississippi Valley Historical Review*, XVI (1929), 81–90.

Reed, William B., ed. *Life and Correspondence of Joseph Reed*. 2 vols. Philadelphia: Lindsay and Blakiston, 1847.

"Revolutionary Army Orders for the Main Army Under Washington, 1778–1779," *Virginia Magazine of History and Biography*, XVIII (1910), 428–34.

Robertson, William Spence, ed. *The Diary of Francisco de Miranda, Tour of the United States, 1783 – 1784*. New York: The Hispanic Society of America, 1928.

Rochambeau, Jean Baptiste Donatien de Vimeur, Comte de. *Memories Militaries, Historiques et Politiques. . . .* 2 vols. Paris: Fain, 1890.

Ross, Charles, ed. *Correspondence of Charles, First Marquis Cornwallis*. 3 vols. London: John Murray, 1859.

Rowan, Archibald Hamilton. *Autobiography*. Dublin: Thomas Tegg and Co., 1840.

Rutland, Robert A., ed. *The Papers of George Mason, 1725 – 1792*. 3 vols. Chapel Hill: University of North Carolina Press, 1970.

Sawvel, Franklin, B., ed. *The Complete Anas of Thomas Jefferson*. New York: The Round Table Press, 1930.

Scheer, George F., ed. *Private Yankee Doodle: Being a Narrative of Some of the Adventures, Dangers and Sufferings of a Revolutionary Soldier, by Joseph Plumb Martin*. Boston: Little, Brown and Company, 1962.

Shepard, Lee, ed. *Journal, Thomas Taylor Underwood, March 26, 1792 to March 18, 1800, An Old Soldier in Wayne's Army*. Cincinnati: Society of Colonial Wars in the State of Ohio, 1945.

Sims, William Gilmore, ed. *The Army Correspondence of Colonel John Laurens in the Years 1777 – 1778*. New York: Bradford Club, 1867.

Smith, Dwight L., ed. *From Greene Ville to Fallen Timbers: A Journal of the Wayne Campaign, July 28–September 14, 1794*. Indianapolis: Indiana Historical Society, 1952.

Smith, William H., ed. *The St. Clair Papers*. 2 vols. Cincinnati: Robert Clarke, 1882.

Sparks, Jared, ed. *Correspondence of the American Revolution*. 4 vols. Boston: Little, Brown and Co., 1853.

Statutes at Large of Pennsylvania from 1682 to 1801. James T. Mitchell and Henry Flanders, comps. 14 vols. Harrisburg: State Printer, 1896–1909.

Steiner, Bernard C. *The Life and Correspondence of James McHenry: Secretary of War Under Washington and Adams*. Cleveland: The Burrows Brothers Company, 1907.

Stevens, Benjamin Franklin, ed. *The Campaign in Virginia, 1781: An Exact Reprint of Six Rare Pamphlets on the Clinton-Cornwallis Controversy. . . .* 2 vols. London: Trafalgar Square, 1888.

——. *Facsimiles of Manuscripts in European Archives Relating to America, 1773–1783*. 25 vols. London: Malby and Sons, 1889–95.

Syrett, Harold C., and Jacob E. Cooke, eds., *Papers of Alexander Hamilton*. 26 vols. New York: Columbia University Press, 1961–79.

Tatum, Edward H., ed. *The American Journal of Ambrose Serle, Secretary to Lord Howe, 1776 – 1778*. San Marino, Calif.: The Huntington Library, 1940.

Trumbull, John. *Autobiography, Reminiscences, and Letters, 1756 – 1841*. New York: Wiley and Putnam, 1841.

Trumbull Papers. Massachusetts Historical Society, *Collections*, Series 5, X, Series 7, II–III. Boston: The Society, 1885–1902.

Votes and Proceedings of the House of Representatives of the Province of Pennsylvania, 1682 – 1776, Gertrude MacKinney, ed. in *Pennsylvania Archives*, Series 8, I–IX. Philadelphia: B. Franklin and D. Hall, 1931–35.

Wayne, Isaac. "Biographical Memoir of Major General Anthony Wayne," *The Casket: Flowers of Literature, Wit and Sentiment*, [IV] (1820), 193–203, 241–51,

297–317, 349–61, 389–411, 445–57, 493–505, 531–40, [V] (1830), 4–14, 61–72, 109–20.

Wilson, Frazer E., ed. *Journal of Captain Daniel Bradley*. Greenville, Ohio: Private Printing, 1935.

Wilson, Rufus R., ed. *Heath's Memoirs of the American War*. New York: A. Wessels Co., 1904.

Wood, Judson P., tr., John S. Ezell, ed.. *The New Democracy in America: Travels of Francisco de Miranda in the United States, 1783–84*. Norman: University of Oklahoma Press, 1963.

Secondary Sources

Abernethy, Thomas P. *The South in the New Nation, 1789 – 1819*. Baton Rouge: Louisiana State University Press, 1961.

Alden, John R. *A History of the American Revolution*. New York: Alfred A. Knopf, 1969.

——. *General Charles Lee: Traitor or Patriot?* Baton Rouge: Louisiana State University Press, 1951.

——. *The South in the Revolution, 1763–1789*. Baton Rouge: Louisiana State University, 1957.

Allen, William B. *A History of Kentucky*. Louisville: Bradley & Gilbert, Publishers, 1872.

Armstrong, John. *Life of Major General Anthony Wayne*. Boston: Hislard, Gray and Co., 1835.

Bald, F. Clever. "General Anthony Wayne Visits Detroit," *Michigan History Magazine*, XXII (1942), 439–56.

——. *A Portrait of Anthony Wayne Painted from Life by Jean Pierre Henri Elois in 1796*. . .Ann Arbor, Mich.: William L. Clements Library, 1948.

Baldwin, Leland D. *The Whiskey Rebels*. Pittsburgh: University of Pittsburgh Press, 1939.

Bemis, Samuel Flagg. *Jay's Treaty: A Study in Commerce and Diplomacy*. New York: Macmillan Co., 1923.

Benton, William A. "Pennsylvania Revolutionary Officers and the Federal Constitution," *Pennsylvania History*, XXXI (1964), 419–35.

Binger, Carl. *Revolutionary Doctor: Benjamin Rush, 1746–1813*. New York: Norton, 1966.

Bolles, Albert S. *Pennsylvania, Province and State: A History from 1609 to 1790*. Philadelphia: John Wanamaker, 1899.

Bond, Beverley W., Jr. *The Foundations of Ohio*. Columbus: Ohio State Archaeological and Historical Society, 1941.

Boyd, George Adams. *Elias Boudinot: Partiot and Statesman, 1740–1821*. Princeton, N.J.: Princeton University Press, 1952.

Boyd, Thomas. *Light-Horse Harry Lee*. New York: Charles Scribner's Sons, 1931.

——. *Mad Anthony Wayne*. New York: Charles Scribner's Sons, 1929.

Brackenridge, H. M. *History of the Insurrection in Western Pennsylvania, Commonly Called the Whiskey Insurrection*. Pittsburgh: W. S. Haven, 1859.

Bradley, Arthur G. *Sir Guy Carleton, Lord Dorchester*. Toronto: Morang & Co., 1907.

Brant, Irving. *James Madison*. 6 vols. Indianapolis: Bobbs-Merrill Co. 1948–53.

Brice, Wallace A. *History of Fort Wayne, From the Earliest Known Accounts of this Point, to the Present Period, With a Sketch of the Life of General Anthony Wayne*. Fort Wayne, Ind.: D. W. Jones & Son, 1868.

Brunhouse, Robert L. *The Counter-Revolution in Pennsylvania, 1776–1790.* Harrisburg: Pennsylvania Historical Commission, 1942.

Burnet, Jacob. *Notes on the Early Settlement of the North-West Territory.* Cincinnati: Derby, Bradley & Co., Publishers, 1847.

Burt, Alfred LeRoy. *The United States, Great Britain and British North America from the Revolution to the Establishment of Peace After the War of 1812.* New Haven, Conn.: Yale University Press, 1940.

Burton, Clarence M. "Anthony Wayne and the Battle of Fallen Timbers," *Michigan Pioneer and Historical Collections,* XXXI (1909), 472–89.

Bush, Martin H. *Revolutionary Enigma: A Re-appraisal of General Philip Schuyler of New York.* Port Washington, N.Y.: I. J. Friedman, 1969.

Butterfield, Consul Wiltshire. *History of the Girtys.* Cincinnati: Robert Clarke & Co., 1890.

Callahan, North. *Henry Knox: General Washington's General.* New York: Rinehart, 1958.

———. *Daniel Morgan: Ranger of the Revolution.* New York: A. S. Barnes and Co., 1961.

Carrington, Henry B. *Battles of the American Revolution.* New York: A. S. Barnes and Co., 1876.

Caruso, John Anthony. *The Great Lakes Frontier: An Epic of the Old Northwest.* Indianapolis: Bobbs-Merrill Co., 1961.

Champagne, Roger J. *Alexander McDougall and the American Revolution in New York.* Schenectady: New York State American Revolution Bicentennial Commission and the Union College Press, 1975.

Charlton, Thomas U. P. *The Life of Major General James Jackson.* Augusta, Ga.: Geo. F. Randolph & Co., 1809.

Cheyney, Edward Potts. *History of the University of Pennsylvania, 1740–1940.* Philadelphia: University of Pennsylvania Press, 1940.

Cleaves, Freeman. *Old Tippecanoe: William Henry Harrison and His Time.* New York: Charles Scribner's Sons, 1939.

Coleman, Kenneth. *The American Revolution in Georgia, 1763–1789.* Athens: University of Georgia Press, 1958.

———, ed. *A History of Georgia.* Athens: University of Georgia Press, 1977.

Collins, Richard H. *History of Kentucky.* 2 vols. Covington, Ky.: Collins & Co., 1882.

Combs, Jerald A. *The Jay Treaty: Political Battleground of the Founding Fathers.* Berkeley: University of California Press, 1970.

Coulter, E. Merton. *Georgia: A Short History.* Chapel Hill: University of North Carolina Press, 1947.

Cress, Lawrence Delbert. *Citizens in Arms: The Army and the Militia in American Society to the War of 1812.* Chapel Hill: University of North Carolina Press, 1982.

Cresson, W. P. *James Monroe.* Chapel Hill: University of North Carolina Press, 1946.

Cripe, Helen, and Diane Campbell, eds. *American Manuscripts, 1763–1815: An Index to Documents Described in Auction Records and Dealers' Catalogues.* Wilmington, Del.: Scholarly Resources, Inc., 1977.

Dawson, Henry B. *The Assault on Stony Point, By General Anthony Wayne, July 16, 1779.* Morrisania, N.Y.: Henry B. Dawson, 1863.

———. *Battles of the United States by Sea and Land.* 2 vols. New York: Johnson, Fry, and Co., 1858.

Downes, Randolph C. "Anthony Wayne." Dumas Malone, ed. *Dictionary of American Biography*, vol. XIX. New York: Charles Scribner's Sons, 1936.
———. *Council Fires on the Upper Ohio: A Narrative of Indian Affairs in the Upper Ohio Valley until 1795*. Pittsburgh: University of Pittsburgh Press, 1940.
Elgeston, Thomas. *The Life of John Paterson, Major-General in the Revolutionary Army*. New York: G. P. Putnam's Sons, 1898.
Flexner, James Thomas. *George Washington: The Forge of Experience, 1732–1775*. Boston: Little, Brown and Co., 1965.
Ford, Worthington C. "Defenses of Philadelphia in 1777," *Pennsylvania Magazine of History and Biography*, XVIII (1894), 1–19, 163–84, 329–53, 463–95.
Freeman, Douglas Southall. *George Washington: A Biography*. 7 vols. New York: Charles Scribner's Sons, 1947–57.
Futhey, J. Smith. "The Massacre of Paoli," *Pennsylvania Magazine of History and Biography*, I (1877), 285–319.
———, and Gilbert Cope. *History of Chester County, Pennsylvania*. Philadelphia: Louis H. Everts, 1881.
Ganoe, William Addleman. *The History of the United States Army*. Revised edition. New York: D. Appleton-Century Company, Inc., 1942.
Gerlach, Don R. *Philip Schuyler and the American Revolution in New York, 1733–1777*. Lincoln: University of Nebraska Press, 1964.
Gifford, Jack Jule. "The Northwest Indian War, 1784–1795." Ph.D. dissertation, University of California at Los Angeles, 1964.
Glenn, Thomas Allen. *Some Colonial Mansions and Those Who Live in Them.* . . . Philadelphia: Henry T. Coates & Company, 1900.
Gordon, Thomas F. *The History of Pennsylvania, from Its Discovery by Europeans to the Declaration of Independence in 1776*. Philadelphia: Carey, Lea & Carey, 1829.
Gottschalk, Louis. *Lafayette and the Close of the American Revolution*. Chicago: University of Chicago Press, 1942.
———. *Lafayette Between the American and the French Revolution, 1783–1789*. Chicago: University of Chicago Press, 1950.
———. *Lafayette Joins the American Army*. Chicago: University of Chicago Press, 1937.
Greene, Francis Vinton. *The Revolutionary War and the Military Policy of the United States*. New York: Charles Scribner's Sons, 1911.
Gruber, Ira D. *The Howe Brothers and the American Revolution*. New York: Atheneum, 1972.
Haiman, Miecislaus. *Kosciuszko in the American Revolution*. Boston: Gregg Press, 1972.
———. *Poland and the American Revolutionary War*. Chicago: Polish Union Daily, 1932.
Hall, James. *A Memoir of the Public Services of William Henry Harrison, of Ohio*. Freeport, N.Y.: Books for Libraries Press, 1836, 1970.
Hargrove, Richard J. *General John Burgoyne*. Newark: University of Delaware Press, 1983.
Harmon, George Dewey. *Sixty Years of Indian Affairs, Political, Economic and Diplomatic, 1789 – 1850*. Chapel Hill: University of North Carolina Press, 1941.
Hatch, Louis Clinton. *The Administration of the American Revolutionary Army*. New York: Longmans, Green, and Co., 1904.
Hawke, David Freeman. *Benjamin Rush: Revolutionary Gadfly*. Indianapolis: Bobbs-Merrill Co., 1971.
———. *In the Midst of a Revolution*. Philadelphia: University of Pennsylvania Press, 1961.

Hay, Thomas Robson. "Some Reflections on the Career of General James Wilkinson," *Mississippi Valley Historical Review*, XXI (1935), 471–94.

——, and M. R. Werner. *The Admirable Trumpeter: A Biography of General James Wilkinson*. Garden City, N.Y.: Doubleday, Doran & Company, Inc., 1941.

Henderson, Archibald. *Washington's Southern Tour, 1791*. Boston: Houghton Mifflin Co., 1923.

Higginbotham, Don. *Daniel Morgan: Revolutionary Rifleman*. Chapel Hill: University of North Carolina Press, 1961.

——. *The War of American Independence: Military Attitudes, Policies, and Practice, 1763–1789*. New York: Macmillan Co., 1971.

Horsman, Reginald. "The British Indian Department and the Resistance to General Anthony Wayne, 1793–1795," *Mississippi Valley Historical Review*, XLIX (1962), 269–90.

Hunt, Samuel F. "General Anthony Wayne and the Battle of 'Fallen Timbers,' " *Ohio State Archaeological and Historical Quarterly*, IX (1900), 214–37.

Hutson, James H. *Pennsylvania Politics, 1746–1770: The Movement for Royal Government and Its Consequences*. Princeton, N.J.: Princeton University Press, 1972.

Jacobs, James Ripley. *The Beginning of the U.S. Army, 1783–1812*. Princeton, N.J.: Princeton University Press, 1947.

——. *Tarnished Warrior: Major-General James Wilkinson*. New York: Macmillan Co., 1938.

Jensen, Merrill. *The New Nation: A History of the United States During the Confederation, 1781 – 1789*. New York: Alfred A. Knopf, 1950.

Jones, Charles C. *The History of Georgia*. 2 vols. New York: Houghton Mifflin Co., 1883.

Jones, Eldon. "The British Withdrawal from the South, 1781–85," in *The Revolutionary War in the South: Power, Conflict, and Leadership: Essays in Honor of John Richard Alden*. W. Robert Higgins, ed. Durham, N.C.: Duke University Press, 1979.

Johnston, Henry P. *The Storming of Stony Point on the Hudson, Midnight, July 15, 1779*. New York: James T. White & Co., 1900.

Kapp, Friedrich. *The Life of John Kalb*. New York: Henry Holt and Co., 1884.

——. *Life of Maj. Gen. Frederick William Von Steuben*. New York: Mason Brothers, 1859.

Killion, Ronald G., and Charles T. Walker. *Georgia and the Revolution*. Atlanta: Cherokee Publishing Co., 1975.

Knollenberg, Bernhard. *Growth of the American Revolution, 1766–1775*. New York: The Free Press, 1975.

——. *Origin of the American Revolution, 1759–1766*. New York: Macmillan Co., 1960.

——. *Washington and the Revolution, a Reappraisal: Gates, Conway, and the Continental Congress*. New York: Macmillan Co., 1940.

Knopf, Richard C. "Crime and Punishment in the Legion, 1792–1793," *Bulletin of the Historical and Philosophical Society of Ohio*, XIV (1956), 232–38.

Kohn, Richard H. *Eagle and Sword: The Federalists and the Creation of the Military Establishment in America, 1783 – 1802*. New York: The Free Press, 1975.

Konkle, Burton Alva. *George Bryan and the Constitution of Pennsylvania, 1731–1791*. Philadelphia: William J. Campbell, 1922.

Lambdin, Alfred C. "The Battle of Germantown," *Pennsylvania Magazine of History and Biography*, I (1877), 368–403.

Leach, Josiah Granville. *History of the Penrose Family of Philadelphia*. Philadelphia: Private Printing, 1903.

Leiby, Adrian C. *The Revolutionary War in the Hackensack Valley*. New Brunswick, N.J.: Rutgers University Press, 1962.

Lossing, Benson J. *The Life and Times of Philip Schuyler*. 2 vols. New York: Sheldon & Company, 1860–72.

———. *Pictorial Field-book of the Revolution*. 2 vols. New York: Harper & Brothers, Publishers, 1860.

MacDougall, William L. *American Revolutionary: A Biography of General Alexander McDougall*. Westport, Conn.: Greenwood Press, 1977.

McLendon, Samuel G. *History of the Public Domain of Georgia*. Atlanta: Foote & Davies Co., 1924.

Mackesy, Piers. *The War for America, 1775–1783*. Cambridge, Mass.: Harvard University Press, 1965.

Mahon, John K. "Anglo-American Methods of Indian Warfare, 1676–1794," *Mississippi Valley Historical Review*, XLV (1958), 254–75.

Main, Jackson Turner. *The Antifederalists: Critics of the Constitution, 1781–1788*. Chicago: Quadrangle Books, 1961.

———. *The Sovereign States, 1775–1783*. New York: New Viewpoints, 1973.

Mellick, Andrew D., Jr. *Lesser Crossroads*. Herbert G. Schmidt, ed. New Brunswick, *Philadelphia, 1765–1776*. Philadelphia: University of Pennsylvania Press, 1978.

Middlekauf, Robert. *The Glorious Cause: The American Revolution, 1763–1789*. New York: Oxford University Press, 1982.

Miller, John C. *Alexander Hamilton: Portrait in Paradox*. New York: Harper & Brothers, 1959.

———. *Triumph of Freedom, 1775–1783*. Boston: Brown and Co., 1948.

Millis, Wade. "A Rugged Patriot: Major General Anthony Wayne." *Michigan History Magazine*, XX (1936), 127–51.

Millis, Walter. *Arms and Men: A Study in American Military History*. New York: G. P. Putnam's Sons, 1956.

Mintz, Max M. *Gouverneur Morris and the American Revolution*. Norman: University of Oklahoma Press, 1970.

Montgomery, Elizabeth. *Reminiscences of Wilmington, in Familiar Village Tales, Ancient and New*. Second edition. Wilmington, Del.: Johnston & Bogia, 1872.

Montross, Lynn. *Rag, Tag and Bobtail: The Story of the Continental Army, 1775–1783*. New York: Harper & Brothers, 1952.

Moore, Horatio Newton. *Life and Services of Gen. Anthony Wayne*. Philadelphia: Leary, Getz & Co., 1845.

Muhlenberg, Henry A. *The Life of Major-General Peter Muhlenberg of the Revolutionary Army*. Philadelphia: Carey and Hart, 1849.

Munroe, John A. "The Philadelawareans: A Study in the Relations Between Philadelphia and Delaware in the Late Eighteenth Century," *Pennsylvania Magazine of History and Biography*, LXIX (1945), 128–49.

Murdock, Beamish. *A History of Nova Scotia, or Acadie. . . .* 3 vols. Halifax, New Brunswick: J. Barnes, 1865–67.

Nelson, Paul David. *General Horatio Gates: A Biography*. Baton Rouge: Louisiana State University Press, 1976.

———. "Guy Carleton versus Benedict Arnold: The Campaign of 1776 in Canada and on Lake Champlain," *New York History*, LVII (1976), 339–66.

Nickell, M. F. "Historic Home of Anthony Wayne," *The Mentor*, XVII (1929), 21–26.

Oberholtzer, Ellis Paxson. *Robert Morris: Patriot and Financier*. New York: Macmillan Co., 1903.

Palmer, John McAuley. *General Von Steuben*. New Haven, Conn.: Yale University Press, 1937.

Pancake, John S. *1777: The Year of the Hangman*. University, Ala.: University of Alabama Press, 1977.

Peckham, Howard. *The War for Independence: A Military History*. Chicago: University of Chicago Press, 1958.

Pennypacker, Samuel W. "Anthony Wayne," *Pennsylvania Magazine of History and Biography*, XXXII (1908), 257–301.

——. *Anthony Wayne*. Philadelphia: J. B. Lippincott Company, 1908.

——. "The Capture of Stony Point," *Pennsylvania Magazine of History and Biography*, XXVI (1902), 360–69.

Pleasants, Henry, Jr. "The Battle of Paoli," *Pennsylvania Magazine of History and Biography*, LXXII (1948), 44–53.

Pratt, Fletcher. "Anthony Wayne, the Last of the Romans," *Eleven Generals: Studies in American Command*. New York: William Sloane Associates, 1949.

Preston, John H. *A Gentleman Rebel: The Exploits of Anthony Wayne*. New York: Farrar & Rinehart, 1930.

Proceedings on the Occasion of the Dedication of the Monument on the One Hundredth Anniversary of the Paoli Massacre in Chester County, Pa. West Chester: F. S. Hickman, 1877.

Prucha, Francis Paul. *The Sword of the Republic: The United States Army on the Frontier, 1783 – 1846*. New York: Macmillan Co., 1969.

Rankin, Hugh F. *The American Revolution*. New York, G. P. Putnam's Sons, 1964.

——. "Anthony Wayne, Military Romanticist," in George Athan Billias, ed., *George Washington's Generals*. New York: William Morrow and Company, 1964.

Read, D. B. *The Life and Times of General John Graves Simcoe. . . .* Toronto, Ontario: G. Virtue, 1901.

Roche, John F. *Joseph Reed: A Moderate in the American Revolution*. New York: Columbia University Press, 1957.

Roosevelt, Theodore. *The Winning of the West*. 6 vols. in three. New York: G. P. Putnam's Sons, 1889–96.

Rossie, Jonathan Gregory. *The Politics of Command in the American Revolution*. Syracuse: Syracuse University Press, 1975.

Rossman, Kenneth R. *Thomas Mifflin and the Politics of the American Revolution*. Chapel Hill: University of North Carolina Press, 1952.

Rowell, Chester Harvey. *A Historical and Legal Digest of All the Contested Election Cases in the House of Representatives of the United States from the First to the Fifty-sixth Congress, 1789–1901*. Washington, D.C.: Government Printing Office, 1901.

Royster, Charles. *A Revolutionary People at War: The Continental Army and American Character, 1775–1783*. Chapel Hill: University of North Carolina Press, 1979.

Ryerson, Richard Alan. *The Revolution is Now Begun: The Radical Committees of Philadelphia, 1765 – 1776*. Philadelphia: University of Pennsylvania Press, 1978.

Sargent, Winthrop. *The Life of Major John André*. New York: D. Appleton and Company, 1871.

Savannah Unit, Georgia Writer's Project, WPA in Georgia. "Richmond-Oakgrove Plantation, Parts I–II," *Georgia Historical Quarterly*, XXIV (1940), 22–42, 124–44.

Sawtelle, William Otis. "Acadia: The Pre-Loyalist Migration and the Philadelphia Plantation," *Pennsylvania Magazine of History and Biography*, LI (1927), 244–85.

Schachner, Nathan. *Alexander Hamilton*. New York: D. Appleton-Century Co., 1946.

Sellers, Charles C. *Benedict Arnold: Proud Warrior*. New York: Minton, Balch and Co., 1930.

Sellers, Edwin J. *The English Ancestry of the Wayne Family of Pennsylvania*. Philadelphia: Allen, Lane & Scott, 1927.

Selsam, J. Paul. *The Pennsylvania Constitution of 1776: A study in Revolutionary Democracy*. Philadelphia: University of Pennsylvania Press, 1936.

Skeen, C. Edward. *John Armstrong, Jr., 1758–1843: A Biography*. Syracuse, N.Y.: Syracuse University Press, 1981.

Smelser, Marshall. *The Winning of Independence*. New York: New Viewpoints, 1973.

Smith, Dwight L. "Wayne's Peace with the Indians of the Old Northwest, 1795" *Ohio State Archaeological and Historical Quarterly*, LIX (1950), 239–55.

Smith, Page. *A New Age Now Begins: A People's History of the American Revolution*. 2 vols. New York: McGraw-Hill Book Co., 1976.

Spaulding, E. Wilder. *His Excellency George Clinton, Critic of the Constitution*. New York: Macmillan Co., 1938.

Spears, John R. *Anthony Wayne, Sometimes Called "Mad Anthony."* New York: D. Appleton & Company, 1903.

Stillé, Charles Janeway. *Major-General Anthony Wayne and the Pennsylvania Line in the Continental Army*. Philadelphia: J. B. Lippincott Company, 1893.

Stokes, Thomas L. *The Savannah*. New York: Rinehart & Co., Inc., 1951.

Stone, Frederick D. "Philadelphia Society One Hundred Years Ago," *Pennsylvania Magazine of History and Biography*, III (1879), 361–94.

Stone, W. L. *Life of Joseph Brant-Thayendanegea*. 2 vols. New York: George Dearborn and Co., 1838.

Stryker, William S., and William Starr Myers. *The Battle of Monmouth*. Princeton, N. J.: Princeton University Press, 1927.

Templin, Thomas E. "Henry 'Light Horse Harry' Lee: A Biography." Ph.D. dissertation, University of Kentucky, 1975.

Thayer, Theodore. *Nathanael Greene: Strategist of the American Revolution*. New York: Twayne Publishers, 1960.

——. *Pennsylvania Politics and the Growth of Democracy, 1740–1776*. Harrisburg: Pennsylvania Historical and Museum Commission, 1953.

Tillotson, Harry Stanton. *The Beloved Spy: The Life and Loves of Major John André*. Caldwell, Ida.: The Caxton Printers, Ltd., 1948.

Tincom, Harry Marlin. *The Republicans and Federalists in Pennsylvania, 1790–1801*. Harrisburg: Pennsylvania Historical and Museum Commission, 1950.

Tower, Charlemagne. *The Marquis de Lafayette in the American Revolution*. 2 vols. Philadelphia: J. B. Lippincott Co., 1901.

Townsend, Sara Bertha. *An American Soldier: The Life of John Laurens*. Raleigh, N.C.: Edwards & Broughton Company, 1958.

Trevelyan, George O. *The American Revolution*. 4 vols. New York: Longmans, Green and Co., 1917–18.

Trussell, John B., Jr. *The Pennsylvania Line: Regimental Organization and Operations, 1776–1783*. Harrisburg: Pennsylvania Historical and Museum Commission, 1977.

Tucker, Glenn. *Mad Anthony Wayne and the New Nation: The Story of Washington's Front-Line General*. Harrisburg, Pa.: Stackpole Books, 1973.

Tuckerman, Bayard. *Life of General Philip Schuyler, 1733–1804*. New York: Dodd, Mead and Co., 1904.

Van Doren, Carl. *Benjamin Franklin*. New York: Viking Press, 1938.
———. *Mutiny in January: The Story of a Crisis in the Continental Army.* . . . New York: Viking Press, 1943.
———. *Secret History of the American Revolution*. New York: Viking Press, 1941.
Van Tyne, Claude H. *The War of Independence*. 2 vols. Boston: Houghton Mifflin Co., 1929.
Wallace, Paul A. W. *Pennsylvania: Seed of a Nation*. New York: Harper & Row, 1962.
Wallace, Willard M. *Appeal to Arms: A Military History of the American Revolution*. New York: Quadrangle, 1964.
———. *Traitorous Hero: The Life and Fortunes of Benedict Arnold*. New York: Harper & Row, 1954.
Ward, Christopher. *The War of the Revolution*. John R. Alden, ed. 2 vols. New York: Macmillan Co., 1952.
Weigley, Russell F. *The American Way of War: A History of the United States Military Strategy and Policy*. New York: Macmillan Co., 1973.
Whitridge, Arnold. *Rochambeau*. New York: Macmillan Co., 1965.
Whittemore, Charles P. *A General of the Revolution: John Sullivan of New Hampshire*. New York: Columbia University Press, 1961.
Wickwire, Franklin and Mary. *Cornwallis: The American Adventure*. Boston: Houghton Mifflin Co., 1970.
Wildes, Harry Emerson. *Anthony Wayne: Trouble Shooter of the American Revolution*. New York: Harcourt, Brace and Co., 1941.
Willcox, William B. *Portrait of a General: Sir Henry Clinton in the War of Independence*. New York: Alfred A. Knopf, 1964.
Wilson, Frazer Ellis. *Arthur St. Clair, Rugged Ruler of the Old Northwest: An Epic of the American Frontier*. Richmond, Va.: Garrett and Massie, 1944.
———. *The Peace of Mad Anthony: An Account of the Subjugation of the North-Western Indian Tribes and the Treaty of Greenville*. Greenville, Ohio: C.R. Kemble, 1909.
———. "The Treaty of Greenville," *Ohio State Archaeolgical and Historical Quarterly*, XII (1903), 128–59.
Wright, J. Leitch. *Britain and the American Frontier, 1783–1815*. Athens: University of Georgia Press, 1975.

INDEX